MIGRATION OF ASIAN WORKERS TO THE ARAB WORLD

Edited by Godfrey Gunatilleke

THE UNITED NATIONS UNIVERSITY

In 1983 the United Nations University launched a project on the Global Impact of Human Migration, with a major focus on migration caused by uneven industrialization in different countries and regions of the world. The impact of large-scale migration is not limited to economic effects but has social and cultural dimensions as well, in both the sending and the receiving countries. The first phase of the project was concerned with surveying the migration flows from seven Asian countries to the Arab region. The second phase studied the problems encountered by Asian migrant workers in the pre- and post-migration periods as well as during their stay in the host countries through questionnaires and interviews with the returnees. Country reports resulting from these studies will be published in 1987.

Migration of Asian Workers to the Arab World, a first product of the project, reports on the present status of migration to the Arab region from the seven countries studied. How many people migrate each year, and for how long? Who are the migrant workers, in terms of their age, sex, profession, and education? What types of work do they perform in the host country, and how much do they earn and send home? What kinds of problems do they face on their return? The book takes a comparative view of these problems, using data from the countries concerned, and provides useful information for both further research and policymaking by governments.

The United Nations University
Toho Seimei Building. 15-1 Shibuya 2-chome, Shibuya-ku, Tokyo 150, Japan
Tel: (03) 499-2811   Telex: J25442   Cable: UNATUNIV TOKYO

Printed in Japan

HSDB-30/UNUP-555
ISBN 92-808-0555-x
United Nations Sales No. E.86.III.A.2
02000 P

CONTENTS

CONTENTS

PREFACE

The United Nations University undertook in 1983 and 1984 a state-of-the-art survey on migrant workers to the Arab world from seven Asian countries as a first step in its project on the Global Impact of Human Migration. The survey was conducted in a comparative framework to cover the common problems of migration both for the workers and for the government agencies concerned, with a view to making policy recommendations.

The migration from these Asian countries to the Arab region is brought about by several factors — primarily, however, by the uneven availability of capital and of material and human resources in the sending and receiving countries. The impact of such large-scale migration is not limited to economic effects but also has social and cultural dimensions in these countries. On the basis of the data and information collected and analysed in the seven country surveys, the project has studied the problems encountered by the Asian migrant workers in the pre- and post-migration periods as well as during their stay in the host countries through questionnaires and interviews with returnees in each country. Results of these studies are expected to be published in 1987.

We are grateful to the United Nations Development Programme (UNDP) for its financial assistance to the project, particularly for the organization of a meeting of researchers and government officials in New Delhi 17–19 February 1984 to review the findings of the survey.

We wish to express appreciation to the researchers and their collaborators in Bangladesh, India, the Republic of Korea, Pakistan, the Philippines, Sri Lanka, and Thailand for their tireless and conscientious work throughout the survey. Our warm thanks go to Mr. Godfrey Gunatilleke of the Marga Institute in Colombo, who has acted as co-ordinator and editor for the project and for the present publication.

INTRODUCTION

Godfrey Gunatilleke
Director, Marga Institute, Sri Lankan Centre for Development Studies, Colombo, Sri Lanka

Characteristics of the Asian Labour Migration to the Middle East

The collection of studies in this volume has been designed to survey the present state of knowledge on the migration of Asian workers to the Middle East. It also reviews and evaluates Asian policies and institutions that are currently dealing with this migration. Although the studies point to the crucial role of migration in the Asian economies, several critical gaps in the available data are also identified. The authors emphasise the urgent need to improve the systems for collecting more reliable data on all aspects of the migration as well as to improve the institutional arrangements and policy frameworks within which this labour migration is managed.

The authors conclude that the labour migration has had far-reaching socioeconomic, cultural, and demographic consequences. The magnitude of the migration is significant enough to make it an important factor in national employment strategies and manpower planning. The workers participating in this flow of migration most often come from the young, reproductive age groups — and this is probably having a significant demographic impact. Remittances from these workers have become a major source of foreign exchange earnings, and most of these countries have come to depend on them heavily to manage their balance of payments. This migration of labour to the Middle East has had a considerable impact on income distribution and, consequently, on the prevailing social stratifications and relationships. Low-income groups are migrating in large numbers and are exposed to new consumption patterns, patterns that were far beyond their reach in the past. This exposure, together with higher income levels, is stimulating changes in life-styles, attitudes, and values at a more rapid pace than other factors that have hitherto been promoting change in the low-income strata. The demonstration effect of a small new-rich group is both dramatic and widespread. In surveying all these aspects of the migration, the authors conclude that the available information is not adequate for a reliable and proper identification of the benefits and costs of the migration. The studies also raise a number of conceptual and theoretical issues about migration. These issues will have to

1

be taken into account in any formulation of national policies on the migration of Asian workers to the Middle East.

Each author notes that the Middle East migration can be clearly distinguished from earlier migrations. Past migrations were often motivated by a desire to establish a permanent or long-term residence abroad, resulting in the movement of entire families and the formation of small migrant communities in the host countries. The motivation to maintain links with the country of origin or to transfer savings to that country is not likely to be strong in such cases. The Middle East migration, on the other hand, is almost entirely temporary and tied to fixed-term contracts of employment, which hold out no prospects for naturalisation or assimilation. Migrants are almost always obliged to return to their home countries after completing their employment contracts, the duration of which will vary according to contract and level of skill. For instance, most migrants to the Middle East are not permitted to take their families with them. From the outset, therefore, the migrant will view his migration in terms of its impact on his economic status and living conditions in the home country. During his employment abroad, separation from his family and his concern for it constantly reinforce his ties with the home country. The contractual limitations on his stay will direct his attention to the situation with which he will have to cope upon his return. These concerns will inevitably influence his patterns of consumption, savings, and transfer of income to the home country.

At each of the different levels — that of the individual migrant, the household, and the community — this single-migrant, temporary flow of labour will have effects that are fundamentally different from past migrations. The long periods of separation will affect family relationships, marriage, and fertility. It will lead to a new disposition of roles within the household. In many cases there will be some enhancement of responsibility for women. But as the following studies show, Asian migration to the Middle East also has important sociocultural and human costs. Adjustment problems for the migrant and his family are likely to impose heavy emotional and psychological strains. The temporary nature of the migration also poses a major problem both to the migrant and the economy. When the migrant returns and re-enters the workforce, his readjustment to a lower level of income and to an occupation commensurate with the skills he has acquired abroad may be difficult and frustrating. At the macro-economic level, the absorption of returnees will require special strategies on the part of the planners and policy-makers.

The Asian labour migration to the Middle East is also distinguished from previous migratory flows by the wide participation of different socioeconomic groups. Whereas past Asian migrations were confined largely to professional and other highly educated strata, the current migration to the Middle East spans the entire range of manpower, from unskilled to skilled and professional employees. Nevertheless, manual workers, both unskilled and skilled, form by far the largest proportion of migrants. They are recruited from the lower-income groups, predominantly from the rural areas. Through the migration to the Middle East these groups have enjoyed access to employment opportunities at relatively high income levels, often surpassing the incomes enjoyed by upper-income groups in their own societies.

A further important feature of the Middle East migration is the special type of interdependence it has created between the countries importing the labour and those supplying it. Most of the economies of the labour-supplying countries have become heavily dependent on their migrant workforce in the Middle East; it helps them manage their balance of payments and it relieves unemployment. The degree of dependence varies from country to country, the Republic of Korea's dependence being relatively low and Pakistan's quite high. On the other hand, the workforce of the labour-importing countries contains an unusually high proportion of migrants. The dependence of these countries on their expatriate workforce is by no means marginal. It can be described as structural. At least for a considerable period in the future, these economies will have to rely on a large stock of migrant workers, both to maintain their levels of consumption and to expand their economies at reasonable rates of growth. We need, however, much more reliable and detailed information on the stock and flow of the migrant workforce, together with shifts in demand in the labour markets of the labour-importing countries, before we can define the exact dimensions of the problems and assess their implications for Asia. Nevertheless, it will be used to devote some space to considering the estimates and data that are available. This should help us to ascertain at least some broad orders of magnitude within which the problem can be perceived.

The Migrant Workforce: Trends and Prospects

The studies in the present volume indicate that, with the exception of the Republic of Korea, there are no firm data on the existing stock of migrants in the Middle East. This applies in particular to Pakistan and India. The estimates made thus far by various scholars and institutions show wide divergences in regard to both the national workforces and the migrant component. If we accept one of the more oft-quoted sources, in 1975 the non-national workforce in the major labour-importing Middle East countries was 1.79 million. This amounted to 48.7 per cent of the total work-force in seven major labour-importing countries, where 20.3 per cent of the migrant workforce, or approximately 350,000, were Asians (see Table 1). Since 1975 the migrant workforce has expanded rapidly. The gross outflow of migrants from the Asian countries alone has multiplied severalfold. It is difficult to estimate the net increment to the migrant stock during this period, because information on the return flow is extremely scanty and unreliable.

Most analysts of the Middle East labour migration have commented on the shrinking supply of labour from the poorer Arab countries and the increasing dependence of the oil-rich Middle East on Asian migrant labour. Most of the initial migration to the rich Arab states came from the poorer Arab countries nearby. By the mid-1970s, however, the labour-importing countries were finding new sources of labour in Asia. Birks and Sinclair have argued that by 1975 the volume of Arab migrant workers represented "a number close to the demographic and economic potential and certainly to the political limits of Arab labour exportation." Moreover, the type of labour migration from Asian countries is likely to be more politically acceptable to the host countries; it could be managed more easily within a temporary enclave that would tend to ensure the return home of the migrants. Therefore, Asian migrant labour probably increased its share of the workforce in the labour-importing Arab countries from 1975 to 1980 and has continued to do so thereafter.

TABLE 1. Population, National Workforce, and Migrant Workforce for Major Arab Labour-Importing Countries, 1975 (in thousands)

	Population			Workforce				
	National	Migrant	Asian	National	Migrant	%	Asian	%
Saudi Arabia	4592.5	1565	93.8	1026.5	773	43	38	2.1
Libya	2223.7	531.4	14.6	449.2	332	42.5	5.5	.7
Oman	550.0	132.2	103.7	137	70.7		58.7	28.2
Kuwait	472.1	502.4	56.1	91.8	208	69.4	33.6	11.2
Bahrain	214.0	56.0	36.5	45.8	30	34.0	16.6	21.9
U.A.E.	200.0	456	311.3	45.0	251.5	84.8	163.5	55.1
Qatar	67.9	97.0	58.2	12.5	53.7	81.1	34.01	51.3
Total	8320.2	3497.9	691.8	1807.8	1719.7		349.9	

Source: Birks and Sinclair.

We could try to get another set of estimates of the stock of migrants in the Middle East as well as their rates of growth by examining first the absorptive capacity of the economies and the feasible limits to the expansion of the migrant workforce. According to World Bank estimates, the labour force of high-income oil exporters grew at approximately 3.8 per cent from 1960 to 1970, and 4.5 per cent from 1970 to 1982. It is expected to grow at an annual average of 3.8 per cent from 1982 to 2000. It is difficult to estimate the foreign component of the incremental workforce. The participation rates of the national population in the workforce is now exceptionally low in these countries, but it would be reasonable to expect a higher rate of work participation as structural changes take place, as the agricultural workforce declines as a share of the total, and as female labour participation increases. Table 2 presents some tentative estimates and projections based on the assumption that the workforce for the labour-importing Arab states has grown up to 1982 at the rates reported by the World Bank and will grow for the period 1982–1990 at 4 per cent per annum. It is assumed that the national workforce will grow at an annual

TABLE 2. Migration of Asian Labour to Arab Countries — Estimates up to 1982 and Projections to 1990 (in thousands)

	1975[1]		1980		1982		1985		1990	
	Number	Growth Rate, %	Number	Growth Rate, %	Number	Growth Rate, %	Number	Growth Rate, %	Number	Growth Rate, %
Total workforce	3539.5	4.5	4394.6	4.5	4807.0	4.5	5403.0	4	6570.0	4
National workforce	1807.8	2.6	2052.7	2.6	2159.6	2.6	2332.3	2.6	2649.4	2.6
Migrant workforce	1719.7	6.6	2341.0	6.4	2647.4	5	3070.7	5	3921.0	5
Asian migrant workforce	349.0	23	971.0	14	1269.0	10.1	1692.0	8.5	2542.0	

1. Birks and Sinclair.

average of 2.6 per cent — the estimate adopted by Birks and Sinclair for their projections for the period 1975–1980. Based on these estimates, the migrant workforce should have grown to 2.341 million in 1980, 2.647 million in 1982, and 3.07 million in 1985. If, for the reasons stated earlier, we assume that the additional supply will come entirely from Asia, then the outer limits for the Asian migrant workforce in the Middle East according to these estimates would be 971,000 in 1980, 1.269 million in 1982, and approximately 1.7 million in 1985.

TABLE 3. Estimates of Gross Annual Flow and Stock of Asian Migrants to the Middle East (in thousands)

	India	Bangladesh	Sri Lanka	Thailand[1]	Philippines[2]	Republic of Korea	Pakistan
1976	Annual average 67.5	6.08	1.5	—	19.2	21.2	—
1977		15.7	7.5	—	31.1	52.24	—
1978		22.8	12.5	5.1	43.2	81.98	—
1979		24.48	24.0	12.9	78.6	99.14	118.3
1980	Annual average 220.0	30.57	27.0	42.3	133.7	127.3	118.3
1981		55.78	55.0	69.7	179.2	153.6	153.0
1982		62.80	55.0	104.0	212.5	159.9	137.0
1983		1st quarter 26.40					
Stock as at 1982[3]	1000.0	118.5	110.0	173.7	391.6	170.0	1250.0

Based on data in country studies.

1. Estimated on total annual flow of remittances and average remittance per worker as given in the study for years 1978-81 (assuming return flow equal to previous year's outflow). Ministry of Labour figure for 1982.
2. Estimated at 85% of the figure for land-based contract workers, as given in study.
3. As estimated in the country studies for India, Pakistan, and the Republic of Korea. For other countries, the stock as at end of 1982 is estimated as the total of the flow for 1981 and 1982.

These estimates are much lower than those derived from the data quoted in the country studies (see Table 3). They are also far below forecasts made by the World Bank in 1979, which estimated that the migrant workforce would grow to approximately 3.8 million by 1985 (see Table 4). The World Bank projections were, however, made when the prospects for the oil-exporting countries were quite favourable, prior to the downturn in oil prices. The high estimates of the stock of migrants derived from the country studies and various other sources — particularly those for India and Pakistan — do not appear to be consistent with reasonable projections of the workforce made on realistic assumptions of growth rates. This situation underscores the urgent need for more reliable and comprehensive information on the stock and flow of migrant workers, which is vital for manpower planning and the management of labour markets, both in the host and the labour-exporting countries.

The long-term scenario will feature major shifts in both the demand and supply of migrant labour; labour-supplying and labour-importing countries need to take this into account. On the one hand, there will be a growing demand for manpower in the labour-supplying countries themselves as their economies undergo structural transformation. These changes will take place at different rates among the different countries, affecting their ability to supply labour to the Middle East market both in terms of volume and skill composition. This would mean that the level of country participation in the migration will change over time. All may not supply the same skills. As domestic wages increase, demand for employment abroad will contract in some countries faster than in others. As the structures of their economies change, the differentials between domestic wages and the wages in host countries will narrow. Even in the current situation, significant differences prevail in regard both to the wage structure within the labour-supplying countries and to the skill composition of the migrant workers. Already in the Republic of Korea we have witnessed the narrowing of the differentials between foreign and domestic wages. Between 1976 and 1980 the ratio of overseas to domestic remuneration decreased from 5.4 to 2.6 for carpenters, 5.1 to 2.3 for welders, and 4.3 to 1.9 for other skilled workers. The migration from the Philippines appears to be largely from among the better-educated and more skilled workers. The largest reservoir of unemployed, low-wage workers is likely to be in the South Asian countries. Therefore, the changes that take place in the economies of labour-supplying countries may enable them to make adjustments among themselves, accommodate the shifts in supply, and manage the migration flow in a less disruptive and less competitive manner over the medium and long term.

The geographical distribution of Asian migration by country of destination in the Middle East varies significantly for these countries (see Table 4). South Korean and Thai migrant workers are mainly in Saudi Arabia. The South Asian countries have a different geographical distribution of the migration. Pakistan, which is the South Asian country with the highest proportion of migrant workers in Saudi Arabia, still has only about half of its workforce in this country, compared to 84.7 per cent for South Korea. The Indian labour migration is lowest in Saudi Arabia and highest in

TABLE 4. Destination of Asian Migrants to the Middle East for Selected Years (percentages)

	Saudi Arabia	Kuwait	U.A.E.	Qatar	Iraq	Libya	Oman	Bahrain	Others
Republic of Korea (1982)	70.8	3.3	0.7	0.8	12.3	10.1	–	–	2.0
Thailand (1982)	84.7	0.58	0.3	2.7	3.0	8.6	–	–	–
Bangladesh (1981/82)	25.6	10.3	8.7	3.4	27.7	6.1	12.3	2.8	3.1
India[1]	14.5	14.5	45.5	4.54	–	–	11.8	4.54	4.54[2]
Pakistan[1]	49.2	–	28.7	–	–	–	–	–	22.4[3]
Sri Lanka (1979)	25.5	24.7	22.2	5.0	–	–	6.4	9.1	6.8

Figures are not available for the Philippines.

1. Refers to the distribution of the stock in Middle East countries.
1. Migrants in Iraq and Libya included here.
2. Migrants in Iraq and Libya included here.
3. Migrants in all countries other than Saudi Arabi and U.A.E. included here.

the United Arab Emirates. The migrant flows of Bangladesh and Sri Lanka are more evenly distributed, with about a quarter moving into Saudi Arabia. In short, each country has different degrees of concentration in the various labour-importing countries of the Middle East. On the basis of the present studies, it is not possible to provide a clear explanation for the variations. They have been influenced by historic ties between the labour-importing and -supplying countries, as in the case of India and the United Arab Emirates. The links between Thai labour and U.S. construction firms established during the Viet Nam war may have been the principal factor in the flow of Thailand's migrant labour to Saudi Arabia. Whatever the causes, the geographical distribution of the migrant workforce will have important consequences for each labour-supplying country. The economic condition in each labour-importing country and its prospects for growth will vary. Policies of recruitment and retrenchment will depend on these internal changes. At least in the short term, labour-supplying countries will be affected according to the present distribution of their workforces in foreign countries.

The host countries, on the other hand, will want to reduce their dependence on a foreign workforce. Their capacity to replace the migrants with local manpower is, however, strictly limited, as it is the overall shortage of manpower that led in the first instance to their recruitment of a foreign workforce. It is only through far-reaching technological change and increased productivity that the host countries will be able to contain the growth of the foreign workforce and their dependence on it. These changes will affect the skill composition of expatriate labour needed by Middle East countries in the future. According to the demand projections made by the World Bank, the major increases will occur in the service, manufacturing, and agriculture sectors. The migrant workforce in the construction sector, which expanded rapidly in the 1970s, was expected to grow only marginally over the 1980–1985 period, increasing from an estimated 737,000 to 770,000. The World Bank estimates, however, projected a rapid increase in the share of the market for professional and subprofessional technical workers, with skilled office and manual workers following close behind. According to these estimates, all office workers in the skilled and semiskilled categories would have together accounted for 698,000, or 62 per cent, of the 1,127,000 additional migrant workers that the Middle East would have required during the 1980–1985 period (see Table 5).

The foregoing discussion indicates that structural changes, both in the countries supplying the manpower and in the host countries, must lead to an equilibrium in the long term which would produce stable and mutually beneficial conditions of interdependence between them. It would be in the mutual interests of these countries to cooperate in working towards such a smooth transition. Both groups of countries need to manage the process of migration so as to realise the fullest benefits from it and to mitigate its inherent economic, political, and sociocultural problems. For the labour-importing countries, the regular turnover of the migrant workforce might be an essential condition to ensure temporary stays for their migrant workers. It would therefore be in their long-term interest to provide incentives for the smooth, homeward-bound flow of migrants via a regular turnover of the workforce. Similarly, the labour-supplying countries should organise and plan their supply of manpower so as to sustain the migration without creating bottlenecks or shortages of the critically important skills required for the long-term structural transformation of their economies. This is particularly important in view of the anticipated changes in the skill composition of the expatriate labour required by the Middle East. These medium- and long-term adjustments will call for greater cooperation and policy coordination between labour-supplying and -importing countries.

TABLE 5. Demand for Expatriate Labour in the Middle East and North Africa, 1980–85 (by occupation)

	1980	1981	1982	1983	1984	1985
Professional and technical	139,405	149,179	159,195	170,730	184,073	210,769
percentage change		7.0	6.7	7.2	7.8	14.5
Other professional	252,636	271,614	291,234	313,506	337,300	380,960
percentage change		7.5	7.2	7.6	7.6	12.9
Subprofessional and technical	200,095	221,327	238,262	254,173	275,317	313,322
percentage change		10.6	7.6	6.7	8.3	13.8
Other subprofessional	115,321	125,245	130,577	133,078	138,399	151,371
percentage change		8.6	4.3	1.9	4.0	9.5
Skilled office and manual	801,148	858,594	914,064	973,108	1,043,997	1,152,784
percentage change		7.2	6.4	6.4	7.3	10.4
Semiskilled office and manual	599,118	660,478	721,919	793,902	882,674	947,988
percentage change		10.2	9.3	10.0	11.2	7.4
Unskilled	474,417	487,044	497,994	512,659	547,874	551,946
percentage change		2.7	2.2	3.0	6.9	0.7
Total	2,582,140	2,773,481	2,953,245	3,151,156	3,409,634	3,709,140
percentage change		7.4	6.5	6.7	8.2	8.8

Projections cover the following countries: Algeria, Bahrain, Iran, Kuwait, Libya, Oman, Qatar, Saudi Arabia, United Arab Emirates.

Source: World Bank, 7 September 1979, cited in World Bank, Labor Migration from Bangladesh to the Middle East, 1981.

A New Conceptual Framework

A definitional and analytical framework that takes full account of the characteristics of the Asian labour migration to the Middle East has to include many new elements. In many past migrations, various noneconomic factors played an important role. Religious persecutions, political upheavals, imperialistic expansion, and disasters such as the Irish famine all led to large movements of people across national boundaries. Much of this migration was involuntary. In addition, these movements took place when the distribution of the population over the earth's habitable surface offered more scope for new habitats and for permanent, large-scale migrations.

The emergence of an international labour market is a more recent phenomenon and has generated equilibrating forces, resulting in the movement of manpower across national boundaries. The growth and expansion of capitalist modes of production in various parts of the world, and the resulting imbalances in the supply of capital and labour are largely responsible for the creation of this new labour market. In the colonial phase of capitalist expansion, large flows of voluntary migration occurred between imperial centres and the colonies as well as among the colonies themselves. These helped, among other things, to supply the manpower needs of the colonial economic system. The Asian countries participated in the migrations by supplying unskilled labour to plantations and mines in Asian countries and by sending high- and mid-level manpower to the African colonies. The voluntary international flows of manpower during the postcolonial phase are of a significantly different order, occuring in the aftermath of the profound global changes and the unprecedented expansion of the world economy following World War II. Even within these changes, the Asian labour migration to the Middle East forms part of the later phase, when economic relations between the developed and developing countries, as well as the relations among the developing countries themselves, underwent major adjustments. The Asian labour migration, therefore, should be analysed within the framework of the more recent developments in the world capitalist system. It must also be considered in the context of the changing North-South and South-South relations.

The changes in the world economic structure must be viewed alongside the vast technological advances in transport and communication. These revolutionary improvements in international travel and communication have to a large extent removed many of the privations formerly associated with the movement of people across vast distances. They have transformed international migration. In many cases, these advances have eased the migrants' problems of adjustment by enabling them to have continuing contact with their families and by vastly extending the potential for mobility and interaction in the modern world. Today, this mobility takes place in a continuum that includes short-term international travel for specific purposes at one end, temporary migration for employment abroad at another point, and permanent migration and resettlement. The sociocultural and human implications of international migration in the modern world, therefore, require a different frame of analysis. Migration has changed; consequently our analytical framework must also change. This task, however, should be undertaken as a separate United Nations University study and might well form a component of the next phase of this project.

An Overview of the National Impact of Migration

The preceding section attempted to define the special character of the Asian migration to the Middle East and referred to its far-reaching social and economic impact. Before we proceed to the country studies, a quick overview of the national situations would be quite useful. Although the labour-supplying countries of Asia share the fact of Middle East migration, they can be distinguished from each other by a variety of features.

TABLE 6. Annual Flow of Remittances from the Middle East as Share of Merchandise Exports, 1982

	Remittances (millions)	Remittances as % of Exports
Bangladesh	US$600[1]	65.8
Pakistan	US$2,580[2]	107.0
Philippines	US$508[3]	10.1
Republic of Korea[4]	US$3,448[5]	20.0
Sri Lanka	Rs 3,000[1]	14.0
Thailand	B 10,326[1]	10.0

1. Estimates in country studies.
2. *World Development Report, 1984,* tables 9 and 14, pp. 234. 244.
3. Estimated from country figures given in country study, as a proportion of total remittances. Figure includes remittances of all land-based contract workers
4. The figures for the Republic of Korea are for 1980.
5. Includes income of firms and migrant workers. Estimates in country studies.

Economic Impact

Understandably, the economic impact of the Asian labour migration varies from country to country. If we look at the data in Table 6, we observe that, when measured as a proportion of export earnings, the support given to the balance of payments through private remittances is largest in the case of Pakistan. In 1982 the receipt of workers' remittances exceeded the earnings from merchandise exports – $2,580 million as against $2,403 million. The Bangladesh study estimates that remittances amounted to 65.8 per cent of export earnings and covered approximately 73 per cent of the value of oil imports. The author observes that the additional flow of remittances in 1979 and 1980 "is seen not only to have compensated for the dramatic fall in the terms of trade but to have gone some way towards mitigating the effects of a reduced aid flow."

TABLE 7. Labour Migration to Middle East as Proportion of Incremental Workforce and Open Unemployed, 1982

	Gross Outflow	Percentage of Incremental Workforce	Number of Open Unemployed	Outflow as % of Unemployed
Thailand	104,000	26	286,000	36.3
Philippines	212,000	31.5[2]	775,000	27.3
Republic of Korea	159,000	31.1[2]	660,000	24.0
Pakistan	137,535	16.8	850,000[1]	16.8
Sri Lanka	55,000	42.2	815,000	6.7
Bangladesh	62,805	4.1[2]	n.a.	—

1. Estimated on the rate of unemployment of 4.4%
2. Estimated from IBRD, *World Development Report, 1984,* Table 21, p. 258.

Source: Country studies.

For India, the flow of remittances amounted to approximately 25 per cent of export earnings for the year 1982. It was somewhat higher for Sri Lanka — about 28 per cent in 1982. In the Philippines, the remittances from land-based contract workers abroad were around $450 million in 1979, amounting to approximately 7.5 per cent of the earnings from exports for that year. In Thailand, the remittances as a proportion of export earnings run around 10 per cent. The Republic of Korea's earnings from foreign contracts and labour overseas amounted to nearly 20 per cent of export earnings in 1980.

These figures, however, are for the total flow of remittances from all migrants abroad. From the information available, we can conclude that the major share of this flow comes from the migrant workers in the Middle East, but there are wide variations. In the case of Sri Lanka it would appear that remittances from the Middle East are not more than 50 to 55 per cent. Similarly, it is likely that in the case of the Philippines the sources of remittance are considerably diversified and include a substantial contribution from workers on non-national ships as well as migrants who have permanently settled in North America. These problems highlight the uncertainties relating to the available data on many aspects of the migration. For most of these countries, the export of manpower and the income from such exports has become as important as their principal commodity exports. Therefore, the data that provide adequate information on the size of the flow, its sources, and its regularity become crucially important for the management of the external sectors.

Most of the studies conclude that migrant workers in the Middle East are remitting a high proportion of their earnings. It is estimated, for example, that Bangladeshi workers remit approximately 70 per cent of their earnings and that there is hardly any gap between potential and actual remittances. According to calculations in the studies, the proportions of earnings remitted are significantly lower for Sri Lanka, and probably lowest for the Philippines. With the exception of South Korea, however, these assessments are based on very rough estimates of the stock of migrants and on assumptions regarding skill composition and average earnings. As stated earlier, the incentive for migrant workers to remit a large proportion of their savings is quite strong. But the extent to which remittances make a positive contribution to a country's balance of payments depends on whether they are sent through official channels. In the case of the Republic of Korea, Korean migrants provide the labour component of a project managed in the Middle East by Korean firms. As a result the remittance of earnings is well regulated and possibilities of leakage are almost non-existent. In countries where there are no large gaps between the official and unofficial exchange rates, there is no strong incentive to channel remittances into the unofficial market. Bangladesh has devised a premium exchange rate to attract remittances into the official market. But in India, the Philippines, and, to some extent, Pakistan there are likely to be considerable leakages of foreign exchange.

Table 8 provides a tentative comparison of average earnings by migrants from

TABLE 8. Average Monthly Earnings of Asian Migrant Workers in the Middle East: Estimates from Country Studies

	Average Monthly Earnings
Bangladesh	Tk 3,500
India, Kerala	
unskilled	Rs 1,500–3,000
semiskilled	Rs 2,500–5,000
skilled	Rs 3,000–7,500
Pakistan	RsP 3,750–6,850
Philippines	US$335–665
Sri Lanka	
unskilled	RsSL 2,200–4,800
skilled	RsSL 2,700–7,300
mid-level	RsSL 6,300–8,000
Republic of Korea	US$756
Thailand	B 12,000

1. Averages for all categories of workers except as indicated.

14

different Asian countries. The differences in average earnings will, among other things, reflect the differences in the skill composition of the migrant workforce from each country. However, it has been the accepted policy of the labour-importing countries to fix the remuneration with reference to the countries of origin and the wage levels prevailing there. Consequently, migrants from the South Asian countries appear to be receiving lower salaries than their counterparts from Southeast Asia. This is reflected in the remittances shown in Table 6. The average earning appears to be highest for the Republic of Korea, and this cannot be explained entirely in terms of its lower proportion of unskilled workers. Thailand, whose workforce has a considerable contingent of unskilled and semiskilled labour, still has an average earning that is significantly higher than that of Pakistan.

There is not enough information to examine how these wage differentials operate in the process of recruitment or how they affect the migrations from each country. The market for migrant labour in the host countries would, under normal conditions, respond to the wage differentials in a manner that favours the cheaper source for the same type of skill. Political considerations and noneconomic preferences might intervene to regulate the market. On the whole, however, it might be expected that with the prevailing wage differentials and the likely upward movement of wages in East and Southeast Asia, the South Asian countries will remain the most economical source of labour for the Middle East.

The use of remittances by the recipient households is related issue. It can reduce some of the benefits that are assumed to accrue from the employment of workers abroad. First, it introduces changes into expenditure patterns and increases the demand for imports. Although migrant workers remit considerable savings in foreign exchange, thereby contributing to the country's balance of payments, a large share of the money is spent on a wide range of imported goods, including modern household appliances and expensive consumer durables. The high incomes earned by migrant workers can lead to major changes in the life-styles of their families, which tend to increase the import content of regular household expenditures, apart from the once-for-all spending on imported consumer durables. These spending patterns tend to reduce the net foreign exchange benefit of the migration. No country study has attempted to examine the net benefit and to quantify it, as the data available are entirely inadequate for such an exercise. All the country studies, however, refer to micro-research that runs counter to the popular belief that the windfall incomes accruing to low-income households of migrant workers are frittered away in wasteful consumption and various forms of extravagant spending. Most studies indicate that the average migrant worker spends his money prudently — his behaviour largely influenced by the knowledge that his employment is temporary and that he must use his resources to plan for a stable future.

The expenditure patterns of migrant households reported in the studies have many features in common. There is no doubt that elements of extravagant expenditure and conspicuous consumption are present. Households are keen on demonstrating their success and achieving a higher social status. This they try to do by acquiring visible social symbols of affluence and well-being. They tend to spend heavily on ceremonies and social occasions through which Asian households and families conventionally demonstrate their standing in the community. These include marriages, festivals, and similar occasions. But apart from expenditures of this type, households spend on items which bring lasting benefits to their members. These include investments in education, housing, and employment — particularly small enterprises that create self-employment. Many studies, however, conclude that much more research is needed on migrant households and their use of remittances from abroad. The studies also caution against simplistic conclusions concerning the demonstration effect of migrant spending. They stress the need to trace the ways in which migrant spending influences nonmigrant households through various types of interaction. On the one hand, the labour migration could create a greater, economy-wide propensity for consumption and higher import demand, both of which are beyond present capacities. On the other, the migrants' higher standards of living may demonstrate the rewards of hard work. Higher expectations and the demand thus generated may help raise the level of activity and productive effort in the community as a whole and eventually contribute to savings, investment, and growth.

Almost all the studies indicate that the data on the return flow of migrants are inadequate for determining the annual net outflow. With the exception of the Republic of Korea, most of the labour-exporting countries do not have enough data at a disaggregated level. Therefore, they cannot determine the impact of the migration on different segments of the labour market. Firm conclusions cannot be made on the impact of the migration on the labour market nor on the employment levels in these countries. The studies reveal that in most of these countries the gross annual outflow amounts to a sizeable share of the annual increment to the labour force.

In Sri Lanka, for example, it constitutes about 40 per cent; it is 16.8 per cent for Pakistan and 26 per cent for Thailand. But this alone is not adequate, as we need more information on the return flow in order to estimate the net addition to employment created by the opportunities provided by the migration. In evaluating the effect of the migration on the labour market, most studies conclude that the migration has had little adverse effect on the supply of labour for domestic needs. In most of the countries, the vast majority of migrants to the Middle East are recruited from the unemployed and the underemployed workforce. Employment abroad and the consequent withdrawal from the workforce can therefore help appreciably to reduce the rates of unemployment. This will be true of a large part of the migrations from Thailand, Sri Lanka, Bangladesh, Pakistan, and India. The exception appears to be the Philippines, where the migrants are reported to be mainly from the employed workforce and from sectors where the skills are scarce. In the case of the Republic of Korea, migration is regulated through firms and is therefore manageable in terms of national priorities.

Furthermore, significant variations exist in the migrants' skills (see Table 9). The effects of the migration on the labour market of the labour-supplying countries will therefore vary according to these differences in skill composition. Although the manual and operative workers appear to comprise the major share of the labour migration, the shares of the skilled and unskilled categories, as well as the types of

TABLE 9. Skill Composition of Asian Migrants in the Middle East (percentages)

Republic of Korea		Sri Lanka		Pakistan	
Construction[1]	48.2	High-level		Professional	4.33
Drivers and		doctors,		Clerical	1.52
mechanics	14.3	engineers,		Service	2.19
Nurses	0.4	accountants	1.9	Skilled	
Sailors	0.3	Mid-level		production	
Unskilled	18.1	technicians,		workers	40.6
Others	18.7	foremen,		Unskilled	42.5
		clerical	7.6	Others	8.8
		Skilled	20.3		
		Unskilled	53.7		
		Others	16.5		

Philippines		Bangladesh		Thailand	
Professional and		Construction[2]	50.5	Unskilled	13.1
technical	10.4	Transport		Carpenters	18.5
Managerial and		equipment		Construction	19.2
executive	3.5	operators	15.3	Mechanics and	
Clerical and		Production	6.4	electricians	9.7
administrative	4.2	Clerical	1.2	Other skilled	7.1
Sales and service	15.9	Technicians	2.6	Drivers	11.4
Production and		Professional	5.5	Foremen	4.1
transport	65.6	Service	8.0	Cooks	3.9
Others	0.4	Others	10.8	Others	8.5

1. Semiskilled and skilled.
2. Includes unskilled.

occupation, vary from country to country. Unskilled workers account for a relatively small proportion of migrants from South Korea and the Philippines, whereas they form a majority in the other countries. One feature specific to the Sri Lankan migration is the large proportion of unskilled female workers going into domestic service in the households of Arab countries. Although most migrant workers are skilled or unskilled labourers, in all cases the migration includes a small proportion of high- and mid-level manpower. Several studies show that even for these higher categories, the output from the national system exceeded the domestic demand and that, therefore, the withdrawal of these professional and mid-level workers did not create any critical shortages. In most of the countries, the impact of the migration was felt mainly in the construction sector. But even here, the workers could be replaced after relatively short time lags. Most countries were in a position to undertake accelerated training programmes to meet some of the shortages.

Sri Lanka found itself in a special situation. For a variety of reasons unique to Sri Lanka, the migration coincided with a massive programme of investment that raised the rates of capital formation to unprecedented levels from 1977 to 1982. This placed unusual demands on the construction sector and led to particularly steep price and wage increases in this sector. The migration of skilled manpower from the construction sector to the Middle East compounded the problems, contributing to the high rate of inflation that prevailed during this period. But in most other countries the migrations took place when the economies were feeling the serious impact of the world recession, when employment had slackened and unemployment risen.

We should not, however, exaggerate the impact of the migration on the employment situation of the labour-exporting countries. We saw earlier that the growth of the migrant workforce in the host countries and the net outflow of workers from the labour-supplying countries must bear some relation to the annual increase of the workforce in the host countries and their absorptive capacity. The shares of each participating country in this increase of the migrant workforce will vary depending on the structural changes that are taking place within the labour-supplying countries themselves as well as their capacity to supply skills according to the changing composition of demand in the host countries. As stated earlier, we could assume that the greater part of the future supply of expatriate labour to the Arab countries may come from the Asian region. But even with an optimistic forecast of economic growth in the Middle East countries, the Asian migrant workforce is not likely to grow at a rate exceeding 10 per cent per annum. During the initial spurt of migration following the massive increases in oil revenues of the oil-exporting countries, the flow of migration from Asia appears to have increased at approximately 25 per cent per annum. The net outflow is likely to stabilise at an annual rate of growth in the region of 10 per cent.

We can apply these assumptions to the migration from Sri Lanka and assess the impact on employment. It is likely that an increasing share of the Asian migration will be taken over by South Asian countries because of their large reservoir of cheap labour. If this happens, we might expect the new outflow of migration from Sri Lanka to be higher than 10 per cent. But even if it rises to 15 per cent, the net addition to employment will be not more than 16,500, or about 12 per cent of the annual incremnt to the workforce. It would, therefore, seem imprudent for the labour-exporting countries to expect the Middle East migration to continue to relieve unemployment in the same manner as it did during the initial phase when the Middle East countries were

compelled to correct the massive imbalance between capital and labour in their countries. This points to the need for labour-exporting countries to obtain the maximum benefit from the migration in terms of employment creation through better use
of remittances and the channelling of workers' earnings into productive employment-
generating investments.

The effects of the migration on income distribution is another aspect explored in the
studies that follow. Undoubtably, the major share of economic opportunities provided
through the migration go to the manual labourers in the low-income sector of the
labour-exporting countries. To that extent the low-income households are the primary
beneficiaries of the migration and are enabled to climb the socioeconomic ladder.
However, the households that gain these opportunities comprise only a small
proportion of the total socioeconomic group to which they belong. Some of the
studies point out that while the migration helps a minority of low-income households,
on the aggregate these substantial increases of income accruing to a few may worsen
economic disparities. But to the extent that even a few households are able to move
out of poverty, the migration must also serve to reduce poverty in aggregate terms.
Also, inasmuch as these income increases occur because of transfers from earnings
abroad, the process does not lead to what might be described as an "extraction of
surplus" from the local groups. The studies also point out that various other factors
should be considered in order to assess the effects of migration on the poor. The flow
of income to these low-income groups has various spillover effects by way of spreading
the benefits to dependents and relatives of the migrants as well as to the community.
It also creates new employment opportunities for those left behind. These opportunities include the vacancies created by departing migrants, as well as the new
employment generated by investments made out of the migrants' savings. The income
gains resulting from the transfer of earnings from abroad may also have an impact on
demand, particularly demand for essential products such as food, which are produced
by the poor. This in turn would help to generate economic activity that raises their
incomes.

But, in discussing the distribution of benefits, all the studies except the one on the
Republic of Korea draw attention to the various forms of exploitation of migrant
workers by the numerous intermediaries that have entered the scene. The labour
migration has become a lucrative business for employment agencies. Most studies
refer to various malpractices: extortionate commission fees, fraud, falsification of
documents, and discrepancies between formal contracts of employment and actual
work conditions. All these drastically reduce the benefits that eventually accrue to the
migrants. The Thai study estimates that, on the average, payments to intermediaries
siphon away as much as two months of a migrant's earnings. Nevertheless, the gap
between the migrant's earnings abroad and his income from employment at home is so
vast that the net gain for the average migrant remains substantial.

The Human and Sociocultural Adjustments

We have only fragmentary information on the sociocultural adjustments of migrants and their families. Some work has been done at the micro-level to ascertain changes in social structures, family relationships, and value systems, and some information is also available on the migrants' problems of adjustment in the host countries. In considering these adjustments it is interesting to note the different types of linkages extant between the labour-supplying and labour-importing countries before the full-scale migration started. In the case of Thailand, the entry into the Middle East appears to have been facilitated by U.S. firms that had previously worked in Thailand during the Viet Nam war and had hired Thai workers in a number of major projects. In the case of Pakistan and India, the links with the Middle East go back much further. The Kerala study describes how small Indian communities are engaged in a number of Middle East countries, participating in different sectors of the economy ranging from public services to business and trade. The Indian presence is mainly concentrated in the United Arab Emirates (see Table 5). According to the Kerala study, it is estimated that the major share of Indian migrant labour in the Middle East is in the United Arab Emirates, in contrast to almost all other countries, most of whose migrant workforce is in Saudi Arabia.

In the case of both Pakistanis and Indians, the migrant workers have a larger migrant community of their own nationals who have long resided in these countries and who provide the new migrants with an immediate community network. The Kerala study refers to the variety of social and recreational activities that are organised by the migrants. The adjustment problems of Indian and Pakistani migrant workers will therefore be less acute. In this respect the migrants from the Philippines, Thailand, and Sri Lanka are less fortunate. Culturally, migrants from Pakistan and Bangladesh and, to a lesser extent, those from India would have closer affinities with the nationals of the host countries. This would be particularly true of Moslem migrants from these countries. The studies have not drawn specific attention to this aspect of cultural adjustment, but the surveys of the Thai and Korean migrations make special mention of the hardships imposed by the customs and laws of host countries that prohibit the consumption of alcoholic liquor and various forms of entertainment that are commonplace and acceptable to Thais and Koreans.

The migration from the Republic of Korea stands apart from the others for a number of reasons. Korean migrant workers are employed abroad in projects undertaken by Korean firms. As a result, the recruitment of workers, their deployment in the host countries, and their living and working conditions all differ markedly from those of migrants from other countries. They live in small Korean enclaves in the Middle East countries, and most of them work for Korean employers. In this respect it might be argued that the Korean migration will not give rise to the same problems of adjustment experienced by workers from other countries. The author of the Korean study, however, argues that the enclave type migration presents serious problems of its own.

Because the Korean workers are recruited by the firms themselves, the whole process of migration is better organised and managed. Corruption, exploitation of workers, and other malpractices that are present in almost all other countries do not appear to afflict the Korean migration. The benefits of the migration both in terms of profits and remittances are better realised because Korea is able to capture both the income from labour and the income from profits. The Korean activities in the Middle East have also promoted trade between the Republic of Korea and the Middle East countries, particularly in the supply of intermediate goods, equipment, and other materials required for the projects undertaken there.

As might be expected, the sociocultural impact of the migration varies widely from country to country. For example, in Kerala, with its rigid social stratification, the migration has acted as an important catalyst for social change. Groups that had been quite low in the social hierarchy have been able to participate in the migration and have improved their socioeconomic status and overcome some of the social barriers inherent in the traditional system. While these developments have helped to loosen the rigidities in the social structure, at the same time, the rapidity and discontinuity of the changes have resulted in a high incidence of mental ill-health; divorce rates have risen; family ties and relationships have weakened; and delinquency among children and young persons has increased. The study points out that these trends are evident in the communities with high levels of migration to the Middle East. Most of the studies highlight the effect of the migration on the personal lives of migrants and their families. The long separations have proved particularly hard on marriage relationships. But, at the same time, there is evidence that the separations have promoted a new appreciation for family ties and have strengthened family relationships.

This brief overview of the studies shows that the labour migration can have many different outcomes. Migration is primarily a human phenomenon, and its outcome depends on the responses of the participating migrants and their households, as well as on the policy framework and institutions of the labour-supplying countries. For many countries, the migration poses new economic and social management problems. The new resource it has brought to the economy has to be given even greater attention than the traditional export sectors. It calls for tools of analysis, modes for promoting markets, development of manpower both to supply the international market and to satisfy domestic demand — all of which calls for new capacities of a different order. As an economic activity, the migration is perceived primarily as an export of manpower with its attendant consequences, but as an activity with human and social dimensions, it requires attention from quite another part of the national system. It calls for disciplines of a different kind. The studies that follow point out that most countries are attempting to grapple with the different problems of migration in a variety of ways. They are still, however, only at the initial stages of the task of creating the required mix of policies and institutions. Some countries have had greater success than others, but in all cases there are large gaps of knowledge and information, insufficient policy responses to the key issues, and meagre institutional frameworks to deal with and coordinate all aspects of the problem. Progress in the three major areas — (1) the information and statistical base, (2) the formulation of policies and measures, (3) the institutional framework and governmental machinery — varies widely. The way in which a country designs an effective system for managing the migration will depend on how these three components of the system function.

The chapters that follow survey the situation in seven Asian countries that are exporting labour to the Middle East: Bangladesh, India, Pakistan, Sri Lanka, the Republic of Korea, the Philippines, and Thailand. These are revised versions of more comprehensive country studies, which have been suitably abbreviated for inclusion in the present volume. The concluding chapter examines some of the main issues that emerge from the studies and discusses the policy responses and institutional improvements that have been suggested by the authors.

BANGLADESH

S. R. Osmani
Senior Research Fellow, Bangladesh Institute of Development Studies

Large-scale human migration is not a recent phenomenon. Since World War II, however, migrations have assumed certain unique features. In the past — before World War II — people migrated mostly to settle permanently in a different land, peopling whole new continents in the process. Most modern migrations, on the other hand, have been temporary. The prime example from recent history is the massive migration into Europe in response to the need to rebuild its war-ravaged economies. A still more recent example is the large influx of labour into the oil-exporting countries of the Middle East.

Such episodes of migration can be described as temporary in two quite different respects. First, the flow of labour can be a response to a specific economic need of the host country — a need arising when the availability of material resources has suddenly outstripped the supply of complementary labour. The second situation relates not to the overall migration but to individual migrants. The overall flow, although temporary, can survive for a considerable span of time, even decades, but the time spent abroad by individual migrants is usually very much shorter.

As far as individual labour-exporting countries are concerned, there is, in fact, a third dimension of "impermanence." Although demand for migrant labour in an aggregate sense continues to thrive in the host countries, particular labour-exporting countries might find that their workers are no longer in demand. This may happen if the particular skill offered by a country's migrant workers becomes redundant because of structural changes in the economies of the labour-importing countries.

This impermanence that is built into modern migrations has in turn led to certain consequences that, again, are unique in history. The most interesting consequences are (1) the volume of remittances, and (2) the lurking fear of mass repatriation. As a rule, the migrants do not perceive themselves as settling permanently in their places of work, so they tend to remit a large fraction of their savings to their households in the home country. Such flows of remittances have grown at a cracking pace over the past decade or so. For a few countries the share of these flows in their foreign exchange earnings is as high as 70 to 75 per cent,[1] opening up new prospects for accelerating domestic economic growth or, at the least, cushioning the shock suffered by some because of the oil price increases. At the same time, such remittances have created worries. When opportunities for employment abroad decline and the migrants begin to return home, the economy will not only have to adjust to a shockingly low level of foreign exchange earnings, it will also have to face the formidable task of reabsorbing the migrant workers, both economically and socially.

Bangladesh has actively participated over the last decade in the exportation of labour and has thus also benefited from flows of remittances. From 1976 up to mid- 1983, about 0.25 million people left Bangladesh to earn wages abroad, mostly in the Middle East. In fiscal year 1982/83, the remittances of these migrant worker equalled about 75 per cent of the country's export earnings. Such a mammoth phenomenon is bound to have wide-ranging repercussions in almost every aspect of the economy. In the event of a mass repatriation, Bangladesh will have to confront massive social and economic upheavals. It is from this twin perspective of present and future that we shall deal with the issue of emigration from Bangladesh.

As might be expected, this paper draws heavily on the recent World Bank study on labour migration from Bangladesh,[2] as this is the only major study of its kind. Very little work has been done in this area since then. We have, however, tried to update data wherever possible, and to utilise whatever additional material was available, especially on the sociocultural aspects of the phenomenon.

Volume and Profile of Migrants

Volume of Migration

Prior to the independence of Bangladesh in 1971, most of the migration was destined for the Western developed world, particularly the United Kingdom. By far a vast majority of these migrants came from a single district of Bangladesh, Sylhet. But this pattern changed dramatically in the 1970s. On the one hand, the United Kingdom's increasingly stricter laws of immigration brought the traditional pattern of migration almost to a standstill. On the other hand, the newfound wealth of the Middle East began to attract the jobless and the poorly paid people of Asia, including those from Bangladesh.

Significant numbers of Bangladeshi nationals are said to have started migrating to the Middle East in 1971. Many of those who were trapped in then West Pakistan during the war of liberation managed to escape to the West to seek their future in the countries of the Gulf region. When the demand for expatriate labour in these countries rapidly expanded after 1973, these migrants brought their friends and relatives, often at their own expense. The flow of migrant labour to the Middle East, therefore, began almost entirely on the private initiative of the early migrants. An official institutional framework came several years later, in the second half of the 1970s.

From 1976 — when large-scale migration of Bangladeshi nationals began — up to May 1983, nearly a quarter of a million people emigrated from the country, the vast majority of them going to the Middle East (for instance, non–Gulf region countries accounted for only 2.6 per cent of the migrants for 1981/82[3]). The migration increased tenfold over this period — from 6,087 in 1976 to 62,805 in 1982 (see Table 1).

TABLE 1. Volume of Bangladeshi Migration, and Composition by Skill Category

	Total Number	Category (%)			
		Professional	Skilled	Semiskilled	Unskilled
1976	6,087	9	29	9	53
1977	15,725	11	41	3	45
1978	22,809	15	36	5	44
1979	24,485	14	29	7	50
1980	30,573	6	40	8	46
1981	55,787	7	40	4	49
1982	62,805	6	33	5	56
1983 (Jan.–May)	26,477	4	34	7	55
Total:	244,748	8	36	6	50

Source: Unpublished documents, Bangladesh Manpower Planning Centre.

Although the gross outflow from 1974 to mid-1983 was a quarter of a million people, the current stock of migrants is considerably less. There is, however, no direct estimate of stock, nor are there any statistics on the magnitude of return flow from which stock might be estimated. There is evidence, though, to suggest that most of those who left the country during the first half of this period have returned to Bangladesh by now. The World Bank study shows that 61 per cent of the employment contracts stipulate a year of work, 25 per cent stipulate two years, and only 4 per cent of the contracts are for three years or more of work.[4] This does not, however, give an accurate picture of the return flow, since it is common knowledge that the majority of the shorter-term contracts are often extended for at least another year. A small sample of returning migrants showed that nearly 90 per cent of them returned within two years and 20 per cent after three years.[5] Yet another study of a micro-region showed that 88 per cent of the migrants returned after two years and only 12 per cent came back after one year.[6]

On the basis of all this, one might hazard a crude estimate of the possible size of the stock. Assume that 80 per cent of those with one-year contracts can have them extended to two years, and that the remaining 20 per cent can extend their contracts to three years; of those with two-year contracts, 20 per cent can extend their contracts to three years. This would mean that roughly 75 per cent of the migrants would return two years after their departure and 25 per cent after three years. On this basis, the stock of migrants at the end of 1982 would turn out to be in the region of 120,000. It would perhaps be safe to conclude that the stock at the end of 1982 probably lies within the range of 100,000–150,000, about 4 per cent of the stock of expatriate workers in the Middle East.

Skill and Occupational Distribution

Half of all the people migrating so far belong to the category of unskilled labour (see Table 1). The small category of semiskilled labour (6 per cent) can also be lumped with this group for all practical purposes as it signifies very low levels of skill, often acquired within a matter of months through apprenticeship. The truly skilled workers constitute the second-largest group, accounting for 36 per cent of all migrants. Although this group possesses reasonable levels of skill, they do not usually learn their trade through any formal training. A sample of migrants surveyed showed that this category of migrants consists of mostly construction workrs (63 per cent), transport equipment operators (19 per cent), service workers (10 per cent), and production workers (8 per cent).[7] Most of these workers in Bangladesh learn their skill through on-the-job training. Those who acquire skill through formal training usually belong to the category of technicians and they have been lumped together with professionals, who also include highly trained people such as doctors, engineers, etc. It is noteworthy that only 9 per cent of the migrants belong to this group.

The migration of labour from Bangladesh is thus seen to be characterised mostly by low- or medium-level skills. The proportions of different skill groups seem to have fluctuated somewhat over the years with the share of professionals rising quite rapidly in the early years but plummeting sharply since 1980. On the other hand, the share of unskilled and semiskilled labour seems to have fallen in the early years, but it has come back to its original level. The share of skilled labour has fluctuated between 29 and 41 per cent without showing any clear trend.

Changes in the skill composition of migrants mainly reflect the changing fortunes of the professionals. Initially, when migration began on the private initiative of the early settlers, very few professionals had a chance to migrate. But as the institutional framework was gradually developed, they began to migrate in increasing numbers through official patronage. But as both government and the public began to fear a possible scarcity of specialised skills, restrictions of various kinds began to be imposed on the movement of certain categories of skills. As a result, the migration of professionals has not grown nearly as fast as that of the rest. Although the total number of migrants in 1981 and 1982 was 250 per cent higher than in 1978 and 1979, for the professionals it has been a meagre 12 per cent higher.

While skill distribution provides an idea of the type and level of labour that is migrating, a more concrete analysis on the impact on labour market requires knowledge about the occupational distribution of migrants. Based on a 10 per cent sample of those who migrated in 1977 and 1978, the World Bank study estimated this distribution (see Table 2). Nearly 50 per cent of the migrants were drawn from the construction sector. Transport equipment operators are a very distant second (15.3 per cent), followed by service workers (8 per cent). The rest are more or less evenly spread out in other occupations.

TABLE 2. Occupational Distribution of Migrants (percentages)

Engineers	2.2
Doctors	1.2
Other professionals	2.1
Technicians	2.6
Construction	50.5
Transport-equipment operators	15.3
Production	6.4
Service	8.0
Fishing and agriculture	3.1
Clerical	1.2
Others	3.2
Skill not known	4.5

In the source, occupational distribution is given by skill category and the division among construction, transport, production, and service is given for skilled workers only. For semiskilled and unskilled categories they are lumped together. We have applied the proportion among skilled workers to the other two categories to arrive at the above figures.

Source: S.A. Ali et al. Labour Migration from Bangladesh to the Middle East (World Bank, Washington, D.C., 1981), pp. 29-30.

We do not have the picture for the whole period up to the present, but later figures seem to broadly correspond to the above. The figures for 1981-82,[8] show that among the skilled workers, the construction sector still accounts for nearly half the migrants. The shares of engineers and technicians have come down to 0.4 and 1.4 per cent respectively. Doctors account for a microscopic proportion, while administrative/ managerial personnel have registered some increases.

This pattern of occupational distribution reflects as much the nature of demand in the host countries as it does the structure of scarcities and surpluses in Bangladesh's domestic labour market. The major impact of enhanced oil revenue in the Gulf region has come in the shape of a construction boom. This structure of demand is also fairly consistent with the structure of surpluses in the labour market of Bangladesh. Although the construction sector employs only about 1.8 per cent of the labour force in Bangladesh,[9] it has also been observed that most of the visibly unemployed people with little literacy or skill first seek employment in this sector. In this sense, this sector contains a large reservoir of unemployed people. To this extent demand and supply of surplus labour have in fact matched each other.

On the other hand, the growing pool of educated unemployed find little scope for seeking their fortune in the Middle East. This is shown by the very low percentages of administrative/clerical posts held by the migrants. This has happened because a mere formal education is not of much help in securing jobs abroad. What is needed is a specific skill obtained through either institutional training or on-the-job experience.

The Origins and Destinations of Migrants

We mentioned earlier that emigration from Bangladesh before 1970 was almost completely monopolised by one small geographical area of Bangladesh, the district of Sylhet. But this has changed dramatically with the advent of migration to the Middle East. Recent migration seems to be confined mostly to 4 out of 21 districts of Bangladesh — Chittagong, Dhaka, Sylhet, and Noakhali (Table 3). Except for Dhaka, the other three districts are in the easternmost region of the country. In observing that the fifth most important district, Comilla, also falls in this division, it is clear that emigration to the Middle East is predominantly a phenomenon of eastern Bangladesh. Within this area, by far the most important subregion is Chittagong, which supplies well over 25 per cent of the recent migrants to the Middle East, although it possesses only about 6 per cent of Bangladesh's population.

The concentration of migrants in a few districts is probably to be explained by the snowballing effect of the first emigrants. The few earlier migrants from Bangladesh, who by historical accident were concentrated in a few districts, played a crucial role in the recent swelling of migration by paving the way for friends and relatives from their own localities. The early pattern of concentration has thus perpetuated itself and is reflected in the recent trends. The initial concentration is, in turn, at least partially explained by the fact that the early migrants were mostly workers on sea-going vessels who landed on foreign shores to seek their fortune, and the Bangladeshi seaport of Chittagong gave the people of the eastern region more opportunities than any other part of the country to secure work on sea-going vessels.

Most of the migrants are of rural origin (77.8 per cent), with the exception of those from Dhaka district, where the proportion of urban migrants is as high as 57.3 per cent. This exception is, however, largely a statistical aberration, because many job-seekers are known to register under an address in Dhaka in order to get foreign employment more quickly. (This also implies, incidentally, that the proportion of migrants from Dhaka district is overstated and the ranking of Dhaka may be lower than is shown in Table 3.) This distortion has partly affected the overall statistics on the rural-urban origins of migrants, which show nearly 22 per cent of the migrants coming from urban areas, while the total urban population constitutes only 10 per cent of the country's population. But this difference is also partly explained by the fact that skilled labour is concentrated in the urban areas.

TABLE 3. District of Origin of the Migrants (percentages)

Chittagong	43.7
Dhaka	19.4
Sylhet	17.4
Noakhali	10.9
Comilla	4.4
Others	4.2

Based on 10% sample of the migrants of 1977 and 1978, as reported in Ali et al., op. cit., p.36. For 35.4% of the sample migrants, originating districts were not known. The table is based on the information relating to the remaining 64.56%.

An overwhelming majority of the migrants are male. For instance, in fiscal year 1981–82, female migrants accounted for only 0.5 per cent of all migrants, and that is the highest percentage achieved so far.[10] The few women who do migrate work as domestic help or as nurses, mostly the former. Islamic religious influence clearly has much to do with the insignificant female share in migration from Bangladesh.

As far as distribution by religion is concerned, Muslims account for 95 per cent of the migrants.[11] The preponderance of Muslims is, of course, quite natural in a country where Islam is the major religion. Yet it is noticeable that while the share of non-Muslims is nearly 15 per cent in the country's population (and a similar percentage in the population of the five main districts where emigrants are concentrated), their share among the migrants is only 5 per cent. Perhaps this discrepancy can be partly explained by the fact that the major religion in the labour-importing countries is also Islam.

Finally, one may note that the majority (93 per cent) of the migrants are in the 20- to 40-year-old age group, and that the educational attainment of most of the migrants is very low. As many as 83 per cent of the migrants have not passed even the secondary-school examination, and only 2.25 per cent possess post-graduate degrees.[12] These figures are, of course, quite consistent with the skill distribution of the migrants discussed earlier. The fact that 83 per cent of the migrants have schooling below the secondary-school level, while as many as 36 per cent are skilled workers (see Table 1), also throws some light on the skill levels normally exported. As has been frequently observed, these are fairly low levels of skill that require little formal education and are attained mostly through apprenticeships and on-the-job experience.

TABLE 4. Distribution of Bangladeshi Migrants by Country of Destination (percentages)

	1977/78	1981/82
UAE	32.3	8.7
Oman	12.7	12.3
Saudi Arabia	12.6	25.6
Kuwait	9.1	10.3
Libya	8.4	6.1
Qatar	8.3	3.4
Iraq	7.3	27.7
Bahrain	4.1	2.8
Others	5.2	3.1

The figures in the first column are based on a 10% sample of workers migrating in the years 1977 and 1978 and are taken from Ali et al., op. cit., p.33. The figures in the second column refer to all workers migrating in fiscal year 1981/82, and are reported in *Manpower Bulletin* (Dhaka), Dec. 1982, p.42.

It would be helpful to compare the distribution of migration by destination from two different time periods (see Table 4). The seven states that comprise the United Arab Emirates (UAE) used to take in the largest proportion of Bangladeshi migrants in the earlier period of 1977/78. Oman and Saudi Arabia trailed far behind, and most of the remaining migrants were divided up among five other countries. Some important changes have taken place in recent years. The dominance of UAE has waned, while Iraq and Saudi Arabia have emerged as the top employers of Bangladeshi labour. Most of the other countries have either retained their share or have shown only minor changes.

Whether this changed geographical pattern of migration represents a sustainable structural break is difficult to say. Year-to-year changes can in fact be quite unpredictable. A successful negotiation with a particular country for a large package deal can significantly alter the shares of importing countries. A more detailed analysis of the changing demand structure in the host countries is required before anything definite can be posited about structural changes in the geographical distribution of migrants.

In comparisons of the geographical distribution of migrants by major occupational groups (for the periods 1977/78 and 1981/82 respectively), the following conclusions emerge. In the first period, the migrants with higher skill and literacy levels (professional, technical, and administrative people) found better job opportunities in Libya, Iraq, UAE, and Saudi Arabia. By 1981/82, UAE, Saudi Arabia, and Iraq continued to remain important, but Libya had lost leading position, although it continues to hold out reasonably good employment prospects. The newly emerging leader is, in fact, Oman, whose early role in absorbing Bangladeshi professionals was not very significant.

In the lower categories of white-collar employment, UAE and Oman have always offered the maximum opportunities, although their relative ranking has changed over the years. In the service sector, four countries were the most important employers in 1977/78: UAE, Saudi Arabia, Oman, and Kuwait. Of these, all but Saudi Arabia have maintained their preponderance in this area, and Iraq has considerably increased its share. The workers in production, transport, and communication — accounting for more than 50 per cent of all migrants — used to be concentrated mostly in UAE and to a much lesser extent in Oman and Saudi Arabia. But UAE now accounts for a very small proportion of workers; Iraq has emerged as the new leader in this sector, with Saudi Arabia also absorbing a much larger share than before. Although Iraq and Kuwait used to take in the bulk of the workers; in the other occupations, they both have now been overshadowed by Oman and UAE (see Table 5).

In summary, UAE has lost its earlier predominant position by bringing in a much smaller proportion of semiskilled workers — e.g. clerical/sales-related and production/transport/construction workers. But they have more or less maintained their share of highly skilled workers. Iraq has emerged as the new leader mainly by raising its share of semiskilled workers, but also to some extent by increasing its levels of high-skill ones. But Saudi Arabia has gained in importance almost exclusively by raising its share of low-skill workers. But, as mentioned earlier, whether these changes represent a genuine structural break or merely a short-term fluctuation is hard to say.

Channels of Recruitment

The main channel of recruitment to the Middle East in the initial migration phase was the early migrants. In the first half of the 1970s, however, a new mode of recruitment was introduced. As the employers in the Middle East began to send out representatives to different countries of South and Southeast Asia, they came into contact with a group of "passage brokers" or unlicensed recruiting agents, who lined up the required manpower for their clients. These unofficial arrangements were often illegitimate operations, in many cases involving extortion and even outright cheating

TABLE 5. Distribution of Migrants by Destination and Occupation, 1977/78 and 1981/82 (percentages)

	Professional/ Technical/ Administrative		Clerical/ Sales		Service Workers		Production/ Transport/ Construction		Others	
	77/78	81/82	77/78	81/82	77/78	81/82	77/78	81/82	77/78	81/82
UAE	14.4	12.5	45.1	20.0	20.1	23.2	38.3	6.3	6.4	22.2
Saudi Arabia	14.4	15.3	10.6	16.2	21.7	11.1	12.1	28.7	6.4	18.6
Libya	32.3	15.0	–	4.8	0.3	2.3	6.4	5.8	14.1	6.8
Oman	5.6	26.2	17.7	31.4	20.1	19.0	13.1	9.6	7.7	43.3
Qatar	1.1	2.1	15.9	2.8	2.7	3.6	9.8	3.5	6.1	3.3
Bahrain	2.5	1.5	5.3	1.9	4.7	4.0	4.6	2.7	0.6	2.6
Kuwait	2.1	6.7	3.5	10.5	21.1	31.7	5.8	8.1	33.3	8.1
Iraq	14.7	20.1	0.9	9.5	1.0	4.9	5.4	31.7	24.4	4.4
Others	12.9	0.6	1.9	2.9	8.3	0.2	4.5	3.6	1.0	–
Total	100	100	100	100	100	100	100	100	100	100

The figures for 1977/78 have been adapted from Appendix Table 4 in Ali et al., op. cit., p.280. The figures for 1981/82 have been compiled from Annexure IV in *Manpower Bulletin,* Dec. 1982, pp.43-46, by aggregating the detailed occupation types into major occupation groups as defined in Ali et al., pp.266-78.

of the recruits. In the mid-1970s, the government set up the Bureau of Manpower Employment and Training (BMET) under the Ministry of Labour to regularise the procedures of labour export. Several important steps were taken at this stage: (1) all foreign employment (except that in sea vessels and international organisations) was required to be cleared by BMET; (2) private passage brokers were allowed to operate as licensed recruiting agents only if they satisfied certain conditions devised to avoid fraudulent deals; and (3) BMET itself started to arrange placement of workers in foreign jobs on the basis of information and requests of foreign employers.

As a result, there now exist three main channels of recruitment: BMET, recruiting agents, and individual efforts. Large employers usually recruit through BMET, while the recruiting agents work for smaller employers who do not have the means to send representatives to look for foreign labour and thus must wait for private intermediaries to offer their services. We have already seen how the individual efforts work.

The proportions of migrants processed through different channels has varied over the years (see Table 6). From 1976 to 1982, just over 50 per cent of the migrants found employment through individual efforts — i.e. through their friends and relatives abroad. Private recruiting agents placed the next most migrants (28 per cent), followed by BMET (20 per cent). In 1976, however, BMET processed the preponderant share of migrants (87 per cent), with individual efforts claiming only 8 per cent. This seems a little incongruous, given the historically pre-eminent role of individual efforts. It is

TABLE 6. Distribution of Bangladesh Migrants by Recruitment Channel (percentages)

	BMET	Recruiting Agents	Individual Efforts	Total
1976	87	5	8	100
1977	36	7	57	100
1978	27	9	64	100
1979	28	12	60	100
1980	19	25	56	100
1981	11	40	49	100
1982 (Jan.–Oct.)	8	10	52	100
1976–Oct. 1982	20	28	52	100

Adapted from *Manpower Bulletin,* Dec. 1982, p.34.

highly probable that when BMET was first formed, it could not maintain proper records of workers migrating through individual initiatives. In any event, the share of individual efforts in the subsequent years is reasonably stable and perhaps reflects the true picture.

The really significant change has taken place in the relative roles of BMET and the recruiting agents. From less than 10 per cent of the share in the early years, recruiting agents are now recruiting as much as 40 per cent of all migrants. This has happened largely at the expense of BMET's share, affecting individual recruiting efforts only minimally. BMET's share of has fallen from one-fourth to one-third of all migrants in the early years (excluding the unusual figures for 1976) to a meagre 8–11 per cent in the recent years.

In absolute terms, however, recruitment through BMET has not fallen. In fact, what has happened is that private agents have begun to exploit the opportunities offered by the smaller employers much more successfully than before. Since the small employers constitute the largest source of employment, the expanding role of recruiting agents has also ushered in a new spurt in the flow of Bangladeshi labour. It should also be noted, however, that the earliest recruitment channel — through individuals — has contributed to this acceleration, as is evidenced by the relative stability of its share.

Return Flow of Migrants

An analysis of the migration and its impact cannot be complete without data on the volume and trends of the return flow of migrants. Because, as mentioned before, the recent migration from Bangladesh is mostly temporary, a return flow is inevitable, and its impact is potentially no less important than that of migration itself. But

TABLE 7. Estimated Return Flow of Bangladeshi Migrants, 1980-1982

	Gross Outflow (actual)	Return Flow (estimated)	Return as % of Gross Outflow
1980	30,573	21,038	69
1981	55,787	24,066	43
1982	62,805	29,051	47

Figures of actual outflow are taken from unpublished materials of the Bangladesh Manpower Planning Centre. See text for the methodology of estimating return flow.

unfortunately, our knowledge in this respect is extremely limited. Although BMET keeps comprehensive records on the labour migrants, it has no such records on the return flow.

One can at best make some informal guesses about the possible orders of magnitude on the basis of certain circumstantial evidence. The employment contract is one source of such evidence, as it stipulates the duration of the work obligation for migrants of different skill-categories. Another is a small sample survey of returning migrants. From these two sources of evidence, it has been estimated that 75 per cent of the migrants return after two years and 25 per cent after three years. On this basis, we can devise a possible scenario of return flow in the early 1980s (see Table 7).

In 1982 the return flow of migrants was possibly somewhat less than half of the gross annual outflow. In 1980 this ratio was much higher, but as gross outflow accelerated after 1980, the ratio fell drastically. If the acceleration in gross outflow continues, the ratio will fall even further, but once the outflow stabilises or starts to decline, the ratio will start to rise again.

Migration and the Labour Market in Bangladesh

In a study on migration, an analysis of the internal labour market is important on at least two accounts. On the one hand, it shows the impact on the balance of demand and supply, and hence suggests the possible loss of production due to withdrawal of labour. On the other hand, it helps to identify specific areas of scarcity and surplus, enabling the country to formulate a rational migration policy based on selective inducement or restriction, as the case may be. Together with an analysis of the emerging structure of the labour market in the importing countries, it also helps to project more realistically the possibility of exporting different types of labour abroad.

In spite of the importance of this exercise, however, we cannot be as comprehensive as we would have liked. Although some useful information was collected in the course of the World Bank study mentioned earlier — there is also some additional data of more recent vintage — the overall availability of data in this area is far from satisfactory. Some tentative conclusions have nevertheless been drawn.

Overall Magnitudes

We have already estimated the stock of Bangladesh migrants in the Middle East as of the end of 1982 to be in the region of 120,000. On the other hand, using a participation ratio of 32 per cent (as used by the Second Five-Year Plan) and projected population based on the 1981 census, we estimate that Bangladesh's labour force at the end of 1982 was nearly 29.76 million. The stock of emigrants thus turns out to be only 0.4 per cent of the total labour force.

Yet another way of looking at the overall picture is to compare the stock of semiskilled migrants with workers in the modern sector, where the former would have sought employment had they not gone abroad. Based on the information that unskilled workers constituted on an average nearly 50 per cent of the migrants over the years, we may safely assume that the remaining half possess skills of some level or other; i.e., an estimated 60,000 migrants have some sort of some skill. If the modern sector is defined broadly to include the whole of the industrial and services sectors, the stock of skilled migrants as a proportion of modern sector employment turns out to be 0.1 per cent. It may be considered more appropriate not to include the whole of the services sector, as people in most services would not find any significant employment opportunities abroad. In another estimate that includes only transport and communication and an arbitrary proportion of 25 per cent of miscellaneous professional services (totally excluding trade services, public administration, banking, and insurance), the stock of skilled migrants is estimated to be about 0.2 per cent.[13]

Thus, whichever way one looks at it, the overall volume of migration does not constitute a sizeable proportion of the labour force in Bangladesh. This is a reflection of the country's vast reservoir of manpower and its relatively modest success in finding jobs for its nationals in the Middle East, compared to other Asian countries.

These overall figures suggest that, at the current levels of emigration, any cost in terms of forgone production can hardly be significant. It is nevertheless possible that specific sectors or activities may still be adversely affected, and it is from this perspective that a more detailed analysis is provided below.

Unskilled Workers

The category of unskilled workers is taken here to include both agricultural labourers and workers in the urban informal sector, in addition to the unskilled workers in the modern sector. As we have seen, this category of workers constitutes nearly 50 per cent of all Bangladeshi migrants. For this vast majority of migrants, the domestic labour market is characterised by excess supply.

This excess, however, does not take the form of visible unemployment. A manpower survey of 1980 shows that only 0.8 per cent of the population (or 2.5 per cent of the labour force) is openly unemployed, with the rural and urban percentages being 0.7 and 1.6 respectively.[14] The true surfeit of labour lies in the phenomenon of "disguised" unemployment. The vast literature on surplus-labour models for typical developing countries has demonstrated that the surplus is hidden by the work-sharing inherent in societies based on the extended family. But, if a worker withdraws from the labour force, the remaining workers compensate by working more intensively to prevent any loss of production. The excess supply of labour is manifested in this absence of any adverse impact on production rather than in any evidence of openly unemployed people seeking work. In the context of Bangladeshi agriculture, however, at least one study has argued that surplus labour is a seasonal phenomenon and that any permanent withdrawal of labour is likely to reduce agricultural output,[15] but the methodology of this study has been questioned. By using a different methodology, the same set of data has been shown to reveal the existence of withdrawable surplus.[16] Moreover, Ahmad and Masum have shown in two independent studies that underemployment in Bangladesh agriculture represents a genuine structural surplus, not just a seasonal one.[17] The relative strength of evidence thus suggests that unskilled workers in Bangladesh agriculture are indeed in excess supply.

As far as the urban market for unskilled workers is concerned, it can be argued in line with the familiar dual-economy models that the existence of a large labour surplus in agriculture also ensures similar surpluses in the urban sector. The crucial link here is the possibility of rural-to-urban migration. If an unskilled labourer is withdrawn from the urban labour market, his position is filled — either directly or through a chain reaction — by a surplus labourer migrating from the countryside. Surplus labour in agriculture thus ensures, through the nexus of rural-to-urban migration, a perfectly elastic supply of labour in the urban market.

It would thus be safe to conclude that unskilled labour is in excess supply in both rural and urban Bangladesh in the sense of having a zero-opportunity cost of withdrawal. Migration of such labour has not, therefore, entailed any loss of production, and Bangladesh can afford to export such labour for many more years without any adverse effect on its productive capacity.

Semiskilled and Skilled Workers

Semiskilled and skilled workers are demanded mostly in the formal urban sector, and they acquire their skills largely through on-the-job training as apprentices. A variety of occupations are included in these categories: e.g. mechanics, electricians, carpenters, masons, welders, plumbers, drivers, typists, launderers, cooks, cleaners, and hotel porters, to name only a few. A detailed analysis of the labour markets for each of these activities is ruled out by the lack of data, and is in any case not necessary for reaching broad conclusions.

A common characteristic of all these labour markets is that the workers are not *potentially* in short supply. This assertion is based on the twin observations that (1) it takes very little time for an unskilled worker to acquire these skills, and (2) there exists a large pool of unemployed and underemployed unskilled workers. The empirical evidence for the latter observation has been discussed earlier. According to the estimates given in one study, an apprentice needs on average about six months to reach the semiskilled status; he requires about three years to become fully skilled. The important thing here is that although there exist a few technical institutions to impart some of these skills, by and large workers acquire skills by working as apprentices for master craftsmen. Therefore, there are no capacity constraints to the uninterrupted generation of semiskilled and skilled workers. Consequently, the continued migration of such workers is not likely to face any significant supply bottleneck, provided the annual outflow does not suddenly become disproportionately large.

Yet one must recognise that such workers are not in excess supply in the sense that unskilled workers are. That is to say, the opportunity cost of such labour is not zero, and its withdrawal from the economy does entail a loss of production. This loss, however, does not consist of the marginal product of the migrating worker. Since a replacement can always be found from among the pool of unskilled workers, his marginal product is not ultimately lost to the society. The true loss consists in the cost incurred in obtaining a replacement. Such replacement cost can be broken down into three components: (1) the marginal output of the replacement worker in his earlier occupation, which is now lost to the society; (2) the resources used up in training the replacement to bring him up to the desired skill level; and (3) the output lost or reduced during the training period.

Since the replacement eventually comes from the pool of unskilled workers who, as argued before, have a zero-opportunity cost, the first of the three components of replacement cost can be taken as zero. Moreover, since hardly any formal training is received by such workers, the second component is also virtually zero. Thus, the only relevant social cost of the migration of semiskilled and skilled workers could lie in the loss or reduction of output during the training period.

One measure of such loss is the difference between the salaries paid to the apprentice and the full-fledged workers. This difference is expected to reflect the employers' private valuation of the output sacrificed by taking in an apprentice in place of a full-fledged worker. One study has shown that, on the average, apprentices for semi-skilled jobs are paid 50 per cent of the regular pay during their period of training. Apprentices for skilled jobs in the industrial units receive 50 per cent less than full salary in the first year, 40 per cent less in the second year, and 30 per cent less in the third year.[18] Given the regular salary of the workers, the loss of output caused by hiring an apprentice can easily be measured. Using appropriate capital recovery factors in order to annualise such losses, the annual social cost of migration has thus been estimated to be close to zero for semiskilled workers and 857 taka for skilled workers at 1979 prices.[19] Compared to the annual remittances of skilled workers, discussed in the next section, this is a fairly negligible social cost, representing as it does only about 2 per cent of remittance.

We may thus conclude that a gradual migration of semiskilled and skilled workers is not likely to be hindered by any supply bottleneck in the near future and that the social cost of such migration in terms of lost production is negligible in comparison to the remittance received.

Professionals and Technicians

We must now analyse the market structure for the remaining 8 per cent of Bangladeshi migrants — the professionals and technicians. They represent the upper end of the skill spectrum of migrants. Public concern about the loss of workers with scarce skills relates mostly to this category of emigrants, and the market structure of various activities in this category therefore deserves much closer examination. Fortunately, quantitative information is relatively more plentiful for this group of migrants.

Unlike semiskilled and skilled workers, these people almost invariably acquire their skill through formal training in relevant institutions. It is therefore tempting to argue that the social cost of their emigration (in terms of output forgone) can be measured by the cost of their training. But this commonsense view turns out to be quite misleading when one examines the education system of Bangladesh. Training cost would be the relevant social cost only if training facilities were consciously created to meet the anticipated demand for replacement resulting from emigration. For only in this case one would say that emigration generates forces of its own replacement, so that it is the cost of obtaining the replacement that matters. But if the extent or nature of training activities is not affected by emigration, then the cost of training is no longer the relevant cost of emigration. It is a sunk cost to the society, and would have been incurred regardless of the emigration.

Such, indeed, seems to be the case in Bangladesh. Other studies have often noted the lack of articulation between the educational system and the labour market, resulting in long lags between changes in demand for and the training and education of professionals.[20] As a result, additional demand for them confronts virtually zero elasticity of supply. Consequently, the cost of emigration of such a person would be measured not by the cost of training, but by the marginal product of the emigrants — provided the market is supply-constrained. If, however, demand is the dominant constraint, the cost is simply nil.

TABLE 8. Demand and Supply of Highly Skilled Manpower in Bangladesh, 1978

	No. of Job Aspirants	No. of Jobs	Surplus or Deficit
Postgraduate doctors	411	506	−95
Graduate doctors	7,071	7,917	−900
Medical technicians	10,105	14,363	−4,258
Engineering graduates	7,856	7,989	−128
Engineering technicians	16,211	17,496	−1,285
Engineering craftsmen	24,877	179,792	−154,915
Fibre technologists	1,041	4,862	−3,821
Agricultural professionals	7,705	8,717	−1,012
Trained school teachers	102,793	267,152	−164,359
Masters in natural sciences	10,232	8,857	+1,375
Masters in economic sciences	11,855	7,079	+4,776
Masters in social sciences	14,080	5,182	+8,958
Masters in humanities	10,427	5,562	+4,865
Generalists	1,181,545	365,559	+815,986

Source: Ali et al., op. cit., p.161

In dealing with the professionals and technicians, therefore, it is crucial to examine the supply-demand balance for different types of activities. This is important for assessing both the potential for emigration and its social cost (see Table 8). The built-in imbalance in Bangladesh's educational system is clearly evident from the data shown in Table 8. Generalists and the top-degree holders are being graduated from the universities in numbers that cannot be absorbed by appropriate professions, whereas specialized professions such as engineering craftsmen or trained educators are too few relative to demand. It is quite unfortunate in this context that only the skills in deficit supply are in demand in the Middle East. From all the surplus categories (shown in Table 8), only 267 professionals (in natural and economic sciences) had migrated by 1978; all the rest were in the deficit categories. Table 9 shows the magnitude of migration along with the deficit in the supply of professionals and the number of vacancies.

It should be noted that trained school teachers, the most heavily deficit profession, have not participated in the migration at all, but engineering craftsmen, who represent the next most deficit skill, have migrated in greater numbers than any other highly skilled profession. The migration of other professionals with engineering and medical training has also clearly exacerbated the existing deficit.

One would theoretically expect to see the combined effect of supply deficit and overseas employment reflected fully in the volume of vacancies. But the number of vacan-

TABLE 9. Migration and Vacancies in Deficit Professions, 1978

	Supply Deficit	Overseas Employment	Volume of Vacancy
Postgraduate doctors	−95	100	166
Graduate doctors	−900	1,025	769
Medical technicians	−4,258	1,301	2,153
Engineering graduates	−128	1,184	1,119
Engineering technicians	−1,285	1,978	2,819
Engineering craftsmen	−154,915	6,436	13,323
Fibre technologists	−3,821	208	538
Agricultural professionals	−1,012	168	611
Trained school teachers	−164,359	−	27,624

Source: Ali et al., op. cit., p.161.

cies is usually much less than one would expect (see Table 9). Apart from possible informational gaps, this discrepancy is explained by the partial filling up of vacancies through inadequate substitutions.

Leaving aside the profession of school teachers, who are not important in a study on migration, the most remarkable degree of substitution seems to have taken place among engineering craftsmen. This shows the extent to which the existing craftsmen are drawn from apprentices who learn through experience rather than through formal training. It is important to keep this in mind while deploring the relatively heavy migration of scarce craftsmen. They are indeed scarce, but finding replacements would not be too difficult if employing enterprises adopted a policy of systematic apprenticeships.

As for the other professions, substitution — even if possible to some extent — is arguably much less desirable. One would certainly not want half-baked doctors and engineers. In this sense, the migration of such professionals in the face of scarcity at home is clearly not desirable. But the figures on highly skilled migrants can be some-what misleading in this respect (see tables 8 and 9, which show data only up to 1978). For many professions, the scarcity that existed in 1978 has ended by now, mostly because the educational institutions have continued to pour out professionals at an accelerating pace, although the slow growth of the economy has inevitably meant only a slow growth in the demand for their skills.

This statement is corroborated by more than one projection (see Table 10). The supply estimates in Table 10 are based on enrolment patterns in the educational institutions, and the two demand estimates are based on alternative assumptions about growth in demand. The lower estimate assumes 50 per cent growth in demand over the five-year period on the strength of the fact that this was the growth rate over five-year periods in the previous decade. The second estimate is based on the overly optimistic assumption that growth in demand will double itself to 100 per cent.

It is remarkable that, leaving aside engineering craftsmen, who are in acutely short supply, no other professional group remains scarce relative to demand even under alternative 2. The demand for postgraduate medical specialists and fibre technicians does seem to outstrip supply by a small margin, but the difference is fairly negligible. Moreover, since a doubling of the growth rate is an unrealistically optimistic assumption given the sluggish growth of the overall economy, one may assume alternative 1 comes closer to reality, which would imply a considerable surplus in all categories (except for craftsmen).

Subsequently, an ILO/ARTEP study on the projected supply and demand for engineers and technicians over the Second Five-Year Plan period (1980–85) added further strength to this conclusion. The study estimated that if the plan targets are completely fulfilled, there will be a small shortfall (6 per cent) of engineering graduates and a sizeable surplus (17 per cent) of technicians.[21] However, plan implementation in the first three years has already fallen considerably short of target. Therefore, it would not be surprising to find surplus among the engineering graduates either. In fact, an April 1982 survey of the five major employers of graduate and diploma engineers in Bangladesh showed that vacancy as a proportion of sanctioned posts was in general no higher than normal levels in other government departments.[22] The only exception was the Power Development Board (PDB), where the proportion of vacancies was unusually high (51 per cent) for the graduate engineers. But it is well known that there are important domestic reasons for this situation at PDB — mainly, the reluctance of engineers to work in power-generating stations and other offices in remote, outlying areas.

TABLE 10. Projected Supply and Demand in Selected Professions, 1978–83

	Additional Demand		Additional Supply
	Alternative 1	Alternative 2	
Postgraduate medical specialists	303	404	400
Graduate doctors	2,284	3,046	12,000
Medical technicians	5,619	7,492	10,000
Engineering graduates	4,645	6,194	6,500
Engineering technicians	9,120	12,160	14,000
Engineering craftsmen	98,448	131,264	35,000
Fibre technologists	1,092	1,456	1,400
Agricultural professionals	5,730	7,640	8,000

Source: Ali et al., op. cit., p. 166.

One may thus conclude that although there were some stresses on the market in the early years of migration, as of this writing, the only professionals who are in short supply relative to demand are formally trained engineering craftsmen. This, incidentally, is also the group that has migrated in greater numbers than any other group. Yet, this is also, perhaps, the only group among the professionals that can be replaced reasonably satisfactorily through proper on-job training of apprentices without formal training. Such substitution has taken place widely in the past and is also likely to mitigate the harmful effects of migration in the future.

Volume and Impact of Remittance Money

The large volume of remittances sent home by the labour migrants is the most important benefit of the migration. Labour-exporting countries realise certain other benefits, such as the reduction in consumption, which releases resources for savings and investment, and the workforce's acquisition of new skills or new attitudes towards employment. But undoubtedly the most important source of benefit is the remittance money.

In this section we shall first trace the growth in remittance over time and the measures undertaken to increase its flow, then discuss the use of remittance money by recipient households, and, finally, analyse the macro-economic effects of remittance on balance of payments, savings, prices, and distribution of income.

Growth of Remittance Flow

Sizeable migrations from Bangladesh occurred before the emergence of the Middle East phenomenon. For instance, nearly 80,000 Bangladeshis were living in the United Kingdom in 1976,[23] as against the estimated stock of 120,000 in the Middle East at the end of 1982. But most of the emigrants to the United Kingdom are more or less permanently settled, so remittances were relatively unimportant to Bangladesh until the labour migration to the Middle East began to grow in the mid-1970s.

There has been a phenomenal growth in remittance income over the last eight years (see Table 11). The distinction between financial remittance and total remittance arises from the fact that until September 1979 the migrants were also allowed to send directly from abroad such goods as could be imported under the Wage Earners' Scheme. In other words, the migrants were allowed to remit in both cash and kind. The proportion of remittance in kind is not known for all the years under discussion. However, from August 1978 to September 1979, the ratio between financial remittance and remittance in kind was 79.21.[24] Applying this ratio to the period between July 1975 and September 1979, we have estimated the flows of total remittance. The dollar value of remittances has been obtained from the World Bank, which used balance-of-payments data. Since an equivalent counter-entry is recorded

TABLE 11. Flow of Remittance from Bangladeshi Migrants, 1975/76–1982/83

	Financial Remittance (taka in millions)	Total Remittance	
		Taka in millions	$US in millions
1975/76	245.9	314.6	29.6
1976/77	744.7	952.7	60.6
1977/78	1,541.4	1,971.6	113.5
1978/79	1,888.3	2,415.8	143.4
1979/80	3,854.5	4,035.5	210.3
1980/81	6197.4	6,197.4	379.4
1981/82	8,296.7	8,296.7	412.4
1982/83	15,000.0	15,000.0	600.0

Source: Column 1 is estimated from unpublished sources of the Foreign Exchange Department, Bangladesh Bank, but data up to 1979 are also available in Ali et al., op. cit. Second column has been estimated by the procedure described in the text. The third column is taken from *Bangladesh: Recent Economic Trends and Medium Term Development Issues* (World Bank, Washington, D.C. 1983), p.121.

under the heading of private transfer against every dollar of remittance in kind that is recorded as merchandise import, we expect that the balance-of-payments estimate refers to total remittance.

In taka terms, the volume of remittance has grown by about 48 times during the eight-year period, implying an annual compound growth rate of 74 per cent. Part of this increase, of course, is not real as it incorporates the effect of exchange-rate depreciation. A better approximation of the real picture is conveyed by the dollar value of remittances, which has grown 20-fold, still implying a spectacular growth rate of 54 per cent.

Not all of the remittance has come from the Middle East, but most of it has — recall that the other major stream of migration, namely to the United Kingdom almost dried up in the early 1970s. If one takes the remittance levels from the mid-1970s as coming exclusively from non–Middle Eastern sources and inflates them by the United Kingdom's wage inflation so as to estimate their current value, they are seen to constitute barely 6–7 per cent of the total remittance in recent years.

Incentive for Remittance

In order to maximise the benefits from labour migration it is of utmost importance that the workers should be induced to remit to their fullest potential. There are basically two issues here. First, the migrants must be induced to increase their savings, thereby raising their potential remittances. Second, adequate incentives should exist to encourage them to remit their money through official channels instead of investing it abroad or remitting through illegal channels.

The first issue, perhaps, is not a paramount concern int the case of the Bangladeshi migrants to the Middle East, most of whom maximise their savings anyway since the vary rationale of short-term migration is to accumulate resources to strengthen their economic base when they eventually return home. We shall discuss later the empirical evidence of the migrant workers' fairly high propensity to save.

The second issue is of much greater concern, especially the threat of remittances through illegal channels. The other form of leakage, namely investment abroad, is again perhaps only a minor problem. Most of the migrants lack the necessary skill to manage relatively risk-free investments abroad. They are more likely to hand over their savings to more experienced intermediaries, who then pay the migrant's nominee at home an equivalent amount in domestic currency at the black-market exchange rate. If the transaction ends there, then the migrant's earning is totally lost to the country, since the payment to the migrant's nominee is merely an internal transfer. It is possible, however, that the intermediaries would use at least part of the foreign exchange to smuggle goods into the country. To that extent, the country would derive some benefit from the earnings of its migrants. But it is still arguable that the benefits derived in this manner would, in general, be less than if an equivalent amount were remitted through official channels. This divergence in benefit arises basically from the difference in the composition of imports that come in through the two channels. Smuggled goods usually enjoy the highest scarcity premiums, but then the very high scarcity premium is enjoyed by the very commodities that have the lowest priority in the eyes of the government and are hence restricted most severely. Moreover, government loses tax revenue when goods are smuggled into the country. And although import tax is a transfer from the importers to the treasury, such loss of revenue must be considered undesirable insofar as public saving is deemed to have at the margin a greater weight than the scarcity premiums reaped by the black-market racketeers.

Maximisation of benefits from migrants' earnings thus requires not only that they remit in full, but also that they remit only through the official channel. Mahmud and Osmani tried to estimate the magnitude of leakage through unofficial channels and concluded that the leakage, if there is any, is probably rather small.[25] This conclusion is, however, at variance with the judgement of some other contributors to the World Bank study. The disagreement basically arises from methodological differences in estimating actual remittances from the Middle East.

Those who believe in the existence of a large leakage have used the official figures of remittances sent from the Middle Eastern countries.[26] But Mahmud and Osmani have pointed out that the official records of remittance by country of origin underestimate the actual remittance from the Middle East because a lot of Middle Eastern money is known to be routed through Western financial channels. (For instance, according to the Bangladesh Bank records, remittances from the Middle East constituted only about half of the total financial remittances from January to June 1979.[27] But, as we shall

TABLE 12. Actual and Potential Remittance per Bangladeshi
Migrant in the Middle East, 1979 (taka per month)

Actual Remittance	
Macro data	
low estimate	3545
high estimate	3223
Household survey	3136
Potential Remittance	
low estimate	3200
high estimate	3820

Source: Mahmud and Osmani, in *Bangladesh Development Studies,*
8, no. 3 (Fall 1980), p.14.

see, under realistic assumptions the share from the Middle Eastern countries should be
close to 76 per cent.) Accordingly, Mahmud and Osmani made an alternative estimate
based on assumptions regarding the possible contribution of non-Middle Eastern
sources. First, because Bangladeshi migration since 1976 has been almost entirely
directed towards the Middle East, the increase in remittance between 1976 and a later
year (1979 in their exercise) can be explained by two factors: (1) remittances coming
from new migrants to the Middle East, and (2) the rise in remittances from those around
the world who had already emigrated before in 1976 because of wage increases. The
authors applied the U.K. wage index for 1979 to the 1976 level of remittance to arrive
at the 1979 remittance levels from non-Middle East sources. The Middle East remittance was then estimated by subtracting it from total remittance. Second, two alternative assumptions were made about the stock of migrants in the Middle East in 1979.
The low estimate was based on official figures of migrants and assumed that the unknown volume of unofficial migration was equal to the similarly unknown number of
returning migrants. The high estimate assumed that actual net migration was 10 per
cent higher than the official figure of gross migration. Matching these figures of
migrant stocks against estimated remittances from the Middle East, the authors then
arrived at two estimates of "actual remittance" per Bangladeshi migrant in that region.
Yet another estimate of "actual remittance" was made on the basis of a household
survey of families receiving remittance money.[28]

The estimates of "potential remittance" were made on the basis of survey data on the
savings and earnings of the migrants. There are again two estimates here, one based
on direct evidence on savings (low estimate), the other on independently gathered
information on earnings and savings propensities (high estimate) (see Table 12).

The estimates are all comfortably close to each other, so there is little to support the
view that there are wide divergences between the amount of remittable funds and the

actual level of remittance. Similarly, one cannot substantiate the frequent complaint that Middle East remittances have been feeding a rapidly expanding black-currency market. We may recall, however, that these estimates of remittance per worker are based on the increments in remittance flows and in the stock of migrants between 1976 and 1979. As such, they cannot tell us anything about the extent of the black-currency market that already existed at the 1976 level of worldwide remittance to Bangladesh.

One could also argue in principle that the migrants' savings propensities as incorporated in the estimates of potential remittance given above do not imply maximum possible savings potential. Hence, "true" potential remittance may be even higher. But this is very unlikely, because, as Mahmud and Osmani showed, the migrants were already saving 65–75 per cent of their income. We do not have similar estimates for the recent years to show whether the full potential is being remitted or not. However, we do know that from 1978/79 to 1982/83, remittance increased 4.2 times in dollar values, whereas the stock of migrants at the end of 1982, as estimated earlier, was only 2.7 times that at the end of 1978 (estimated by adding up the gross outflow of 1976, 1977, and 1978). This shows that there must have been a considerable increase of remittance per worker. Since we know that the relative share of highly skilled migrants has tended to decline in the recent years, this increase cannot be explained by changes in the composition of the stock of migrants and must therefore represent a genuine increase in remittance per worker. It may thus be inferred that any slack in the savings propensities of workers, or any leakage that still might have existed in 1979, must have disappeared by now. Therefore, now, more than in 1979, actual remittance through official channels must be approximating the potential remittance very closely indeed.

It is arguable that the special exchange-rate incentive, known as the Wage Earners' Scheme (WES), was largely responsible for channeling most of the remittance through the official route. Introduced in mid-1974, WES is based on the same principle as the Bonus Voucher Scheme used by Pakistan in the 1960s. The WES enables migrant workers to sell their foreign exchange in Bangladesh to importers at a premium over the official rate and thus provides an incentive to use offical channels for sending money home. While most imports in Bangladesh are subject to exchange controls, the WES essentially relies on the operation of a relatively narrow but nevertheless free market for foreign exchange. Under exchange controls, imports are allowed at the officially fixed exchange rate, but the quantities imported are controlled by import licenses. The supply of foreign exchange available for import licenses comes from export earnings and foreign aid.

In the free market, the supply of foreign exchange comes mainly from the remittances of Bangladeshi nationals working abroad. On the demand side, imports can come in freely (without any quantitative restrictions) from a wide range of items importable under this scheme. The price of foreign exchange in the WES market is thus determined by the free interaction of supply and demand. Given the restrictions on imports in the official market and the consequent overvaluation of the official rate of exchange, the interaction of supply and demand in the WES market naturally leads to a higher taka rate of foreign exchange. The resulting premium represents a partial transfer of scarcity margins from the importers to the remitters from abroad. This is what constitutes the incentive for remitting money through legal channels. Until recently, the rate of premium in the WES market has mostly varied within a range of 25–35 per cent. The margin has narrowed very considerably in the last year or so as a result of significant depreciation in the official exchange rate. Currently, the WES rate is hovering around Tk 26 per U.S. dollar, while the official rate is just under Tk 25.

The narrowing of the premium has been causing worries in some quarters as to the future effectiveness of WES in attracting remittances. This worry is somewhat misplaced. If the narrowing of the gap were caused by the slackening of demand by importers in the WES market — leading to a drop in the WES rate (also called the importers' premium rate or IP rate for short) — then one could be legitimately worried about a disincentive effect. But, as it happens, the rise in the official rate, not a slackening in the WES rate, is what has led to the narrowing of the gap. This should not dampen the supply of remittance money as long as WES imports are still freer than official imports and the list of WES imports is not tilted more heavily in favour of commodities that earn a smaller scarcity premium in the domestic market.

Here, incidentally, lies a dilemma in the operation of the Wage Earners' Scheme. Although we have characterised the WES market as free, it is not, in effect, completely so. It is true that WES are sets no quantitative restrictions on imports, but there are tariffs, and, more importantly, there are restrictions on the type of items that can be imported under this scheme. Importers' demand for WES foreign exchange can be manipulated by variations in tariff rates as well as by changing the composition of the list of importables. For instance, if the list is more heavily loaded with commodities that earn a very high scarcity premium, importers will naturally rush in to push up the WES rate. This may provide an incentive for larger remittances, but only at the cost of distorting Bangladesh's import structure. The commodities earning the highest scarcity premiums are usually least essential for the country's development needs. The whole principle of selective import restrictions will therefore be jeopardised if the aim is to maximise the premium for the WES rate. Moreover, given the present rate of remittance and the evidence regarding the proximity of potential and actual remittances, it is likely that remittance flows would now be fairly inelastic to the WES rate. It would not be worthwhile, therefore, to marginally improve the incentive at the cost of distorting the import structure.

A more fruitful line of attack at this stage would probably lie in streamlining the financial mechanisms and banking procedures. Much has been done over the years to improve these procedures. But much still remains to be done.[29]

Use of Remittance Income

Remittance money, by itself, is merely a potential resource; its exact benefits depend crucially on how it is utilised by those who receive it. The only source of information on the spending behaviour is a household-budget survey conducted by R. Islam in connection with the World Bank study.[30]

Separate samples were taken from rural and urban areas. In each area there were two sub-samples of equal size (201 households for rural and 76 for urban areas). Sub-sample A comprised remittance-receiving housholds, and sub-sample B comprised other households of roughly comparable incomes. In practice, it was hard to find exactly comparable sub-samples, and the difference in their average incomes turned out to be quite high. In the rural sample, the average monthly household incomes of sub-samples A and B were Tk 5,201 and Tk 2,685 respectively; for the urban areas these averages were Tk 5,354 and Tk 5,201. The households in the remittance-receiving sample had thus, on the average, a higher income. This makes any comparison between the two groups somewhat complicated, but certain interesting findings still come out quite clearly.

The survey shows that the remittance-receiving households (sub-sample A) save a much

TABLE 13. Savings of Rural Households (in taka)

Household Income Group	Monthly Income	Monthly Savings	Average Savings Ratio	Marginal Savings Ratio
A. *Remittance-receiving households*				
I	1,304	−180	−0.14	—
II	1,807	403	0.22	1,16
III	2,480	667	0.27	0.39
IV	3,959	1,322	0.33	0.44
V	6,056	2,865	0.47	0.74
VI	8,462	4,683	0.55	0.76
VII	12,238	7,998	0.65	0.88
VIII	18,590	14,163	0.76	0.97
B. *Other households*				
I	634	−1,136	−1.79	—
II	1,235	−629	−0.51	0.84
III	1,719	−213	−0.12	0.86
IV	2,472	21	0.09	0.31
V	3,814	588	0.15	0.42
VI	5,663	766	0.14	0.10

Source: Mahmud and Osmani, op. cit., p.19.

TABLE 14. Monthly Expenditure on Domestic Servants, Recreation, and Festival-Ceremonies

	Domestic Servants		Recreation		Festivals, etc.	
	A	B	A	B	A	B
Rural	138	179	27	12	153	139
	(5.2)	(6.9)	(1.0)	(0.5)	(5.8)	(5.3)
Urban	152	185	110	88	159	210
	(4.7)	(6.0)	(3.4)	(2.9)	(4.9)	(6.8)

A, remittance-receiving households. B, other households. Figures in parentheses express expenditures on the item as percentage of total consumption expenditure.

Source: R. Islam, chap. 3 in Ali et al., op cit.

larger proportion of income than their counterparts in sub-sample B. In the rural areas these households save 50 per cent of their income as against only 1.8 per cent by the other households; in the urban areas, these ratios are 39.2 and 4.2 respectively. These results are not, however, exactly comparable because, as mentioned before, the A households have a higher average income and are expected to have a higher savings ratio anyway. But the most interesting fact is that even for given income groups, the remittance-receivers are found to save more (see Table 13). For groups with comparable household incomes, both average and marginal savings ratios are higher for remittance-receiving households in the rural areas (and, although we have not reproduced the urban tables here, the same is true there as well). This finding flies in the face of the popular belief that remittance money is mostly squandered in frivolous consumption. In fact, it is possible to think of a number of very cogent reasons for the propensity of remittance-receivers to save more. First, there is the well-known Duesenberry lag in the adjustment of consumption in response to a sudden increase in income. It takes time to catch up with consumption patterns of those who are long accustomed to higher income levels. Second, the households are unlikely to treat remittance as a permanent income. They would rather treat it as a windfall and want to save as much as possible, as long as it lasts. Finally, since the emigrant worker (usually the head of the family) is away, the total consumption of the migrant's family is likely to be less than the consumption of other families at similar income levels.

It is, however, arguable that although the remittance-receivers have greater propensities to save, the wastefulness with which remittance money is spent may be revealed by a closer look at the composition of consumption and savings. In order to test this hypothesis, Islam[31] separated out three consumption expenditures that may be considered luxury items — domestic servants, recreation, and festival ceremonies (see Table 14). Differences between remittance-receiving (A) and other (B) households

TABLE 15. Average Monthly Expenditure of the Migrant's Family on Land, House Construction, and Consumer Durables (in taka)

	Land Purchase	House Construction	Consumer Durables
Professionals	1,556	1,556	1,400
	(10)	(10)	(9)
Subprofessionals and technicians	991	914	381
	(13)	(12)	(5)
Skilled	600	525	112
	(16)	(14)	(3)
Semiskilled and unskilled	457	400	86
	(16)	(14)	(3)

Figures in parentheses show expenditure per item as percentage of monthly remittance.

Source: Mahmud and Osmani, op. cit., p.24.

are rather small in both rural and urban areas. In fact, the only statistically significant difference is in the amount spent on recreation by the rural households. On the whole, the hypothesis of disproportionate luxury-item consumption by remittance-receivers is once again given the lie.

The composition of savings, however, does reveal a picture that is closer to popular notions. Islam's survey includes expenditures on such items as consumer durables, real estate, and house repair and construction under the rubric of savings. Nearly one-third of the income from remittances is spent on land, the construction and improvement of houses, and consumer durables. If we assume that the expenditure of the migrants' families on these items was negligible at the pre-migration level of income, the entire amount of these expenditures can be taken to have resulted from remittances (see Table 15).

Macro-economic Impact of Remittances

The role of migrants' remittances in economic development can be conceptualised by using the traditional two-gap models of the role of foreign aid. To the extent that remittance provides foreign exchange to the government, it helps bridge the trade gap; and insofar as the remittance-receivers save part of their additional income, it also helps relax the savings-investment gap. To what extent it ultimately helps to accelerate the pace of development depends on its contribution in relaxing the dominant gap at particular points in time. A comprehensive analysis of the developmental impact of remittance through such a two-gap framework is, however, beyond the scope of this paper. Instead, we shall limit our discussion to analysing the available evidence about its impact on the two gaps separately; this would provide the ingredients needed for a more comprehensive analysis.

In addition to the impacts on balance of payments and savings, we shall also look into the impact of remittance on prices and the distribution of income. (The macro-economic impact of migration, as distinct from that of remittance as such, also includes the possible adverse impact on "absorptive capacity" which results from the loss of skilled labour. We have already noted this in our discussion of the labour market in Bangladesh and concluded that this effect is probably quite manageable at present.)

The Impact of Remittances on Bangladesh's Balance of Payments

Remittances have had a considerable role in easing the foreign exchange constraints in the Bangladesh economy (see Tables 16 and 17). Compared to merchandise exports, the role of remittance as a source of foreign exchange grew at a spectacular rate between 1975 and 1982 (see Table 16). Remittance as a ratio of export earnings shot up from a lowly 7.9 per cent in 1975/76 to an impressive 65.8 per cent in 1981/82. With a remittance income of nearly US$600 million in 1982/83, this ratio is expected to have exceeded 80 per cent by now. The possibility of remittance flow surpassing the earnings from merchandise exports in the near future seems quite likely.

Such a tremendous upsurge in the flow of remittance inevitably had a salutary effect on Bangladesh's capacity to import. Bangladesh has always been heavily dependent on foreign aid for financing its imports, and aid still provides the major source of import finance. But remittance flow has enabled the country to achieve some success in reducing this dependence in a relative sense. Own foreign exchange resources — i.e. the combined contribution of remittances and exports — financed somewhat less than one-third of its imports in 1975/76, but since 1979/80 they have accounted for nearly 40 per cent of the country's imports. In 1982/83 this share is likely to have exceeded the halfway mark.

TABLE 16. Remittance and the Balance of Trade of Bangladesh (in million $US)

	Remittance	Export	Import	Remittance as % of Exports	Remittance as % of Imports
1975/76	29.6	371.9	1275.0	7.9	2.3
1976/77	60.6	404.6	875.0	15.0	6.9
1977/78	113.5	489.8	1349.0	23.2	8.4
1978/79	143.4	609.7	1556.0	23.5	9.2
1979/80	210.3	722.3	2372.0	29.1	8.9
1980/81	379.4	710.7	2533.0	53.4	15.0
1981/82	412.4	627.0	2587.0	65.8	16.0

Source: Bangladesh: Recent Economic Trends . . . , p.120.

TABLE 17. Importance of Remittance in Relation to Other Items of Balance of Payments

	Remittance as a Percentage of		
	Jute Export Earnings	Foreign Aid	Oil Imports
1975/76	9.8	3.7	23.5
1976/77	21.0	11.4	41.5
1977/78	33.0	13.7	65.4
1978/79	34.2	13.9	80.0
1979/80	39.8	17.2	54.9
1980/81	79.7	33.0	75.4
1981/82	107.1	33.4	73.6

The absolute figures of remittance are given in Table 16. Jute export earnings include earnings from both raw jute and jute products. Foreign aid refers to long-term loans and grants only and does not include IMF financing. Oil imports include import of both crude petroleum and petroleum products.

Source: The table has been derived from tables 3.1-3.5 in *Bangladesh: Recent Economic Trends. . . .*

The importance of remittance income for Bangladesh's economy was never more dramatically illustrated than in the first two years of the 1980s. Bangladesh faced a severe balance-of-payments crisis in 1980/81 and 1981/82 owing mainly to (1) a drastic deterioration in its terms of trade, and (2) a simultaneous stagnation in external aid inflow. A sharp decline in the export prices of jute and jute products and of non-traditional exports such as leather and fish products together with an increase in average import prices led to a 16 per cent deterioration in Bangladesh's terms of trade in 1980/81. Although import prices remained relatively stable in 1981/82, export prices declined again owing to the continued stagnation of demand for raw jute and jute goods; the terms of trade deteriorated further by 17 per cent in 1981/82. Thus the cumulative deterioration in the terms of trade amounted to an alarming 30 per cent in a two-year period.

At the same time, Bangladesh suffered from a reduction in the quantum of external assistance. Disbursements of external aid to Bangladesh in real terms fell in 1980/81. Although there was some recovery in 1981/82, in real terms it was only 4 per cent higher than in 1978/79. In addition, the International Monetary Fund suspended in July 1981 an Extended Fund Facility arrangement that had been agreed upon in December 1980.

The only redeeming feature in this overall picture of gloom was the spectacular growth of remittance. It grew 80 per cent between 1979/80 and 1980/81. After another year it stood at nearly twice the 1979/80 level. In these two years it gave

Bangladesh nearly US$370 million more than it would have if it had remained at the 1979/80 level. On the other hand, if the terms of trade had remained at the 1979/80 levels, Bangladesh's current account deficit for these two years would have been US$250-350 million less than it actually was.[32] Thus, the additional inflow of remittances in these two years is seen not only to have compensated for the dramatic fall in the terms of trade but to have gone some way towards mitigating the effects of a reduced aid flow.

Further quantitative perspective of the importance of remittances, from a somewhat different angle, shows that jute and jute products (long the single most important foreign-exchange earner for Bangladesh, and previously for combined Pakistan) have very recently relinquished pride of place to migrants' remittances (see Table 17). The relative decline in the dependence on foreign aid is demonstrated by the fact that remittances as a proportion of foreign aid have risen from a negligible 3.7 per cent in 1975/76 to about 33 per cent in recent years. Finally, since the remittance boom is essentially a consequence of the oil price explosion in the early 1970s, it is interesting to see how the two conflicting effects stand in relation to each other in the context of the Bangladesh economy. Oil imports have proved a severe strain on Bangladesh's balance of payments over the last decade. While the oil bill accounted for only 4 per cent of the country's total imports in 1972/73 (and 10 per cent in 1973/74), it has claimed a share of 20-22 per cent in 1980/81 and 1981/82. However, remittance income has increasingly compensated for the pressures of a mounting oil bill. Remittances financed less than one-fourth of the oil bill in 1975/76, but in the 1980s they have been financing nearly three-fourths of the cost.

We have discussed at some length the overall impact of remittances on the balance of payments of Bangladesh. But apart from increasing the country's overall import capacity, remittances can also have important consequences for the economy through the structure of imports. We pointed out during our discussion on the Wage Earners' Scheme that the efforts to attract remittances by boosting the importers' premium rate may lead to a sub-optimal import structure by encouraging greater import of inessential goods than is warranted by the developmental needs of the country. In that event, an increase in overall import capacity would be of little help.

Indeed, a prevailing concern in Bangladesh is that an unduly high proportion of remittances is being squandered through the import of inessential commodities. In our view, however, there is not enough solid empirical evidence with which to judge this issue one way or the other. The relevant concern is often the result of faulty methodology. The usual way of judging the effect of remittances on import structure is to look at the composition of imports through the Wage Earners' Scheme. For instance Ali reports[33] that in 1978 the breakdown of WES imports was as follows: 13 per cent for essential consumer goods, 17 per cent for inessential consumer goods, 9.4 per cent for capital goods, and 64 per cent for raw materials. On estimating the proportion of raw materials used for the production of luxury goods, he concludes that roughly 50 per cent of the total value of imports under this scheme is directly or indirectly used for luxury goods. This leads him to conclude that, "viewed in the context of the elaborate supervision and control over imports into Bangladesh under the Cash Licensing Scheme, the *laissez faire* attitude under the Wage Earners' Scheme appears to be rather paradoxical."

Yet there is nothing essentially paradoxical here. In order to shore up the exchange rate in the WES and thereby to attract new remittances, it is only natural for the authorities to allow a relatively free import of inessential goods or of the raw materials that typically enjoy the highest-scarcity premiums. The important question here is whether the authorities are shifting such inessential imports from the regulated Cash Licensing Scheme to the free WES marker or are allowing a net addition in their import. If it is basically a shift, then there is no reason for concern. On the other hand, if it represents a net addition in inessential imports, one may have reason to worry. What is, therefore, required is an analysis of the total import structure in relation to the country's priorities, and not just an isolated breakdown of WES imports.

In fact, even an analysis of the import structure alone will not be adequate. The relative proportion of inessential imports may go up because of the Wage Earners' Scheme, but it may merely represent a shift of consumers' preference from domestic goods to imported ones. The total domestic absorption of inessential goods may not rise. The issue of the compositional effect of remittances can therefore be analysed only within a framework comprising the overall trade structure and the structure of domestic demand and production. Such an integrated analysis has not yet been made.

The Impact of Remittances on Savings

We have already discussed the savings propensities of remittance-receiving households. But the savings of these households cannot be taken as an estimate of savings out of remittance income. There are several reasons for this. First, there is considerable evidence of dissaving at low-income levels in Bangladesh. Insofar as the migrant's family used to dissave at pre-migration level in income, savings generated by remittance would be higher than the apparent current savings. Second, the observed current income and savings of the migrants' households have probably been boosted not only by the current remittance but also by the return on assets acquired from past remittances. This latter effect must be eliminated in order to answer the question of how much the receivers save of the remittance.

On the other hand, the estimated savings propensities cannot be applied directly on the remittance income to estimate the volume of savings out of remittance. This is because these propensities relate to total income and not to remittance income alone. These two incomes can be different for any number of reason. We have already noted the possibility of asset income created by past remittance. It is also possible that there are other earners in the family besides the migrant.

To circumvent these problems, Mahmud and Osmani adopted the following methodology to estimate the volume of savings out of remittance:

Let y_1 be the pre-migration level of income of the household. In order to eliminate the effect of asset income generated by past remittance, current remittance is added to y_1 to estimate the income-boosting effect of current remittance. But from this the previous income of the migrant is subtracted, since this income is now lost to the family. In other words, the net income effect of remittance is actual remittance (r) minus migrant's previous income (m).

Post-migration income y_2, shorn of the income-generating effect of past remittance, is then given by

$$y_2 = y_1 + r - m$$

The difference in savings at y_2 and y_1 then gives the net savings effect of current remittance.

We have noted earlier that the remittance-receiving households have a different consumption function from that of other households. Let the corresponding savings functions of the two groups of households be denoted by s_2 (y) and s_1 (y) respectively. It is reasonable to assume that the savings function of other households will be applicable for estimating savings out of the pre-migration income (y_1) of the migrants' households.

The required savings impact of current remittance is then given by

$$S = s_2 (y_2) - s_1 (y_1)$$

Following this methodology, Mahmud and Osmani arrived at estimates of savings for households of different skill-categories of migrants (see Table 18).

TABLE 18. Estimated. Net Increase in Income and Savings of Migrant's Family, 1979 (in taka)

	Net Increase in Income	Net Increase in Savings	Savings Increase as % of Net Increase
Professional	13,198	7,458	57
Subprofessional and technical	6,170	3,947	64
Skilled	2,897	2,041	70
Semiskilled and unskilled	2,358	1,722	73

Adapted from Table V of Mahmud and Osmani, op. cit., p.22.

The estimates in Table 18 show that about 60–70 per cent of the net increase in income is saved by migrants' families. However, as seen earlier, expenditures on housing, land, and consumer durables together account for nearly one-third of the income from remittances. This would mean that these three items are responsible for committing about 55–60 per cent of the estimated savings out of the net increase in income due to remittance. If one wants to treat them as totally unproductive expenditure, then truly "productive" savings would turn out to be about one-third of remittance income.

The Impact of Remittances on Prices

We are unable to address this issue with the rigour it deserves, largely because of the difficulty involved in isolating the effect of remittances from the general inflationary pressures extant in Bangladesh. But some qualitative remarks can certainly be made. For one thing, it should be clear that, contrary to popular belief, the "spending spree" of the remittance-receivers cannot be held responsible for adding to the *general* price inflation in the country. This is so for the simple reason that corresponding to the additional expenditure, an equivalent amount of commodities is also imported within the country with the remitted foreign exchange.

However, it is quite possible that such expenditure would have a significant impact on the structure of relative prices due to a very likely mismatch between the expenditure pattern and the structure of additional imports. In particular, the prices of the non-tradables that are specially favoured by the remittance-receivers must have risen much more than they would have in response to general inflation alone.

The most important of such non-tradables are land and housing. Of all the components that go into the cost-of-living index, the cost of housing in Bangladesh has gone up more than any other commodity group. For instance, for the low-paid government employees of Dhaka the housing cost towards the end of 1982 stood at 10.4 times that of 1969/70, while the overall cost-of-living index was 7.6 times as high.[34] The picture is similar for the cost-of-living index of industrial workers. It is also worthy of note that ever since 1973/74 (when large-scale migration had not yet begun), the house rent index for Dhaka has been higher than any other cost or price index for the country, with the sole exception of the price index for land.[35] The consumer price index for Dhaka in 1981/82 was 287 (with 1973/74 as base), but the house rent index was 488. On the other hand, the price index for urban land for Bangladesh as a whole was 1,013, while that for rural land was 516.

This astronomical rise in the price of land was not due to remittance money alone. The general inflationary environment was a strong inducement for anyone with excess liquidity to invest in land. The prevalence of this tendency is evidenced by the land prices, which went up faster than the general price level in almost all of the 21 districts of Bangladesh, not just in the four or five districts that supply migrant

TABLE 19. Pre- and Post-migration Monthly Income of Migrants and Their Families, 1979 (in taka)

	Migrant's Previous Income	Migrant's Income Abroad[1]	Family's Previous Income	Value of Remittance[1]
Professional	2,360	23,994	2,645	15,558
Sub-professional/technical	1,450	12,900	1,668	7,620
Skilled	850	7,353	1,445	3,747
Semiskilled and unskilled	500	4,902	850	2,858
All groups	762	7,146	1,178	4,090

1. Migrant's Income abroad and valve of remittance are evaluated at WES exhange rate for Jan.-June 1979.

Compiled from tables II and III, Mahmud and Osmani, op. cit.

labour. On the other hand, in three of the five districts (Dhaka, Comilla, and Noakhali), the land price index was considerably higher than the average for the country.[36] This shows that remittance money probably exacerbated the tendency to buy land. But the fact that Chittagong and Sylhet had a lower land price index than the national average indicates that other factors were also at work.

The Impact of Remittances on Income Distribution

Income distribution is thought to be most adversely affected by remittances from migrant workers. There is hardly any doubt that emigration has the ability to create a new elite class by causing the migrants' families to jump several rungs on the income ladder at once (see Table 19).

The income of migrants is nearly ten times their previous earnings, and the remittance their families receive is nearly four times their previous income. (The estimates of the families' previous income for the last two categories of workers in Table 19 are upper bounds. Mahmud and Osmani also submitted lower estimates which would imply that average remittance income for all groups is nearly five times their previous income.) To appreciate fully the distributional consequences of this change in the income class of the migrants' families, we may compare these incomes with the average household income in the economy. Mahmud and Osmani made two estimates of average household income in 1978/79 — one based on national-accounts figures and the other on the Household Expenditure Survey of 1976/77. These estimates are Tk 754 and Tk 888 per month respectively. Whichever estimate we accept, it may be seen that even for unskilled workers, the estimated remittance is more than three times as large as the average household income in the economy; it is nearly twenty times as large for the professionals.

It is thus quite clear that migration and remittance have catapulted a fortunate few into the uppermost end of the income-distribution spectrum. An even better perspective can be obtained by looking at the relative positions from which these families originated. According to Table 20, all categories of workers came from households with income higher than the national average. However, as mentioned before, the estimates of previous household income for the last two categories are upper bounds. The lower bounds are Tk 977 and Tk 565 respectively.[37] Comparing these figures with the national average, one finds many of the semi-skilled and skilled workers have probably come from households with income slightly lower than the national average. This would still mean that at least 40–42 per cent of the migrants were originally above the national average. Even the semi-skilled and unskilled workers do not typically come from the poorest of families, since the lower estimate of their previous income is only slightly below the national average.

The evidence thus supports the hypothesis that emigration is helping only the relatively better-off families to move further up in the income scale. In contrast, the poorest households do not appear to have benefited much from emigration. (The main reason, perhaps, is that the poorest people cannot manage the cost of airfare and other necessary expenses — which would amount to a small fortune for such people.)

Apart from this direct impact on nominal income distribution, remittances can also be said to have adversely affected the real income distribution by changing the structure of relative prices. However, this issue requires caution, as fact and myth often become hopelessly entangled.

The tendency of migrants' families to tie up their fortunes in land — pushing up its relative price more than any other non-tradable good in Bangladesh — has already been seen. It is often alleged that this massive land hunger is aggravating the problem of landlessness and income inequality in Bangladesh. But there is hardly any factual evidence to support this contention. Although landlessness is increasing in Bangladesh, there is no reason to believe that remittance money has anything to do with it. In fact, some theories lead one to expect the contrary. Most land sales in Bangladesh are distress sales. People part with their plots of land only as a last resort in order to meet some given needs of an urgent nature. When the sale is meant basically to meet a *given* need, the supply curve will slope downwards, because at a higher price the same need can be met by parting with a smaller piece of land. So, if remittance income has pushed up the price of land, it should lead to fewer and not more land sales.

However, other relative price changes have certainly had adverse distributional consequences. We have already noted the relatively sharp rise in the cost of housing in the urban areas, and the migrants' demand for accommodations is very likely to have added pressure to this trend. This has helped the propertied class enormously, but it has also made a substantial dent into the real income of the poor and middle class, for whom the price elasticity of the demand for housing is probably not very high. Moreover, although it is difficult to prove, the remittance-induced rise in the relative prices of other relatively inessential non-tradables, such as milk, meat, etc., has adversely affected the real income of the middle class, especially where there are dense concentrations of migrants.[38]

Sociocultural Effects of Migration

Although the total volume of migration from Bangladesh may not yet be a sizeable proportion of its labour force, its effect on particular localities has been quite significant. When large numbers of people migrate from a village or a cluster of villages, the social consequences for that particular community can be enormous. There are also wider social implications for the country as a whole. Yet the sociocultural consequences of migration remain the least-researched aspect of labour migration from Bangladesh.

The only published work on the sociocultural impact of the labour migration that has come to my notice is a study by M. Islam of a rural commnity in the district of Chittagong,[39] and even this study is basically exploratory, based as it is on a very small sample and on mostly anecdotal evidence. The main sociocultural consequences observed in Islam's study can be classified under the following headings: social impact of wasteful expenditure, apathy towards work, dampening of educational aspirations, and marital problems such as polygamy, divorce, etc.

The over-spending by returning migrants or their families for social and religious ceremonies has set a prohibitively high standard of expenditure, which others attempt to emulate. A particularly pernicious development in the survey area was the malignant spread of the dowry system, previously confined to a minority of the community. Encouraged by the examples set by migrants' families, which provide their sons-in-law with luxury consumer-durables such as T.V., refrigerator, etc., other bridegrooms have also come to expect such dowries from their would-be fathers-in-law regardless of their economic status. Consequently, it has become quite difficult for middle-class and poor families to find husbands for their daughters. In addition to setting expensive standards of expectation, migration has also given rise to incipient social tensions by affecting the distribution of purchasing power. The prices of many commodities have gone out of the reach of ordinary people as a result of the migrants' ostentatious consumption. The resultant deprivation has naturally sown the seeds of resentment among the non-migrants.

Employment in the Middle East has become so alluring that the search for a job opening becomes an obsession for many people. If the opening continues to elude them, frustration inevitably results. Both the original obsession and the resulting frustration lead to disinterest or apathy towards work. Islam's study notes the

59

frequent occurrence of this worker apathy. If it becomes widespread, it will not only worsen production losses resulting from migration but will cause long-term damage to Bangladeshi society through the degeneration of its work ethic.

A related phenomenon is general devaluation of education and a lowering of educational aspirations. People with general college and university educations have little chance of finding employment in the Middle East, while semi-literate people are seen to be returning with a small fortune after a few years' stay abroad. This has not only caused frustration among the growing number of the educated unemployed; it is disillusioning a part of the younger generation about the utility of formal education. If this attitude should lead to a restructuring of the educational system to give greater prominence to vocational and technical education, it might turn out not to be such a bad thing for the country after all. But there is a danger that higher education may itself fall out of grace, and that can only harm the society in the long run.

M. Islam also noticed an increased incidence of divorce and polygamy in the area he studied, and this he believes to be a direct result of migration. Divorces are primarily granted by wives whose husbands have spent year after year in the Middle East, leaving their families behind. In addition, many migrants, after returning home with a pocketful of money are known to have married more than one woman. Although these findings are based on a limited sample, the tendencies are such as to be generally prevalent wherever substantial migration is concentrated.

Apart from localised effects, migration also has social implications for the country as a whole. One such effect is the increase in corruption. Corruption begins in the office of the recruiting agents. In theory, agents are to receive no payment from the migrants; they are paid a commission by the employers for recruiting on their behalf. But there is a large scope for economic rent in this transaction, as the demand for jobs far outstrips supply, and the agents take full advantage of it. It is an open secret that there are fixed rates that prospective recruits must pay the agents for different categories of employment. What is worse, fake agencies proliferated in the early migration years and simply vanished after collecting money from a number of prospective recruits. This fraudulent activity ruined many families, as they had to sell all their assets, often including their last piece of land, to raise the required funds. The resulting destitution of a large number of families is itself a social problem of considerable dimensions. Frequent occurences of such incidents have given the manpower export business such a bad name that recruiting agents have popularly come to be known by the pejorative term *"Adam Bepari,"* which literally means a dealer in human cargo.

But extortion is not a monopoly of the recruiting agents. The Bureau of Manpower Employment and Training, in its role as an intermediary for recruitment and as authority for giving clearance, is also not supposed to take any money from employers or employees. But it is also common knowledge that the migrants can seldom get away without lubricating the bureau's official machinery. The chain of bribery can often go quite high in the hierarchy. A scandalous political uproar broke out a few years ago when the then minister of state for manpower export was openly accused in the parliament for his involvement in illegitimate deals. More importantly, the involvement of a particular minister is not to be viewed as an isolated incident. The granting of agency rights has been used systematically in the past to distribute political patronage. It has also been alleged that a part of the money raised by such agencies has flowed into the coffers of the political party in power.

Manpower export threatens to rend the social fabric in still other ways. Remittance money provides easy, short-term solutions to what basically are problems of fundamental structural disequilibrium. It can also have a long-term detrimental effect on the social will to deal with the fundamental issues. This argument is not dissimilar to the one often voiced regarding the disincentive effect of foreign aid. It is much more relevant in the context of remittance, which is likely to be a much more transient phenomenon than foreign aid. But transient or not, the very fact that a nation has to survive by sending its people to earn abroad is not a morale-raising thought for any self-respecting nation. One may accept this as a temporary expedient, but if a nation continues to fail in utilising its human resources for its own productive activities, it can be anything but a proud nation.

Issues Related to the Return Flow of Migrants

There are two aspects of the problem of return flow of migrants. The first relates to the temporary nature of the migration: since the workers are not allowed to settle permanently in the host countries, there is a continuous return flow even when the gross outflow is growing rapidly, and this raises various issues. The second aspect relates to the transient nature of the overall migration process. Some day, as the oil economies acquire the ability to fully use their own human resources, their need for migrant workers will cease. The end of the migration may come later for some labour-exporting countries than for others; it may come gradually, or it may come to a sudden halt. But the eventuality of an end to this process must be envisaged as real. This raises some very difficult issues, many of which are simply accentuated versions of the problems associated with the regular return flow, but some are unique to itself.

The prospects for a country such as Bangladesh already begin to look a little dim. Bangladesh has abundant unskilled and semiskilled labour. Yet, it is precisely this category of labour that the importing countries are going to import less and less in the coming years. This is a natural consequence of structural changes taking place in the labour-importing countries because of their attempts to diversify their economies and to employ more and more of their own labour forces. The construction boom which attracted most of the unskilled migrant labour in the initial migration years is gradually tapering off. Some of the importing countries have taken steps to improve their indigenous supply of skilled technicians and professionals, but, because of the inevitable time-lag, these efforts will not yield immediate fruit. On the other hand, the effort to diversify the economy is constantly pushing up the demand for skilled personnel. Consequently, prospective migrants with professional and technical expertise have a much brighter opportunity now than ever before.

But unfortunately, Bangladesh is not in a position to take advantage of this trend. Our earlier analysis of the labour market in Bangladesh has shown that the present migration rate of highly skilled workers renders the domestic situation just manageable in most cases. Any attempt to increase migration to any appreciable degree is bound to face supply constraints, given Bangladesh's existing capacity to produce skilled labour. One could argue that it may be worthwhile to augment the supply capacity of educational institutions so as take advantage of the expanding market in the Middle East. But this may turn out to be a counsel for abortive investment unless there is absolute confidence in Bangladesh's ability to sustain an increased rate of migration for a considerable period of time.

It is, in fact, doubtful that Bangladesh will be able to sustain even its current export levels of skilled or unskilled labour, even though no absolute reduction is envisaged in the aggregate demand for expatriate labour by Middle Eastern countries. The cause of concern lies in two trends in the structure of demand. First, as the total stock of expatriate workers is growing, the importing countries are becoming increasingly concerned about the social and cultural consequences of harbouring large pockets of an alien workforce. This may induce them to rely more on inter-Arab migration, which can only restrict the opportunities for the countries of South and Southeast Asia, including Bangladesh. Second, both in construction and in manufacturing activities, the importing countries are increasingly showing a preference for package deals or "turn-key" projects through contracting firms. The firms supply the technology and labour from their own countries. As a result, the ability of different countries to maintain or enhance their share of the expatriate labour market will depend very much on the success of their contracting firms in bidding on such turn-key projects. Bangladesh is doing rather poorly in this regard. As of 1982 only 12 Bangladeshi firms were working in the Middle East, with a workforce of only about 5,000; most of them were subcontractors engaged in labour management under general contractors. In contrast, 25 Pakistani and 70 Indian firms were at that time engaged in major Middle East projects.[40] Bangladesh, therefore, must seriously contemplate the possibility not only of an accentuated return flow but also of a gradual drying up of new openings.

Consequences of Return Migration

Leaving aside for the moment the eventual possibility of a complete halt to the migration process, the regular return flow of migrants itself can be seen to pose quite a few problems for policy-makers.

The immediate economic problem is the reabsorption of the returning migrants in the productive labour force. There exists no study in Bangladesh on the reabsorption problems actually faced by returnees. One can, however, speculate that the migrants with special skills — e.g. doctors, engineers, etc. — will not find re-entry particularly difficult. But the skilled workers and technicians, in whose absence employers tend to hire inadequate substitutes in the form of apprentices, may find it hard to get their jobs back. If they succeed, it may be at the cost of laying off the apprentices. However, a systematic study on the reabsorption problem needs to be undertaken before anything more concrete can be said.

One aspect of the reabsorption problem is to enable the returnees to engage in productive self-employment in industry or commerce on the strength of their accumulated capital. This is particularly important for unskilled workers, who may loathe returning to their pre-migration work, especially in view of their aspirations to advance their social status in keeping with their improved financial circumstances.

The institutional and financial measures required to provide the necessary incentive for this purpose are going to prove a serious challenge to the policy-makers in the days to come. The incentive problem is not specific to the group of returning migrants; it is in fact part of the general problem of private-capital formation in Bangladesh. The existing incentive structure induces the owners of finance capital to invest in quick-yielding speculative activities more than in productive investment. Short of a general restructuring of the incentive system, some specific measures aimed at the returnees are not going to be of much help. What the existing institutions have been failing to do, the special institution will fail to do equally. For it is not just a matter of institution, but of the incentive system, as it is influenced by the interest rate structure, the inflation rate, and related factors.

All these problems will be magnified many times over if the migration process ceases and all the workers return home. In addition, a particularly serious problem will arise in the management of the balance of payments, which has become so heavily dependent on remittance money. Having relied for years almost exclusively on jute for its foreign exchange earnings, Bangladesh has had bitter experience with the volatility of an economy sustained by just one source of foreign exchange. There are now two predominant sources with the emergence of remittance. But the disappearance or even a drastic diminution of remittance income may bring about a much bigger catastrophe than anything wrought so far by the volatile golden fibre.

Much depends on how the remittance money is utilised while it lasts. Herein, however, lies a probable dilemma. Everyone agrees that the bonanza of foreign exchange earned through remittances should not be frittered away on consumption goods but should instead be used to build up the productive base of the economy. If that means setting up industries based on raw materials imported with the newly acquired foreign exchange, the eventual adjustment problem will be much more serious than if most of it were really to be spent on consumer goods. In the event of a foreign exchange crisis, it is exceedingly difficult to decrease imports of industrial raw materials, as it would lead to unused capacity, unemployed labour, and loss of production. This is not to be taken as counsel for liberalising the import of consumer goods. The best strategy would perhaps be to utilise the remittance income for importing capital goods to be used for activities based on indigenous raw materials (of which natural gas springs first to mind).

In any case, this is a problem whose solution, unlike that of reabsorption, cannot wait until the labour migration actually ceases. Appropriate strategies must be adopted now; adjustments later on will be too late.

Notes

1. G. Swamy, *International Migrant Workers' Remittances: Issues and Prospects*, World Bank Staff Working Paper no. 481 (Washington, D.C., 1981).
2. S. A. Ali et al., *Labour Migration from Bangladesh to the Middle East*, World Bank Staff Working Paper no. 454 (Washington, D.C., 1981). The present author was one of the co-authors of this report.
3. *Manpower Bulletin* (Bangladesh Manpower Planning Centre, Dhaka), Dec. 1982, p. 42.
4. Ali et al., p. 39.
5. Ibid., p. 349.
6. M. Islam, "Socio-economic Consequences of Manpower Export" (Department of Management, University of Chittagong, 1982, mimeo), p. 23.
7. Ali et al., p. 29.
8. *Manpower Bulletin*, Dec. 1982.
9. *Statistical Pocketbook of Bangladesh, 1981* (Bureau of Statistics, Dhaka), p. 401.
10. *Manpower Bulletin*, Dec. 1982, p. 37.
11. Ali et al., p. 39.
12. Ali et al.
13. Estimates based on official figures of sectoral employment in 1981; see *Statistical Pocketbook of Bangladesh, 1981*, p. 399.
14. Ibid., p. 376.
15. M. Muqtada, "The Seed-Fertilizer Technology and Surplus Labour in Bangladesh Agriculture," *Bangladesh Development Studies*, Oct. 1975.
16. R. Islam and R. I. Rahman, "Surplus Labour in Bangladesh Agriculture: A Comment," in *Bangladesh Development Studies*, Summer 1978.
17. I. Ahmad, "Employment in Bangladesh: Problems and Prospects," in E. A. G. Robinson and K. Griffin, eds., *The Economic Development of Bangladesh* (London: Macmillan and Co., 1974); also, M. Masum, "Unemployment and Under-employment in Agriculture: Case Study of Bangladesh" (Ph.D. dissertation, University of Delhi, 1977).
18. M. Farashuddin et al., "Shadow Prices for Bangladesh" (Boston University, Boston, Mass., USA, 1979, mimeo).
19. Ali et al., p. 208.
20. See, for example, Farashuddin et al.
21. Quoted in *Manpower Bulletin*, Aug. 1982.
22. Ibid.
23. M. Islam, "Bengali Migrant Workers in Britain" (Ph.D. dissertation, University of Leeds, 1976).
24. S. A. Ali, "Home Remittances by Bangladesh Nationals Working Abroad," chap. 2 in Ali et al.
25. W. Mahmud and S. R. Osmani, "Impact of Emigrant Workers' Remittances on the Bangladeshi Economy," *Bangladesh Development Studies*, vol. 8, no. 3 (Fall 1980).

26. See Ali, "Home Remittances"; and A. M. A. H. Siddiqui, "Policy Implications for Bangladesh in Respect of Promoting Foreign Employment of Bangladeshi Worker" (paper presented to the Asian Regional Project on Strengthening Labour Administration, sponsored by the International Labour Organisation, Bangkok, 1979).
27. Ali, "Home Remittances."
28. R. Islam, "Export of Manpower from Bangladesh to the Middle East Countries: The Impact of Remittance Money on Household Expenditure," chap. 3. in Ali et al.
29. A good discussion of the existing procedures may be found in S. A. Ali, "Utilization of Remittance," in Ali et al.
30. R. Islam, "Export of Manpower."
31. Ibid.
32. World Bank, *Bangladesh: Recent Economic Trends and Medium Term Development Issues* (Washington, D.C., 1983), p. 3.
33. Ali, "Home Remittances."
34. World Bank, *Bangladesh: Recent Economic Trends*, p. 208.
35. *Statistical Pocketbook of Bangladesh, 1981*, p. 330.
36. Ibid., pp. 364–365.
37. Mahmud and Osmani, p. 17.
38. M. Islam, in his 1982 study (op cit.), provides some anecdotal evidence in support of this hypothesis.
39. Ibid.
40. *Manpower Bulletin*, Dec. 1982.

INDIA

P. R. Gopinathan Nair

Professor of Economics, University of Kerala, Trivandrum, India

This study endeavours to bring together the fragments of information scattered about in research summaries, government publications, and press reports that have a bearing on the migration of Indian workers to the Middle East. Information on this phenomenon is scanty in India since no detailed and in-depth studies have been conducted by any of the country's institutions or agencies, national or state governments, international institutional agencies, or research institutions. Unfortunately, therefore, this survey can hope only to present the broad contours of the problem and highlight the need for an in-depth study. Such a study appears to be most essential particularly because the peak phase of migration has already come to an end. The attendant problems of rehabilitation and re-employment of repatriates are expected to present formidable challenges to India in general and the states that account for considerable proportions of the migrants (e.g. Kerala) in particular.

Indian Labour Migration to the Middle East: Volume and Distribution by Destination

Emigration from India to countries in the Persian Gulf region is generally known to have been taking place on a substantial scale during the past ten years. The rough magnitudes can be determined by various sources: pronouncements made by the ministers of the government in the parliament, press reports, and estimates made by a few authors in studies on the labour situation in the Gulf countries. The drawback of such sources is that they are, at best, only conjectures.

Besides these sources, there exists information on the number of passports issued annually throughout India. Passports are, of course, issued for many different travel purposes and destinations, not only to countries in the Gulf region. The number of passports issued would therefore be a poor base on which to construct estimates of the annual flows to any particular region.

Another possible source would be the Protectorate of Emigrants, which issues clearance to the emigrants and registers their employment agreements. This source has not been accessible to us.

A third source would be data on air traffic, the number of passengers travelling by the different airlines from India to the Gulf countries and back every year. The difficulties with this source are manifold. The information is not available for all the various airlines that operate between India and the Gulf countries; vast numbers of persons are known to have emigrated from India to the Gulf region through third countries; many emigrate by sea and land routes; and passengers to the Gulf countries include not only new emigrants but also those returning from leave, as well as those who are making short visits, such as the Haj pilgrims.

Yet another source might be the Indian embassies in the different host countries, but information from this source is not available in India.

Until 1977/78, the Reserve Bank of India (RBI) issued "P" forms to persons travelling abroad, and the information used to be reported in *Currency and Finance*, published annually by the bank. The practice of issuing "P" forms has since been discontinued with the relaxation of the rules regarding travel abroad.

Prakash C. Jain[1] has observed that the migration of Indians to the Gulf region was minor until the end of World War II. He cites an earlier study on the number and distribution of Indians in that region in 1948, which claimed the total number to be around 14,000, with about 40 per cent concentrated in Aden. Jain notes that during the next two decades, the total number increased to only about 40,000 and that the distribution of the migrants among the different countries had undergone some change. About 60 per cent of these migrants were distributed equally between Iraq and Kuwait.

Indians have migrated to almost all the capital-rich Arab states that entertain Asian immigrants. The trade contracts of Indian merchants with the Middle East countries have existed for several centuries. The United Arab Emirates (UAE — comprising Abu Dhabi, Dubai, the small Emirate of Sharjah, and the "village states" of Ras-al-Khaimah, Umm-al-Quaiwain, Ajman, and Fujairah) imported Indian goods and redistributed them throughout the Arabian peninsula.[2] Dubai served as the major centre in the UAE in this redistribution trade. The Indian merchants and their Arab partners also used to carry out extensive illegal trade with India in goods on which the government of India had placed import restrictions, such as gold, watches, tape recorders, and transistor radios. It is estimated that about 3,000 Indian merchant families live in Dubai, and that they had arrived there well before the 1970s. These traditional links probably account for the fact that the largest flow of Indian migrants to the Middle East has been to the UAE.

Bahrain had some special Indian connections during the British rule in India. It was made a British protectorate and was controlled by the government of India. During that period Indian merchants settled in Bahrain and imported rice, tea, sugar, and shoes, helped Arab traders who were smuggling gold and pearls, and shared in the trade in hashish and opium.[3] Indians began to arrive to work as clerks and technicians and nurses during the 1930s with the development of the Bahrain Petroleum Company.

Subsequent to the hike in world oil prices, the volume of migration from South Asian countries began to swell and the migrants were employed mostly in construction work and shipping and banking services.

Oman, like Bahrain, had a special Indian connection during the British rule of India. During the first half of the present century, British officials of the government of India policed this region, and members of the Indian political service and civil service were posted in Muscat as agents and residents.[4] The Indian merchant community had dominated the economy of Oman even during the nineteenth century. Indian merchants were not only wholesale and retail traders and import and export agents for Western companies; they were also the bankers. These merchants came from the northwestern regions of the Indian peninsula that now are partly in Pakistan and partly in India. The Hindu merchants who had emigrated to Oman from Kutch in Gujarat experienced persecution in the 1860s, and many of them left for safer areas along the East African coast. Those who remained behind had, of course, a secure place in Oman's economy. They imported food to Oman, exported dates to India, managed the pearl trade from Bahrain, and developed trade links between Oman, on the one side, and Zanzibar, Somalia, and Mozambique, on the other. The Indian merchants had close ties with government officials, provincial governors, and the ruling family.

According to Birks and Sinclair,[5] there were 247,700 Asian workers in the Arab region in 1970, distributed in Bahrain, Kuwait, Qatar, and the UAE. The number of Indian migrant workers increased quite rapidly after 1970, and in 1975 stood at about 154, 000 (see Table 1).[6]

A more recent estimate gives a figure of 599,500 in 1981.[7] According to this source, the largest concentration of Indian migrants was in the UAE; Saudi Arabia and Kuwait were next with 80,000 each (see Table 2).

The latest estimate of the number of Indian workers in the Gulf countries came from Mr. A. A. Rahim, external affairs minister of India, who visited the region in May 1983 to study and find solutions to the problems faced by Indian labour. According to him, there were nearly one million Indian workers in the Gulf countries, including Saudi Arabia and Iraq.[8] If the work participation rate of the Indians remains at its 1975 level, namely 57.6 per cent (see Table 5), the total Indian population in the Gulf region is likely to be on the order of 1.7 million. A large proportion — say, more than 50 per cent — of the Indian migrants come from the small state of Kerala, which accounts for less than 4 per cent of the total population of India.[9]

TABLE 1. Indian Migrant Workers in Countries of the Arab Region, 1975

	Number of Indian Workers	Indians as % of All Asian Workers in Country
Saudi Arabia	15,000	1.9
Libya	500	0.2
UAE	61,500	24.5
Kuwait	21,475	10.3
Qatar	16,000	29.8
Bahrain	8,943	30.5
Oman	26,000	36.8
Iraq	5,000	7.6
Total	154,418	8.5

Source: Birks and Sinclair, International Migration and Development in the Arab Region (Geneva, 1980), p.137.

TABLE 2. Indian Workers in Countries of the Arab Region, 1981

	Number of Indian Workers (approximate)
Saudi Arabia	80,000
Kuwait	80,000
UAE	250,000
Oman	65,000
Libya	40,000
Bahrain	25,000
Iraq	25,000
Qatar	25,000
Yemen Arab Republic	5,000
Jordan	3,500
Yemen	1,000
Total	599,500

Source: Statement before Parliament by the Indian minister of external affairs, on 26 March 1981.

Annual Rate of Outflow

No reliable data exist on the annual migration flow to the Gulf countries. However, it is possible to get a rough idea from the stock of workers for the different years: 40,000 in 1971; 154,400 in 1975; 559,500 in 1981; and 1,000,000 in 1983. The annual net outflow would have been, therefore on the average around 28,500 from 1971 to 1975; 67,500 from 1975 to 1981;[10] and 220,000 from 1981 to 1983.[11]

Emigration from India to the Gulf countries takes place mainly from seven states — Kerala, Andhra Pradesh, Punjab, Gujarat, Goa, Maharashtra, and Tamil Nadu. Of these seven states, Kerala is supposed to account for not less than 50 per cent of the migrants. The bulk of the migrants from Bombay (in the State of Maharashtra) are actually from Kerala and Goa. Tamil Nadu is the latest entrant into the exodus. No surveys are known to have been conducted about the volume of annual flow of migrants for any state in India other than Kerala. According to a survey conducted in Kerala from January to March 1980, there were 207,800 persons employed abroad, of whom 186,500 (90 per cent) were in Middle Eastern countries. This figure includes only the workers, not their non-working spouses, relatives, or children who live with them abroad. There are reasons to believe that this figure is low and that the present volume of Keralites (workers and non-workers combined) in the Gulf countries could be not less than 800,000.[12]

The vast majority of the migrants are rural people. The townsfolk among the migrants are the engineers, doctors, contractors, and other professional workers, whose proportion among the migrants is likely to be extremely small, about 10 per cent at the most.

Stock and Annual Rate of Returnees

Apart from the occasional reports in the press about repatriation, actual or potential, of the migrants, no information exists on the returnees. The inflow of return migrants, however, has not occurred at a rate and in a volume large enough to pose any major problems for the state governments concerned. Enquiries made at the employment exchanges in Kerala have revealed no instances of a Gulf repatriate registering with the employment exchanges. Only an extensive household survey would reveal the magnitude of the stock of returnees and their annual inflow.

Composition of Migration

The Indian workers in the Gulf regions may be grouped into five broad categories — construction workers, employees in private firms, employees in government and other public-sector institutions, traders and businessmen, and domestic servants.[13]

Construction workers form the single largest category. Indian workers are employed in a variety of jobs such as unskilled workers, skilled craftsmen, civil engineers, and managers. The major construction companies are Indian, British, American, Cypriot, and Arab. Private-sector firms in industry and services employ Indians as factory workers; clerks in department stores; waiters, clerks, receptionists, and managers in hotels; engineers in oil companies; clerks, accountants, and managers in banks; and in various clerical and sales jobs in business. A large number of Indians are employed in government departments and other public-sector institutions as well.[14] India, particularly Kerala, is the major supplier of doctors and nurses to hospitals in the Gulf countries. The fourth category of Indians in the Gulf region is the trading and business community. Even though their numbers are not large, economically they are a powerful section, particularly in Dubai, Abu Dhabi, and Oman. Indians are also employed by Arab famillies as cooks, sweepers, and gardeners. Their numbers are limited, however, since the government of India in recent years has completely banned the emigration of Indian women for purposes of domestic service in Persian Gulf countries.[15] This ban was not successful owing to the large clandestine movement of migrants; the government reiterated its decision in 1973.[16]

No extensive surveys have been conducted in the labour-supplying Indian states; therefore, the distributional patterns of the emigrants by age, education, occupation, etc. discussed below are based on the findings of a few sample surveys conducted by private agencies and individual researchers in Kerala in recent years. Most of these sample surveys were conducted during 1977 and 1978.[17]

Age

The majority of the Gulf migrants are young at the time of their first emigration (see Table 3). Migrants in age groups below 35 years dominated in all the case studies, accounting for 78 to 87 per cent of the total migrants.

Education

Migrants to the Gulf countries possessed, on the average, far fewer educational qualifications, general and special, than their counterparts going to Western countries and Africa. Even illiterates formed part of them, although, according to the surveys conducted in Kerala, they did not exceed 10 per cent. The distribution of the migrants according to educational levels as shown by the case studies is shown in Table 4.

The majority of the migrants from all except two of the regions surveyed either were matriculates or had university degrees and professional qualifications. The proportion of highly qualified personnel, however, was small, not exceeding 10 per cent for most of the regions. The Gulf migration did not, therefore, constitute a serious problem of

TABLE 3. Age Composition of Migrants from Selected Regions of Kerala to the Gulf Countries (percentages)

	Elakonam	Koipram	Kadakkavur	Perumathura	Puthukurchi	Chirayinkil, Chengannur, Chavakkad, Tirur
Below 20	6.5	5.4	0.7	18.5	9.1	0.6
20–25	33.9	41.9	24.5	33.8	36.4	24.9
25–30	27.4	24.3	40.1	20.8	22.7	34.2
30–35	19.4	13.5	21.1	13.1	11.4	18.1
Subtotal	87.2	85.1	86.4	86.2	79.6	77.8
35–40	3.2	2.7	6.8	4.6	11.4	11.3
40–45	6.5	9.5	3.4	7.7	4.5	5.8
45–50	3.2	2.7	2.0			3.3
50 & above	—	—	1.4	1.5	4.5	1.8
Subtotal	12.9	14.9	13.6	13.8	20.4	22.2
Total	100.0	100.0	100.0	100.0	100.0	100.0

TABLE 4. Education of Migrants from Selected Regions of Kerala to the Gulf Countries (percentages)

		Literate			
	Illiterate	Non-matriculate	Matriculate	Postgraduate, Engineers, Doctors, etc.	Total Literate
Elakonam	—	51.5	43.5	5.0	100.0
Koipram	—	9.5	55.4	35.1	100.0
Chavakkad	6.6	77.9	11.8	3.7	93.4
Kadakkavur	—	44.5	42.1	13.4	100.0
Perumathura	4.6	43.2	41.4	10.8	95.4
Puthukurichi	—	35.7	55.5	8.9	100.0
Chengannur, Chirayinkil, Chavakkad, and Tirur	10.5	39.7	34.0	15.8	89.5

brain drain; rather, it was predominantly a flow of excess operative and manual labour which has been evident in Kerala as in the rest of India over the past several decades.

Occupational Status

The majority of Keralite migrants during the 1970s came from among the unemployed. The proportion of the unemployed varied, however, from one region of emigration to another. In the relatively poor areas in which the income and educational status of the population was low, the proportion of the unemployed among migrants was as high as three-fifths or more. In other regions, they formed slightly more than one-third. Unskilled and skilled workers accounted for between one-eighth and half of the total, again depending on the income-educational status of the migration regions. We should observe that professionally qualified and highly educated Indian migrants to the Gulf region were rare and came primarily from a specific area that has sent similar migrants to countries in the West and to Africa. Otherwise, the migrants were workers, unskilled and semiskilled. Emigrants destined for white-collar jobs such as clerks, typists, teachers, nurses, and telephone operators comprised on the average of 5–6 per cent, even though the percentage of white-collar workers was also high in areas with high educational and income levels (see Table 5).

TABLE 5. Distribution of Migrants from Selected Regions of Kerala by Occupational Status before Emigration (percentages)

	Elakamon	Koipram	Chavakkad	Kadkkavur	Chengannur, Chirayinkil, Chavakkad, Tirur
Unemployed, incl. students	37.1	33.8	36.0	69.4	62.6
Unskilled workers	16.1	5.4	35.3	8.8	11.3
Skilled & semiskilled workers	12.9	6.8	12.5	10.2	11.6
Technical and professional	8.1	29.7	—	—	1.0
Petty traders, businessmen, and cultivators	19.4	2.8	5.9	2.7	6.9
Clerks, typists, teachers, nurses etc.	6.5	21.6	—	2.0	6.6
Not known	—	—	10.3	6.8	—
Total	100.0	100.0	100.0	100.0	100.0

Marital Status

Since the migration to the Gulf countries is almost entirely a youth phenomenon, a significant proportion of migrants are unmarried at the time of migration. The marital status of migrants was researched in only one study made during the late 1970s in Kerala. According to this study, migrants younger than 25 were, for the most part, unmarried. Thus, in areas with high proportions of unskilled and semiskilled young workers, who had low educational qualifications, the proportion of unmarried persons among the migrants was correspondingly higher. On the average, it was found that nearly one-third of the migrants were unmarried at the time of their first migration.

Household Income

The occupational and educational attainments of the migrants are also a reflection of the income status of their families. Most migrants come from poor, rural families that are engaged in low-productivity traditional activities such as fishing, agricultural labour, cottage industry, and service-sector jobs, such as helpers in rural teashops and salesmen in grocery stores. Only a few migrants come from well-to-do families of plantation owners, or professionals such as engineers, doctors, and college teachers, and mid-level industrialists and businessmen. Some of the village studies conducted in Kerala throw light — albeit only indirectly — on the income levels of the migrant families.

For instance, according to the study conducted by Mathew and Nair, more than four-fifths of the migrants' fathers earned their livings from unskilled manual labour; 33.5 per cent were engaged in petty commodity production; 37.4 per cent in trading; 4.5 per cent in semiskilled work such as masons, carpenters, and blacksmiths; 4.5 per cent in small-scale cultivation; and 4.5 per cent in low-income occupations such as priests, barbers, and soldiers. Only 15.5 per cent had worked in supervisory and managerial

TABLE 6. Landholdings of Emigrant Households

Acres	Percentage
Less than 1	41
1–2	28
2–3	7
3–5	5
More than 5	1
Not reported	18
Total	100

jobs; and 5.8 per cent held professional and technical positions. The percentage of migrants from households with middle-income, white-collar jobs such as clerks, typists, stenographers, teachers, and nurses was 9.7 per cent. Nearly 15 per cent of the fathers were illiterate, and among the literate, 74 per cent had never matriculated. Thus, only around 11 per cent had matriculated. The survey conducted by the Commerce Research Bureau made the following observation: "By and large the migrants originally hail mostly from poor homes. . . . About 41 per cent of the households have land below one acre. Households holding more than 5 acres are negligible." (See Table 6.) Another indication that this study gives about the economic status of the families at the time of migration is their indebtedness. About 60 per cent of the migrants' families were heavily in debt, even though it may be noted that part of the debt was incurred specifically to meet the cost of migration itself.

Domestic Demand and Supply of Labour

From the national point of view, the emigration of two or three million persons does not perceptibly affect the labour situation in India since unemployment is severe and the population growth rate is high. The goal of full employment has remained elusive.

During the decade 1971–1981, India's population grew by 24.8 per cent. The work-participation rate has remained at around 33 per cent of the total population during the past two decades, with a male work-participation rate of about 52 per cent and a female work-participation rate of about 12–14 per cent. Even a small state like Kerala, which accounts for more than 50 per cent of the total migration to the Gulf countries and whose population accounts for less than 4 per cent of the total population of India, has not been able to improve its work-participation rate from 1971 to 1981. In 1971 the rate was 29.1, and declined to 26.5 in 1981. The decline was higher among men (from 45 to 41) than among women (which remained around 13 in both the years). The tardy rate of growth of employment opportunities in the industrial sector of the state economy and the stagnation of employment opportunities in the agricultural and allied sectors have rendered an increase in the state's work-participation rate virtually impossible. This is despite the mass migration of males from Kerala and the sharp fall in the population growth rate from 26.3 per cent for the decade 1961-1971 to 19.0 per cent for 1971-1981. The work-participation rates in the localities which have had particularly heavy migration to the Gulf countries are not in general higher than in Kerala as a whole (see Table 7).

The fact that even with the heavy exodus of population, Kerala's work-participation rate remains very low (it has had the lowest participation rates among all Indian states from the beginning of the twentieth century) is an indication of the high level of unemployment that prevails in the state and the economic stagnation that the state has been facing.

TABLE 7. Work-Participation Rates in Selected Regions (*taluks*) of Kerala Which Have Had Heavy Migration to the Gulf Countries (percentages)

	1971			1981		
	Total	Males	Females	Total	Males	Females
Trivandrum	28.1	44.2	11.8	26.8	41.6	12.2
Chirayinkil	30.4	43.4	18.1	25.8	37.8	15.1
Quilon	29.6	42.5	17.0	22.1	34.8	9.7
Pathanamthitte	25.8	45.2	6.4	26.0	44.8	8.0
Chengannur	26.9	43.8	10.7	23.9	38.9	10.1
Tiruvalla	25.7	43.1	9.0	24.5	40.4	9.7
Mukundapuram	28.1	42.1	14.8	26.0	38.6	14.2
Trichur	27.9	41.6	14.9	27.7	40.7	15.5
Chavakkad	25.7	39.3	14.1	22.4	33.6	12.9
Talappally	32.2	44.8	20.8	29.8	41.2	19.6
Ponnani	29.2	45.1	14.4	21.4	21.4	14.5
Tirur	24.9	43.5	7.3	19.3	34.3	5.3
Badagara	25.2	41.8	9.2	21.4	34.6	8.8
Cannanore	28.6	45.3	12.3	25.7	42.0	10.0
Kerala State	29.1	45.0	13.5	26.5	40.8	12.8

Source: Census of India, 1981, Ser. 10, paper 2 (Trivandrum, Kerala: Director of Census Operations, 1981).

TABLE 8. Job Availability for University Graduates in India, 1977–1978

	Available Jobs, 1978	University Graduates, 1977	Available Jobs as % of Graduates
Engineers (degree, postgraduate degree, & diploma holders)	21,932	43,158	50.8
Technologists	840	2,907	28.9
Agriculture & allied scientists	2,742	9,258	29.6
Medical personnel	6,736	21,347	31.6
Natural scientists (postgraduate only)	5,768	14,716	39.2
Social scientists & teachers (postgraduate only)	16,827	208,240	8.1
Other graduates and diploma holders	12,881	527,134	2.4
Total	67,726	826,760	8.2

76

However, unemployment is not confined to Kerala alone. It is a spectre that haunts all the states in India. Nor is unemployment confined to the less educated or rural populations. Unemployment among the educated is as acute as among the less educated. According to a government study in 1980 on the job opportunities for highly qualified manpower in India, the number of vacancies arising annually are much lower than the annual output of such manpower from the educational system.[18] In 1976 there were 765,588 graduates, whereas the vacancies for highly qualified manpower were estimated at 60,705. The corresponding figures for 1977 were 826,588 and 62,071, respectively. On the average, Indian universities are graduating 11 times more persons than there are jobs available (see Table 8).

In such a situation where annual supply exceeds several times the annual absorption capacity, an outflow abroad in considerable numbers does not lead to domestic shortages. In fact, without job opportunities commensurate with their qualifications, highly qualified job seekers will be constrained to take jobs that require lower qualifications. Thus, the migration of labour and highly qualified personnel has not created general shortages of manpower, either for the national economy or for the particular labour-supplying states. The impact, however, has been felt in special sectors, particularly the construction industries, as will be seen later. But even here, given the large unemployed workforce, it should not be difficult to make good the shortages after brief time-lags. The flow of highly qualified personnel cannot in the ordinary sense of the term be called a "brain drain." The phenomenon is more a case of "brain overflow." This does not, however, mean that the Indian economy is not in acute need of their services; it means only that the market demand for their services has not developed adequately. The heavy costs India has incurred by producing such high-level manpower must be considered in determining the losses sustained by the national economy in allowing them to emigrate.

Even though in terms of total numbers India can readily supply the requisite number of migrants from its pool of the unemployed, it is likely that shortages of personnel with specific skills may arise from time to time. Even within the domestic economy persistent shortages of manpower in certain categories have occurred. For instance, Kerala is reported to have experienced shortages in the following occupations: refrigeration mechanics, machine operators (harbour engineering), mines foremen, telex operators, punch-card operators, radiographers, pharmacists, electricians, nurses, midwives. Most of these shortages are, it should be noted, for those with significant work experience. Most of the training in these trades is being undertaken by private-sector agencies, since the government has not found it worthwhile to start training institutions, and the excess demand for such personnel in Kerala is not extensive or persistent.

In the case of foreign demand for skilled personnel, the government or other public-sector agencies are not fully informed. There does not exist in India or abroad any governmental agency to monitor the demand for manpower by labour-importing countries. In this respect, as well as in others relating to migration, the government of India and the state governments have been following a laissez-faire policy.[19]

The costs involved in training in the manpower categories that are in short supply are not likely to be high since there already exists a vast reservoir of unemployed, educated Indians with qualifications of the level of matriculation and above, and who hold science and commerce degrees and certificates and diplomas of different intermediate levels of technology. The government of India has initiated a industrial training program throughout the country designed to cater to the need for trained and skilled industrial workers. Training is imparted in engineering and non-engineering trades. This scheme does not envisage the supply of skilled manpower to countries abroad. However, many of those who are trained in the industrial training institutes do find employment in the Gulf countries. If the government had some arrangements to apprise itself of future manpower needs and the possible trends it could have designed courses and enrolled sufficient trainees so as to anticipate and thus cater to both domestic and foreign demand.

The impact of migration is to be expected in the wage structure of workers in short supply. We have seen that, in general, shortages do not exist in most of the educated categories and among skilled and unskilled workers. However, owing to the increasing migration of construction workers — particularly skilled masons and carpenters — and the rise in the domestic demand for them consequent on the housing boom in Kerala during the past several years, there exists in Kerala a dearth of these workers. The rate of entry of skilled masons and carpenters into the labour work force has lagged far behind the rate of increase in the demand for them. Consequently, the wages for skilled masons and carpenters have increased at a much higher rate than they have for other workers (see Table 9).

A part of the rise in wages is, of course, due to rises in the general price levels. However, in the case of skilled workers, inflation does not explain the entire increase. Similar increases have been registered in the wage rates of painters, plumbers, electricians, and other technically skilled categories.

The Process of Migration

The government of India has passed emigration acts that lay down the procedures for emigration. According to the Emigration Act of 1952, emigration of unskilled workers was prohibited. Skilled workers were permitted to emigrate after clearance by the Protectors of Emigrants at the ports of embarkation on compliance with the formalities prescribed in the act. These included the signing of employment agreements in standard forms prescribed by the government, forms that stipulated the terms and conditions of employment for the emigrant and the employer.

These standard forms were revised from time to time in the light of the experience gained in the disposal of complaints dealt with by the emigration authorities.[20] Until 1964 all skilled emigrants had to travel abroad by sea. In February 1964 the airports at Bombay, Calcutta, Delhi, and Madras were declared airports from which skilled migrant labour could lawfully depart.[21] Even after this declaration, the majority of emigrant workers continued to go abroad by sea.

Until 1974/75, there existed only five regional passport offices in India, located in the cities of Bombay, Madras, Delhi, Calcutta, and Lucknow. For the thousands of prospective emigrants, most of whom lived in remote rural areas, it was next to impossible to obtain either passports from the passport offices or clearance from the protectorates of emigrants situated in only a few urban centres in the country.

As a result of the rising number of applications for passports from Kerala consequent on the opening up of Gulf countries for massive emigration, a new passport office was opened in April 1974 exclusively for handling Kerala's labour exodus. However, the new office did not help the Keralites much since it was located not in Kerala but in Madras.[22] It was only in 1978/79 that the new office meant for Kerala was shifted to Cochin (within Kerala itself). That year a second passport office for Kerala was opened in the city of Kozhikode. New passport offices were opened in some other cities (in other states) that same year, and by 1979/80, the number of passport offices in India had increased to 18.[23]

In the meantime, the government was adopting measures to ensure fair terms and conditions of employment for Indian workers abroad and to protect workers from exploitation both in India and abroad at the hands of unauthorised agents. Individual migrants who obtained jobs through their own efforts were allowed to emigrate on the completion of registration formalities without paying the required security deposit. Two more embarkation points with airports, at Trivandrum (in Kerala) and Amritsar (in Punjab), were declared lawful emigration points in order to help emigrants from Kerala and Punjab. In addition, the migrants were allowed to secure

TABLE 9. Wage Rates of Carpenters, Masons, and Agricultural Labour: Kerala, 1973/74 to 1983/84 (rupees per day)

	1973/74	1977/78	1981/82	1983/84
Carpenters (agl. sector)	9.38	13.94	22.42	35.0
Masons (agl. sector)	9.38	14.10	22.50	35.0
Field labourers (men)	6.67	8.67	12.74	17.0
Field labourers (women)	4.45	6.06	8.83	12.0

Source: For 1973/74, 1977/78, and 1981/82, Directorate of Economics and Statistics, Government of Kerala; for 1983/84, the figures are rough estimates and purely provisional.

emigration clearance from any of the notified embarkation points declared lawful by the government. The protectorates of emigrants were strengthened to enable them to grant emigration clearance to prospective emigrants within 72 hours. Further, around-the-clock emigration checks were introduced at important embarkation points to ensure that the emigrants left the country only after obtaining clearance from the authorities. The government thought these steps helped secure better terms and conditions of employment for Indian job-seekers.[24] Subsequent to the introduction of these measures, the number of emigration applications received by the various regional protectorates increased substantially.[25] However, illegal emigration and circumvention of government rules have also risen year by year.

By 1977 there were many illegal Indian immigrants in most Gulf countries. The punishments meted out by the host-country governments came to the attention of the Indian government. One such instance took place in Oman. The government of Oman arrested 2,500 Indian workers and marched them through the streets because they had asked for their wages and benefits as agreed upon before their recruitment. The Indian government also heard reports of clandestine agencies that used fake passports and visa seals of foreign governments.[24]

India responded by asking all the recruiting agencies in the country to register with the government in the hope that the proliferation of illegitimate agencies would be curbed. The government also insisted that each agency have a minimum bank balance of Rs.10,000. Foreign firms seeking to recruit Indians were required to go through these licensed agencies. Indian companies engaged in construction projects abroad were, however, allowed to recruit their workers directly. The government also barred recruiting agencies from levying fees on candidates seeking jobs that were advertised by those agencies. When foreign governments approach the government of India for personnel, all requests are circulated to all the employment exchanges in the country. The lists of names sent up by the employment exchanges are then given to the External Affairs Ministry, which in turn forwards them to the missions of the countries concerned. Some foreign governments also utilise Indian recruiting agencies. In order to ensure that the Indian workers are paid according to the terms and conditions agreed upon with the employers, the recruiting agencies are required to execute a contract specifying the terms and conditions of employment. The guidelines issued by the Ministry of Labour also stipulate that the employers, or their agents in India, must offer the same salaries and perquisites to Indian recruits as are offered to workers of other nationalities engaged in similar work. The Labour Ministry is assisted in this respect by the Indian missions in the host countries, which verify the bona fides of companies employing Indians. The missions try to stay informed about the different countries recruiting Indian labour.[27]

These guidelines, however, have not been altogether effective. Clandestine emigration continues unabated, and there are even reasons to suspect that the outflow of Indian workers through illegal channels has increased in recent years. At present Indian emigrants in the Gulf countries fall into four categories.[28]

The first category of Indian migrant labour includes those who left legally with work visas or who are running businesses in partnership with Arab nationals (partnerships in which the Arab is, in most cases, a sleeping partner). In Dubai, expatriates are allowed to run businesses even without Arab partnership. Professionals such as business executives engineers, bankers, bureaucrats on specific contracts, journalists, and a vast army of clerical workers also are included in this first category. The tenure and conditions of work for this category are relatively secure. Workers in this category commonly bring their spouses and children to the countries of employment, as the Gulf states allow migrant workers who earn above a certain salary level to do so.

In the second category we may include workers who arrived in the Gulf states with regular, legal work visas but who left their original employer in search of better and more remunerative work. If they manage to find new employment, they can get a new visa after cancelling their original labour card. Several companies in Kuwait and the UAE reportedly are engaged in this visa trade, which has developed into a lucrative, illicit business.[29]

A third category of migrant labour, which is very large in the Gulf countries, includes workers who enter the host country on visitors' visas and stay on in the hope of earning their fortunes before they are caught and expelled. Others who entered the country illegally and continue to stay as illegal immigrants fall in the fourth category. They have flouted all rules and regulations for emigration from India and have usually reached the "promised land" by land routes or in *dhows* (single-masted Arabian Sea ships of about 200 tons). Such immigrants are found in large numbers in most Arab states, particularly in the UAE, eking out a subsistence living by doing all kinds of odd jobs such as selling newspapers on streets and in marketplaces and vending vegetables or other retail goods.

We have noted in the foregoing discussion that stringent regulations are in force in India to oversee the process of emigration and to prevent illegal emigration. Recruitment can be made by foreign firms only through the licensed agencies in India; foreign governments must negotiate through the government of India; and Indian firms abroad are alone allowed to recruit directly in India. The Protector of Emigrants is the custodian and authority of the entire emigration process. Foreign private employers are required to give power of attorney to their recruiting agent in India in addition to a demand letter showing the personnel categories required, conditions of work, salaries, etc. (such letters must first be reviewed by the Indian embassy in the country concerned). When this document is received by the recruiting agent, he obtains recruitment sanction from the relevant regional Protector of Emigrants. Then the recruitment is carried out by the agent and finalised with the employer. Meantime, the visa and the ticket are given to the agent. Once the emigration is cleared by the Protector, the recruit leaves the country.

It should also be noted that all the agreements entered into between the employer and the worker and registered by the Protector of Emigrants must conform with the labour laws in the country of immigration. The employers are also required to supply return fare to the recruits *at the time of their emigration*. The employers are also required to provide accommodations for the lower categories of workers.

The original contracts can be renewed if the employer has a continuous contract and the migrant worker is acceptable to the employer[30] As stated earlier, the Indian government stipulated that no fees of any kind can be levied on those seeking jobs advertised by the agents. Employment agencies were charging an application fee of a rupee or two for job applications made in response to advertisements. Thus, in the eyes of the law, enrolment for employment in the Gulf countries is absolutely free for the emigrants. The practice, however, continues to be far different.

Spurious recruitment agencies have mushroomed in all of the important emigration regions of India. All regions in Kerala and the cities of Bombay and Delhi report almost daily dozens of cases in which unsuspecting emigrants have been defrauded of thousands of rupees by such agencies and "employers." The practice has been growing in spite of the passing of regulations and efforts at stricter controls by the government of India. Emigrants "sponsored" by such unauthorised agents and imaginary employers play into the hands of ruthless contractors in the Gulf countries and are put through harrowing experiences of hard work, miserable working conditions and negligable remuneration. These conditions will be discussed in a later section.

Terms and Conditions of Work Abroad

The Government of India has laid down rules and regulations for the recruitment of different categories of workers destined for jobs in the Gulf region. The authorised recruitment agencies are: public sector agencies (e.g. Overseas Employment Promotion Corporation of Kerala) and Indian firms and organisations engaged in consultancy or execution of works on contract or on subcontract basis. The policy of the Indian government in the recruitment of highly qualified experts is that such recruitment should be made on a government-to-government basis. The interest of the government of India was aroused in 1976 after it heard numerous complaints about discrimination against Indian workers abroad. Wages and salaries, working conditions, work security and welfare facilities were reported to be discriminatory. The burden was greater on the skilled and unskilled workers than on the highly qualified professional and technical personnel. The Indian government was deluged with complaints about the miserable working conditions, especially from migrant workers who were recruited by unauthorised agencies that used false passports, visas, and work permits. Contractors and subcontractors in the Gulf countries were able to employ Indian workers on terms very unfavourable to the workers because many Indian migrants who had entered the various labour-importing countries with invalid documents were willing to work on terms and conditions that were not acceptable to Arab workers and migrants from other countries. There were also many complaints about the prohibitively high fees charged by unauthorised recruiting agents.

In response, the Labour Ministry has prepared a draft model agreement use by migrants and recruiting agents. Foreign employers are required to provide — according to the model agreement — among other things, free roundtrip passage, free furnished accommodation commensurate with the category of work, free medical care, free transportation, and other benefits. The employment contracts contain, in addition, provisions for overtime wages, hours of work, terminal benefits, compensation for accidents, etc.

In spite of these requirements, however, malpractices and contract violations continue. According to a report published on 25 May 1983, the Indian government received 274 complaints in a six-month period (from October 1981 to March 1982) relating to "a wide variety of subjects including cheating by recruiting agents, substitution of contracts, and poor working and living condition." There are frequent complaints that the agreed terms and conditions are not honoured by the employers. Most often, workers are forced to sign new employment contracts upon their arrival in the host country. These contracts are normally drawn up in Arabic and are seldom explained to the workers. As a result, unscrupulous recruiting agents and employers are able to violate the original contracts and undertakings with impunity. These abuses include lower wages, more menial work assignments (e.g. unskilled labour instead of skilled), and reduction of benefits, such as home-leave, accommodations, air fare, and so on.

Wages for Indian Migrant Labour

Wages and salaries for the different occupations in the Middle East are not determined by the direct operation of the market forces of supply and demand.

> The Gulf governments can decide how many migrants to admit, what qualifications they must have, how long they can stay, what wages should be paid, what rights and benefits should be provided, and whether they should be imported from India, Pakistan, other parts of Asia or from Arab countries. For all practical purposes, the power to regulate is primarily in the hands of the labour-importing, not the labour-exporting countries.[31]

In each of the labour-importing countries, wages offered to the workers for the same job have varied depending on their countries of origin and economic status and the wage policies of the employing agencies. The trend in the wages has been downward. In addition, there are different wage and salary levels among the Gulf countries themselves. For example, the highest levels of wages among the countries in this region are found in Saudi Arabia, Kuwait, and Bahrain; the next in order is the UAE; and Oman is reported to be paying wages and salaries at roughly half the rates obtaining in the rest of the region.

Published data do not exist on the wage of Indian workers employed in the different Gulf countries. There occur stray references to wage levels of Indian workers in a few of the studies conducted in the Arab countries on migrants and in the press reports. Table 10 presents information gathered from such sources and in consultation with recruitment agencies.

TABLE 10. Monthly Earnings of Indian Migrant Labour in the Middle East (thousands of rupees)

	Minimum	Maximum
Professional, technical, scientific, and managerial		
(a) highly specialised	10	20
(b) other	7	10
Technicians	8	10
Paramedical	5	10
Clerks, typists, stenographers, etc.	3	7.5
Skilled	3	7.5
Semiskilled	2.5	5
Unskilled	1.5	4
Household workers (e.g. ayahs, nannies, housemaids)	1	3

Exclusive of subsidies on food, accommodation, medical care etc. and earnings from overtime work.

Work and Living Conditions of the Migrant Labourer

Migrants from Asian who are working in the Gulf region are a part of its economy but do not enjoy rights of political or social participation. They live in their own enclaves, and cannot obtain citizenship, own property, or join trade unions; they have restricted access to social benefits and are excluded from participation in the political system.[32]

Labour legislation and administration as well as social security institutions are not yet fully developed in most Gulf countries; therefore, the working and living conditions of Indian workers — as well as of other migrant workers — depend on the nature of employment contracts and the honesty and integrity of the employers in honouring the terms and conditions of the agreements. Even in cases where employers violate the terms — say by paying wages lower than those stipulated in the agreements, demanding excessive hours, denying overtime allowances, providing inadequate accommodations, denying free or subsidised food, or even cancelling visas before the termination of the contract period — the workers have no access to legal redress.

In general, however, workers with valid passports, visas, and work permits who are employed either by well-established and large firms or by the governments directly in their own services, receive wages which are severalfold higher than those they might receive in India for similar work; they also receive free or subsidised housing, food, and medical care.[33] Workers are therefore able to save a large part of their earnings.

The fear of repatriation lurks in the mind of every Indian migrant. Indians know fully well that their stay and work abroad are temporary and that they can hardly expect protection against mistreatment by the host countries from the government of India. Within these constraints, however, the Indian community, particularly the middle-class migrants, do their utmost to create congenial communities for themselves. Sports clubs, schools, literary and debating associations, film societies, libraries and reading rooms, and centres for other cultural activities have sprung up in all the Gulf countries. Perhaps Saudi Arabia is one major exception. The government there strictly regulates the migrants' activities to the extent of prohibiting non-Muslims from bringing the scriptures of their own religion. Other countries have permitted some degree of religious freedom. For instance, Kuwait has allowed the construction of a large church for the Catholic Christian community. Other governments in the Gulf region have also given permission to Christian churches to function. Hindus have had fewer opportunities to build their own places of worship in these countries until very recently. The two temples — the 100-year-old Balakrishna Temple near the souk (marketplace) in Bahrain, and the new temple being built near the palace compound of the sultan of Oman in Kuwait — are exceptions.

There have also been serious complaints that Arab countries discriminate against Indians on the ground of nationality. These complaints appear to be caused by the remuneration policies adopted by the Gulf countries for migrant workers. The salary scales and wages offered to migrant workers vary according to the migrants' country of origin and the levels of wages there. Therefore, wage differentials exist between East Asian and South Asian migrants. The complaint is, therefore, not specific to Indian nationals. In fact, Indian nationals who have emigrated to countries in the West and acquired citizenship would receive the wages relevant to those countries if they were recruited for Middle Eastern employment.

Indians are also distressed by the contempt directed at them by host-country nationals. Indians are reported to be the "ABCs" of the Gulf — i.e. ayahs, barbers, and cooks. The epithet is not undeserved, since Indians do predominate in these fields.[34] Despite such complaints, the trek towards the Gulf for such menial occupations is increasing through both legal and clandestine channels.[35]

In response to more widespread complaints among Indians about mistreatment, underpayment, discrimination, and contempt, the sole device with which the government of India has sought to control malpractices and ensure fair and reasonable terms of employment for migrants is the employment agreement. Several South and Southeast Asian countries have centralised institutions for recruitment of candidates for employment abroad. India has no centralised recruitment agency. Instead, a few states, including Kerala and Orissa, have "overseas employment development corporations." There are also many other public-sector agencies recognised by the government of India as recruiting agents, such as the Beas Project Employees Welfare Society (Himachal Pradesh), Caltex Oil Refining (India) Limited (Bombay), and Madras Fertiliser (Tamil Nadu). The number of emigrants sponsored by the state corporations and other public-sector agencies form only a tiny proportion of the total. For instance, the Overseas Development and Employment Promotion Consultants, Ltd., of Kerala, formed in 1977, had deployed only 1,441 workers as of 31 December 1982. Almost the entire volume of recruitment is therefore handled by the thousands of private agencies, both authorised and unauthorised, spread out among all the states in India, but mainly in Kerala, Maharashtra, Gujarat, Punjab, and Andra Pradesh.

If India is to ensure fair working and living conditions for its citizens, it may have to control the flow more effectively than it has done up to now. Only citizens with valid passports and visas and who have signed employment contracts cleared by protectorates of emigrants should be allowed to migrate. The government should also see to it that the terms and conditions in the contracts signed in India are respected by the employers and governments in labour-importing countries. If the government of India were to insist that recruiting agents stand guarantee for the employer, it is possible that most complaints of mistreament could be avoided. However, it is uncertain that recruiting agencies would be able to do this, given the highly volatile employment situation in the Gulf countries. The practical and legal difficulties would also be considerable. Agencies would be hard-pressed to recoup the damages paid to the employees, especially in view of the fact that the financial strength of most private recruiting agencies is nominal. However, it appears that some discipline and order have been instilled into the entire recruiting procedure. The Indian government announced in early 1983 its decision to introduce legislation for streamlining and regularising the recruitment of Indian emigrants to Gulf countries.[36] The promised legislation was enacted as the Emigration Act, 1983 (no. 31 of 1983), in September of that year.

Social and Psychological Problems

The social and psychological problems of migrant workers are caused by a variety of factors. Among them, job security is perhaps the most serious. Not only are the work permits of most workers for limited, specified periods, but the spectre of sudden job loss and forced repatriation constantly haunts them. The workers are always painfully aware of the discrimination in wages and salaries shown by employers toward workers of different countries. Most labourers engaged in construction work are destined for lives in work sites and "enclaves" that deprive them of the enjoyment of a satisfying social existence. The majority of married workers from India are not able to bring their wives and children along with them. The inhospitable and enervating climate of the Gulf region saps their energies, and the chances of seeking better and more lucrative employment opportunities have almost disappeared with the introduction in these countries of highly restrictive rules. Indian workers are also keenly aware of the fact that they (as well as other Asian migrant workers) are treated as socially inferior by the nationals of the host countries. In sum, their problems are the problems of a total outsider facing a future full of uncertainties.

Renewing Contracts: Possibilities and Problems

Indian migrants have varying expectations about their ability to renew their contracts of employment. Expectations are higher among middle-class workers in private-sector industry and business.[37] Employment in government has less job security since the Gulf governments have decided to staff their government services with Arabs.[38] However, it may take a few years before this "Arabisation" policy succeeds, since the effects of education take time to materialise.

The jobs of migrant construction workers — both skilled and unskilled — are beset with uncertainties. Among the Asian migrant workers, construction workers form the largest proportion. If construction in the Gulf had continued at the same rapid pace, these workers would have no serious problems with job security. In the past the Gulf countries permitted repeated renewals of work contracts for as long as the employers required the migrants' services. Even when the original employers no longer required their services, the migrants were allowed to seek work with other employers. The new labour law passed in the UAE in 1979 put an end to this freedom by prohibiting all foreign workers from changing their jobs unless they leave the country for a year. This law was passed in order to address the problem of a casual, floating, or unemployed work force — workers were not returning home after the termination of their employment contracts. Reports indicate, however, that Asian migrants in this category, particularly those from India, can be found in significant numbers in Dubai, Abu Dhabi, and Sharjah searching for jobs. They do so in constant fear of being caught by the police, sent to jail, or deported straightaway. The numbers of unemployed Indian workers seeking work permits are also reported to be high in Saudi Arabia. With the passing of new legislation in the host countries making it necessary for expatriates to return home once their work is over, the number of returnees has increased. However, most of these returnees manage to secure new No Objection Certificates and re-emigrate after a stay at home for the minimum period required.

The demand trends in the past for Indian labour in the Gulf region were highly in favour of skilled and unskilled construction workers. When the construction activity drops — as it is now doing — and the new industries and service-sector establishments are launched, the composition of demand is likely to undergo significant changes; the demand for skilled and unskilled construction workers will decline sharply. In keeping with their employment policies, Gulf countries are also likely to increase their Arabisation policies. At the same time, they are likely to shift to more capital- and technology-intensive methods, thereby reducing their dependence on an expatriate workforce.

Advertisements placed by recruiting agents in Indian newspapers on behalf of employers in the Gulf countries reveal the shift in manpower requirements. The demand is now mainly for managerial, professional, and technical personnel and for workers with more modern and multiple skills (such as mason-cum-mixer, welder-cum-driver) and significant work experience. Computerisation and automation are also revolutionising the composition of demand for labour in the Gulf region. The process of reducing the number of construction workers has already started in the Middle East. According to the minister for labour and social affairs of the UAE, the demand for unskilled labour is likely to be nil by 1985, while the need for skilled manpower to operate industries, power stations, and petroleum companies will grow. According to him, most construction projects were likely to be completed in about two years, thus ending the construction boom that began in the mid-1970s.[39] These trends in the demand for expatriate workers in Middle East countries will have significant implications for the educational, manpower development, and emigration policies of the labour-exporting Asian countries.

Savings and Remittances

The major attraction of employment in the Gulf countries for all occupational groups is the possibility of saving a substantial proportion of earnings, despite the high cost of living in these countries. The migrant workers are not seriously affected by the cost of living since their employment contracts entitle them to free or highly subsidised housing, food, transportation, and medical facilities.[40] The near absence of bars and gambling houses, where a great deal of money could be spent, and non-existence of consumer durables also enable migrant workers to save a substantial portion of their earnings. The incentive to save is also great, particularly among those in mid- and low-level occupations, since most of them bought employment at exorbitant prices, incurring debts at home or selling property and jewellery. Besides, every Indian migrant worker is constantly aware that his employment in the Gulf countries is temporary and that his work permit could by cancelled any moment. Above all, the migrant worker sees the employment in the Gulf countries as perhaps his only chance to accumulate enough money to purchase some land, construct a house, educate his children, give his sisters and daughters in marriage, and save funds with which to start some independent career at home upon repatriation. There are, however, no legal compulsions for the migrant worker from India to save out of his earnings or send his savings home.

According to knowledgeable sources, expenditure per month of an average Indian migrant in the Gulf countries may not come to more than Rs.500. If this figure is approximately correct, then an average Indian worker would be in a position to save not less than Rs.2,000 per month. Of course wide variations in savings will exist because income levels vary a great deal. However, even the most unskilled and the most low paid workers reportedly remit about Rs.1,000 per month.[41] More accurate estimates of savings can be made only after more detailed investigations. Myron Weiner's cursory interviews with Indian workers reveal that they remit about one-third to one-half of their income.[42]

These figures obviously would apply only to migrants with valid work permits and whose original employment agreements remain in effect. Of course, they do not apply to those without work permits, or working for wages far below those stipulated in India, or working casually on miscellaneous jobs to earn a meagre living (washing cars, selling peanuts on streets, etc.). Some of these migrants might have spent their entire savings in order to make payments under the table for purchasing new work permits from employers or their agents in the Arab countries. In such cases, the proportion of savings would be low and the remittance nominal. There may be even cases in which no remittances at all are received by their families in India.

Whether all the savings are transferred to India or deposited elsewhere depends, *inter alia*, upon the employment status of the workers. For employees in high-level jobs drawing salaries above a minimum level, the urge to transfer all their savings home may be much less pronounced because such workers are often accompanied abroad by their families. Besides, their chances of continuing to work in the Gulf countries are much less uncertain. Furthermore, when their employment in the Gulf region ends, they may migrate to other countries — say, in the West — where they may hope to secure jobs on the strength of their special qualifications, skills, and experience. Such migrants, therefore, remit — if they remit at all — only a small fraction of their savings to maintain their dependants still in India, or they send gifts to friends and relatives. The rest of the savings is usually deposited in Western banks.

Mid-level employees and skilled and unskilled workers save the maximum out of their earnings and transfer their savings home by way of bank remittances or money orders or in the form of cash, jewellery, and consumer durables during their home visits.[43] In other words, there probably is not much difference between actual and potential remittances for this category of workers. Since no studies have been conducted in the labour-importing countries on the migrants' earnings and savings, it is not possible to present estimates.

Remittances

It is widely acknowledged among government authorities and in banking circles in India that foreign remittances have been rising at an unprecedented rate in recent years. Evidently such an increase must be attributed mainly to remittances from the Gulf states and Saudi Arabia; Indians living in other parts of the world generally send only a small portion of their savings to India, as the bulk of their savings are kept in Western banks. Migrants to other countries, particularly developed countries, consist for the most part of highly educated and qualified persons. They usually migrate with their families and enjoy opportunities of settling down in the countries of immigration. They would not have strong reasons to transfer their savings to India. On the other hand, migrants to the Gulf countries are purely temporary migrants; most of them have not taken their families with them, and they have few educational qualifications and little knowledge of banking practices.

Indians migrated in large numbers to Great Britain, the United States, Canada, and some African countries seeking jobs as teachers, doctors, engineers, and nurses during the 1950s and the 1960s. With the exception of Great Britain, these streams of emigration have not dried up. Such emigration did not result in substantial increases in the transfer payments in India's balance-of-payments accounts until the early 1960s. For instance, private-transfer payments in the current accounts in India's balance of payments — which stood at Rs.400 million in 1950/51 — rose only marginally during the 1950s, and reached Rs.449 million in 1960/61. By the beginning of the 1970s they had increased to Rs. 1,364 million. The bulk of the increases could be due to remittances from migrants abroad, including migrants to the Gulf countries, since the flow of migration to that region began on a sizeable scale at the beginning of the 1970s. But the increase also included unilateral transfers such as maintenance remittances, receipts of missionaries, and credits in lieu of contra-entries for imports from the United States under the PL 480 (titles II and III) programme. A disaggregation of the amount under private transfers into migrants' home remittances and the other components is, however, not available.

The credit side of the balance of payments (current account) under private-transfer payments increased steadily during the 1970s. As our preceding discussion indicated, it was from 1975 onwards that the flow of Indian migrants to Arab countries increased substantially. Consequently, we find a sudden rise in the amount under private-transfer payments to India from the year 1975/76; the increase has continued

TABLE 11. Receipts under Private-Transfer Payments (Current Account of the Balance of Payments), 1950/51 to 1980/81 (millions of rupees)

	Total Receipts	Receipts from the Sterling Area	Sterling-Area Receipts as % of Total
1950/51	408	355	87.0
1960/61	449	320	71.3
1970/71	1,364	372	27.2
1971/72	1,622	571	35.2
1972/73	1,653	458	27.7
1973/74	2,033	763	37.5
1974/75	2,799	1,108	36.0
1975/76	5,412	2,481	45.8
1976/77	7,457	3,452	47.5
1977/78	10,293	6,157	59.8
1978/79	10,593	6,075	57.3
1979/80	16,320	9,784	60.0
1980/81	22,688	15,286	67.4
1981/82	22,371	13,169	58.9
1982/83	25,410	—	—

Source: Reserve Bank of India bulletins.

during the subsequent years as well. Table 11 presents the amounts under private-transfer payments published by the Reserve Bank of India for the year 1981/82. The table also shows the amounts received under this rubric from the sterling area, which includes the Gulf countries (but excludes Canada) along with the rest of the Commonwealth countries. Since remittances from the rest of the Commonwealth countries would not have increased significantly, the increase shown under this item would broadly reflect the increase of remittances from the Gulf countries.

The table shows a sharp break in the trend of remittances after 1974/75. In 1950/51, when the bulk of the migrants from India lived in the United Kingdom and other Commonwealth countries, the sterling area accounted for 87 per cent of all the receipts under private-transfer payments. With the increase in the migration flows to non–sterling areas, the percentage share of the sterling area declined to nearly one-fourth of the total remittance in 1972/73. Thereafter, presumably with the beginning of the large-scale migration flows to the Middle East, its percentage share began to increase and by 1980/81 accounted for more than two-thirds of all the receipts of the country under private-transfer payments. The percentage declined, however, in 1981/82 to 58.9. The government of India has referred to a decline in remittances (and has expressed apprehension about it) as due largely to a considerable return flow of workers from some important countries because of a slowdown in economic expansion in oil-surplus countries of the Gulf region.[44]

TABLE 12. Per-Capita Deposits in Scheduled Commercial Banks, by State, 1971–1981 (selected years)

	1971		1974		1975		1976		1978		1980		1981		Change in Rank, 1971–1981
	Rs.	Rank	Rs.	Rank	Rs.	Rank	Rs.	Rank	Rs.	Rank	Rs.	Rank	Rs.	Rank	
Maharashtra	335	1	499	1	570	1	728	1	1048	1	1380	2	1292	2	Decline
Punjab	252	2	396	2	494	2	620	2	944	2	1441	1	1440	1	Rise
West Bangal	222	3	350	3	412	3	500	3	710	3	933	4	912	3	No change
Gujarat	217	4	319	4	369	4	470	4	705	4	961	3	896	4	No change
Karnataka	126	5	190	5	229	6	299	5	458	7	660	7	662	8	Decline
Tamil Nadu	109	6	199	6	231	5	284	7	438	8	612	9	616	10	Decline
Jammu and Kashmir	107	7	179	8	212	8	287	6	603	5	818	5	651	6	Rise
Haryana	104	8	168	10	196	10	264	10	426	9	651	8	631	7	Rise
Kerala	102	9	171	9	207	9	266	8	488	6	682	6	672	5	Rise
Himachal Pradesh	94	10	184	7	208	7	265	9	404	10	595	10	610	9	Rise
Uttar Pradesh	69	11	72	15	140	11	180	12	270	12	405	12	394	12	Decline
Bihar	57	12	96	12	112	13	140	14	189	15	276	15	277	14	Decline
Andhra Pradesh	56	13	110	11	137	12	185	11	294	11	428	11	429	11	Decline
Rajasthan	55	14	87	13	102	14	142	13	219	13	327	13	300	13	Rise
Madhya Pradesh	43	15	76	14	95	15	128	15	190	14	281	14	270	15	No change
Assam	38	16	69	16	83	16	111	16	172	16	227	16	222	16	No change
Orissa	26	17	45	17	58	17	74	17	120	17	196	17	207	17	No change
India	132		212		250		322		484		675		647		

Source: Reserve Bank of India, Annual Report on Trends and Progress of Banking in India (various years).

92

We would expect the inflow of remittances to have increased the bank deposits in the Indian states that have supplied the most migrant labour for the Gulf states. As mentioned at the outset of this chapter, the major emigration flows have taken place from Kerala, Andhra Pradesh, Punjab, and Gujarat. Kerala, as noted earlier, has pride of place among them, accounting for more than 50 per cent of total emigration to the Gulf region. Bank deposits present some difficulties as an indicator of foreign remittances. First, since the nationalisation of the major banks in India in 1969 the Reserve Bank of India has been engaged in an intensive deposit mobilisation drive by opening branch offices of banks in both rural and urban areas. It has placed particular emphasis on the former and offers various incentives to people for depositing their cash savings in banks. Second, bank deposits increase — even without additional deposit mobilisation drives — where and when economic activities (and therefore incomes) rise. Third, not all foreign remittances are channelled through the banks. It is well known that sizeable amounts of migrant savings flow through non-banking and illegal channels. The money received via these illegal channels — through agents of foreign purchasers of the migrants' savings (in foreign currency) who offer them higher rates of exchange than the official rates — is known in Kerala households as "tube money." The size of this flow again is not at all known, even though frequent reports appear in the press about individual cases of such illegal transfers. These limitations must be borne in mind while looking at the growth of bank deposits in the different states in India shown in Table 12.

The table suggests that Kerala is unique among the states in that its rank in per-capita bank deposits has risen from ninth (1971-1976) to fifth in 1981. Besides, the per-capita bank deposits in Kerala, which stood below the all-India average until 1976, have exceeded it since then. Another state that has improved its position is Andhra Pradesh. Andhra Pradesh is also known to have sent many migrant workers to the Middle East, even though its role is considerably less than that of Kerala in this respect.[45] Gujarat and Punjab also have marginally improved their ranking in respect of per-capita bank deposits. Part of this improvement may be attributed to foreign remittances, but the major cause is the rising economic activities and the growth of income in these two states.

The improvement in Kerala's ranking may be attributed almost entirely to the flow of inward remittances, particularly because its domestic per-capita income has been rising much less rapidly than the Indian average and its rank among the states in terms of per-capita income has been declining, (see Table 13). The foregoing discussion shows that Kerala is one of the states in India whose economy has substantially benefitted from remittances. In fact, a substantial part of its per-capita national (as against domestic) income — say, about 15 per cent — is considered to arise from remittances received from abroad.

The increase in remittances will be partially reflected in bank deposits. As argued

TABLE 13. Per-Capita Domestic Incomes, by State

	1969/70		1975/76		1977/78		1981/82		Change in Rank, 1969/70– 1981/82
	Rs.	Rank	Rs.	Rank	Rs.	Rank	Rs.	Rank	
Punjab	945	1	1597	1	1962	1	3122	1	No change
Haryana	811	2	1274	3	1600	3	2574	2	No change
Maharashtra	752	3	1377	2	1628	2	2519	3	No change
Gujarat	696	4	1215	4	1340[1]	4	2211	4	No change
Himachal Pradesh	586	5	1078	6	1178	6	1659	5	No change
Kerala	541	6	907	8	987	10	1445	10	Decline
Tamil Nadu	536	7	846	12	1036	8	1373	13	Decline
Uttar Pradesh	522	8	730	16	916	14	929	16	Decline
West Bengal	522	9	1116	5	1268	5	1595	7	Rise
Andhra Pradesh	521	10	903	9	999	9	1536	8	Rise
Rajasthan	497	11	850	11	948	12	1417	11	No change
Karnataka	495	12	1005	7	1129	7	1458	9	Rise
Orissa	491	13	747	15	857	16	1147[2]	15	Decline
Assam	491	14	776	13	932	13	1380	12	Rise
Jammu and Kashmir	–	15	883	10	986	11	1630	6	Rise
Madhya Pradesh	469	16	769	14	905	15	1217	14	Rise
Bihar	403	17	661	17	735	17	870	17	No change
India	598		1021		1189		1741		

1. Refers to 1976/77.
2. Refer to 1980/81.

Source: Government of Kerala, *Statistics for Planning, 1980,* Directorate of Economics and Statistics, Kerala, 1980, p.79; and Government of Kerala, *Economic Review, 1984,* State Planning Board, Kerala, p.105.

earlier, bank deposits will be affected by several other factors, such as the availability of banking facilities, the population's banking habits, the sectoral distribution of income, and the level and the growth rates of income. In general, districts with higher per-capita incomes and a large urban population are likely to have well-developed banking facilities. In such areas, the growth of incomes and the growth of bank deposits may take place at comparable rates. However, in areas where the levels and the growth rates of per-capita income are low, the growth rates of bank deposits are likely to be correspondingly low. If in such an area we

TABLE. 14. Per-Capita Domestic Income, Bank Deposits and Proportions of Emigrants by Districts, Kerala, 1975 and 1980

	Per-Capita Income			Outstanding Bank Deposits		
	1975 (Rs.)	1980 (Rs.)	% Increase	1975 (Rs.million)	1980 (Rs.million)	% Increase
Kottayam	1123.0	1140.4	28.3	371	1159	212.4
Quilon	1063.9	1022.8	-3.9	372	1295	247.9
Idukki	1035.6	1517.5	46.5	52	169	230.0
Ernakulam	1016.1	1744.0	71.6	1035	2930	183.0
Trivandrum	908.3	1251.8	37.8	613	2195	258.3
Kozhikode	844.7	1488.1	76.2	276	910	229.6
Allappey	828.1	1251.9	51.2	446	1685	227.6
Cannanore	806.5	1260.2	26.3	312	1054	238.2
Palghat	804.8	1214.4	50.9	334	893	167.0
Trichur	753.0	1184.8	57.3	518	1833	254.2
Malappuram	683.3	875.6	37.2	95	427	349.5
Kerala State	882.7	1311.8	48.6	4423	14,550	229.0

| | Emigrants from District in Relation to Total from State | | Rank | | | | | |
| | | | Per-Capita Income | | | Bank Deposits | | |
	%	Rank	1975	1980	Increase	1975	1980	Increase
Kottayam	2.2	10	1	4	10	6	6	9
Quilon	10.2	5	2	5	11	5	5	5
Idukki	0.1	11	3	2	7	11	11	7
Ernakulam	2.0	9	4	1	2	1	1	10
Trivandrum	11.2	4	5	8	8	2	2	3
Kozhikode	9.1	6	6	3	1	9	8	8
Alleppey	9.1	7	7	7	5	4	4	2
Cananore	13.4	3	8	6	4	8	7	6
Palghat	3.7	8	9	9	6	7	9	11
Trichur	20.3	1	10	10	3	3	3	4
Malappuram	18.7	2	11	11	9	10	10	1

TABLE 15. Growth of Outstanding Bank Deposits in Selected Centres of Emigration, Kerala, 1975–1980

	Percentage Increase
Malappuram District	*349.5*
Kuttipuram	331.3
Malappuram	348.0
Tanur	366.7
Tirur	514.8
Trichur District	*254.2*
Chavakkad	490.4
Kerala State	229.00

find, on the other hand, a high rate of growth of bank deposits, this can plausibly be attributed to remittances from labour migrants if a large number of such migrants have gone out from the area.

Table 14 shows the ranking of the districts of Kerala in terms of per-capita incomes and bank deposits in 1975 and 1980 and their percentage increases over that period, and of each district's proportion of emigrants.

A more disaggregated analysis of the deposit figures shows clearly the impact of re-mittances on bank deposits in the emigration pockets. During the five-year period 1975–1980, the percentage increase in bank deposits in the centres of migration has been in the range of 330–514, against the state average of 229 (see Table 15).

A study of the size and distribution of bank deposits in a few centres of emigration in Kerala was conducted in 1980[46] using the data on monthly remittances during the periods January–October 1978 and January–October 1979. The centres were selected from districts that together accounted for nearly 60 per cent of the total emigrant workers from Kerala. They fall into two categories: Malappuram, Chavakkad, Kunnamkulam, and Varkala, which are well-known centres of emigration to the Gulf countries; and Chengannur, Tiruvalla, and Kumbanad, from where the proportion of persons migrating to regions other than the Gulf countries is slightly higher.

The data for the study were collected from all the 43 commercial banks functioning in these centres. The following conclusions emerge from the data:
— The average amount per remittance was Rs.3024 (for a full year, this would work out to Rs.23,629) (see Table 16).
— The total remittances were distributed in the following proportions: 13.2 per cent of the amount was received in individual remittances of less than Rs.1000; 31.3 per cent in the range of Rs.1000–5000; 22.2 per cent in the range of Rs.5000–10,000; and

TABLE 16. Average Amounts of Remittances by Range in Selected Centres of Emigration, Kerala, January–October 1978 and 1979 (rupees)

	Below 1000	1000–5000	5000–10,000	Above 10,000	All
Malappuram	772	2446	6213	14,087	2236
Chavakkad	817	2733	6955	14,110	2276
Kunnamkulam	752	2577	7194	24,483	2986
Varkala	846	3002	7024	19,504	2940
Chengannur	704	2680	7240	22,824	3551
Tiruvalla	740	2317	6896	21,695	4392
Kumbanad	761	2813	7186	22,698	4866
Average	781	2767	6927	20,336	3024

TABLE 17. Distribution of Total Amounts of Money Remitted by Size Range of Remittances (percentages)

	Below Rs. 1000	Rs. 1000–5000	Rs. 5000–10,000	Above Rs. 10,000	Total
Malappuram	18.1	38.4	27.0	16.4	100.0
Chavakkad	19.6	42.8	20.7	16.8	100.0
Kunnamkulam	13.0	31.0	19.1	36.9	100.0
Varkala	14.7	36.2	23.3	25.8	100.0
Chengannur	9.9	24.7	20.8	44.6	100.0
Tiruvalla	7.7	19.3	23.4	49.5	100.0
Kumbanad	6.7	18.8	19.3	55.5	100.0
Average	13.2	31.3	22.2	33.3	100.0

TABLE 18. Distribution of Number of Foreign Remittances by Size Range (percentages)

	Below Rs.1000	Rs. 1000–5000	Rs. 5000–10,000	Above Rs.10,000	Total
Malappuram	52.5	35.1	9.7	2.6	100.0
Chavakkad	55.0	35.6	6.8	2.7	100.0
Kunnamkulam	51.6	35.9	7.9	4.5	100.0
Varkala	51.0	35.4	9.8	3.9	100.0
Chengannur	50.1	32.7	10.2	6.9	100.0
Tiruvalla	45.8	29.3	14.9	10.0	100.0
Kumbanad	42.6	32.5	13.1	11.8	100.0
Average	51.1	34.2	9.7	5.0	100.0

TABLE 19. Distribution of Foreign Remittances by Country of Origin (percentages)

	United Arab Emirates	Saudi Arabia	Oman	Qatar	Kuwait	Bahrain	Total Gulf Countries	Other Countries	Total
Malappuram	31.3	54.0	1.9	4.2	2.1	2.2	95.7	4.3	100.0
Chavakkad	53.6	4.6	8.2	11.2	11.1	0.5	89.2	10.8	100.0
Kunnamkulam	49.3	7.5	7.2	16.1	3.6	2.7	86.4	13.6	100.0
Varkala	70.6	4.4	6.6	1.1	0.9	1.0	84.6	15.4	100.0
Chengannur	26.0	13.7	11.3	9.4	17.7	7.6	85.7	14.3	100.0
Tiruvalla	21.6	9.2	9.9	6.5	22.4	4.8	74.4	25.6	100.0
Kumbanad	24.4	11.0	8.5	17.3	18.1	6.9	86.2	13.8	100.0
Average	43.8	11.3	7.8	8.1	10.6	2.9	84.6	15.4	100.0

33.3 per cent in the range above Rs. 10,000 (Table 17).

— The average amounts per remittance in the different ranges were Rs.781 in remittances below Rs.1000; Rs.2767 in remittances in the range of Rs. 1000-5000; Rs. 6927 in remittances in the range of Rs.5000-10,000; and Rs.20,336 in remittances above Rs. 10,000 (Table 16).

— The percentage distribution of the number of foreign remittances was 51.5 per cent less than Rs.1000; 34.2 per cent in the range of Rs. 1000-5000; 9.7 per cent in the range of Rs. 5000-10,000; and 5.0 per cent of more than Rs. 10,000 (Table 18).

— The percentage distribution of foreign remittances according to countries of origin was United Arab Emirates, 43.8 per cent; Saudi Arabia, 11.3 per cent; Kuwait, 7.8 per cent; Qatar, 8.1 per cent; Oman, 10.6 per cent; Bahrain, 2.9 per cent; total (Gulf countries): 84.6 per cent. Remittances from other countries amounted to 15.4 per cent, to bring the total to 100 (Table 19).

Savings are transferred home through legal as well as illegal channels, even though the importance of the latter has declined in recent years. In the former are included remittances made through banks either in the form of bank drafts or cheques, deposits made in the banks in India in the non-resident external (rupee) accounts and the foreign currency (non-resident) accounts,[47] money brought home by the migrants during their visits home, and goods and jewellery sent or brought in person by the migrants. Transfer of savings through illegal channels is done mainly by smuggling[48] in gold biscuits and gold jewellery, wristwatches, video cassette recorders, television sets, and textiles and by sending their savings home in the form of "tube money". The proportion of savings transferred through these different channels is unknown. Nevertheless, it is well known that the amounts remitted via banking channels form only part — though the major part — of the total savings reaching India from the Indian migrant workers in the Gulf region.

Neither the migrants nor their families in India seem to experience any difficulty

TABLE 20. Expenditures of Emigrants' Households on Other than Current Consumption, Perumathura and Puthukkurichi villages, Kerala, 1977 (percentages)

Business investment	0.3
Livestock investment	0.5
Financing migration of close relatives	4.9
Real estate	27.2
Construction	46.9
Property renovation and repairs	2.0
Automobiles	2.5
Ornaments and jewellery	2.7
Consumer durables	1.4
Celebrations, festivals, ceremonies	11.5
Total	100.0

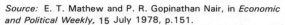

Source: E. T. Mathew and P. R. Gopinathan Nair, in *Economic and Political Weekly,* 15 July 1978, p.151.

arising from bank procedures or exchange practices. The migrants do not enjoy any special consideration regarding exchange rates as do migrant workers from Pakistan and Bangladesh. Banking facilities are quite widespread in the rural areas of the country, particularly in Kerala, which accounts for more than half of India's migrant population in the Gulf countries.

Remittances are received by migrants' family members — the father or older brogher in the case of unmarried migrants, and the spouse in the event the migrant is married.

Use of Remittances

The migrants' remittances constitute the major source of income for their households. A survey conducted in 1980/81 in a centre of migration (Chavakkad *taluk* of Trichur District) in Kerala showed that such households spent about 52 per cent of the remitted incomes on current consumption.[49] Of the total current consumption expenditure, more than 70 per cent was spent on food and 9 per cent on clothing. Expenditure on medicine formed 4.5 per cent, and educational expenditures lay in the range of 1–5 per cent. It was observed in the survey that a steep increase had occurred in expenditures on education and medicine in both absolute and relative terms.

Another survey[50] conducted in 1977 in two labour-supplying villages (in Chirayinkil and Trivandrum taluks of Trivandrum District) in Kerala provided a break-down of expenditures on items other than current consumption (see Table 20). According to this survey, 4.9 per cent of such expenditures were on financing the migration of the close relatives of the migrant already in Gulf countries. The purchase of consumer durable such as vehicles,[51] ornaments, and jewellery, and gadgets like radios, refrigerators, and

TABLE 21. Private-Sector Vehicles in Kerala, 1975/76–1981/82

	Goods Vehicles	Stage Carriages	Taxi Cars	Auto-rickshaws
1975/76	15,880	4,620	11,580	3,730
1978/79	18,520	5,240	15,200	5,720
1981/82	27,660	7,500	21,570	12,730
Increase (%)				
1976/76–1978/79	26.4	6.2	36.2	19.9
1978/79–1981/82	91.4	22.6	63.7	70.1

Source: Bureau of Economics and Statistics, Government of Kerala, Trivandrum.

other electrical appliances together accounted for 6.6 per cent. About 12 per cent was spent on marriage and other ceremonial functions. But the highest proportion (74 per cent) was spent on land and buildings.[52]

One of the important items of expenditure of migrants' households, particularly the poorer among them, is repayment of debts incurred to raise the money required for financing emigration. On the average, it takes about two years for such households to repay the loans.

In the two villages surveyed by Mathew and Nair in 1977, total deposits in banks in the name of the emigrant or members of the emigrants' household were divided almost equally between ordinary (demand) and non-resident (external) accounts. Information on the average amounts held per household was not available.

Migrants from Kerala have been reluctant so far to invest in public-sector projects for two major reasons: First, public-sector projects in Kerala are notoriously inefficient; very few among them earn profits. And, second, there exists a widespread, erroneous impression that Kerala is not an attractive place to invest because of incessant labour troubles.[53] It should be noted, however, that migrants would not hesitate to invest in projects if they had faith in their organisational efficiency and profitability.[54]

There are reasons to believe that in recent years migrants have been investing an increasing share of their savings in business. The main avenues of investment are taxi cars, lorries, trucks, and vans, and private buses; constructing and running cinema houses, producing films, and constructing and running hospitals.[55] Table 21 shows the increase in the number of vehicles for transport of goods (lorries, trucks, and vans), buses (stage carriages and contract carriages), taxi cars, and auto-rickshaws from 1975/76 to 1978/79 and 1978/79 to 1981/82. Here again, the proportions of these purchases financed by remittances from migrants and out of other incomes have to be ascertained.

Migrants in the Gulf countries have contributed generously to public and private philanthropic campaigns for the rehabilitation of victims of natural disasters such as droughts and floods and for helping the destitute and handicapped. Both individuals and migrant associations have offered such donations and contributions. They are also known to have contributed liberally for the renovation of religious institutions and the construction of temples, mosques, and churches in their home villages. No quantitative information is available on the magnitude on such expenditures.

Migrants, as noted earlier, bring foreign goods on their home visits, paying heavy customs duties.[56] Such goods include television sets, radios, and transistors, tape recorders, video recorders, cameras, electronic calculators, and wristwatches. These items are imported not because domestically produced goods are not available, but because the foreign goods still command more prestige at home. Non-migrants do not have opportunities to import them owing to governmental restrictions. A comparison of migrants' and non-migrants' households would disclose the difference in the proportions of foreign and domestically produced goods. But such a study has yet to be undertaken in India.

Propensity to Consume: Migrants and Non-migrants

The widely held opinion in the country is that migrants spend larger amounts on consumption than non-migrants. However, it is not clear that the migrants' propensity — particularly the marginal propensity — to consume is higher. Expenditures on several items, such as consumer durables, is incurred during the early years of emigration. The bulk of the goods imported by migrants are consumer durables. If the migrants bring the same gadgets even after they have already purchsed them for their own use, it is for resale in India. The availability of "foreign goods" has led to the development of a ready market, and the migrants or their families get a handsome margin on such resales. Thus, the large influx of foreign goods is affecting the consumption pattern of the non-migrant families as well. However, this craze has not infiltrated all economic groups; the lower and upper middle classes in society are the more fashion-conscious, and it is therefore their expenditures that have increased.

A household's decision to invest its income or keep it in the form of cash or jewellery, land and buildings, or bank deposits would depend not only on the source of income. (i.e. whether it is earned abroad or domestically) but also on the aptitude and experience of the household in making and managing the investments. One of the difficulties encountered by most migrant families is that they do not have any experience in a business line, except investment in agricultural land. Besides, often in such families, the members left behind are mostly children, women, invalids, and the elderly. Migrant households are mostly poor and not well educated and are not aware of the possibilities of investing in shares and securities of private or public corporations. This applies to most non-migrant families as well. In fact, except for a few selected business communities and very rich business families in urban areas, investment in stocks and shares is a totally strange proposition.

Social, Psychological, and Cultural Problems

We referred in a preceding section to the social, psychological, and cultural problems of migrant workers in Gulf countries. We shall now briefly touch upon the problems faced by the migrants' families back home.

Family members left at home also live tension-ridden lives for a variety of reasons. The seriousness of their problems and the policies that might possibly assuage them can be discussed only if reliable information on an adequate scale is available. Unfortunately, such information does not yet exist. Here we shall only mention in passing some references made by leading psychiatrists in Kerala to the psychological problems faced by the migrants' families.[57] Problems arise for the male adults of the migrants' household in India, most often caused by frustration at the income disparity between them and their relations abroad. The wives of emigrants are troubled by anxieties arising from the long separations from their husbands. Psychiatrists in Kerala report that the Gulf boom has taken a toll on the mental health of the people. They report an unprecedented increase in the number of persons falling ill, with at least half of them belonging to the "Gulfite" homes.

According to the superintendent of the Government Mental Hospital, Trichur (Trichur District has sent the maximum number of migrants to the Gulf countries from Kerala), almost every second family with a relative in the Gulf has a history of mental illness. The superintendent of the government hospital in Calicut observed that the entire family situation seems to be heading for a total breakdown in the Gulf-emigrating belts of the state. In Chavakkad taluk, one of the most important emigration pockets in Kerala, nearly 60 per cent of the cases of mental illness came from "Gulf families." Most of the cases reported from Trichur came from young Muslim wives in the age group of 15 to 25 years, the most important reason for the illness being incompatibility with their in-laws. The problem is most serious among Muslims because of their low levels of education.

"Gulf marriages" are another factor. Workers in Gulf countries coming home on leave marry in haste, have a quick and short honeymoon, and leave their wives with their (the husbands') parents for long intervals. The sharing of the migrant's remittances between parents and wives becomes another bone of contention. The wife usually gets very little. In the ensuing quarrels among families the main victims are the young wives.

Psychiatrists also point out that prolonged post-marital separation has led to deviant sexual behaviour by both partners, ending in guilt and tension. Separation has also

102

fuelled suspicions about the partner's fidelity, and some marriages have disintegrated. The break-up of marriages is more common among Muslims, for whom the divorce procedure is quite simple. Mosque meetings are reported to be full of discussions of marital disputes.

The children of "Gulf families" also have psychological problems. Such children, it is reported, are becoming delinquents and turning to alcohol and drugs. Mothers who have to take full control of the children are finding it difficult in the absence of the supporting presence of the fathers. Psychiatrists have even coined a new term: the "Gulf syndrome."

Apart from the psychologists and psychiatrists, social scientists are also worried about the harmful effects of Gulf money in promoting wasteful expenditure and raising the prices of all consumer goods, real estate, and labour. Gulf money has brought about drastic changes in the demand patterns for consumer goods as well. Cotton clothes are discarded for synthetics; private cars, not public conveyance, are used for travel; convenience foods are preferred over food made from scratch; and so on. Extravagance is becoming the status symbol.

But Gulf migration has had positive effects also. Educational levels had remained miserably low in several areas from which migration of unskilled workers has taken place in large numbers. A visible change is now taking place in the attitude of people in such areas towards education. There is a rising demand for educational facilities. An increasingly larger percentage of children, particularly among girls, now attend school and college. A larger proportion of young men turn to training centres for various technical skills. Women are eschewing low-paid, menial occupations. This process may lead to a decline in their work-participation ratio for an interim period until the younger generations find avenues of better employment. Social mobility has increased. Several families with whom the so-called aristocratic families would not seek marital affiliation are now sought after. Families that until recently were disdained are now consulted in social functions. The migrants' families have by their consumption patterns instilled into the society around them an awareness of modern ways of life and an urge to strive for them.

Even though there exists a general awareness of the problems that the migrants and their families face, as well as the impact of migration on the society, no institutions have emerged at any level — social, cultural, religious, or other — to deal with such problems.

The psychological problems associated with the Gulf migration should not be ex-aggerated. Separation, absence of a parent, disparities in household income levels among families in the same locality, sudden riches that lead to ostentation, etc. are not problems exclusively confined to the Gulf migration. Besides, its positive aspects also have to be readily conceded. Since the bulk of the migrants come from poor homes, their employment and the flow of income to their families has had a levelling effect. Poverty-stricken, desolate villages are suddenly becoming prosperous. A sizeable proportion of the former houseless population now own houses. Demand for more schooling, health care, street and domestic electrification, sanitation and transport facilities is rising from previously backward areas. Welcome changes are taking place in the attitudes of the "Gulf families" towards customs, habits, and life-styles. Their rise in social and economic status has automatically led to the diminution of privileges and power wielded by certain sectors of society in the past. These sectors are now looking askance at the challenging, defiant attitudes of the new rich. One may note, however, that social tensions do often-times lead to conflicts and change and growth. Gulf migration seems to have acted as a catalyst for change in Kerala society.

Scenarios for the Returning Migrants

The present indications are that the peak phase of construction activities in the Gulf is fast coming to an end. The repatriation of workers, therefore, particularly those in the construction industry, is likely to accelerate.[58] The possibility of a sharp decline in the demand for construction workers and of the consequent inflow of returnees exceeding the generation of employment opportunities was envisaged by researchers as early as 1978.[59] The decision of the Gulf labour ministers in December 1979 to follow a policy of "Arabisation" is another factor compounding the problem of returnees.[60]

The burden of repatriates is likely to be heavy in countries like India since there already exists the threat of an imminent massive inflow of returnees from Iraq, Libya, and Nigeria.[61] The exact number of Indian workers in the UAE is not known, but the general impression is that they make up about 50 per cent of all the Indian workers in the Gulf countries. Since the total number of Indian workers in the Gulf countries exceeds 1 million (and the total Indian population there is nearly 1.7 million), there are probably 500,000 Indian workers in the UAE. Not less than 75 per cent of the Indian workers would be construction workers. In case most of them are repatriated by 1985, India will have to receive back not less than 300,000 workers (plus their dependants in the UAE) by then. The bulk of these repatriates, not less than 50 per cent, will come back to Kerala and the rest to the other states in India such as Punjab, Andhra Pradesh, Maharashtra, Gujarat, Goa, and Tamil Nadu. After 1985, in addition, India should expect a sizeable number of repatriates if the present indications are to be taken as reliable harbingers.[62]

Besides, as the construction projects in Saudi Arabia, Kuwait, and Oman are completed, significant changes will likely emerge in the composition of demand, with the construction workers getting repatriated and managerial, professional, and secretarial workers being in demand in larger numbers.

The volume of actual repatriates is likely to be still more because of the numerous illegal migrants (or migrants whose contract periods are over) in the Gulf countries, particularly in the UAE. Their numbers are not known, but the general impression is that they run into several thousands. The UAE has recently intensified the crackdown on illegal migrants, and a few thousands are already in jail. All illegal migrants are likely to be deported soon.[63]

It is unlikely that repatriated construction workers will be able to return to Gulf countries on new visas since construction activities are slowing down throughout the Gulf region.

Rehabilitation of Returnees

In the absence of any demographic study on the returnees, it is not possible to furnish in this chapter any information on this aspect. Nor is it possible to report on their present employment status or the problems involved in their social and psychological rehabilitation. It is possible to report, however, that the employment of the repatriates has not yet become an important public issue and that no reports have appeared on the problems of the repatriates in rehabilitating themselves in their home society.

Nevertheless, we hasten to add that the dimensions of the repatriate problem are likely to become formidable in the next few years, especially for a small state like Kerala, which has to reabsorb more than half the total number of repatriates. The problem for Kerala will be all the more serious since it has been plagued by chronic unemployment in all categories of labour for several decades. Unfortunately the government of India has no resettlement schemes for the returning emigrants from the Gulf countries.[64]

The government of Kerala also has been remaining complacent on the question of employment of the Gulf repatriates. The interest of the government has been focused more on the mobilisation of the migrants' savings for investment in public-sector enterprises. However, in May 1983 the minister for industries in Kerala stated that the state government was considering a plan to establish industrial estates in different parts of the state to provide employment for repatriates. According to him, 100 units were proposed to be started in the electronics industry of which one-third would be reserved for Gulf repatriates. He also spoke of starting television assembly units in some emigration pockets in the state.[65] However, such small endeavours are likely to attack at best only a fringe of the problem. For all practical purposes, it would seem that the Gulf repatriates will have to fend for themselves.

Notes

1. "Indians Abroad: A Current Population Estimate," *Economic and Political Weekly*

(20 February 1982), 299-304.

2. Myron Weiner, "International Migration and Development," *Population and Development Review* 8 (March 1982): 13.

3. Weiner, op. cit., p. 17.

4. Ibid., p. 18.

5. J. S. Birks and C. A. Sinclair, *International Migration and Development in the Arab Region* (Geneva: ILO, 1980), 31.

6. Ibid., Table 13, p. 137.

7. On 26 March 1981 the Indian minister of external affairs informed the Lok Sabha (the Indian Parliament) that there were an estimated 559,500 Indians working in the major countries in the Gulf region.

8. *Indian Express*, 27 May 1983.

9. "Estimates are that there are five lakh [500,000] Keralites working in the Gulf region," *Indian Express*, 10 April 1983. If the work-participation rate among Keralites is the same as among Indians as a whole, the total Keralite population may come to about 870,000.

10. These figures are not to be taken as exact. Some reports place the total number of migrants during the two-year period 1976–77 at 300,000. Pavan Sharma, "Biased Propaganda Against Indians in West Asia," *Commerce*, 1 July 1978, p. 20.

11. According to a press report, the magnitude of the annual flow of workers to the Gulf countries during 1980 was 236,200; in 1981 it increased to 276,000; in 1982 there was a slight decline to 239,500. It is reported that during the first six months of 1983 more than 110,000 persons migrated to the Gulf countries. *Kerala Kaumudi*, 29 August 1983.

12. According to an official source (whose identity we have not been permitted to disclose), the total number of persons from Kerala who are outside India at the end of 1982 was about 800,000. The same source also reported that about 40,000 left Kerala during 1982–83 alone for employment in the Gulf countries. A sizeable number of Keralites migrated also from Bombay. Besides these, we may add about 20% as those constituting illegal emigrants.

13. Weiner, op. cit., 8-9.

14. It was reported that the total number of Indians employed in government service in the UAE was 97,700; *Indian Express*, 1 July 1983.

15. "In view of the many complaints received by the government about the maltreatment of domestic female servants in Kuwait and other Persian Gulf territories, executive orders have been issued completely banning the emigration of Indian women to those territories for domestic service." *Report of the Ministry of External Affairs, Government of India, 1961–62*, p. 71.

16. "As a result of unprecedented affluence in recent years in the Gulf countries (mainly Kuwait, Muscat, Bahrain, and Dubai), the demand there for Indian domestic staff, e.g. maidservants, cooks, ayahs, has been growing rapidly. Unscrupulous touts and 'agents' in India have, reportedly, been clandestinely exploiting the situation by luring the needy and susceptible Indian women to the area, with exaggerated promises of lucrative jobs and attractive living conditions there. With a view to curbing any surreptitious outflow of Indian women in this manner, *inter alia*, all the state governments have been requested to tighten up security arrangements at all possible exit points. Additionally, they have been requested to give extensive publicity, particularly among the uneducated and the poorer sections of society, to the hazards to which women leaving India illegally are inevitably exposed abroad." *Report of the Ministry of External Affairs, Government of India, 1972-73*, p. 99.

17. The case studies include Raju Kurien, "Patterns and Effects of Emigration from Kerala: A Study of Two Villages" (M. Phil. diss, Trivandrum: Centre for Development Studies, 1978); E. T. Mathew and P. R. Gopinathan Nair, "Socio-economic Characteristics of Emigrants and Emigrants' Households: A Case Study of Two Villages in Kerala," *Economic and Political Weekly*, 15 July 1978; B. A. Prakash, "Impact of Foreign Remittance: A Case Study of Chavakkad Village," *Economic and Political Weekly*, 8 July 1978; Commerce Research Bureau, *Emigration, Inward Remittances and Economic Growth of Kerala, Report of a Survey* (Bombay: 1978); C. Radhakrishnan and P. Ibrahim, "Emigration, Inward Remittances and Economic Development," *The Manpower Journal* (New Delhi: Jan.–Mar. 1981); Agro-Economic Research Center, Madras, "Impact of Foreign Remittances on the Economy of a Rural Area in Kerala," *Agricultural Situation in India* (Delhi: October 1982).

18. *Bulletin of Job Opportunities in India, 1978*, vol. 15, no. 5 (New Delhi: Central Inst. for

Research and Training in Employment Service, Ministry of Labour, 1980). Vacancies were calculated for all sectors — local, state, and national government, quasi government, local bodies, and private agencies.

19. The Ministry of Labour has lately decided to set up a panel to train workers who are going for jobs; *Indian Express*, 14 June 1983.

20. *Report of the Ministry of External Affairs*, Government of India, 1955-56 (Delhi, 1956), 33-36.

21. *Report of the Ministry of External Affairs*, Government of India, 1964-65 (Delhi, 1965), p. 95.

22. *Report of the Ministry of External Affairs*, Government of India, 1974-75 (Delhi, 1975), p. 115.

23. *Report of the Ministry of External Affairs*, Government of India, 1979-80 (Delhi, 1980), p. 99.

24. Ibid., p. 65.

25. Ibid., p. 71.

26. Nitish Chakravarthy, "West Asia Lure: Protecting the Migrant Labour," *Hindu*, 13 November 1978, p. 7.

27. Ibid.

28. Dilip Bobb, "Chasing A Mirage," *India Today*, 1-15 April 1980, p. 37.

29. The UAE minister for labour and social affairs stated on 31 August 1983 in Dubai that the corrupt practice followed by nationals and companies of selling visas to foreigners who just come to the UAE to look for jobs would be stopped and heavy penalties imposed on visa traders, firms which employ foreigners with illegal sponsorship, and foreigners who take visas from employers other than those with whom they had originally entered into agreement. *India Express*, 1 September 1983.

30. In Abu Dhabi a new rule has come into force recently which stipulates that at the expiry of one contract, the worker has to go back to his home country and may re-enter the same country only after the expiry of six months from the termination of the original contract.

31. Weiner, op. cit., pp. 7 and 8.

32. Weiner, op. cit. p. 4.

33. Recent reports indicate that the UAE has discontinued the system of free medical facilities to expatriates. The prohibitive cost of medical care has compelled many expatriates to send their families back.

34. Dilip Bobb notes that "In Kuwait, for instance, every prominent Kuwaiti from the Emir downwards has at least one domestic. They either come from Kerala, Maharashtra or Goa. The overall result is that most Indians are looked down upon by Arabs." Op. cit., p. 38.

35. "Five sub-inspectors were suspended from active duty in connection with what is now known as the slave trade between Bombay and West Asia. Investigations reveal that these policemen were hand in glove with reputed recruiting agencies in sending a flow of illegal migrants into the Gulf. The charge for visas and emigration endorsement varied between Rs.12,000 to Rs.15,000. The surprise check on Saudi flight No. SV338 revealed seven passengers travelling on forged endorsements. According to police officials, most of these migrants would not have had a job waiting for them after landing in Saudi Arabia. However, certain influential men in Saudi Arabia had evolved a scheme for using these "slaves" as unskilled labour and make quick money. The minimum wages for an unskilled worker in Saudi Arabia is 1200 rials (about Rs.3000). The same job is offered to the helpless job seeker for 200 rials. Take it or go back to the unemployment that awaits him back home, the job seeker invariably succumbs to this kind of blackmail," *Indian Express*, 27 August 1983.

36. "Indians in the Gulf Countries Are Safe." Speech by the minister for external affairs, Government of India, *Kerala Kaumudi*, 19 April 1983. The promised legislation was enacted as the Emigration Act, 1983 (No. 31 of 1983) in September 1983.

37. "Indians are employed as factory workers, department-store clerks, hotel staff, engineers for oil companies, bank officials and in clerical jobs for business. These private-sector jobs are among the most prized, not only because the wages are good but also because they provide opportunities for staying in the Gulf for an extended period," Weiner, op. cit., p. 8. "The category which includes executives, engineers, bankers, bureaucrats on specific contracts, businessmen, journalists, and a vast army of clerical staff, is comparatively

secure," ibid., p. 37.

38. "At the Gulf Labour Ministers' Conference in December 1979, there was a collective call for 'Arabisation' of the region, which meant that future employment should be confined to Arab nationals. The employment of Indians and Pakistanis has slowed down considerably and they are being replaced by Palestinians, Egyptians, Syrians and Iranians," ibid., p. 36.

39. *Indian Express*, 1 September 1983.

40. Free medical facilities are no longer available in the UAE. The Federal National Council of the UAE approved a draft law in May 1983 abolishing free medical services provided by the government. *Indian Express*, 15 May 1983. The draft has been passed into law and the UAE has become the first Gulf country to charge for all kinds of government-run medical services.

41. Weiner, op. cit., p. 15.

42. Ibid., p. 6.

43. A considerable number of migrant Indian workers — particularly those from Kerala — in the recent past deposited part of their savings (which they would take home personally on annual leave) in exchange firms, some of which were run by Keralites. The major incentive for the expatriates to deposit in such firms was the high rates of interest. Following the collapse of a few such exchange firms in the UAE, many Indians lost their hard-earned savings. The Gulf governments have in recent months taken several steps to control the functioning of exchange firms.

44. Government of India, *Economic Survey, 1982–83,* p. 59. A recent report has, however, pointed out that according to government sources in Delhi the level is expected to have been higher in 1982-83; see Minhaj Barna, Kuldip Nayar, and K. Nadaraj, "Waiting for the Fallout," *South*, August 1981, p. 69.

45. Andhra Pradesh has other connections with the Arab world, particularly through what are known as "Arab marriages" — instant marriages performed between Arabs who visit the country and Andhra girls mostly in their early teens — conducted with the help of the poor and money-crazy parents of the girls. Syed Majeedul Hasan, "The New Arab Slave Trade," *Sunday, 30* November 1980, pp. 16 and 17, and *Indian Express, 6* July 1982.

46. The survey was conducted by a reliable official agency for its internal use.

47. With a view to encouraging remittances from abroad, the Reserve Bank of India introduced a new facility in 1975. Under this scheme, non-residents and persons of Indian origin resident abroad are permitted to open and maintain foreign currency (non-resident) accounts in US dollars or in pounds sterling with initial remittances received from abroad or by conversion of already existing (external) rupee accounts held with banks authorised to deal in foreign exchange in India. The interest accruing on these balances is free from Indian income tax. The balance including the interest accrued is freely repatriable in the designated foreign currencies without reference to the RBI. Balances held in non-resident (external) rupee accounts or in designated foreign currencies are exempt from India's wealth tax. Reserve Bank of India, *Annual Report on Trend and Progress of Banking in India, 1975–76*, pp. 100–101.

48. Smuggling is quite common with Indian workers on their home visits. The press frequently reports cases of unsuccessful smuggling at the various airports — particularly at Bombay and Trivandrum — the entry points from the Gulf countries.

49. Agro-economic Research Centre, "Impact of Foreign Remittances on the Economy of a Rural Area in Kerala," *Agricultural Situation in India,* 37 (October 1982): 452.

50. Mathew and Nair, op. cit. (see note 17 above), p. 151.;

51. Investment in vehicles for direct use and for business seems to have increased substantially in recent years. In Kerala, during the period 1975/76 to 1981/82, the number of cars purchased for private use increased by nearly 20,000.

52. Laurie Baker, an English architect domiciled in India and an admirer of indigenous architecture of the Orient, has observed that in Kerala houses are no longer built in the traditional way. The beautiful houses built with local natural materials which were functionally the ideal for the Kerala climatic conditions are yielding to reinforced concrete, terraced, and coated with chemical, glossy colours — "angry reds and purples, metallic greens and blues, startling oranges and yellows — deposited on the ground like a spoiled child's toy blocks, defiantly spread across the floor." Baker attributes this change mostly to the naivete of new-rich Gulf expatriates. *Indian Express,* 22 May 1983. The rising demand for housing sites

had led to the conversion of large areas of rice field into plots for the construction of buildings. A typical report says, "Paddy fields are cheaper than land and the cost of converting them is not high. Field owners, attracted by Gulf money, are answering the increasing demand for land in many places." *Indian Express*, 13 August 1983.

53. Weiner, op. cit., fn. 9, p. 32.
54. For example, in 1976 Keltron, a public-sector corporation producing electronic goods, was able effortlessly to raise Rs. 1.2 million from Keralites in the Gulf countries. Kurien, op. cit., 88.
55. Rechard Thomas, *India's Emergence as an Industrial Power — Middle East Contracts* (Delhi: Vikas Ltd., 1982), p. 54.
56. The migrants are not given any concession in customs duties. Rather, their complaint has been that they are penalised.
57. Raj Chengappa, "The Mental Gulf," *India Today*, 15 September 1982, pp. 58–61.
58. The trends in the demand for manpower in the Gulf countries are uncertain. "Some of the official studies have given conflicting trends, with a few indicating a fall in the labour market demands whereas others predicting an increase for about another 20 years." Ibid.
59. Birks and Sinclair wrote in 1978: "The problems to be faced by all countries of origin is that probabaly the international demand for their migrant labourers will eventually fall. The decline will be sharp enough for workers to return home more quickly than employment can be created for them in their country of origin," op. cit., p. 101.
60. Dilip Bobb, op. cit., p. 36.
61. In Iraq and Libya several thousand Indian workers are employed in construction companies run by Indians. The governments of these two countries are finding it difficult to finance the completion of the projects already taken up. The government of India has been taking steps to ensure that the workers engaged by the construction companies are paid their wages and salaries that have already fallen into arrears. It is almost certain that the workers engaged by the construction companies will be repatriated immediately after the completion of their present assignments. In addition, large numbers of Indian professionals, scientists, and teachers employed in Nigeria are expected to return home permanently on the expiry of their present contracts as a result of the economic crisis in Nigeria following the fall in the oil prices.
62. The governments of most Gulf countries have presented in 1983 the tightest budgets ever in recent years. *Bankers' Magazine* in June 1983 reported: "Undeniably, growth is going to slow down over the next few years. The explosive increase in construction-related finance of the early to mid 1970's is over," *Bankers' Magazine*, 227 (June 1983): 18–32; A. K. N. Mohammad has reported from Washington still more recently that the outlook for development in Saudi Arabia is dismal. "Only recently during fiscal year 1983 the Saudis were forced to slash their original spending plan of US$90 billion to $70 billion as oil revenue fell. In fiscal year 1984 they are planning to spend only US$75 billion. Yet they face a deficit of at least $10 billion. This projected deficit may be on the lower side since it is based on some optimistic assumptions. Some independent analysts calculate the level of deficit will be between $21 billion and $26 billion instead of the projected $10 billion. The economic retrenchment that began last year will continue in fiscal year 1983–84. Few new development projects were funded last year and fewer are expected this year. This in turn will imply foreign firms, particularly construction firms, will feel the squeeze deeper and deeper." "Saudi Arabia, Oil Glut and Poor World," *Commerce*, 20 August 1983.
63. *Indian Express*, 1 September 1983.
64. Announced by India's labour minister before Parliament on 2 August 1983.
65. *Indian Express*, 29 May 1983.

PAKISTAN

M. Fahim Khan

Director of Research, International Institute of Islamic Economics, Islamabad, Pakistan

The Annual Volume of Migration: Emigrants and Returnees

There are always movements of people across national boundaries for a variety of
reasons. Such movements go unnoticed as long as they do not attain a sizeable
volume in relation to the total population, particularly in relation to the total
labour force of the country. As migration reaches a sizeable volume, however, it starts
to pose various socioeconomic problems and begins to have a significant impact on the
society as a whole. For the economy, the implications of migration are seen in its
effects on the labour market and the inflow of remittances from abroad in cash and
kind. For the society, its implications arise, among other things, out of the exodus of
active, working members of families, new patterns of social mobility, the demonstration effect of the changed consumption patterns of migrant families, and the
changes in individual attitudes as a result of exposure to the rest of the world.

The significance of the impact, whether economic or social, direct or indirect,
short-run or long-run, will depend on (a) the total stock of emigrants, i.e. the cumulative total of the migrants who are abroad (for employment); (b) the annual rate of
migrant outflow; (c) the annual rate of inflow (returns); and (d) the total stock of
returnees, i.e. the cumulative total of those who have returned permanently (from
employment abroad).

Volume of Emigration from Pakistan

In 1979 the Pakistan Institute of Public Opinion (PIPO), a private organisation,
estimated the total number of emigrants abroad to be 1.8 million, among whom
1.25 million were estimated to be in the Middle East. A study conducted jointly

---

See the Appendix for a discussion of the various research studies and sources of data referred to
in this paper.

by the Pakistan Institute of Development Economics (PIDE) and the World Bank evaluated all other available sources of information on the subject and accepted the institute's figures. Since 1979 reliable figures have been supplied by the Bureau of Emigration regarding the annual outflow. On the basis of these figures, the total stock of migrants abroad can be estimated at 2 million. PIPO data also provide information on the provincial and rural-urban origins of the migrants (see Table 1).

Table 2 shows the distribution of Pakistani migrants (by their rural and urban origins) in the Middle East and the rest of the world as a whole.

TABLE 1. Pakistani Migrants by Home Province and Rural or Urban Origin

	Rural		Urban		Total	
	Millions	%	Millions	%	Millions	%
Punjab	0.83	73.6	0.43	64.7	1.26	70.4
Sind	0.10	9.2	0.15	22.9	0.25	14.0
NWFP	0.16	14.1	0.05	7.8	0.21	11.7
Baluchistan	0.04	3.1	0.03	4.6	0.07	3.9
Total	1.13	100.00	0.66	100.00	1.79	100.00

Source: PIDE-World Bank Study.

TABLE 2. Pakistani Migrants by Country of Migration and Rural or Urban Origin

	Rural		Urban		Total	
	Millions	%	Millions	%	Millions	%
Saudi Arabia	0.445	39.5	0.162	24.6	0.608	34.0
UAE	0.236	20.9	0.122	18.5	0.358	20.0
Other Middle East countries	0.153	14.0	0.122	18.5	0.280	15.6
Total Middle East	0.840	74.4	0.406	61.6	1.245	69.6
All other countries	0.289	25.6	0.255	38.4	0.544	30.4
Total	1.129	100.00	0.661	100.00	1.790	100.00

Source: PIDE-World Bank Study.

Statistics on the stock of migrants are reported by official agencies too. For example, Pakistan's embassies provide statistics, although these statistics have certain limitations in that illegal migrants are not included and many legal migrants do not register with the embassies. The Ministry of Labour and Manpower provides statistics about emigrants based on the registrations with the Bureau of Emigration. These statistics also have shortcomings because registration with the bureau was not mandatory for emigrants until 1979 and, consequently, most emigrants did not register. Also, illegal migrants or migrants who first emigrate on a non-migrant visa and then secure employment after their arrival in the host country generally are not accounted for by the bureau. The figures proffered by the various international agencies are also inadequate because they use the official records of the host countries, which are also incomplete, particularly with respect to illegal immigrants. In addition statistics that show a breakdown of immigrants by nationalities have raised a politically sensitive issue in some countries and their release, therefore, is not permitted. The most reliable figure, however, would be the one collected by the 1981 census. The final figures have yet to be released; a preliminary release on the total number of migrants, however, does not differ significantly from those estimated by PIPO.

The PIPO figures, adopted by the PIDE-World Bank study, have now gained recognition in official circles, particularly after the 1981 census. These figures, however, do not seem to be accepted in host countries such as Saudi Arabia, whose official figures are much less. This could be partly attributed to a reluctance on the part of these countries to reveal their excessive dependence on expatriate labour and the very high proportion of such labour in the total workforce.

Annual Outflow of Emigrants

The only source for information on the annual outflow is the Bureau of Emigration, which by law registers every emigrant going abroad for a job. The bureau publishes monthly and annual figures of outflows in its official publications, with details about occupations, origin by district, and destination. The bureau reported that during 1981 (which was the peak year) a total of 168,403 migrants obtained jobs abroad. Out of these, 119,771 went through the private recruiting agents; 33,370 obtained jobs through their own private sources; and 15,322 utilized government sources to get a job abroad (see Table 3).

Returning Migrants

The only attempt to estimate the stock of migrants who have returned was made in the Fahim Khan and Munawar Iqbal study conducted at PIDE. They estimated that as of 1980 a total of 42,000 emigrants had returned permanently from the Middle East. Though it is true that returning migrants have not yet reached a sizeable number, the PIDE's method of estimating this figure was very indirect (due to lack of data), which makes its reliability doubtful. No official agency exists to keep records on permanently returning migrants. The situation regarding information on the annual return flow is similar. An estimate, through not very reliable, was made in the PIDE study on returning migrants, which put the figure at 21,672 for the year 1979/80, which was less than 10 per cent of the annual rate of outflow of workers to the Middle East.

TABLE 3.   Official Estimates of the Flow of Overseas Migration

	Private[1]	Public[2]	Direct	Total
1971	3340	194	—	3534
1972	3359	1171	—	4530
1973	7654	4646	—	12,300
1974	14,652	1676	—	16,328
1975	21,766	1311	—	23,077
1976	38,516	3174	—	41,690
1977	77,664	2683	60,175	140,522
1978	78,685	4238	47,602	130,525
1979	80,615	10,306	34,586	125,507
1980	91,482	13,564	24,801	129,847
1981	119,711	15,322	33,370	168,403
1982	99,119	15,410	38,416	152,945
1983	73,837	8175	46,194	128,206
1984	68,129	2703	29,575	100,407

1. Through overseas employment promoters.
2. Through government channels.

Source: Pakistan Economic Survey 1984–85.

Characteristics of Pakistani Migrants

Occupations

The Bureau of Emigration is the official agency that collects and provides data on migrant's occupations. In Table 4, 24 occupations have been grouped into four categories: unskilled labour, skilled labour, professional and managerial workers, and clerical staff and service workers. In addition, there is a "miscellaneous" category of workers which accounts for about one-fifth of the outflow. The presence of this category, therefore, introduces some uncertainty regarding this analysis of occupations.

The PIDE–World Bank study presented its own set of statistics on migrants' occupations, which it derived from data it collected from airport surveys. Approximately 12,500 passengers going to the Middle East were interviewed during the airport surveys. The distribution of workers going to the Middle East by major

113

occupational categories as obtained from these airport surveys is shown in Table 5. Production workers constituted 83 per cent of the migrating labour force, of whom more than half were unskilled. The remaining 17 per cent were mostly professional workers, business executives or sales workers, service workers, and clerical staff.

TABLE 4. Occupational Profile of Pakistani Labour Migrants in the Middle East

	Number	%
Production workers	*112,421*	*71.5*
Unskilled labour	54,746	34.8
Skilled labour	57,735	36.7
masons	10,579	6.7
carpenters	11,840	7.5
steel erectors	6269	4.0
painters	1943	1.2
foremen	2478	1.6
electricians	3485	2.2
plumbers	1630	1.0
welders	2380	1.3
cable jointers	682	0.4
technicians	11,085	7.0
mechanics	5364	3.4
Other workers	*44,985*	*28.5*
Professional and managerial	3773	2.4
engineers	1040	0.7
accountants	487	0.3
managers	306	0.2
teachers	396	0.2
nurses	904	0.5
doctors	640	0.4
Clerical staff	4422	2.8
stenographers	541	0.3
clerks/typists	2776	1.8
storekeepers	1105	0.7
Service workers	2852	1.8
cooks	2030	1.3
waiters	822	0.5
Miscellaneous	33,938	21.5
Total	157,466	100.0

These figures represent only those migrants who migrated through the Bureau of Emigration.

TABLE 5. Major Occupational Groups of Pakistani Migrants
(percentages)

Production workers	83.2
Unskilled	42.6
Skilled	40.6
Professionals	4.3
Clerical	1.5
Service	2.2
Sales/business	6.0
Miscellaneous	2.9
Total	100.0

Source: IMP Survey.

Table 6 gives a more detailed analysis of the data by individual occupations. About 12 per cent of the unskilled workers emigrating to the Middle East (5.12 per cent of the total) were reported to be destined for agricultural labour. The remaining 88 per cent of the unskilled labour included general labourers and loaders. Among skilled labour, the prominent emigrating occupations were drivers, masons, electricians, carpenters, and tailors, constituting 28 per cent of the migrating labour (70 per cent of skilled migrating labour). The other skilled workers migrating to the Middle East were machine operators, mechanics, welders, steel binders/fixers, denters, etc. Among professional workers, engineers were the major migrants. Accountants and teachers ranked next, although the proportion was very small. Cooks and security guards/watchmen were the main service workers going to the Middle East.

The airport surveys also showed the distribution into occupational groups by province of origin (Table 7) and the distribution of the migrants according to the length of their stay abroad (Table 8).

The data in Table 9, showing a breakdown into occupational groups by date of migration, indicate that the proportion of unskilled labour has gone up over time relative to that of skilled labour. Unskilled workers made up only 30 per cent of Pakistanis who migrated to the Middle East before 1973 but nearly 51 per cent of those who migrated in 1979, while the proportion of skilled workers declined from 47 per cent to 38 per cent.

It has to be noted, however, that since the PIDE–World Bank study was made, substantial changes may have taken place in the occupational composition.

Marital Status

The PIDE–World Bank study estimated that 70 per cent of Pakistani migrant workers were married. With a total figure of 1.2 million migrants in the Middle East, it was

TABLE 6. Distribution of Migrants by Occupation (percentages)

Production workers	*83.16*
Unskilled labour	*42.55*
agricultural	5.12
nonagricultural	37.43
Skilled	*40.61*
drivers	7.85
carpenters	6.23
masons	6.08
tailors	4.72
electricians	3.34
steel binders/fixers	2.47
mechanics	2.44
machine operators	2.22
painters	1.57
welders	1.38
plumbers	1.32
denters	0.38
goldsmiths	0.31
blacksmiths	0.12
turners	0.09
watchmakers	0.07
furnace fitters	0.04
Service	*2.19*
cooks	1.11
security guards	0.47
bakers	0.31
peons	0.17
laundry	0.14
Clerical	*1.52*
accounts clerks	0.54
storekeepers	0.37
typists	0.29
site clerks	0.17
telephone operators	0.14
Professionals	*4.32*
engineers	2.67
accountants	0.55
teachers/professors	0.35
nurses	0.20
computer programmers/operators	0.19
doctors	0.18
executives	0.09
photographers	0.08
Sales/business	*5.95*
Miscellaneous	*2.85*
Total	100.0

Source: PIDE-World Bank Study.

TABLE 7. Major Occupational Groups of Migrants by Province of
Origin (percentages)

	Punjab	Sind	NWFP	Other Provinces/Areas[1]
Production Workers	82.4	71.2	92.1	87.9
Unskilled	33.9	33.8	58.8	53.0
Skilled	48.5	37.4	33.3	35.0
Professional and managerial	4.4	8.4	1.7	2.1
Clerical	1.7	2.6	0.5	1.1
Service	2.0	2.5	1.8	3.7
Sales/business	6.3	12.0	1.8	2.8
Miscellaneous	3.1	3.5	2.1	2.3
Total	100.0	100.0	100.0	100.0

1. This includes Azad Kashmir, federally administered areas, and Baluchistan.

TABLE 8. Distribution of Migrants by Length of
Stay Abroad (percentages)

Less than 1 year	33.3
1–2 years	30.5
3–4 years	18.9
5–6 years	7.8
More than 6 years	9.5

estimated that this implied that about 3 million women and children were separated
from their husbands and fathers. No other information is available.

Employment Status before Migration

The PIDE–World Bank study showed only 7 per cent of the migrants as unemployed
before migration. This is the only information available on this issue. In countries like
Pakistan, however, a substantial portion of the "employed" labour force is, in fact, in
disguised unemployment. A more detailed investigation is required to determine what
type of work the emigrants were doing before migration and how much they were contributing to the actual output of agriculture, industry, or the other sectors in which
they were working.

Household Incomes

Ascertaining the family income of migrants at the time of departure (which in
most of the cases was several years ago) is one of the most difficult tasks.

TABLE 9. Distribution of Migrants by Occupation and Date of Migration

	1979	1977–78	1975–76	1973–74	Before 1973
Unskilled	50.6	46.4	39.3	39.6	30.2
agricultural	3.0	8.1	3.7	0.0	3.9
nonagricultural	47.6	38.3	35.6	39.6	26.5
Skilled	38.2	44.6	48.6	45.3	47.0
carpenters/masons	11.6	14.6	16.1	11.8	11.7
technicians/mechanics	17.9	19.5	20.8	15.2	17.4
tailors	4.6	4.0	3.9	7.5	9.3
drivers	4.1	6.5	7.8	10.8	8.6
Clerical	0.6	0.7	2.7	3.8	3.5
Professional and managerial	4.4	2.6	2.7	2.8	3.1
Business	4.4	4.6	5.8	6.6	10.9
Service	1.8	1.1	2.9	1.9	5.1
Total	100.0	100.0	100.0	100.0	100.0

First, the precise definition of "family income" is elusive, and the collection of data according to that definition poses numerous problems. Second, an analysis of the migrant outflow according to household incomes — in order to be meaningful — must be based on pre-migration incomes. Only then will questions such as the effects of migration on income distribution, poverty, and underdevelopment be adequately answered. The PIDE–World Bank study is the only project that has tried to collect such information, and elaborate questions were included in the questionnaires to this end. The data, however, could not be processed properly, and hence this information could not be published in their reports. During the project, a preliminary exercise was carried out to determine the distribution of migrants by pre-migration family income. It was observed that the migrants' households had income levels above the national average, implying that emigration has been taking place from the relatively more affluent part of the population. This could have negative consequences for income distribution. This type of analysis, however, must be supported by a deeper analysis of the issue. We know that emigration is taking place mostly from the unskilled and semiskilled labour and from the rural areas. This, therefore, must improve the conditions of lower-income groups in Pakistan. No other study has generated data on the pre-migration incomes of migrant households.

Social Status

No information on the social status of Pakistani migrants has been published. The PIDE-World Bank and the OPF-PIPO studies did collect data on this subject, but it has not been processed or published. An anthropological study was conducted during the PIDE–World Bank study regarding the social status of migrants' families.

The results of this study, though very limited in scope (inapplicable on a national basis), are available in the form of a research report at PIDE.

Domestic Supply and Demand for Labour in Pakistan

The Labour Supply

The last labour-force survey whose results were available for this study was conducted in 1974/75. Though another survey was undertaken in 1978/79, its results were not available. All the information on the employment situation in the economy here is therefore based on the 1974/75 survey. The Planning Commission and the Manpower Division have made their own projections up to 1979/80 on the employment situation. These projections are not very rigorous in that they simply inflated the 1974/75 statistics on the basis of the Planning Commission's investment programme without taking into account the changes in labour productivity, real wages, or technology. For example, between 1970 and 1975 real wages increased substantially, which might have created a bias towards capital-intensive technology. Also, there was a considerable decline in labour productivity during the 1970s owing to non-economic factors, causing a shift towards capital-intensive technologies. On the supply side, considerable structural changes might have taken place since 1974/75. Up to the early 1970s there was substantial disguised unemployment in the country. Such employment declined considerably after 1975. The labour-supply situation as depicted by the available statistics is therefore questionable.

Another shortcoming of the available statistics was reported to be in the collection of unemployment statistics. In developing countries there are always many workers who do not report themselves to be in the workforce because they believe there are no jobs available for them. Similarly, there are many who report themselves to be working, whereas they are not gainfully employed. This disguises the real extent of unemployment in the economy. With emigration, not only is the disguised unemployment declining, but those who were not part of the labour force are now entering it because they are now hopeful of getting a job. It was on these grounds that the PIDE–World Bank study concluded that the growth of labour supply in Pakistan's economy during the late 1970s was substantially higher than the 3 per cent annual growth rate shown by the official statistics. Some idea of the labour supply in Pakistan can be obtained from the available official data based on the projections of the Planning Commission, Manpower Division (see Tables 10 and 11).

The workforce participation rate is estimated at about 31 per cent. It is low in comparison with 36.6 per cent for Indonesia and 48.8 per cent in Thailand. In most developed countries, the workforce participation rate is around half of the population, whereas in Pakistan it is less than one-third.

119

TABLE 10. Pakistan's Workforce: Employment and Productivity, 1977/78 to 1982/83

	Workforce (millions)	Workforce growth (%)	Employment (millions)	Productivity (rupees per worker)[1]
1977/78	22.22	2.9	21.84	600
1978/79	22.93	3.2	22.54	609
1979/80	23.68	3.3	23.13	637
1980/81	24.45	3.2	23.81	657
1981/82	25.24	3.3	24.50	681
1982/83	26.06	3.2	25.21	—

1. Value added (GDP) per worker per month at 1977/78 prices.

Source: Manpower Division.

TABLE 11. Workforce Participation Rates by Province — Urban-Rural, Male-Females, 1978/79

	Total	Rural	Urban	Male	Female
Punjab	31.12	32.30	27.39	27.15	3.97
Sind	33.44	38.67	27.00	28.64	4.81
NWFP	24.96	24.97	24.90	23.54	1.48
Baluchistan	32.34	33.71	26.04	21.28	2.00
Pakistan	31.02	32.55	27.06	27.23	3.79

Source: Labour Force Survey

Labour Supply and Demand According to Occupation, and the Impact of Emigration on the Labour Market

Unemployment is not uniform across all occupations and professions in the Pakistani economy. A number of skills and professions are believed to be scarce in the country, and it is generally believed that there is excess demand rather than unemployment in all skilled and professional occupations. Any unemployment in these occupations is only minor or reflects the job-search period. Though there was substantial unemployment among engineers during the 1960s, it is believed that this has long been eliminated by the emigration of the 1970s. There is, however, still believed to be substantial unemployment among the educated labour force with only general education. The Labour Force Survey, 1974–75, reported the highest unemployment rate for those with nontechnical educations of 10 to 14 years of schooling.

Unfortunately, no official statistics are available on the unemployment rate by occupations. The Labour Force Survey provides only the demand side; information about the supply of jobs in major occupations is not available, so unemployment by occupation cannot be determined. And the estimates of the occupational composition in employment by the Planning Commission and Manpower Division for the current year are given only by major occupational groups (see Table 12). No official statistics are available on the supply and demand for labour in the domestic market according to the detailed occupational classification used earlier in analysing the occupational distribution of emigrants. In these circumstances it is difficult to assess the varying impact of emigration among the various occupational categories.

TABLE 12. Employment Opportunities by Major Occupational Groups, 1978/79 (millions)

Professional, technical, and related	1.07
Administrative and managerial	0.18
Clerical and related	0.96
Sales	1.95
Service	1.77
Agriculture, animal husbandry, forestry, fishermen, hunters	11.93
Production and related	
Transport-equipment operators and labourers	4.62
Unclassified	0.06
Total employed	22.54
Total unemployed	0.39
Total labour supply	22.93

Source: Manpower Division Ministry of Labour and Manpower, Government of Pakistan

An official of the Manpower Division and I have both made efforts to estimate labour supply and demand for as detailed a list of occupations as possible in order to determine the occupations where emigration has created excess demand. Both these attempts were made on the basis of information on past trends that are likely to have changed significantly. Nevertheless, using the growth rates implied in the Manpower Division's estimates and the detailed occupational composition published for the 1961 census, I conducted a crude exercise on domestic demand for major emigrating occupations for the PIDE–World Bank study. In Table 13 the estimated increase in domestic job opportunities is compared with the estimated number of migrants by major emigrating occupations.

According to these estimates, the skills required for Pakistan's construction and manufacturing sectors are emigrating excessively as compared with the growth in their domestic supply. The transport sector can also be seen to be facing shortages of drivers when the increase in domestic demand is compared with the number of

121

TABLE 13. Estimated Domestic Demand for Major Migrating Occupations (thousands)

	1961[1]	1971/72[2]	1974/75[2]	1978/79[3]	1982/83[4]	Increase 1971/72– 1978/79[3]	Emigrants to the Middle East[5]
Mason	69	171	229	244	278	73	73
Carpenter	59	147	197	210	239	63	75
Electrician	24	59	79	84	96	25	40
Plumber and pipefitter	4	10	13	14	16	4	16
Painter	11	27	36	38	43	11	19
Machine operator	15	21	25	27	31	6	27
Mechanic	64	80	106	113	130	24	29
Blacksmith	84	117	139	148	170	31	1
Driver	183	504	551	574	649	70	94
Tailor	126	247	361	394	445	147	57
Goldsmith	41	80	117	128	145	48	4
Engineer	11	20	31	53	60	33	32
Doctor, medical worker, medical technician	35	62	99	166	188	104	5
Teacher	94	167	261	466	504	279	4
Executive	90	98	148	180	203	82	1
Clerical and related	374	440	560	960	1085	520	18
Service worker, barber, peon, cook, launderer	709	710	931	1770	2000	839	26
Business/sales	130	387	349	327	380	22	7

1. Census figures.
2. Based on the growth rates implied in the labour force surveys of 1971/72 and 1974/75.
3. Estimates.
4. Projections as implied by Planning Commission and Manpower Division statistics on employment.
5. Estimates. Almost all of this emigration was during the 1972–1979 period.

Source: PIDE – World Bank Study.

drivers who have migrated. An important factor that these statistics fail to reflect but which has been mentioned by employers is that the workers who are emigrating are more capable and experienced than those who remain in Pakistan. This results not only in reduced output but also in declining quality of production and service. Scarcities exist for engineers also. Since it takes much longer to educate and train an engineer than the skilled workers mentioned above, the emigration of engineers is creating more serious shortages for the economy. In occupations like teachers, clerical workers, business executives, and service workers, however, the migration is not causing serious problems as the proportion of their emigration to the increase in demand for them is not yet very significant. The emigration of doctors and medical personnel is also not very significant, but government control of their migration might be the reason for this.

The Impact on Pakistan's Economic Output

The PIDE–World Bank study also analysed the effect of emigration on output of the economy. They estimated that the emigration to the Middle East constituted 7.7 per cent of the total recorded labour force of the country and concluded that, keeping in view the peculiarities of the labour-supply situation in Pakistan, the migration had not yet assumed an alarming proportion of the workforce.

This was, however, considered to be true only in the aggregate. At the micro-level, there were shortages in certain professions. Most of Pakistani labour is illiterate, possessing no substantial skills. Technical, skilled, and professional labour is scarce in the country. Therefore, the migration of workers with scarce skills will obviously have a harmful effect on the labour-supply situation of the country and will slow down Pakistan's economic development.

The fact that about 83 per cent of the migrants are production workers is likely to adversely affect this part of the domestic workforce if adequate and appropriate replacements are not forthcoming at the same rate. The changes that occurred in the composition of the labour force by major professions from 1972 to 1979 are shown in Table 14, along with the occupational distribution of the migrants. The "production and related" category, which includes skilled and unskilled labour working in the non-agricultural sector, accounts for 78 per cent of migrating labour, which may create bottlenecks for the development of Pakistan's nonagricultural sector. The emigration of production workers, therefore, means a reduction of output in Pakistan's non-agriculture sector, particularly in the sectors of construction, manufacturing/mining, transport, and communication.

TABLE 14. Occupational Breakdowns for Pakistan's Domestic and Migrant Workforce (percentages)

	Labour Force		Migrants, 1979
	1972	1979	
Professional and technical	2.1	4.7	4.2
Clerical and administrative	2.8	5.0	1.6
Sales	12.1	8.6	5.6
Service	3.7	7.9	4.7
Farmers, fishermen, etc.	57.2	53.3	4.8
Production and related	22.1	20.5	78.9

We can assume that surplus unskilled labour is available for employment. Therefore, the loss of output in the agricultural and non-agricultural sectors will depend upon the extent of emigration from among skilled labour, which is assumed to be fully employed. (Any reported unemployment in the skills can be assumed to be only a reflection of the search period for suitable jobs.) With 40.6 per cent of the emigrants as skilled labour and with a total of 1.2 million Pakistani emigrants in the Middle East, the total number of skilled emigrants in 1979 was 487,000.

According to the composition of the labour force given in the 1961 census, skilled and unskilled workers were employed at a ratio of 4:1 in the non-agricultural sector. On this basis, the withdrawal of skilled labour would mean the loss of output of 122,000 unskilled workers along with that of the 487,000 skilled workers. Alternatively, however, it can also be assumed that since it is not too costly in terms of time and money to acquire the relevant skills, the large number of unemployed, unskilled labour can always be upgraded into skilled labour to meet the full skills requirement. Hence, the emigration of even skilled labour may non-agricultural any loss of output in Pakistan. However, large differences (100–200 per cent) between the wages of unskilled and skilled labour indicate that the replacement process and the acquisition of skills have not been smooth. The number of unskilled workers out of the total 1.2 million emigrants to the Middle East is in the region of 511,000. According to this analysis, 76 per cent of the emigrating unskilled labour will not cause any loss of output to the economy because this percentage of the workforce was either unemployed or part of the disguised unemployment in the agricultural and traditional sectors.

There is no evidence of unemployment among professional workers, and the economy has therefore lost the output of 52,000 professional workers who accounted for 4.3 per cent of total emigrants from the country. The labour force survey of 1974/75 indicated a 5.7 per cent unemployment in the educated (general-degree certificate) labour force, which generally represents Pakistan's clerical workforce. The emigrants have been found to include 18,000 clerical workers, or 1.6 per cent of the total emigrants. It can be inferred that the emigration of clerical workers does not cause any appreciable loss of output.

Service workers (cooks, laundrymen, watchmen/guards, barbers), though they are not unskilled, can be assumed to have caused no loss of output by their emigration, mainly because these skills can be acquired easily and quickly.

In view of the unemployment among people with general education, the supply of salesmen/business workers, who required only general education, can also be assumed to be elastic. Thus, their emigration should cause no substantial loss of output.

The Impact of the Labour Migration on Wages in Pakistan

The PIDE–World Bank study in examining the impact of the emigration on wages made the following analysis. According to the data collected by the Census of Manufacturing Industries, wage increases during the 1970s have been much higher than the increase in the cost of living. This increase in real wages is unprecedented and is furthermore unaccounted for by the domestic demand for labour. The wage increases during the 1960s in real terms were not as marked as the increases during the 1970s despite the fact that during the 1970s economic activity in general and industrial activity in particular were considerably slower than during the 1960s. Though between 1969 and 1975 there was massive government intervention in the form of labour/wage policies, most of the wage hikes during the 1970s are generally attributed to the international migration of workers. Not enough data, however, are available to support this hypothesis. Some evidence can be culled from the data on wage rates of skilled and unskilled labour in the construction sector that have been provided annually by the Statistics Division since 1969/70 (see Table 15).

It can be seen that the spurt in the wage rates of both skilled and unskilled labour started in the mid-seventies, which is also when the migration gained momentum. It can also be noted that the higher rate of the wage increase of unskilled labour compared to that of skilled labour in Karachi and Peshawar corresponds to the ratio of unskilled labour migration to the skilled migrants (masons and carpenters) from Sind and NWFP.

If the hypothesis regarding the positive impact of emigration on real wages is accurate, then its implications for Pakistan's industrial sector are significant — over and above the output forgone. A substantial part of the manufacturing sector is export-oriented, so it does not have much leverage to increase its prices without concomitant price increases in the international market. The wage increases, by raising production costs, not only decrease employment in these industries but also adversely affect industrial development — one of Pakistan's major development objectives. Also, in the presence of increasing wages, industrial development becomes biased towards capital-intensive technology, which conflicts with the objectives of improving exports, employment, and income distribution in the country. There are indications that capital-intensive and non-export industries (e.g. cement, fertiliser, vegetable ghee) are growing more than export industries (e.g. textiles). These adverse consequences will continue to intensify unless the wage increases are backed up by a corresponding increase of labour productivity through massive training programmes.

The statistics on wages are not complete enough to reveal the impact of migration on the labour market. The Census of Manufacturing Industries publishes periodical data on wages, but the last published data are for 1975/76. The Statistical Division publishes statistics on the daily wage rates of labour in the construction sector. Without statistics on the days per year a labourer has been

employed, conclusions will be of limited use. If we can assume that days of
employment for all labour have remained constant during the last five years,
then the statistics indicate significant improvements in the real wages of both

TABLE 15. Wage Rates of Skilled and Unskilled Labour in Pakistan's
Construction Sector, 1970–1978 (rupees per day)

	Lahore	Karachi	Peshawar
Carpenters			
1969/70	10.00	14.50	10.31
1970/71	10.67	15.33	9.62
1971/72	11.75	16.01	9.94
1972/73	12.09	16.15	11.09
1973/74	17.82	19.33	13.65
1974/75	22.68	27.42	17.17
1975/76	28.12	31.90	24.92
1976/77	33.16	40.74	30.80
1977/78	38.79	51.25	37.68
Percentage increase	287.9	252.4	265.5
Masons			
1969/70	10.67	15.25	10.13
1970/71	11.17	15.86	11.00
1971/72	12.00	17.08	11.88
1972/73	12.09	17.84	11.88
1973/74	17.82	20.20	14.12
1974/75	22.68	27.54	17.76
1975/76	28.12	31.86	25.36
1976/77	35.94	40.70	32.31
1977/78	41.38	51.56	39.05
Percentage increase	287.8	238.1	278.8
Unskilled			
1969/70	4.65	5.48	3.00
1970/71	4.75	5.98	3.54
1971/72	5.21	5.53	3.65
1972/73	5.52	5.80	3.80
1973/74	9.20	7.96	4.96
1974/75	11.25	12.41	6.87
1975/76	14.07	15.00	9.68
1976/77	17.34	18.48	11.01
1977/78	17.49	25.17	13.88
Percentage increase	276.1	359.3	362.7

skilled and unskilled labour. It is intriguing that wages have increased in the face of substantial unemployment among the unskilled.

A number of factors have been cited to explain rising real wages in Pakistan. Reservation wages (based on per-capita income) are mentioned by Fahim Khan, and Guisinger and Irfan posit the importance of rural wages. If rural wages are a factor in the rising urban wages, we still would have to find a reason for the rising rural wages. The rising reservation wage, however, can be explained by the rising per-capita income in rural areas resulting from remittances from abroad. Though non-market factors, such as government intervention, have also been used to explain the wage increases, government intervention in wage determination was effective mainly during the 1969–1975 period. Beyond 1975 it could not be the main determinant of wages.

Vocational Training in Pakistan:
A Response to the Shortages

As explained earlier, the manufacturing sector and (to a lesser extent) the construction industry are facing shortages of suitably trained workers. The shortages refer specifically to the absence of appropriate training for unskilled or under-skilled workers who pass for skilled workers. Their training periods, the data show, have been minimal. The PIDE–World Bank study recommended several solutions. It suggested that extensive arrangements were required to accelerate training in order to upgrade the quality of workers. Such training programs would enable them to become skilled mechanics, machine operators, electricians, masons, and carpenters. The study also recommended extensive training programs to meet future manpower requirements in the Middle East without jeopardising domestic production — and to absorb returning unskilled migrants into the domestic market.

Regarding Pakistan's migration policies, the study recommended that some occupational groups be restricted, others be allowed to determine their own migration levels, and still others actually assisted in their migration efforts.

An important policy proposal discussed in the PIDE–World Bank study concerns educational facilities. It appears that high-migration communities will soon be faced with a serious shortage of schools for children. At present there is no reported crisis because of the peculiar demographic profile of migrants: 75 per cent of them are less than 30 years old and 30 per cent are single. But in a few years they may get married and the younger couples will have school-age children. It is shown by survey results that all migrants are keen to educate their children, almost universally in the case of boys and 80 per cent for girls. They also have the resources to back up their desires. Consequently, they will either move to nearby towns with schools or demand schools in their own communities.

The study also suggests an interesting proposal for funding schools in such communities. It shows, on the basis of another anthropological study of migrant families, that migrant families in the rural areas indulge in conspicuous consumption because they generally come from socially lower-caste groups (manual castes). By showing off their newly acquired prosperity, they seek entry to higher social groups. This explains their expenditure on social gatherings, feasts, etc. The study suggests that the channelling of some of this money into contributions for local schools and dispensaries is perhaps possible. It would give the donors social prestige and at the same time channel remittances into a socially productive cause.

The Process of Migration

The following institutions have a part in controlling or regulating the flow of migration from the country:
— the Bureau of Emigration and Overseas Employment,
— the Overseas Employment Corporation,
— the Private Employment Promoters group,
— labour attachés in Pakistan embassies,
— the Overseas Pakistanis Foundation.
The first of these institutions controls the flow of migrants, whereas the fourth looks after the welfare of the migrants in host countries, and the fifth one looks after the welfare of migrants and their families.

The Bureau of Emigration and Overseas Employment was established in 1971 and operates under the Manpower Division of the Ministry of Labour. The Manpower Division is principally responsible for increasing control over overseas employment promoters. It attempts to prevent the exploitation of migrants and to establish a regular, up-to-date flow of data on foreign employment and migration. The bureau has been quite effective in handling these responsibilities, but the procedures remain complicated, leading to exploitation of the emigrants by unscrupulous agencies and individuals.

The Overseas Employment Corporation's general responsibility is to assist Pakistanis in finding jobs abroad. It maintains liaison with foreign employers, and whenever they request labour, the corporation advertises the job openings and selects suitable workers. The corporation also negotiates salaries/wages and their terms and conditions. Workers who migrate through the OEC usually earn much higher salaries and wages and obtain much better terms and conditions than other workers.

The Private Employment Promoters group is a private institution comprising private employment promoters and agencies that arrange jobs for the local workers abroad. Before 1979 a number of unscrupulous promoters exploited prospective migrants, causing serious financial losses and suffering for the migrants. Their abuses became so pervasive that the government was forced intervene. These promoters are now regulated and controlled by the Bureau of Emigration and Overseas Employment. The bureau now requires all private promoters to register with the bureau, and the conditions of registration are stringent enough to keep unscrupulous agents away. The complexity of procedures, however, still permits the migrants' exploitation at the hands of private employment promoters.

The labour attachés in Pakistani embassies look after the welfare of Pakistani workers in the host countries. Their effectiveness is limited by local laws and lack of resources. Inadequacies in the agreements on which migrants come to serve in the host countries often prevents the attachés from taking effective steps.

The Overseas Pakistanis Foundation (OPF) was established to look after the welfare of Pakistani expatriates and their families, both within the country and abroad. Every emigrating worker now has to become a member of the foundation by paying a fee of Rs.550 at the time of emigration. This sum is invested in various welfare and productive projects, the profits of which go toward ensuring the welfare of migrants and their families. Some of these welfare activities include the opening of counters at airports to assist migrants, a transport service from the airport to various rural and urban destinations, aid to widows and children of expatriates in case of death abroad, insurance schemes, housing projects, etc. The OPF also runs schools and training centres for the children of the migrants. It has increased its effectiveness substantially during the last three years, but its impact on the migrant population is still not significant. Only about one-fourth of the overseas Pakistanis are aware of the foundation. Although since 1970 each migrant has had to contribute to the foundation funds, most of the migrants, because they are illiterate, do not know why they are contributing.

The Cost of Migration:
Government Fees/Fund Contribution

The amounts listed below are deposited by the emigrants in the bank under various headings. These are the only official or bona fide payments to be made by emigrants.
— Government adhesive stamps of the value of Rs.10 each are affixed on two copies of the foreign service agreement, and a copy each is given to the migrant and the employer after clearance by the Protectorate of Emigrants.
— The overseas employment promoter deposits a fee of Rs. 25 per worker in the government treasury for stamping agreements in case of group or block visas.
— A fee of Rs. 1450 is deposited in the government treasury for stamping agreements by those who have been given Protectorate of Emigrants clearance under individual or direct visas.
— Every person cleared by the Protector for foreign employment in the public, private, or individual sectors must deposit Rs. 550 toward a welfare fund.

Other Financial Costs

Besides these official payments, the migrants must pay substantial sums in order to find employment through a private recruiting agency. The PIDE–World Bank study estimated that, on average, a migrant spent Rs. 7000 to go abroad (rupee of 1979). For a manual labourer the fee was less, but office jobs commanded fees of around Rs. 18,000-20,000, and this did not include airfare or other travelling expenses. This cost has increased steeply during the last five years. Now no job can obtained from a private recruiting agency for less than Rs.35,000, which again does not include airfare.

Work Conditions Abroad

Most research on the labour migration that is conducted by Pakistan and other labour-exporting countries focuses focuses on the effects of migration on the home economy or society, i.e. on those left behind. Not much interest has been shown in the migrant's adjustment to conditions abroad. A full inquiry into the work conditions of the emigrants abroad would include: (1) a comparison of wages before and after emigration; (2) a comparison of jobs held before and after emigration and the worker 's attitudes about the job he acquired abroad; (3) work and living conditions abroad compared with pre-migration contracts and expectations; (4) job satisfaction and enhancement of the worker's skills through specialised or on-the-job training while abroad; (5) social and psychological problems faced by emigrants (alienation, home-sickness, etc.); and (6) insecurity vis-à-vis employment, repatriation, nonrenewal of contract.

Research on these questions is very weak in Pakistan. Most of the research can be done by surveys and investigations in the host countries. Some such surveys have been planned by a few official agencies, but the results have not been published. Some data have been collected by PIDE–World Bank and PIPO-OPF through surveys within Pakistan. Part of the data is accessible. What follows is based on what limited information is available.

Wage Structures Before and After Migration

As might be expected, there are substantial differences between wages earned at home and abroad. The discrepancy, of course, is what encourages workers to migrate. The calculations made by the PIDE–World Band study regarding wages, however, are not entirely reliable, because very indirect methods were used to determine migrant wages. The information on wages was collected from the migrants' households in Pakistan and therefore reflects guesses rather than facts. No other study has been made on this issue. The collection of statistics, however, will not be a major problem now because the Emigration Bureau is keeping records of contracts of all the emigrants. Wage data can be obtained from these contracts and compared with the domestic wage statistics as published by the Statistics Division.

Jobs Before and After Migration

Data have been collected by PIDE and World Bank, by PIPO and OPF, and by PIPO, but they have not been processed or published. Therefore, no data are readily available. During the PIDE–World Bank study, it was very clear that many emigrants found employment abroad that was completely different from and unrelated to their jobs in Pakistan. Conversions from white-collar to blue-collar jobs were common. Occupational advances were also in evidence in the sense that an unskilled worker was able to find a semiskilled job and a semiskilled worker could acquire a skilled position. A comparison of pre- and post-emigration jobs and how the workers respond to the change is important not only for planning the welfare of the emigrants but also for planning jobs for the returnees. Such a study could be conducted in Pakistan among migrants on home-leave.

The Recruitment Channels and Resulting Work Conditions

Work conditions abroad also depend on how workers were recruited. There are different channels for recruitment. Some emigrants enter the host country illegally and get jobs illegally. Another category comprises emigrants who — after entering either illegally or on a non-work visa — find jobs that provide work visas. A third kind of emigrant obtains jobs through private recruitment agents in the home country. The fourth group consists of those who obtain jobs through a government-sponsored agency, such as the Overseas Employment Corporation. Terms and conditions of the agreements are different (for the same specific job) for each these categories; they improve in the order in which the channels of recruitment were enumerated above. In general, employment contracts will be the worst in the first category and the best in the fourth.

It has been observed that workers emigrate in great numbers through the first and second recruitment channels. An estimated one-third of emigrants get jobs through personal efforts or their friends and relatives abroad, and the bulk of these fall into the first or second recruitment category — the percentage is higher for workers migrating from urban areas. No data are available on the degree of variation among the agreements in these different categories. In fact, none of the studies conducted in Pakistan has focused specifically on this issue. The relevant data, however, can be readily collected. The Emigration Bureau requires that copies of employment agreements be deposited with it. A sample of these agreements could be studied in order to determine the relationship between work conditions and the channel of recruitment.

Contractual and Actual Work Conditions

We may safely observe that, in general, migrant workers do not get what they were promised or what they contracted for at the time of emigration. This is exactly what prompted the government of Pakistan to establish the Protectorate of Emigrants and the Bureau of Emigration.

The PIDE–World Bank study collected substantial information on the issue, particularly from interviews with permanently returned migrants and the emigrants on home-leave. These, have not yet been analysed.

Apparently, there are numerous cases in which the original terms of a contract were abrogated and where workers ended up on jobs that were different from those agreed on during recruitment. More investigation is obviously needed here. Also, little is known about the migrants' work and living conditions abroad compared to those at home. Since most Pakistani migrants are unskilled or semiskilled and are employed in the construction sector, conditions must be difficult. Whether the work conditions are worse than in Pakistan is yet to be determined. The general conclusion of the PIDE–World Bank study was that work conditions are much harder abroad than at home. This needs further investigation. Nevertheless, it should be noted that most workers do get fringe benefits such as housing, utilities, transport, and medical care. This is likely to have provided them better living conditions than most of these workers have in Pakistan.

Job Satisfaction and Enhancement of Skills

This is yet another area that requires research. What skills are migrants learning abroad, and how they can best be utilised in the home country when they return? The data are not sufficient for a competent analysis of the issue. A survey of the migrants returning permanently or on home-leave can help determine skills acquired abroad.

Social and Psychological Problems

The PIPO-OPF study alone included these issues in their investigation. They tried to explore the following:
— the emigrant's outlook on life in general, as well as with respect to income, social relations, health, occupation, and family relations;
— the attitude of overseas employees;
— the attitude of the host-country population;
— perceived social problems on return.
The data and results are yet to be released.

132

Trends in Labour Demand in the Middle East

The growth of demand for labour in the Middle East is slowing down. However, there is no indication that the absolute demand for foreign labour will decline in the Middle East. Such a decline would result in a mass return-inflow into the exporting countries. Alongside these changes in the volume of demand are changes in the composition of demand. A World Bank study (Amena-Ded) forecasts labour demands by occupation in major Middle Eastern countries for the next five years. According to the table, the total demand for expatriate labour in the Middle East will increase 44 per cent from 1980 to 1985. If Pakistan succeeds in maintaining its share in the labour markets of the Middle East, this would mean that the stock of Pakistani workers abroad would continue to increase.

The demand for unskilled labour is slowing down considerably, however, although a decline in the demand may not occur soon. Thus, in view of the trend of the labour demand abroad, a substantial segment of the migrant workforce is in constant fear of repatriation. The trends in demand need to be examined with greater specificity in each labour-exporting country. Besides an overall decline in certain occupations, there are declining trends in the demand for labour from some countries on various grounds such as costly labour, political considerations, etc. No such investigations have been made in Pakistan, though there have been indications that demand for Pakistani labour in some countries is declining.

Earnings Abroad and Home Remittances

One of the main benefits afforded by the labour migration is the migrants' remittances. But, in order to derive the maximum benefits from emigration, measures are required to mobilise maximum remittances and to utilise them optimally. This chapter reviews the research on such efforts in Pakistan to mobilise home remittances.

Formulation of policies to mobilise maximum remittances requires statistics on (1) the income levels of emigrants abroad, (2) the capacity to save abroad and, hence, potential remittances, and (3) actual remittances made and the factors that restrict remittance of savings.

It is also important for the economy that all remittances be received through the official channels. In most South Asian countries, inefficiency and lack of institutional facilities for the remittance of foreign exchange usually force the workers to remit their savings through unofficial channels. In some countries, overvalued foreign exchange creates a black market, so remittances get channelled through the black market instead of through official channels. Remittances that do not pass through the official channels create several problems for the economy, the balance of payments being the major one. The policymakers, therefore, are interested in knowing how much of the remittances do not pass through official channels and what can be done to redirect them. It is therefore necessary to study both the channels of remittances and the reasons (if any) for using other than official channels.

The nature and effectiveness of the policies on remittances will also depend on who receives these remittances and who uses them.

Migrant Savings and Remittances

Only the PIDE-World Bank study has attempted to derive some estimates of the average earnings of emigrants by occupations (see Table 16).

The PIDE-World Bank study also estimated the average expenditure of a labour migrant and subtracted it from his average earnings (see Table 17). According to these figures, emigrants generally save 60 to 70 per cent of their earnings. Since all labour migrants in the Middle East are, almost by definition, temporary emigrants, all of their savings are potential remittances. The figures on average savings shown in Table 17, therefore, also indicate potential remittances by occupation.

It is appropriate to mention again that these figures are based on information obtained from migrants' families, who have no direct information on these matters. Therefore, all inferences should be drawn with caution. The PIDE-World Bank study data collected directly from the migrants remains unprocessed. This data, if available, could be used to study the issue of savings abroad more precisely. No other attempt has been made in Pakistan to generate statistics relating to the incomes of emigrants abroad. The Emigration Bureau's records, which include information on salaries and fringe benefits, will not be very helpful in this respect. Most of the Pakistani labour (almost 85 per cent) is in unskilled and skilled jobs, all of which require substantial overtime work. The amount of overtime done and earnings received from it will obviously not be reflected in the employment contract.

TABLE 16. Average Migrant Earnings by Occupational Group (thousands of rupees per worker)

Unskilled	45.06
Skilled	53.80
Professional	117.60
Service and clerical	60.16
Business	77.92
Miscellaneous	82.50

TABLE 17. Average Income, Expenditure, and Savings, by Occupational Group

	Income (Rs. '000)	Expenditure (Rs. '000)	Savings (Rs. '000)	Savings Propensity
Unskilled	45.06	13.31	31.75	.70
Unskilled	45.06	13.31	31.71	.77
Skilled	53.80	19.44	34.36	.64
Professional	117.60	31.52	86.08	.73
Service and clerical	60.16	20.80	39.36	.65
Business	77.92	28.71	49.21	.63
Miscellaneous	82.50	19.25	63.25	.77

Source: PIDE-World Bank Study.

Information on average earnings abroad is likely to change each year in response to inflation, wage patterns, and occupational-demand composition. These statistics therefore require frequent updating. A simpler way to generate these statistics could be to use the Bureau of Emigration data on wages/salaries adjusted by a factor that converts them to total earnings. The adjustment factor could be obtained from a sample survey of emigrants returning home permanently or on home-leave.

The Level of Remittances and Related Issued

The PIDE–World Bank project conducted an elaborate study of this issue, focusing on the following questions:
— What is the proportion of migrants who send any remittances at all? Are there systematic differences in this behaviour across occupational groups?
— What was the average amount remitted or brought home by a migrant in one year preceding the survey?
— What is the average monetary value of "remittances in kind"? (These may be substituting for cash remittances.)
— What are the causes of significant differences, if any, in remittance behaviour among different types of migrants? Some factors that may cause differences in the average level of remittances are the following:
  (i) *Occupation.* This determines income as well as consumption abroad.
  (ii) *Origins: rural or urban?* This will be a factor if there are regional differences in consumption and saving habits. Even within rural areas, migrants from *barani* (areas that are rain-fed — i.e. almost wholly dependent on rain for irrigation) and irrigated areas may have different consumption/saving habits, and thus may remit differing amounts. The same considerations may require one to consider as well the size of an urban migrant's city.
  (iii) *Education.* This may not only determine the migrants' earnings abroad but may also affect the emigrants' willingness to remit money. Better-educated

emigrants may invest their savings abroad, whereas uneducated emigrants, unaware of investment opportunities, may remit all of their savings.

(iv) *Number of dependents left behind*. Those with fewer dependents left behind may remit less money. Thus, young and unmarried migrants are likely to remit less.

— What is the trend in average remittances? Whether the current average level of remittances will continue in future is an important issue for the cost-benefit analysis. The answer will depend on the behaviour of the various factors that affect remittances.

The PIDE–World Bank analysis of these issues is summarised below.

A total of 972 households were reported to have received some amount as remittances since the migration of a member from their household. This constituted 84.3 per cent of a sample of 1152 migrant households. There were 140 households (12.1 per cent of the sample) that had not received any remittances so far, while there was no information on the remaining 40 respondents. It may be noted that included in the 180 households in the last two categories were those who had been abroad for a year or less. Hence, a flow of remittances can be expected in the future from some of these migrants, because people who have been abroad for less than a year may not yet have had the opportunity of remitting any money home despite their intention of doing so.

Total cash remittances received by a family from the earnings of an emigrant worker comprise money sent through a banking or other channel (R1) and money brought by the migrant on home-leave (R2). Out of the 1152 households in the sample, 881 reported the receipt of a positive amount in the year preceding the survey, while another 108 reported the receipt of no money that year. No information was available on the remaining 163 households. The total amount received by the 881 households in 1979 came to Rs.21,039 million. Excluding the respondents who gave no information on this question, the average amount remitted per migrant worker in the Middle East came to Rs.21,273. (If we take an average for only those who actually sent some money home, the figure comes to Rs.23,880. Note, however, that the sampling problems discussed above may bias both these estimates unless the different errors cancel each other out. Also note that all these figures refer to the year 1979/80.)

Regarding remittances brought by migrants on home-leave, 697 respondents indicated the migrant had visited home. Of the remaining 455 migrants, 313 had not done so, while there was no information on the other 142. A total of Rs.7.77 million was reported to have been brought home by 532 migrants, while another 165 brought no money on the previous visit. Again, the average inflow, excluding the households that did not give information on this issue, came to Rs.7,693. Note, however, that the average amount brought by the people who brought any money at all came to Rs.14,605 per migrant.

In any case, taking these two figures at their face value, an average annual inflow of Rs. 28,966 per migrant in 1979 was arrived at. The most important point that emerged was that a significant part (27 per cent) of the average inflow of emigrant workers' remittance was brought by the migrant himself on a visit. Since a large part of this inflow may not be channelled through the banking system, it is likely that the balance-of-payments statistics substantially under-report the total inflow.

In addition to cash remittances, remittances in kind (R3), such as durable consumer goods, having a total value of Rs.10,336 million were reported to have been sent or brought home by migrant workers in the sample since they went abroad. Taking the average stay of a typical migrant as 3.5 years, and allowing for non-response, an average annual value of Rs.2,637 per migrant was obtained.

The differences in remittance behaviour were examined in the context of the migrants' origins (province and rural or urban) and occupation. The occupation of a worker may influence his remittance behaviour both because it reflects his social background and because it correlates with his income. The social background of the worker is also important for a variety of reasons. Strong kinship bonds impose strong obligations on employed family members and thus encourage savings and remittances. Social status also will affect the rate and magnitude of savings accumulated abroad; those with a higher status and income may have knowledge of and desire investment possibilities in foreign countries, thus reducing the flow of remittances to the home country.

The figures presented in Table 18 indicate that while there are significant differences in average remittances across occupations, there is no significant difference in the proportion of the earnings remitted. The differences in average remittances arise mainly from differences in earnings. Average remittances as a proportion of average earnings are quite similar except perhaps for those in the business sector who appear to be remitting a lower percentage of their earnings.

Another factor that may affect remittance behaviour is the average expenditure of the migrants abroad. Average expenditure will affect not only the average level of remittances but also the relative remittance behaviour of different occupational groups. Table 19 compares savings and remittances of different occupational groups. The pattern of savings is very much in line with the theoretical expectation: The higher-income professions have a greater propensity to save. As for remittances, it is evident that skilled and unskilled workers remit a higher percentage of their savings than professionals and business workers. In general, most of the migrants' savings abroad are being remitted. It must be pointed out that remittances in kind have not been included in the above figures. If that is done, then clearly 80-90 per cent of the savings of a large majority of workers are being sent home. Businessmen and professionals, however, retain 30-40 per cent of their savings in their host country.

TABLE 18. Average Earnings and Remittances of Migrants by Occupational Group

	Earnings (Rs. '000)	Remittances (Rs. '000)	Remittances as % of Earnings
Unskilled	45.06	23.74	53
Skilled	53.80	28.34	53
Professional	117.60	53.68	46
Services and clerical	60.16	33.84	56
Business	72.92	31.94	41
Miscellaneous	82.50	46.10	56

TABLE 19. Average Savings and Remittances by Occupational Group (thousands of rupees)

	Savings	Remittances
Unskilled	31.75	23.74
Skilled	34.36	28.34
Professional	86.08	53.68
Services and clerical	39.36	33.84
Business	49.21	31.94
Miscellaneous	63.25	46.10

TABLE 20. Average Remittances, by Migrants' Place of Origin (thousands of rupees per worker)

	Rural	Urban	Total
Punjab	15.56	25.41	22.54
Sind	5.00	26.11	25.92
NWFP and tribal area	16.14	15.59	15.92
Baluchistan	11.95	15.02	13.94
Azad Kashmir	18.47	18.80	18.54
Pakistan	15.64	23.78	21.27

TABLE 21. Average Remittances, by Occupational Group and Place of Origin (thousands of rupees per worker)

	Unskilled	Skilled	Professional	Service	Clerical	Business	Miscellaneous
Punjab							
Rural	16.10	13.38	8.00	31.00	20.67	12.00	0.00
Urban	19.70	18.68	56.81	21.22	16.50	96.60	17.50
Total	17.92	17.29	51.38	23.03	17.46	91.31	17.50
Sind							
Rural	5.00	0.00	0.00	0.00	0.00	0.00	0.00
Urban	18.20	21.95	32.62	28.50	30.33	85.00	0.00
Total	14.42	21.95	31.96	28.57	30.33	85.00	0.00
NWFP							
Rural	13.65	15.15	31.00	50.00	18.00	27.67	34.00
Urban	10.00	19.83	1.00	8.86	8.33	10.75	0.00
Total	12.62	17.29	21.00	18.00	15.58	18.00	34.00
Baluchistan							
Rural	8.00	15.20	0.00	0.00	0.00	0.00	0.00
Urban	9.72	21.12	0.00	0.00	6.67	0.00	40.00
Total	8.78	19.71	0.00	0.00	12.50	0.00	40.00
Azad Kashmir							
Rural	17.40	20.58	0.00	5.00	12.00	0.00	0.00
Urban	0.00	22.75	0.00	0.00	0.00	3.00	0.00
Total	17.40	21.12	0.00	5.00	12.00	3.00	0.00
Pakistan							
Rural	14.37	14.74	19.50	32.50	19.00	23.75	34.00
Urban	15.91	19.01	38.09	19.70	20.50	69.37	25.00
Total	15.03	18.30	37.01	21.88	20.00	62.86	28.60

Source: PIDE-World Bank Study.

The influence of the migrants' origins on their pattern of remittances was also studied (see Table 20). Urban remittances are on an average considerably higher than rural remittances, perhaps because urban households cannot survive monetary hardships as well as rural households. Another reason could be higher average incomes for urban workers because they constitute a greater proportion of professionals and skilled workers. Thus, the above figures may, in part, reflect the effect of skill composition rather than that of the emigrants' origins. This effect can be assessed by examining the figures for each occupation (see Table 21).

It is evident from these figures that, with a couple of minor exceptions, the conclusions reached earlier remain unchanged. In all occupations and in all provinces, urban remittances are higher than rural remittances. One exception, however, is in the NWFP, where rural remittances exceed urban remittances in all occupations except skilled workers.

A detailed examination of the time trend of remittances should use the analysis of the different influences outlined above. Not all data were processed to assess the trend along these lines. To present the aggregate figures and to suggest some broad trends in the data, the information on remittances was broken down according to the duration of the stay abroad (see Table 22). Although remittances during the first year of migration are clearly lower than the average, there is no significant trend after the first year. The unusually high figure for those who have worked abroad for eight or more years may be due to a few exceptional cases.

TABLE 22. Average Annual Remittances, by Duration of Migrants' Stay Abroad

Duration of Stay (years)	Number of Migrants Surveyed[1]	Annual Remittances (Rs. '000)	
		Total	Per Migrant
Up to 1	146	1765	12.09
1–2	225	4679	20.80
2–4	365	7317	20.05
4–6	116	2582	22.26
6–8	47	969	20.62
More than 8	90	3727	41.41

1. Excludes migrants who sent no remittances, since their inclusion would lower all figures for average remittances.

Source: PIDE-World Bank Study.

Channels of Remittances

Again, only the PIDE–World Bank study has made a major contribution in the area. The results of this study clearly indicate that the bulk of the emigrants (85.5 per cent) used official (banking) channels to send their money home (see Table 23). In fact, if NWFP is excluded, the percentage of other migrants who used the official channel rise to 93.9 per cent.

TABLE 23. Numbers of Migrants Using Various Remittance Channels by Place of Origin

Province	Bank	Hundi[1]	Home-leave	Others	Total
Punjab					
Rural	126	1	0	4	131
Urban	314	8	5	4	332
Total	440	9	5	8	462
Sind					
Rural	0	1	1	0	2
Urban	208	6	2	1	217
Total	208	7	3	1	219
NWFP					
Rural	54	43	9	6	112
Urban	47	24	6	4	81
Total	101	67	15	10	193
Baluchistan					
Rural	19	2	1	0	22
Urban	30	4	6	0	40
Total	49	6	7	0	62
Azad Kashmir					
Rural	18	0	0	1	19
Urban	5	0	0	0	5
Total	23	0	0	1	24
Pakistan					
Rural	217	47	11	11	286
Urban	604	42	19	9	674
Total	821	89	30	20	960

1. Informal bill of exchange.

The major divergence from this picture appears only in the case of NWFP, where 48 per cent of the migrants used channels other than banks to remit money. Of these, 34 per cent used the informal bill of exchange (or *hundi*) for this purpose. The major explanation for this has to do with the existence of a developed foreign exchange market in the tribal areas of NWFP. There are well-developed markets of smuggled foreign goods in these areas, which implies the existence of a demand for foreign exchange by the shopkeepers. Since Pakistan's legal restrictions on smuggled goods are fairly relaxed here, it is quite likely that the major part of the scarcity premium on imported goods is captured by the smugglers. As such, they are in a better position to offer a premium to migrant workers for converting the foreign currency into rupees.

The PIDE–World Bank study argues that the use of informal channels has not spread to other parts of the country mainly because the exchange rate is fairly close to its equilibrium level. This reduces the size of a potential premium which can induce the shift to informal channels. The informal system has established its credibility in the NWFP, but may not yet have done so in the rest of the country. Furthermore, the demand for such "illegal" foreign exchange may be sufficiently limited, rendering unprofitable any expansionary actions on the part of the informal market.

The implication of the informal channels of remittance, together with the large amount brought by migrants on home visits, is that the total foreign exchange inflow is significantly under-reported in the balance-of-payments statistics that refer only the bank figures for this purpose. It is true, however, that the diversion of this money to the illegal market means that it finances an equivalent amount of imports, or of capital outflow. Hence, this under-reporting does not have any implication for the true balance-of-payments constraints, although it may influence the estimates of domestic savings rate, marginal propensity to import, etc. The relative insignificance of this channel also suggests, as mentioned above, that the rupee exchange rate is not very far from equilibrium. If the divergence in domestic and international inflation rates increases the disequilibrium, we may expect the size and activity of this sector to grow.

The Use of Remittances

Although remittances in foreign exchange are a major boon for a country like Pakistan, it is argued that the pattern of use of remittances by the emigrants' families erodes most of the gains from the inflow. A large part of the remittance money is spent on raising current consumption (largely of imported consumer goods) and on unproductive investment such as real estate, homes, and consumer durables. Such expenditures, apart from being inflationary, can be characterised as nonessential, and may therefore have a strong demonstration effect on the consumption of non-migrants as well. This has an initial inflationary impact and is also likely to lead to other social problems, such as frustration among those who were not fortunate enough to migrate. Another aspect of the consumption-oriented use of remittances is the relatively high import content of the consumption demand generated by remitted funds. If this is true, then some of the balance-of-payments gains are offset by the higher import demand. Similarly, since the migration is taking place from relatively

less affluent sections of society, the remittances are expected to bring an improvement in the income distribution. But the beneficial effects on income distribution
may also not be fully realised if a major proportion of migrants do not come from
the lower-income groups and if the consumption and investment patterns generated
by remittances favours the richer classes. For example, the higher demand for real
estate favours the propertied classes by pushing up asset prices.

In the category of consumption, the PIDE–World Bank study included items like
food/fuel, electricity/gas, transport, house rent (or, where the family owns its own
house, its imputed value), clothing/shoes and other household needs. In other words,
normal, recurrent household expenditures have all been included in consumption.
A fairly high proportion of households indicated an increase in expenditure on various
consumption items after the migration of a member of the family (see Table 24).

TABLE 24. Effect of Remittances on Pakistani Migrant Household Expenditures

	Number of Households			
	Increased Expenditure	Decreased Expenditure	No Change	Total
Milk	345	42	488	875
Dry milk	98	4	96	198
Meat	353	49	523	925
Sugar	317	57	568	942
Ghee	331	36	564	931
Tea	283	57	553	893
Eggs	205	35	368	608
Fruit	226	30	431	687
Fuel	217	22	366	605
Cloth	577	55	36	668

Source: PIDE-World Bank Study.

The emigration of a family member should tend to reduce total household consumption (especially since in the Pakistani family structure, adult males consume a
relatively larger proportion of the total). On the other hand, remittances should raise
the consumption of all items. The evidence seems to indicate that the latter is
stronger. The exceptions should be relatively small families in which the proportionate
effect of the migration is larger. This is supported by the fact that the households in
urban Sind (predominantly, the city of Karachi) — which are likely to be smaller
than average because of urbanisation, commercialisation, smaller houses, etc. — have
a significantly higher than average representation of households whose food expenditures decreased. The other issue in this analysis is that of comparing the

consumption propensities of the migrant group and those of the control group. Tables 25 and 26 show the incomes and consumption of migrants and control-group households broken down by rural/urban location and income class (the two major determinants of consumption behaviour). A few minor exceptions apart, the consumption propensities of the migrant group do not appear significantly different from those of the control group. It appears, therefore, that either the general impression that migrant households spend lavishly is not true (at least as far as recurring consumption expenditure is concerned) or that the control group is mimicking the migrants because of the demonstration effect. It should be remembered that lumpy consumption expenditures, such as on marriages, consumer durables, and land, have not been included in the figures reported in Tables 25 and 26 because the time base for such expenditures is different. It is quite possible that the migrant families spend more on such items, especially because these are "prestige goods." Some of these will be analysed later.

We must now determine the proportion of remittances spent on consumption. To arrive at that figure, we need an estimate of the marginal propensity to consume, which can be applied to the increase in migrant families' income due to remittances

TABLE 25. Income and Consumption of Migrant Families

Income Group	No. of Households[1]	Average Income (Rs. '000) y	Average Consumption (Rs. '000) C_1	C_2 [2]	Propensity to Consume $C_2 y$
Rural					
Under 10	30	6.5	13.77	15.98	2.46
10–20	86	14.1	19.25	22.33	1.58
20–40	100	28.0	21.77	25.12	0.90
40–70	38	50.5	24.54	28.10	0.56
70–100	4	78.5	40.03	41.87	0.53
Over 100	6	139.8	37.81	42.61	0.30
Urban					
Under 10	57	6.3	16.76	21.37	3.40
10–20	166	14.2	22.12	25.48	1.80
20–40	205	27.7	25.43	30.80	1.11
40–70	129	51.6	37.65	42.88	0.83
70–100	29	80.8	38.07	44.07	0.54
Over 100	36	166.6	45.90	54.32	0.33

1. The cases for which either consumption or remittances is not reported have been excluded.
2. This includes only recurring consumption expenditure and is equal to C_1 plus average annual expenditure on health and education.

Source: PIDE – World Bank Study.

to get the amount spent on consumption. In order to get an estimate of marginal propensity to consume, we had to estimate the consumption function. This was not done by the PIDE–World Bank Study. In the absence of such a function, nevertheless, we can offer the following crude estimates.

A migrant household's average income without remittances works out to be only Rs.11,338. Average consumption, however, works out to be Rs.27,850. We assume that the household's entire domestic income would have been consumed (i.e. average propensity to consume is unity). The rest of the consumption is, therefore, the amount consumed out of remittances. Thus, it appears that Rs.16, 512 (Rs.27,850– Rs.11,338) out of the average remittance of Rs.28,966 is being consumed, yielding an average of 57 per cent.

A summary of the expenditure on other items as well as savings and investments made by migrant households (as estimated by the PIDE–World Bank study) is shown in Table 27, which shows that 62 per cent of expenditure goes into current consumption, 22 per cent into real estate purchases, 11.5 per cent into real physical investments, and 1.4 per cent into financial investments.

TABLE 26. Income and Consumption of Non-migrant Families

Income Group	No. of Households[1]	Average Income y	Average Consumption (Rs. '000)		Propensity to Consume $C_2 y$
			C_1	C_2 [2]	
Rural					
Under 10	80	5.12	10.63	12.94	2.53
10–20	48	12.41	16.88	19.93	1.60
20–40	26	25.04	22.72	29.16	1.16
40–70	10	48.20	24.63	28.19	.58
70–100	4	63.00	15.73	16.23	.26
Over 100	3	144.33	67.18	70.51	.48
Urban					
Under 10	90	5.11	14.65	17.59	3.44
10–20	86	13.17	17.51	21.12	1.60
20–40	38	28.05	31.64	35.14	1.25
40–70	22	51.50	38.71	44.37	.86
70–100	7	78.00	42.34	46.78	.59
Over 100	6	214.66	65.53	70.61	.33

1. The cases for which either consumption or income are not reported have been excluded.
2. This includes only recurring consumption expenditure and is equal to C_1 plus average annual expenditure on health and education.

Source: PIDE – World Bank Study.

TABLE 27. Uses of Remittances

	Amount (Rs. '000)	%
Consumption	*18,012*	*62.19*
Recurring consumption	16,512	57.00
Weddings	680	2.35
Consumer durables	820	2.84
Real estate	*6280*	*21.68*
Construction/purchase of residence	3516	12.14
Improvements	658	2.27
Commercial	1658	5.72
Agricultural	448	1.55
Investment/savings	*3752*	*12.05*
Agricultural investment	957	3.30
Industrial/commercial investment	2378	8.21
Financial investment/saving	417	1.44
Residual	*922*	*3.18*
Total	28,966	100.00

Source: PIDE-World Bank Study.

The Macro-economic Effects of Remittances

Remittances from migrant workers have a variety of macro-economic effects. We have already discussed the impact of remittances on domestic wage levels, consumption patterns, and the propensity to consume from remitted funds rather than from domestic income. A higher propensity to save remittance income will generate more savings and thus contribute more to the economic development of the country.

Another macro-economic issue is income distribution — i.e., are remittances from abroad making already-rich families more affluent, or are they improving the economic conditions of the people further down the ladder? Also, the demonstration effect of migrant households' consumption patterns throughout Pakistani society must be considered. It is generally believed that the demonstration effect motivates non-migrant families to spend more. If this is true, then remittances will cause savings to decline and will therefore adversely affect Pakistan's economic development. The same demonstration effect described above may also trigger a demand for imported goods, such as electronics and modern domestic gadgets. If this happens, remittances will create balance-of-payments problems, too. Remittances must not only be saved; they must be channelled to productive areas such as investments in profitable ventures for Pakistan's economic development. If remittances are not being used in productive ventures, this may be because they are being managed by those who are not aware of proper investments or are afraid to lose the funds. The fears and hesitations about investment need to be identified so that remedial measures can be taken to render remittances more productive.

The PIDE–World Bank study took great pains to analyse the propensity of migrant households to consume out of remittances and out of domestic income. The propensity to consume out of remittances was estimated to be 0.63, whereas the propensity to consume out of domestic income stood around 0.96. These figures were considered fairly reliable. They were, however, based on three-year-old data, so these consumption patterns need to be reassessed according to current trends. However, if current trends cannot be ascertained, the above figures can be reliably depended upon, as propensities to consume are fairly constant parameters.

As far as assessment of propensities to consume out of remittances is concerned, enough information is available for Pakistan. But no systematic attempt has been made to trace the consequences of the existing propensities to consume in the macro-economic framework, the possibilities to improve the consequences by changing the existing realities, and the policy measures to bring about such change.

Effects of Remittances on Income Distribution and Poverty

S. M. Naseem has commented on the effects of remittances on income distribution and poverty. According to him, the beneficiaries of this profitable avenue (emigration) usually comprise a small group in each village or community with close kinship ties. Such ties are useful in identifying employment and in helping to emigrate. The benefits accruing to the rest of the community, Naseem observes, depend on the extent to which emigrants' remittances help create employment opportunities or social services in the community. Little is known about these important issues. However, Naseem drew some conclusion on the basis of the statistics collected by the Punjab study. According to this study, the remittances per farming household are, on average, more than twice those for landless households. The difference is about 3:1. What is more, the "overseas" emigrants' households among the landless are only 14 per cent, whereas in the remaining combined categories their percentage is twice as high. Naseem has shown that if the ability or propensity to emigrate is highly positively correlated with income, then a rural community is likely to experience worsened income distribution after emigration.

Income distribution depends crucially on the ability of all the different classes to emigrate. Since overseas emigration involves a substantial amount of investment (which is far beyond the capacity of all but an insignificant minority of the rural poor), the profitable avenue of emigration is exploited mostly by the more affluent groups, leading to a deterioration in income distribution. Similar conclusions had already been drawn in the World Bank study conducted in Bangladesh. The

PIDE–World Bank study also identified a similar phenomenon. It noted in the first draft that most of the emigration (and thus receipt of remittances) was taking place in the families with pre-migration incomes above the national average — evidence that remittances are worsening income distribution. The fact, however, is that there is a highly unequal distribution of income in Pakistan: The majority are very, very poor and the remaining few are very, very rich. Most of the very, very poor live in the countryside and have no assets or education or qualifications. Emigration is taking place from among the illiterate rural population who possess no skills at all or only artisan skills (66 per cent of Pakistani emigrants come from rural areas, and 85 per cent are unskilled or have artisan skills like masonry, carpentry, etc.). The emigration, therefore, is providing opportunities for low-income households to improve their lot. The shifts in income distribution caused by migration, therefore, can benefit low-income groups. Although it may be true that emigration requires financial resources, it should not be ignored that the migrating workers are unskilled or semiskilled. Their jobs will become available to the more deprived who were hitherto simply surplus labour.

Second, there is no objective way to compare income distribution after remittances with income distribution before remittances. Remittances have increased the average income level. It will be a mere value judgement to say that the worsening of income distribution has wiped out the benefits of higher income. A better way to evaluate the income-distribution effect would be to compare it with the effect of an alternative transfer payment from abroad (say, that of foreign aid) that would increase the average income level to the same extent. Such a comparison requires formulation of a macro model with home remittances from abroad linked with different endogenous variables in the system.

The Demonstration Effect

All studies inquiring into the consequences of migration in Pakistan have mentioned the demonstration effect. When families receiving remittances raise their consumption levels and improve their standard of living (with modern consumer durables such as television sets, air conditioners, refrigerators, and cars), it induces their neighbours who have no income from abroad to raise their own standard of living. They can do so only by reducing their savings or by borrowing against their future income. Such an increase in the propensity to consume is undesirable for countries like Pakistan which require resources to invest in development projects. The demonstration effect, therefore, not only needs to be measured, but its macro-economic consequences must be assessed.

The PIDE–World Bank study refers to the demonstration effect as one socioeconomic cost of emigration. However, it made no attempt to measure the magnitude of the effect or to trace its macro-economic consequences. Although the Punjab study claims to test the hypotheses that "foreign remittances have transformed the consumption pattern of emigrant families and the consequent demonstration effect has pushed the local non-migrant households in the same direction," no valid evidence has been provided to validate this. The area thus remains open for research. Unless the issue is properly studied, any attempt to determine the macro-economic consequences of the emigration will remain incomplete. The demonstration effect has to be studied not only in regard to consumption but in regard to work effort and productivity. A possible hypothesis is that since it has been demonstrated that it pays to work hard and since the demonstration of higher standards of living by the migrant families induces non-emigrants to spend more, it will induce the latter to work harder in order to earn and consume more.

Trends in the Import of Consumer Goods

No research has been done in this area. Neither the PIDE–World Bank study nor the Punjab study make any reference to this aspect, and S.M. Naseem makes only the following observation:

> A large proportion of remittances is transferred through unofficial channels and through import of certain categories of goods which the emigrants have been allowed to import out of their foreign earnings (e.g., transistors, television sets, other consumer durables, cars, tractors and bus chassis) and which command considerable premium in the open market. This serves to augment the supplies of consumer goods, household durables, buses and tractors — items primarily used for elite or urban consumption and for the adoption of more capital-intensive methods of farming.

This is obviously not enough to determine the extent to which emigration has increased demand for imports and thus put pressure on the balance of payments. Home remittances are considered to provide balance-of-payments benefits to the country, but these benefits will be offset to the extent that the remittances generate additional demand for imported goods. Data are required to determine the proportion of remittances used to finance the imports — a demand created in the first instance by remittances.

The Propensity to Invest Out of Remittances

The PIDE–World Bank study extensively discussed the issue of investment out of remittances; the Punjab study also provided data. The information and statistics are sufficient for a study of the macro-economic consequences of remittances in the investment and development of an economy. An analysis of the macro-economic consequences of these propensities, however, has yet to be undertaken. Without such an analysis, we cannot draw useful policy conclusions for developing institutional structures to channel remittances into appropriate investments.

The PIDE–World Bank study collected data on factors that inhibit migrant investment of saved remittances, but the data have not been analysed. It is likely that the propensity to invest out of remittances is low because there are few opportunities for safe investment, although it appears that investment in real estate is considered to be highly safe. All other savings are thought to be far less secure than real estate. An institutional framework that encourages the small investor to invest and gives him a reasonable degree of security is essential if remittances are to be mobilised for investments that contribute to economic development.

Social, Psychological, and Cultural Aspects of the Labour Migration

Most of the studies on international migration have tried to bypass the social, psychological, and cultural issues and have mainly focused on economic issues. The importance of social, psychological, and cultural issues can hardly be over-emphasised. The impact of migration on values, the behaviour of children (because of a parent's emigration), disorders, and psychological stresses of migrants or their families are as costly to Pakistani society as the loss of output. On the other hand, the migration can bring various economic and social benefits if it promotes favourable changes in various social attitudes such as female education and the participation of women in the labour force. The following major studies conducted in Pakistan have discussed social, psychological, and cultural issues:

1. Ijaz Gilani prepared a paper for UNICEF during the PIDE–World Bank study; her paper addressed the impact of migration women and children.
2. During the PIDE–World Bank study, an anthropological paper was prepared by Faiz Bilqees on a few selected villages.
3. The Punjab report devoted one chapter to social effects and discussed issues relating to family structure, family ties, education, marriages, social status, and changes in work behaviour.
4. The PIPO–OPF study discussed social, psychological, and cultural issues in much greater detail. They included the impact of migration on discipline among children, the impact of emigration on the wives, the dislocation of residence, the impact on decision-making roles of migrants' wives, and the "contentment" of emigrants with life.

The PIDE–World Bank study found that the emigrants' families were more keen to provide their children general education in formal schools. On the other hand, nonmigrant families were inclined to see their children learning some skills either by working at blue-collar jobs or by joining some formal or informal institutions where they could quickly learn some skill such as carpentry, masonry, or welding. The study also indicated that the attitude towards female education was more positive in the emigrant families than in nonmigrant families.

Little information is available on changes in work attitudes. Although there is not any

150

statistical evidence available, it is thought that emigration has softened Pakistani attitudes towards female participation in the workforce. There may be several reasons for this. First, exposure to the rest of the world tends to change one's approach to social issues. Second, the demonstration effect of migrant families' increased consumption is causing nonmigrant families to send their females to work (in order to raise family income). This is particularly happening where there are not enough males in the family. Third and more importantly, the emigration has caused wages to go up very substantially. They rose during the 1970s from Rs.3 per day to Rs.10 per day in real terms (i.e., after accounting for inflation). This is a very steep increase in relation to the previous trends. It is possible that, whereas Rs.3 per day may not be enough incentive for women to leave their household duties, Rs.10 may provide enough incentive. Such attitudinal changes have important consequences for the labour market and hence for the economy of the country; further studies need to be conducted.

Social Mobility and Modernisation

An anthropological study conducted at PIDE as a part of the PIDE–World Bank project provides enough evidence of horizontal as well as vertical social mobility. Similar evidence was also provided by the Punjab report. By spending remittances on the welfare of their locality or community, emigrant families try to acquire a higher social status. The families also have been found to be moving from one village to another in order to change their social status. Evidence of conspicuous consumption and use of modern appliances also indicates a tendency towards modernisation. The exact dimensions of this attitude, particularly towards such aspects as have socioeconomic consequences, are yet to be studied.

Pakistan does not have an agency or institution to deal with social problems arising out of the migration, although, to some extent, OPF is taking care of some social problems of emigrants and their families at the micro level.

Returning Migrants

The labour migration to the Middle East is not permanent. The workers going to these countries are not given an immigrant status, and the workers do not sever their links with the home country. The PIDE–World Bank study showed that of the 70 per cent of the emigrants who are married, 66 per cent leave their families behind, indicating their intention to return at some stage. But even for those who would like to stay on permanently in the host country, it may not possibly because of shifting demand conditions abroad.

The return of the migrants requires attention, at the macro level, on several grounds. First, their emigration brought certain benefits to the economy, particularly the remittances of the foreign exchange and relief to the labour market. Return of the migrants would eliminate these benefits, and the economy will have to adjust accordingly. Second, the returning migrants have experienced higher wages and a different work environment. They may face problems in adjusting to the domestic market. The intensity of problems will increase with the increase in the number of returning migrants.

The PIDE study on returnees is the only research available in Pakistan that has focused on the return flow of migrants. It used an indirect method to determine the number of persons who have so far returned permanently after working in the Middle East from information gathered in the two surveys conducted by the PIDE-World Bank study. Although the surveys were not designed to elicit this particular information, they did contain some useful information.

The total figure for permanently returned Pakistani migrants was estimated to be only 42,000, however, which appears to be far too low if the return flow is estimated on the basis of the annual outflow and the likely duration of employment.

The figure of 42,000 refers to the total number of persons who (up to 1980) had returned permanently after working in the Middle East. For policy purposes, a more relevant variable, perhaps, would be the annual number of returnees. The annual number will obviously depend on the total stock of Pakistani emigrants in the Middle East and the annual outflow. As the stock increases, the annual return flow will also increase.

The effects of labour inflow will mainly depend on the rate of inflow in relation to the rate of outflow of workers. Unfortunately, a reliable time series for the outflow of labour is not available. The annual inflow according to the PIDE study was 21,672 for 1979/80. The study put the figure for the outflow in 1979/80 at 300,000. According to the Bureau of Emigration, around 200,000 workers left for the Middle East in 1979/80. The annual inflow is, therefore, somewhere between 10 per cent and 7 per cent of the annual outflow of the workers. Some unofficial reports, on the other hand, recently claimed that as many as 100,000 workers are returning annually. A study to assess the annual inflow is urgently required.

The current rate of return as estimated in the previous section comes out to be a quite insignificant part (1.7 per cent) of the total stock of the emigrants abroad and about 7-10 per cent of the annual outflow. One reason for this may be that the migration is a recent phenomenon and workers have not yet started coming back. Thus, the natural rate of return may increase as the migrants' own time-profile for anticipated return approaches maturity.

The time-profile of the migrants' anticipated return needs to be determined in order plan for the absorption of returning migrants. This will require a suitably designed survey of the migrants. From the survey of migrant workers who have returned thus far it was found that only 9 per cent returned of their own accord after having fulfilled the objective for which they had migrated. Another 31 per cent returned because of various domestic reasons. Even if we count this as a second category of "voluntary" returnees, a large majority of them returned because they could not manage to stay abroad. These may be of two kinds: (a) illegal migrants, and (b) those who could not extend their contracts (or seek new contracts) owing to labour-market conditions.

Illegal migrants are obviously in a very vulnerable position. The possibility of their deportation by the host countries always exists. Unfortunately, illegal migrants constitute that segment of the migrant population about which there is the least amount of information. There is absolutely no estimate of the number of illegal migrants in the Middle Eastern countries, and one has to rely on a rough estimate. One such estimate occurs in the PIDE study on returnees and was based information about the mode of transportation used by the migrants on their first journey to the Middle East. This information indicated that 4.4 per cent of the total emigrants journeyed illegally by see. They were quite likely to be illegal emigrants. The percentage implies that there are 55,000 illegal Pakistani workers in the Middle East.

Another bit of information from the PIDE–World Bank study that points to the extent of illegal emigration from Pakistan is the proportion of emigrants who were unemployed for some time after their arrival in the Middle East. These emigrants obviously had made no work arrangement before entering the host country and hence could not have work visas. Such emigrants constitute about 25 per cent of the migrant population — about 300,000 emigrants. Not all of these, however, continue as illegal residents. Many originally arrive on visit or pilgrim visas but soon find work and are eventually regularised. If we assume that half of the migrants succeed in regularising the terms of their stay, then perhaps there are around 150,000 illegal Pakistani migrants in the Middle East.

The Rate of Return Due to Changes in Demand Abroad

The growth of demand for labour in the Middle East is slowing down as compared to its momentum during the second half of the 1970s. However, there is no indication that the absolute demand for foreign labour in the region will decline, resulting in a mass return flow into the labour-supplying countries. However, the *composition* of demand is changing. The World Bank's forecast of labour demand by occupation in major Middle East countries for the next five years was discussed earlier in this chapter. According to this study, the total demand for expatriate labour in the Middle East will increase by 44 per cent from 1980 to 1985. If Pakistan succeeds in maintaining its share in the labour markets of the Middle East, the stock of its migrant workers will continue to increase.

The demand for unskilled labour is slowing considerably. Even though a decline in demand may not occur in the near future, the return of unskilled labour is inevitable. In view of the trends, no mass returns in response to simple changes in demand were foreseen by the PIDE study.

We should also note the opinion of some researchers that demand for Pakistani labour in the Middle East has fallen because of the availability of cheaper labour from other countries. No study has been conducted in this context in Pakistan. A study of the wage structure for migrant workers in the Middle East — broken down by nationality — needs to be conducted.

Issues Related to the Migrants' Return

The types of work performed by Pakistani emigrants in the major Middle Eastern countries are shown in Table 28. In order to identify the problem areas, this occupational profile has to be compared with the demand conditions in the domestic labour market. In this regard, the PIDE–World Bank study found evidence of excess demand in the case of skilled labour, whereas there was no evidence of excess demand in the case of unskilled labour and clerical workers. If unskilled and clerical workers return, they may find it difficult to get a job in their occupations.

In the presence of excess demand, the skilled labour, theoretically, should not face any employment problems. However, the return of migrants will put a downward pressure on the wages of the workers in their respective categories. If the wages are not flexible downwards (which is quite likely to be the case), then the skilled persons may also face unemployment problems.

Another relevant item of information in this regard is the regional background of the migrants. About 60 per cent of the migrants are from rural areas. If they decide to return to the rural areas, their absorption, in a sense, may not be problematic. The agricultural sector is characterized by an institutional arrangement whereby surplus labour can be absorbed so as to avoid open unemployment. This absorption saves workers from many social problems, but from a national point of view it cannot be considered fully productive. Moreover, the rural migrants may not all like to return to the agricultural professions. On the other hand, some of the returnees may not enter the labour market, as they may like to go into business. Thus, the problem of the absorption of returnees depends on the type of work they intend to do. The PIPO-OPF study provided further details, which are given below.

TABLE 28. Distribution of Emigrants by Occupation

	%	Number[1]
Doctors	0.6	7500
Engineers	2.8	35,000
Accountants	1.1	13,750
Teachers/professors	0.7	8750
Bank officers	0.5	6250
Executives/managers	0.4	5000
Salesmen	0.6	7500
Businessmen and shopkeepers	2.6	32,500
Typists and clerks	2.5	31,250
Storekeepers/supervisors	0.8	10,000
Telephone operators	0.5	6250
Miscellaneous white-collar	2.4	30,000
Carpenters	4.1	51,250
Masons	3.2	40,000
Plumbers	0.4	5000
Electricians	3.8	47,500
Painters	1.0	12,500
Steel binders and fixers	0.8	10,000
Mechanics	6.3	78,750
Machine operators	2.1	26,250
Welders	2.2	27,500
Denters	0.7	8750
Laboratory technicians	0.6	7500
Air-conditioner mechanics	0.5	6250
Miscellaneous blue-collar	2.0	25,000

1. Assuming a total stock of 1.25 million emigrants.

Source: PIDE-World Bank Study.

Pre- and Post-migration Employment

The occupational demands of the returning migrants (see Table 29) are obviously entirely different from their occupational composition abroad. As mentioned earlier, about 43 per cent of Pakistani workers abroad are engaged in unskilled labour, but only 8 per cent seek unskilled jobs upon their return to Pakistan. Only about half of the returnee migrants are able to find gainful employment immediately. Some find employment after a year or so, but a significant number of the returnees remain unemployed for much longer periods of time. Almost 30 per cent are unable to find employment even two years after their return.

The problem of persistent unemployment seems to be more acute in Mirpur and Kohat districts. Most of the unemployed returnees are willing to go out of their localities in search of a job. However, 20 per cent express a preference for jobs in

TABLE 29. Returning Migrants' Occupational Demands

	% Seeking Work	Total Number of Jobs Required[1]
Unskilled	8.1	1700
Skilled	37.1	7790
Construction (mason, carpenter, electrician, plumber, etc.)	(13.1)	(2730)
Industrial (mechanic, welder, machine-operator, steel fixer, etc.)	(10.0)	(2100)
Other (drivers, tailors, barbers, service, etc.)	(14.1)	(2960)
Clerical	5.3	1110
Business	29.5	6195
Agriculture	12.4	3603
Professional	7.6	1600
Total	100.0	21,000

1. Based on current annual level at 21,000 returnees.

Source: PIDE-World Bank Study.

their own neighbourhoods. This ratio is particularly high in Mirpur. Perhaps the returnees are now too old and they have stayed away for too long to want to do it again.

It appears that more than half of those who remained temperarily unemployed did not actively seek a job during that period. The most frequent reasons for this were: no desire to work (45 per cent), and physical or mental illness (33 per cent). The most frequently mentioned problems faced by the returnee migrant in seeking employment are: shortage of capital to start self-employment business (15 per cent); lack of ability or training to start a new business (11 per cent); disorientation from work (8 per cent); finding it hard to make a living through legal means (8 per cent); and inflation (6 per cent). Half of those who had remained unemployed (55 per cent), however, said their unemployment was not related to any specific problems. Those who continued to be unemployed mentioned shortage of capital (22 per cent), lack of education (9 per cent), ill-health (12 per cent), and being short of proper references (4 per cent). Again, half the respondents attributed their unemployment to lack of effort on their part or other miscellaneous reasons.

Shortage of capital and ill-health are mentioned as the principal problems faced by the unemployed returnees. At the same time, their responses do not indicate a situation of helplessness. Half of them feel they have still not made a genuine enough effort and do not blame anyone else for their present state. Nor do we trace a sense of cynicism shown by the fact that only 4 per cent attribute their unemployment to lack of proper references.

Those returnees who are employed wish to continue with their present jobs, except for a few (12 per cent) who plan to change their economic activity over the next year. Members of this group are possibly dynamic and want to improve their economic position by going into business or enlarging their current enterprises.

Even though the returnees were not very explicit in expressing disappointment at the steep decline in their earnings upon their return, it is indeed true that they want much higher incomes than they are enjoying today. When asked to mention a desired income, the figures were at least four times their current incomes, or nearly equivalent to what they were earning abroad. The difference between actual and desired income given by the general population was much smaller than the one given by the returnees. This shows the latters' dissatisfaction with their current incomes.

About 42 per cent of the returnees expressed their intention to go into business or the agricultural sector. For these people, the employment problem does not appear to be serious. Business is usually a self-employed occupation, and traditional agriculture has institutional arrangements that can absorb surplus labour. Certainly, this kind of absorption is not fully productive, but the arrangements do help to relieve the immediate pressure on the employment situation. It may also be mentioned here that the return of migrants to agriculture at the present rate will not seriously aggravate the problem of disguised unemployment in the agricultural sector and, therefore, does not require separate policy measures.

The absorption of professionals such as engineers and doctors will also pose no problem, first, because they are in short supply in the country and, second, because they do not form a large proportion of the emigrants.

TABLE 30. Employment Status of Returnees by Occupation (percentages)

	Returnees Doing Job (1)	Returnees Seeking Job (2)	Col. 1 as % of Col. 2
Professional	6.2	1.4	22.5
Skilled and semiskilled	23.1	13.8	59.5
Clerical	2.4	2.9	120.8
Unskilled	6.7	2.4	36.0
Business	21.9	7.6	34.7
Agriculture	12.7	28.1	38.6

As mentioned already, skilled workers are also in excess demand and hence should be able to find jobs easily. This, however, assumes downward flexibility of wages, which does not seem to be very realistic. If wages are not flexible, then the skilled workers will also face difficulties in finding jobs. The information on the employment status of the returnees lends support to this hypothesis (see Table 30).

The small percentage of the professionals looking for jobs constitutes only "search unemployment," which is not serious. However, the unemployment of skilled and semiskilled workers is puzzling because there are no indications of excess domestic supply in these occupations. This cannot all be considered as "search unemployment," as the proportion of those unemployed is quite large (60 per cent).

Unemployment History of Returnees

It can be seen in Table 31 that returnees remained unemployed for considerably long periods after their return. This lends support to the hypothesis that wages in these categories are rigid downward. Thus, unskilled, skilled, and clerical workers will have to be provided jobs. These groups comprise 50 per cent of the returnees.

TABLE 31. Returnees' Job Searches (percentages)

Job-Search Period	Construction	Other	Total Skilled and Semiskilled
Less than 6 months	25.0	38.5	33.3
6 months to 1 year	37.5	23.1	38.6
More than 1 year	37.5	38.4	38.1
Total	100.0	100.0	100.0

Post-migration Standards of Living

Families of migrants receive substantial remittances. When the migrants return, even if they find suitable work, their income cannot ensure their families the same standard of living. Domestic wages/incomes in different occupations are compared with wages earned abroad by Pakistani migrants in Table 32.

Except for skilled and professional workers, all other workers normally earn only about 30 per cent of what they remitted from abroad. Skilled labour and professionals would be in a little better position, but they still will be earning only 44 per cent, respectively, of their remittances. Thus, after allowing for the returnees' personal expenses, very little would remain for their families as compared to

TABLE 32. Comparison of Annual Domestic and Remittance Incomes by Occupation

	Domestic Wages/Income (Rs.)	Cash Remittances (Rs.)	Domestic Income as % of Remittances
Unskilled	4700	15,035	32
Skilled	8000	18,301	44
Service	6500	21,978	30
Clerical	6300	20,000	31
Professional	14,500	38,014	38

what was remitted from abroad. We must, however, allow for the possibility of savings out of remittances. If the propensity to save out of remittances is quite high, then the families of the returning migrants may be able to maintain a standard of living closer to their old standard simply by cutting down their savings. Unfortunately, however, the propensity to save out of remittances is not very high for most occupations (see Table 33).

It is evident from the data given in tables 32 and 33 that even if the returnees spend their entire income from domestic jobs on consumption, the level of consumption of their families will be about 50 to 60 per cent of their previous levels in most cases. The unskilled workers will be even worse off, while the professionals will be slightly better off. Failure to earn an income that is enough to maintain their standard of living is likely to be quite frustrating. This may also be one reason for their unemployment on their return, as they will be looking for better emoluments.

TABLE 33. Comparison of Annual Domestic Wages/Incomes with Consumption out of Remittances

	Domestic Wages/ Incomes (Rs.)	Remittances (Rs.)	Propensity to Consume out of Remittances	Consumption out of Remittances (Rs.)	Domestic Income as % of Remittance Consumption
Unskilled	4700	15,035	0.8	12,028	39
Skilled	8000	18,301	0.7	12,811	62
Service	6500	21,978	0.6	13,187	50
Clerical	6300	20,000	0.6	12,000	52
Professional	14,500	38,014	0.5	19,007	76

Source: PIPO-OPF report on returning migrants.

Appendix. A Note on the Research Done in Pakistan on the Labour Migration to the Arab Countries

Migration from Pakistan to the Middle East is a recent phenomenon, dating from the mid-1970s. The research in the field is therefore quite limited. It was only around 1980 that the issue was recognised and efforts were made to study it. Since then two types of studies have been conducted.

The first has concentrated on collecting facts and providing primary data by conducting field surveys. Four main agencies have conducted such surveys:
— the Pakistan Institute of Development Economics,
— the Pakistan Institute of Public Opinion,
— the Punjab Economic Research Institute, and
— the Overseas Pakistanis Foundation.
These agencies have published most of the results of their surveys. Though their reports have also made some analyses, they generally serve as data sources for further analysis and research. Besides these, the Bureau of Emigration also maintains and publishes statistics on the basis of the registration of emigrants with them. This registration was made mandatory in 1979. The census conducted in 1981 is another source of statistics on the total number of emigrants abroad.

The other type of research has concentrated on analysing the problems and issues related to migration to the Middle East. These studies did not generate their own data and instead depended for their research on the data generated by the agencies mentioned above.

ILO-ARTEP also organised a seminar on recruitment procedures. The participants from South Asian countries presented papers in the seminar. The country paper from Pakistan made useful contributions to the literature.

A brief description of the objectives and scope of these studies, along with the methodology adopted by them is given below:

1.   The PIDE–World Bank Study. This study was conducted at the Pakistan Institute of Development Economics and was sponsored by the World Bank. The author of this chapter was also a principal member of the team responsible for this study. The main objective of the study was to estimate costs and benefits of emigration and to identify productive and non-productive used of the remittances. Because of insufficient data, the members decided to collect original data on the socio-economic aspects of emigrants working abroad, their families left behind, and permanently returned emigrants.

Five sample surveys were designed to collect the data. Elaborate sample designs were prepared for these surveys, which were unique in the sense that they provided a selection of nationally representative samples in the absence of any statistical frame. The following samples were selected:

— A sample of 12,500 emigrants: The interviews of these emigrants were conducted at the airport at the time of departure. This list of 12,500 addresses also served as a frame to select a sample of families left behind for detailed inquiry.
— A sample of 2500 families was selected from this list. This sample was considered to constitute a nationwide probability sample for the purpose of drawing inferences.
— Another sample was selected of about 1100 households in which there was at least one permanently returned migrant from the Middle East (irrespective of the time of his return).
— A sample of 600 non-migrant households was also selected. This group was selected to serve as a control group so that behavioural deviations in migrant families could be identified.
— Another sample of returning migrants was obtained by meeting them at the airport at the time of their arrival in the country. This was done to get most recent trends in the returning migrants' behaviour.

A report in three volumes (based on part of the data) prepared by the three senior members of the team — namely, Ijaz Gillani, M. Fahim Khan, and Munawar Iqbal — was published by the Pakistan Institute of Development Economics and the World Bank and entitled *Labour Migration from Pakistan to the Middle East and Its Impact on the Domestic Economy.* The report analysed the data collected from the first three samples mentioned above. The first volume of these reports presented and analysed statistics relating to various issues such as the volume of the migration, its occupational composition, its impact on the domestic labour market, wages and output, remittances and their uses, etc. The second volume tried to conduct a cost-benefit analysis in a simplified framework. Owing to the time constraints, elaborate exercises on cost-benefit analysis could not be done; this is one of the areas where further analysis is needed. The third volume described in detail the methodology of sampling employed during this study.

Another study was later conducted at PIDE by M. Fahim Khan and Munawar Iqbal using the survey results for the sample of 1100 households with at least one permanently returned migrant. Their study was entitled *Economic Implications of the Return Flow of Emigrants from the Middle East.* They focused on estimating the total number of returned migrants and the annual rate of inflow and also highlighted main problems and issues arising out of their return.

The information collected from the airport survey remains completely unprocessed and unanalysed. The information in the questionnaire can provide answers to several questions relating to returning migrants, such as regional composition of the migration, its occupational composition, the duration of the migrants' stay abroad, the reasons for their return, and their return plans.

Even from questionnaires for the first three samples, which have already been elaborately analysed by Ijaz Gillani et al., there is still scope for further analysis. Some aspects requiring further analysis are:
— social and psychological changes brought about by the emigration, such as social mobility, attitudes towards female education and employment, attitudes towards cultural and social norms;
— impact on women and children left behind, particularly the education and training of children;
— macro-economic effects of emigration and remittances received.

2. The Pakistan Institute of Public Opinion (PIPO) conducts periodical opinion surveys based on statistically selected nationwide samples. In these surveys various socioeconomic facts are also collected. In some of their surveys, PIPO included questions relating to emigration and return of migrants. Being derived from nation-wide surveys, based on scientifically selected samples, their statistics are highly reliable for the purpose of drawing inferences. Most of their data, however, have not been analysed and are lying in raw form on the computer tapes. The only information that they have processed and published concerns the total number of Pakistani migrants in the Middle East.

3. The Punjab Economic Research Institute conducted an elaborate study on the utilisation pattern of emigrants' remittances and their socioeconomic impact on rural Punjab. The study generated original data regarding the uses of remittances by conducting sample surveys in selected rural areas of Punjab. The study also tried to generate a time series of statistics regarding the amounts of remittances received. The researchers, however, took a case-study approach.

A total of 362 emigrant respondents and 242 family respondents were surveyed. The report covered the utilisation and pattern of remittances and the socio-economic changes consequent to remittances.

On the basis of secondary data, analyses have also been made on the size of migration and potential migration, skill composition of emigrants, regional distribution of emigrants, destination of emigrants, and wage structure.

4. The Overseas Pakistanis Foundation (OPF) is a semigovernmental institution looking after the interests and the welfare of migrants, their families left behind, and the returning migrants. The foundation hired PIPO to conduct research to identify the areas where the OPF can contribute to the welfare of migrants. PIPO has recently completed this study. They conducted fresh surveys in the form of case studies of selected villages from the areas where there was concentration of migrants' families. These surveys were conducted to get a basis for making policy recommendations for OPF. The three main reports prepared by PIPO for OPF related to (1) overseas Pakistanis: profile, problems, plans, and proposals; (2) those left behind:

a study of families left behind by overseas Pakistanis; and (3) returnees: a case study of Pakistani workers returning from overseas. These reports are not available for circulation.

5.   The Bureau of Emigration is the only official agency that maintains regular data on emigration since 1972. Up to 1979 its coverage was very limited, and hence the statistics were inadequate and incomplete. It was only in 1979 that it was made mandatory for all the emigrants to obtain clearance from the Protector of Emigrants of the bureau. The registrations with the Protector's office are then processed, and the statistics thus obtained are published regularly by the bureau. The publication is entitled *Emigration Statistics of Pakistani Manpower* and is issued yearly but includes monthly statistics also. The data provided by the bureau's publications are limited in scope, as they provides only occupation, country, and month/year breakdowns of migration. Besides compiling the figures of bureau-registered emigrants, the bureau carried out an exercise with the assistance of diplomatic missions abroad to determine the total number of Pakistanis living/working abroad. These figures are also included in the publication mentioned above.

6.   The 1981 census of Pakistan included a question designed to determine the number of emigrants who migrated during the period when the exodus to the Middle East started.

7.   The book *Under-development, Poverty and Inequality in Pakistan*, by S. M. Naseem, included a brief analysis of the problem of overseas migration from Pakistan and its impact on the economy. It was based on data collected by the Punjab Economic Research Institute, the Bureau of Emigration, and the PIDE-World Bank study. The book discussed the following aspects of the problem of overseas migration: (a) occupational and skill composition of Pakistani emigrants; (b) brain drain and human-resource development; (c) education and manpower policies affecting the brain drain; and (d) the effect of overseas migration on Pakistan's economy, including the effects on income distribution. The book was published by Vanguard Publications, Ltd., Lahore.

8.   The ILO-ARTEP report "Employment and Structural Changes in Pakistan — Issues for the Eighties" was prepared for the Pakistan Planning Commission in preparation for the sixth plan for the economy. The report discussed in detail the emigration and related issues in the context of its impact on the labour market and its implications for the anticipated employment strategy for the sixth plan. The main data source for issues relating to emigration was the PIDE–World Bank study.

9.   The ILO working paper "Emigration of Scarce Skills," by Mansoor Ahmed, presented its analysis of the emigration problem from the viewpoint of employment issues. Apart from reworking some of the existing data, Mansoor Ahmed directed several specially designed surveys for this study in Islamabad and nearby rural towns.

The reliability of these survey results is limited, as Islamabad and the nearby rural towns are not representative of national behaviour. The paper of May 1982 is available from the International Migration for Employment Branch of ILO, Geneva.

10. Two papers presented at seminars organised by ILO/ARTEP/ARPLA in collaboration with the government of Pakistan have made useful contributions to the research on emigration: "External Migration of Labour from Pakistan (Overseas Employment Issues)," by Zulekha Zar, which explains the recruitment procedures and other processes through which migrants must pass before emigrating, and "Repatriation and Self-employment," by Syed Iqbal Imam, director-general of the Overseas Pakistanis Foundation, which analyses the prospects of generating self-employed business activities for the returning migrants as a measure of their gainful absorption in society. The analysis was done in light of the studies conducted by PIPO for the foundation. A paper by Muhammad Akbar (which has also been published in the Proceedings of the Symposium on Recruitment Procedures) highlighted the malpractices in the recruitment procedures and how they should be addressed.

References

Ijaz Gillani, M. Fahim Khan, and Munawar Iqbal, "Labour Migration from Pakistan to the Middle East and Its Impact on the Domestic Economy," Research Report Series nos. 126, 127, and 128 (Islamabad: Pakistan Institute of Development Economics, 1981).

M. Fahim Khan and Munawar Iqbal, "Economic Implications of the Return Flow of Emigrants from the Middle East," Research Report Series no. 132 (Pakistan Institute of Development Economics, 1981).

Habibur Rehman, "Utilization Patterns of Emigrants' Remittances and Their Socio-economic Impact on Rural Punjab," publication no. 185 (Lahore: Punjab Economic Research Institute, 1981).

"Emigration for Employment," Report of ARPLA Symposium on Overseas Recruitment Procedures for Senior Officials of South Asian Countries, Islamabad, May 1981.

"Emigration of Scarce Skills," working paper, International Migration for Employment, (Geneva: ILO).

M. Akbar, "Country Paper: Pakistan" in Report on ARPLA Symposium.

Zulekha Zar, "External Migration of Labour and Self-Employment: Overseas Employment Issues." Paper presented at ARPLA Symposium, May 1981, Islamabad.

Syed Iqbal Iman "Repatriation and Self-Employment." Paper presented at the Self-Employment Seminar, Islamabad, April 1983.

S. M. Naseem, "Underdevelopment, Poverty and Inequality in Pakistan" (Lahore: Vanguard Publications Ltd., 1981).

Bureau of Emigration, "Emigration Statistics of Pakistan Manpower" (Islamabad).

PIPO-OPF, "Left Behind or Left Out," Migration Report no. 1 (Islamabad: Pakistan Institute of Public Opinion, 1983).

PIPO-OPF, "Returnee Migrants," Migration Report no. 2.

PIPO-OPF, "Overseas Migrants," Migration Report no. 3.

PIPO-OPF, "The Affluent Villages," Migration Report no. 4.

A. R. Kamal and M. Irfan, "Employment and Manpower Projections for the Sixth-Plan Period." Paper presented at the ARTEP/PIDE Seminar "Employment and Structural Changes in Pakistan's Economy," April 1983, Islamabad.

M. Fahim Khan, "A Study into the Cause of Fluctuations in Real Wages in the Labour-Surplus Economy of Pakistan," Ph. D. diss. (Boston: Boston University, 1978).

SRI LANKA

Godfrey Gunatilleke

International migration of Sri Lankans for employment abroad, on a significant scale, has been a relatively recent phenomenon. In the pre-independence period, a small number of Sri Lankans migrated to different parts of the British Empire. Of these outflows, the migration to the Malay Peninsula for employment in government was fairly significant. Others migrated to undertake business and trade in Singapore and Hong Kong, where they established enterprises in the gem trade that have continued to this day.

The outflow of Sri Lankans for employment abroad first reached significant proportions in the late 1960s and early 1970s That migration consisted almost exclusively of professionals and included doctors, engineers, and accountants. They initially found employment in the United Kingdom, Western Europe, Australia, New Zealand, Canada, and the United States. A considerable Sri Lankan migration to East and West African countries followed and included school teachers, university lecturers, and scientific personnel. The emigration of Sri Lankans from 1970 to 1976 resulted in a severe depletion of the country's stock of professionally qualified manpower. The largest single category of such emigrants was that of medical practitioners, followed by engineers, accountants, and teachers. It has been estimated that the labour migration during this period accounted for more than 15 per cent of the total number of doctors and engineers in the country. The United Kingdom absorbed the largest proportion of this outflow, although exodus to the developing countries was also quite substantial, accounting for about one-third of the total migration for this period. The latter stream of migration, however, was in many respects different from the former, since migrants to the developed countries most often migrated with the intention of permanent settlement, whereas the migrants to developing countries sought only temporary employment abroad and an eventual return to Sri Lanka. The of the composition of the two streams was also significantly different. A larger proportion of doctors migrated to the developed countries, while the outflow to the developing countries consisted mainly of accountants and engineers.

The low professional salaries in Sri Lanka and the very wide differentials between these and what was offered in the international market were perhaps the principal incentives for the migration of these professionals. Besides, the opportunities and the facilities available for high-level research in developed countries was an added attraction to some of them. But apart from the pull of external factors, there were several internal changes in Sri Lanka during the period 1956–1977 that appear to have contributed to the migration. The introduction of Sinhala as Sri Lanka's official language and the displacement of English from the predominant position it held during the colonial era was one such change. Some of the English-educated elite in every community found it difficult to adjust to the new conditions. The Tamil community, in particular, regarded the language legislation as a serious act of discrimination that placed them at a disadvantage in gaining employment in public service, as well as in obtaining access to higher education. Meanwhile, in the 1960s, the country began to face increasingly grave economic problems. The economy was not expanding fast enough to provide jobs for the rapidly increasing workforce, including the graduates of universities and professional institutions. The constrains imposed on the budget prevented the expansion of public-service cadres in health and construction, and as a result, in the early 1970s, even engineers and doctors were faced with the prospect of unemployment. At the same time, in an effort to manage a steadily worsening balance of payments, Sri Lanka introduced a strict regime of import and exchange controls. The impact was most severe on the living conditions of the elite. All these problems combined to create disincentives that reinforced the motivation among professionals to migrate.

The Sri Lankan government was seriously concerned about the sizeable drain on professional talent which was resulting in a shortage of personnel to meet the country's development needs. As a first response, the government implemented policies designed to restrict the exodus. It introduced legislation requiring compulsory service for some of the professional grades, such as doctors and engineers, whose training was borne by the state educational system. These measures, however, were not effective. In the mid-1970s the government introduced a more liberal set of measures which increased the incentives to professionals by permitting them both to proceed abroad for employment for a stipulated period of leave and to return to their former occupations without loss of either seniority or advancement prospects. These policies, too, have not been altogether successful in stemming the outflow of professionally trained personnel. There is some evidence, however, that there is a freer return flow than previously.

The Sri Lankan migration to the Middle East which commenced in the mid-1970s was an entirely different phenomenon from earlier outflows. The temporary nature of the migration has been more strictly regulated by the host countries than was the case in previous migrations. There is little if any prospect of permanent settlement in the labour-importing countries. The composition of skills and income groupings also has been very different. Whereas the main beneficiaries of the migration in the earlier phase were the professional elite, the large proportion of the migrants to the Middle East come from low-income groups, particularly those engaged in skilled and unskilled manual occupations. The withdrawal of considerable numbers of migrants from this segment of the workforce has had the immediate effect of reducing the rate of unemployment, which in the mid-1970s was exceptionally high in Sri Lanka.

Unlike past migrant flows, the Middle East migration has contributed substantially to the country's balance of payments through the remittances of workers. At the same time, the benefits brought by the migration have been accompanied by various other, adverse developments. Shortages of labour and rising wages and costs in particular segments of the labour market — as in the case of construction labour — have had mixed results. The regular turnover of migrant employment, while it has its advantages, creates special problems of re-entry and re-absorption that were not a feature of past migrations from Sri Lanka. At another level, the separation of families for long periods has social and human costs that cannot be neglected. The government has realised that the Middle East migration has wide-ranging consequences for the social and economic life of the country as a whole. The present government machinery is not yet fully equipped to cope with the multiplicity of problems arising out of the Middle East migration, but efforts are being made to develop the required institutional framework.

In this chapter we will survey selected aspects of the Sri Lankan migration to the Middle East. In the process, no doubt, areas will be identified where further knowledge and more effective policy formulation and management are needed. The present study brings together information from several studies and analytical papers on the Middle East migration. These were produced mainly by agencies and researchers concerned with managing as well as with monitoring the migration. The main sources of the data for the present study are the papers prepared by Ruhunage and Korale of the Ministry of Plan Implementation, the paper presented by G.D.G.P. Soyza of the Labour Ministry at the ILO/ARPLA conference on South Asian countries held in Islamabad in May 1981, and the study of four Sri Lankan communities by Malsiri Dias. A full list of references on which the present study has drawn is appended. It must be emphasised here that many aspects of the migration have yet to be researched adequately, that the present state of knowledge and information on the migration is incomplete, and that what is available is often not entirely reliable.

Sri Lankan Migrants: Number, Skills, and Socieconomic Characteristics

The Volume of the Migrant Outflow

The migration of labour from Sri Lanka to the Middle East assumed significant proportions only in the second half of the 1970s. Sri Lanka entered the labour market in the oil-exporting Middle East countries later than most of the other South Asian countries. Available data indicates that the outflow of labour in an organised form commenced sometime in 1976 and increased rapidly in the years that followed. There has been no systematic collection of data that would enable us to estimate accurately either the annual flow of migrants to the Middle East or the total migrant population which is at present employed in Middle East countries.

Three main sources of information are available for estimating the volume of Sri Lankan migration to the Middle East: (i) the data available with the Ministry of Labour regarding employment obtained through the ministry; (ii) the data supplied by private employment agencies that recruit labour for employers in Middle East countries; and (iii) the data recorded on the embarkation cards of Sri Lankans travelling abroad. The first two sources do not provide information on the entire migrant outflow, as many migrants have obtained employment through unlicensed agencies as well as through the network of relations and friends already employed in the Middle East. Therefore, the embarkation cards are the most reliable source. However, even the information obtained from embarkation cards does not include the persons who travel to India by surface transport and subsequently reach the Middle East.

The statistical analysis presented in this section relies heavily on the detailed work done by the director of the Manpower Division, Ministry of Plan Implementation, R.B.M. Korale and his colleagues, who have constructed as reliable an estimate of the outflow as is possible and have identified the migrants' occupational and socio-economic characteristics. The Manpower Division, which made a detailed analysis of the data available in the embarkation cards for one year (1979), found that out of 86,000[1] Sri Lankans who travelled *by air* during that year, 25,000 were going abroad for employment; this includes all destinations. The figure for the Middle East countries amounted to 20,980. The total number of Sri Lankan departures, however, was 122,197, which included 34,696 passengers who travelled to India by rail and ferry and were not required to state the purpose of travel on their embarkation cards. Any estimate of the proportion destined for Middle East employment out of the number travelling to India would be entirely speculative.

From the evidence available, there is no doubt that a significant number would travel via India for a variety of reasons, including economies in cost of travel and intermediary arrangements that are made through agencies in India. The proportion of Middle East migrants among those who travelled by air according to the embarkation cards, was approximately 24.3 per cent. If we assume a much lower estimate of 10 per cent of the total number travelling to India as persons who eventually proceed to the Middle East for employment, then the number of migrants to the Middle East for the year 1979 will increase by a further 3460. This illustrates the uncertainty and margin of error in any estimate derived from available information.

Given these deficiencies, Table 1 presents the information collected so far in the

169

TABLE 1. Flow of Sri Lankan Migrants to the Middle East, 1976–1982

	Gross Outflow						
	Private Employment Agencies	Department of Labour	Total	Estimate from Embarkation Cards	Total (estimate)	Return Flow (estimate)[1]	Net Outflow (estimate)
1976	526	—	526	n.a.	1500	—	1500
1977	5082	2551	5633	n.a.	7500	—	7500
1978	6141	1941	8082	n.a.	12,500	750	11,750
1979	8614	809	9423	20,980	24,000	4500	19,500
1980	—	—	—	24,053	27,000	10,000	17,000
1981	—	—	—	55,000	18,250	36,750
1982	14,193	900	23,193	52,000	55,000	19,250	35,750
Total					182,500	52,750	129,750

1. Based on average employment contract of 30 months, and on the assumption that the outflow is spread evenly throughout the year.

Sources: R. B. M. Korale et al., "Migration of Sri Lankans for Employment Abroad"; and Foreign Employment Division, Department of Labour.

various exercises conducted by the Ministry of Plan Implementation, supplementing them with some estimates that indicate the broad magnitude of the outflow of migrant labour from Sri Lanka to the Middle East. The increase in workers' remittances from the Middle East is a rough indication of the rapid rate of growth of the migration: Remittances more than doubled between 1980 and 1981 and increased again by a little over 50 per cent in 1982 (see Table 8). Given certain assumptions, the gross outflow during the period 1976 to 1982 is approximately 180,000. This figure, of course, does not represent the number who are at present resident and employed in the Middle East. One special characteristic of Middle East employment is that its tenure is restricted and that, consequently, there is a high labour turnover. At present there is no reliable information on the number of migrants who have returned to Sri Lanka after completion of their contracts. Assuming that the average contract of employment will be in the region of two and a half years, approximately 50,000 migrants would have returned to Sri Lanka in the period from 1979 to 1982. Of these, some would have succeeded in negotiating new contracts and obtaining a second term of employment. When allowance is made for these returnees and renewals, the net outflow of migrants as of the end of 1982 for the period 1978–1982 is likely to be in the region of 130,000.

It has to be emphasised that these are very rough approximations. They only indicate the possible magnitude of the outflow and provide some basis on which much more work will have to be done. This information has now become crucially important for employment policies and manpower-development strategies. It is estimated that the net annual increments to the workforce are in the region of 125,000. This is expected to increase to approximately 160,000 in the mid-1980s. The information recently available on the labour migration indicates the outflow has risen to more than 50,000 per year. The migration to the Middle East appears to have doubled between 1978 and 1979, and doubled again between 1980 and 1981. According to Korale the preliminary data for 1982 record the same level as for 1981. In the recent past, the outflow to the Middle East has become by far the largest regional component of international migration. In 1979 it accounted for 81 per cent of the total migrant outflow, and in 1980 84 per cent.

Migrant Skills and Occupations

The information on the skills and occupations of the labour migrants is also not entirely reliable. The most authentic data in this regard is supplied by the Ministry of Labour and the registered employment agencies. The embarkation cards are likely to provide unreliable information for a variety of reasons. Designations such as "technician," "supervisor," and so on easily cover a wide gradation of skills. There is also no assurance that the occupation shown on the embarkation card is the occupation for which the migrant has contracted in the Middle East. For example, in any number of instances a skilled employee is ready to take up employment in a lower grade because of the vast wage differentials between Sri Lanka and the Middle East. The data in Tables 2–4 were extracted by the Manpower Division from available sources.

TABLE 2. Sri Lankan Migration to the Middle East, 1976–1979

	1976		1977		1978		1979	
	Number	%	Number	%	Number	%	Number	%
High-level	15	2.8	51	0.9	200	2.5	162	1.7
Mid-level	75	14.2	343	6.1	609	7.5	709	7.5
Skilled	222	42.3	3208	57.0	3613	44.7	2449	16.0
Unskilled	214	40.7	2031	36.0	3660	45.3	6103	64.8
Total	526		5633		8082		9423	

Data obtained from the Department of Labour and registered recruitment agencies only.

Sources: L.K. Ruhunage, "Migration of Sri Lankans to the Middle East Countries"; and David Soysa, Country Paper, Sri Lanka Overseas Employment Administration, ILO/ARPLA Symposium, Thailand, 1984.

TABLE 3. Migration of Labour to All Countries and to the Middle East, by Skill Level

| | All Countries | | | | | | | Middle East | | |
| | 1978[1] | 1979 | 1980 | | 1981[2] | | | 1978[1] | 1979 | 1980 |
			Male	Total	Male	Female	Total			
High-level	200	1657	1160	1357	1725	265	1990	200	544	455
Mid-level	609	2374	1917	2199	3080	280	3360	609	1743	1819
Skilled	3613	6110	5799	5895	10,960	240	11,200	3613	5171	4890
Unskilled	3552	12,803	3180	14,501	7400	24,500	31,900	3552	11,502	12,929
Not classified	108	2931	2045	4692	4100	4800	8900	108	2020	3960
Total	8082	25,875	14,101	28,644	27,265	30,085	57,350	8,082	20,980	24,053

1. Based on data collected from Ministry of Labour and registered recruitment agencies only.
2. Provisional.

TABLE 4. Comparison of Migration to Middle East with That to Other Countries

| | Middle East | | | | Other Countries | | | | Middle East Migration as % of Total | |
| | 1979 | | 1980 | | 1979 | | 1980 | | 1979 | 1980 |
	Number	%	Number	%	Number	%	Number	%		
High-level	544	2.6	455	1.9	1113	22.8	902	19.6	32.8	33.5
Mid-level	7743	8.3	1819	7.6	631	12.8	380	8.3	73.4	82.7
Skilled	5171	24.7	4890	20.3	939	19.2	1005	21.9	84.6	92.9
Unskilled	11,502	54.8	12,929	53.7	1301	26.5	1572	34.3	89.8	89.1
Not classified	2020	9.6	3960	16.5	911	18.7	732	15.9	68.9	84.3
Total									81.0	83.9

Source: R. B. M. Korale, "Migration for Employment to the Middle East."

net annual increments to the workforce are in the region of 125,000. This is expected to increase to approximately 160,000 in the mid-1980s. The information recently available on the labour migration indicates the outflow has risen to more than 50,000 per year. The migration to the Middle East appears to have doubled between 1978 and 1979, and doubled again between 1980 and 1981. According to Korale the preliminary data for 1982 record the same level as for 1981. In the recent past, the outflow to the Middle East has become by far the largest regional component of international migration. In 1979 it accounted for 81 per cent of the total migrant outflow, and in 1980 84 per cent.

Migrant Skills and Occupations

The information on the skills and occupations of the labour migrants is also not entirely reliable. The most authentic data in this regard is supplied by the Ministry of Labour and the registered employment agencies. The embarkation cards are likely to provide unreliable information for a variety of reasons. Designations such as "technician," "supervisor," and so on easily cover a wide gradation of skills. There is also no assurance that the occupation shown on the embarkation card is the occupation for which the migrant has contracted in the Middle East. For example, in any number of instances a skilled employee is ready to take up employment in a lower grade because of the vast wage differentials between Sri Lanka and the Middle East. The data in Tables 2–4 were extracted by the Manpower Division from available sources.

TABLE 2. Sri Lankan Migration to the Middle East, 1976–1979

	1976		1977		1978		1979	
	Number	%	Number	%	Number	%	Number	%
High-level	15	2.8	51	0.9	200	2.5	162	1.7
Mid-level	75	14.2	343	6.1	609	7.5	709	7.5
Skilled	222	42.3	3208	57.0	3613	44.7	2449	16.0
Unskilled	214	40.7	2031	36.0	3660	45.3	6103	64.8
Total	526		5633		8082		9423	

Data obtained from the Department of Labour and registered recruitment agencies only.

Sources: L.K. Ruhunage, "Migration of Sri Lankans to the Middle East Countries"; and David Soysa, Country Paper, Sri Lanka Overseas Employment Administration, ILO/ARPLA Symposium, Thailand, 1984.

TABLE 3. Migration of Labour to All Countries and to the Middle East, by Skill Level

	All Countries							Middle East		
	1978¹	1979	1980 Male	1980 Total	1981² Male	1981² Female	1981² Total	1978¹	1979	1980
High-level	200	1657	1160	1357	1725	265	1990	200	544	455
Mid-level	609	2374	1917	2199	3080	280	3360	609	1743	1819
Skilled	3613	6110	5799	5895	10,960	240	11,200	3613	5171	4890
Unskilled	3552	12,803	3180	14,501	7400	24,500	31,900	3552	11,502	12,929
Not classified	108	2931	2045	4692	4100	4800	8900	108	2020	3960
Total	8082	25,875	14,101	28,644	27,265	30,085	57,350	8082	20,980	24,053

1. Based on data collected from Ministry of Labour and registered recruitment agencies only.
2. Provisional.

TABLE 4. Comparison of Migration to Middle East with That to Other Countries

	Middle East				Other Countries				Middle East Migration as % of Total	
	1979 Number	%	1980 Number	%	1979 Number	%	1980 Number	%	1979	1980
High-level	544	2.6	455	1.9	1113	22.8	902	19.6	32.8	33.5
Mid-level	1743	8.3	1819	7.6	631	12.8	380	8.3	73.4	82.7
Skilled	5171	24.7	4890	20.3	939	19.2	1005	21.9	84.6	92.9
Unskilled	11,502	54.8	12,929	53.7	1301	26.5	1572	34.3	89.8	89.1
Not classified	2020	9.6	3960	16.5	911	18.7	732	15.9	68.9	84.3
Total									81.0	83.9

Source: R. B. M. Korale, "Migration for Employment to the Middle East."

TABLE 5. Migration to the Middle East by Occupation

	1978	1979	1980
High-level			
doctors	7	15	15
engineers	66	168	146
scientists and social scientists	—	8	15
accountants	85	129	142
university and school teachers	n.a.	69	50
administrators and managers	30	96	54
Mid-level			
nurses	16	107	136
technicians	87	258	255
foremen	118	115	134
surveyors	25	52	75
draughtsmen	18	33	34
clerks	116	557	581
secretaries and stenographers	18	144	146
store keepers	74	116	145
hotel industry	n.a.	95	89
Skilled			
carpenters	755	760	541
masons	647	525	486
plumbers	78	83	43
bar benders	148	95	84
welders	68	161	152
painters	96	129	120
mechanics	302	492	538
electricians	190	331	243
fitters	79	126	81
drivers	247	837	1051
heavy vehicle operators	397	226	75
cooks and chefs	201	275	290
roomboys and bellboys	n.a.	139	233
stewards	n.a.	152	142
tailors/dressmakers	n.a.	103	89
Unskilled			
female domestics	1384	9152	10,118

Source: Korale, op. cit.

For purposes of manpower assessment and planning, the Employment and Manpower Planning Division of the Ministry of Plan Implementation recently attempted to compile adequately detailed statistical data on the skill distribution of migrants. The consolidated data for each manpower level for all countries for the period 1978–1981 are given in these tables. Data for the skill profile of the Middle East migration have been obtained for 1979 and 1980, and the various occupations classified under four levels — high-level, mid-level, skilled, and unskilled. Table 5 lists some of the representative occupations for each level. The data for 1976 are limited to the information obtained from registered employment agencies, and, as this accounts for only a part of the migration, it is not comparable with the information available for 1979–81, which was derived from emigration documents.

Over the years, the skill composition of the migrant outflow has changed quite significantly. The proportion of unskilled labour, which was approximately 41 per cent during the period 1976–78, increased to 54 per cent in 1979. Skilled labour dropped from 49 per cent to 25 per cent for the corresponding period, and the proportions of mid-level manpower and professional manpower have also declined. This does not, however, mean that there has been a decline in absolute numbers. In absolute numbers, there are increases in all categories. For example, the number of doctors migrating to the Middle East had increased from 1 in 1977 to 7 in 1978, and to 15 in 1979; the number of engineers from 13 in 1977 to 66 in 1978, and to 152 in 1979. However, here again the comparisons have to be taken with some reservations: the figures available for 1977 and 1978 are limited to those obtained from the Ministry of Labour and the employment agencies, whereas the 1979 figures reflect the information obtained from embarkation cards. If we use the 1979 figures from the Ministry of Labour and the employment agencies, we find a decline in the number of professionas. It is therefore likely that, for the years 1977 and 1978 as well, there were far more high-level workers migrating than is indicated by the data from the Ministry of Labour. However, even if we allow for discrepancies in the data, it is clear that the migration profile changed considerably as regards both skill and gender.

A comparison of the skill composition of the Middle East migrants with the outflow to other parts of the world reveals that the major share of the professional manpower — approximately 67 per cent in 1979 and 66.4 per cent in 1980 — migrated to destinations other than the Middle East. The non–Middle East migration includes small numbers of skilled and unskilled categories, but these figures include the residual figure for migrants who have not given their destination. The Middle East migration, we can see, predominantly comprises skilled and unskilled manual labour. These two categories accounted for 79.5 per cent of the total outflow in 1979 and 74 per cent in 1980. The unskilled component made up more than 50 per cent of the total number of migrants each year. However, when the mix of skills in the migration is examined, it can be seen that the Sri Lanka's migrant workforce, although relatively small, contains skills ranging from the professional level to unskilled labour (see Table 5).

Therefore, its contribution of manpower to the economies of the host countries is not negligible.

Distribution by Sex

An unusual feature of the Sri Lankan migration is the large proportion of female workers. Up to 1978 the proportion of females in the labour migration was 12 per cent. In 1979 the proportion was as high as 47.3 per cent, and more than 80 per cent of this was concentrated in the unskilled category, e.g. housemaids. In the high-level, middle, and skilled categories, males had the predominant share. The numbers as well as the proportion of females in the total migration have continued to increase over the years, with the Middle East being the destination of more than 90 per cent of them. Almost all other countries in South and Southeast Asia have placed restrictions on the migration of female workers. and as a result Sri Lanka became the main source of supply for female domestic workers. The number of female migrants more than doubled between 1980 and 1981. The share of female workers in the migration has continued to increase in 1981, according to provisional figures available.

Distribution of Sri Lankan Migrants by Country

Saudi Arabia absorbed nearly a quarter of the migrant flow in 1979 and 21 per cent in 1980, with Kuwait and the United Arab Emirates close to this level (see Table 6). In 1980 the emigration to Kuwait slightly exceeded the flow to Saudi Arabia. These three countries together account for more than 70 per cent of the total migrant flow to the Middle East. The major part of the balance is distributed in Bahrain, Qatar, and Oman. In terms of skills, Saudi Arabia had the highest proportion of high, middle, and skilled levels. In 1979 Saudi Arabia absorbed 30 per cent, 34.5 per cent, and 45 per cent of the total number of migrants in these three categories, respectively, and accounted for similar shares in 1980. Its share of unskilled labour was relatively low — approximately 14.8 per cent of the total of unskilled migrants. In the total migrant outflow to Saudi Arabia, unskilled labour made up only 31 per cent, whereas in all other countries the unskilled component was much higher. For Kuwait it was 83 per cent. Female labour migration was concentrated in a few countries. The proportion absorbed in Saudi Arabia is relatively low. Kuwait received the highest proportion of female labour for domestic service, with the United Arab Emirates following.

The Distribution of Sri Lankan Migrants by Origin

From the analysis for the years 1979 and 1980 (see Table 7) in regard to the place of origin of the migrants, it is clear that a large proportion of the migrants are from Colombo and the outlying districts in the southwest of Sri Lanka. Colombo, Gampaha, and Kalutara are contiguous districts in the southwestern coastal belt and are the most urbanised areas in the country, accounting for approximately 77 per cent of the total migration. Kandy, Galle, and Jaffna each provided 4 per cent of the total

TABLE 6. Migration to the Middle East by Skill Level and Country

	High-level	Mid-level	Skilled	Un-skilled	Not Classi-fied	Total	% Total Migration
Saudi Arabia							
1979	164	602	2373	1711	515	5365	25.6
1980	140	650	2085	1775	623	5253	21.8
UAE							
1979	126	444	620	3032	422	4644	22.1
1980	106	441	686	2932	828	4993	20.8
Kuwait							
1979	31	136	225	4303	465	5160	24.6
1980	28	126	405	4423	900	5882	24.5
Bahrain							
1979	50	171	344	1158	354	2077	9.9
1980	62	218	541	2141	936	3898	16.2
Qatar							
1979	13	40	191	714	102	1060	5.0
1980	10	33	173	642	186	1044	4.3
Oman							
1979	109	246	541	326	106	1328	6.3
1980	83	246	436	201	132	1098	4.6
Iraq							
1980	4	34	301	78	45	462	1.9
Iran							
1980	1	4	4	8	–	17	0.1
Lebanon							
1980	4	11	119	537	241	912	3.8
Other Middle East countries							
1979[1]	51	104	877	258	56	1346	6.4
1980	17	56	140	212	69	494	2.0
Total							
1979	544	1743	5171	11,501	2020	20,980	
1980	455	1819	4890	12,929	3960	24,053	

1. Data on "other Middle East countries" for 1979 include migration to Iraq and Iran.

Source: Korale, op. cit.

number; the balance was distributed among the other 21 districts. The contribution made to the migration stream by the dry-zone districts such as Anuradhapura, Polonnaruwa, Vavuniya, Mannar, Moneragala, and Mullaitivu was quite low. It is, however, interesting to note that every district has participated in the migration flow, even though migrants from the more remote regions are very few. It can be further observed that in the 1980 migration there is a significant increase in rural migrants (see Table 7). This same trend is observed for the year 1981. It would seem, therefore, that the opportunities for high-income employment in the Middle East in all

TABLE 7. Distribution of Migrants by District of Origin

	1979		1980	
	Number	%	Number	%
Colombo	14,907	57.6	15,169	53.0
Gampaha	4090	15.8	4548	15.9
Kalutara	990	3.8	1044	3.7
Kandy	1028	4.0	1675	5.8
Matale	232	1.0	285	1.0
Nuwara Eliya	111	0.4	89	0.3
Galle	1007	4.0	1192	4.2
Matara	254	1.0	269	0.9
Hambantota	183	0.7	272	1.0
Jaffna	1043	4.0	1615	5.6
Mannar	26	0.1	14	0.
Vavuniya	15	0.1	31	0.1
Mullaitivu	3	0.	6	0.
Batticaloa	90	0.4	158	0.6
Ampara	62	0.2	82	0.3
Trincomalee	134	0.5	165	0.6
Kurunegala	341	1.3	455	1.6
Puttalam	268	1.0	441	1.5
Anuradhapura	61	0.2	57	0.2
Polonnaruwa	10	0.	10	0.
Badulla	150	0.6	200	0.7
Monaragala	11	0.	11	0.
Ratnapura	89	0.3	86	0.3
Kegalle	252	1.0	368	1.3
Address illegible	164	0.6	181	0.6
Address not stated	354	1.4	221	0.8
Total	25,875	100.0	28,644	100.0

Source: Korale, op. cit.

occupational categories are being perceived even in the remote areas of the country and are likely to create incentives for migration on a more widespread basis than at present.

Educational Levels of Migrants

The data available do not provide much information regarding the migrants' educational levels apart from what could be inferred from the different levels of employment. All high-level migrants have a secondary education in addition to a degree or professional qualifications. Mid-level workers such as clerks and storekeepers also have a secondary education, and most of them have GCE (ordinary level) certificates. Technicians, foremen, nurses, etc. have undergone mid-level technical training and obtained some formal qualifications in addition to secondary-level schooling.

Given the high rate of literacy in Sri Lanka — 85 per cent — and the high level of participation in the educational system, it can be inferred that most of the skilled and unskilled migrants have had at least a few years of schooling at the secondary level. Female domestic helpers are very likely to have at least a primary education, if not more.

Other Characteristics

There is little information regarding the income levels and social status of the migrants prior to migration. Considering the occupational categories, one could broadly conclude that all migrants in the unskilled category and a majority of skilled labour would fall into the bottom four deciles in the structure of income distribution, where the mean income of households was below Rs.600 per month according to the consumer finance survey 1978/79.[2] From the occupational distribution it is also clear that the large majority of the migrants are from these four low-income deciles and that, consequently, the migration flow to the Middle East has been particularly beneficial to these classes. The mid-level occupations and a small proportion of skilled labour would fall into the next 40 per cent, where mean monthly household incomes were between Rs.600 and Rs.1000 at 1978/79 wage levels. Professional and high-level manpower would be in the highest two deciles, with incomes well above Rs.1500 per month.

The available data have not been analysed according to ethnic and religious groups. From the distribution of migrants according to regions and districts, it appears that migrants come from all ethnic groups in the country, although their relative proportions have not been precisely ascertained.

Accurate information on the ages of migrant workers is not available. The conditions of employment, however, clearly stipulate minimum and maximum ages, according to which workers of most grades must not be below 20 years of age or above 50 years. The maximum age is 55 years for professionals, and 45 years for female domestic help, according to information provided by recruiting agencies. Although the maximum age is specified, the average age would be well below this. Most unskilled and skilled workers are between 25 and 40 years old. Within this span the average age of unskilled workers would be less than that of the skilled workers. They would all be in the peak of physical performance and productivity in their working life. Almost all female workers would be in the reproductive age group. Employers would prefer workers who are physically capable of adjusting to the rigours of the Middle East climate as well as to the demanding nature of the work, which in the construction or domestic-service sectors often requires long hours.

The Economic Impact of the Middle East Migration

Volume of Remittances

Like most other labour-exporting countries, Sri Lanka has benefited substantially from migrant remittances. According to the available estimates of such remittances, there is no doubt that their contribution to the external account has been quite significant. Private transfers as a whole have increased very rapidly in the second half of the 1970s and have overtaken all other items except tea as a single source of foreign exchange income. Tables 8 and 9 provide information on private transfers and their breakdown for the years 1979 and 1982. The phenomenal increase in private transfers coincides with the outflow of migrants to the Middle East in the second half of the 1970s. We saw that Sri Lanka had already experienced a sizeable stream of migration from the professional categories in the late sixties and the early seventies. This outflow, however, did not immediately result in any substantial addition to Sri Lanka's external income.

The remittances of the first half of the 1970s were negligible in comparison with those of the late 1970s and early 1980s, when the Middle East migration had got under way. Statistics from the Central Bank of Ceylon show that net private transfers — a very high proportion of which consist of remittances from Sri Lankans abroad — were as follows from 1973 to 1977: 1973, Rs.2 million; 1974, Rs.2 million; 1975, Rs.19 million; 1976, Rs.56 million; 1977, Rs.112 million. After 1977, when the migration of lower occupational categories began to gather momentum, net private transfers soared from Rs.342 million in 1978 to Rs.5170 million in 1982. The slow growth of remittances prior to 1977 can apparently be explained by the fact that migration in this period was predominantly for permanent residence abroad. The migrants had little motivation to repatriate their savings since they were normally accompanied by their families and needed their income to support a household at the standard of living available in the countries to which they had migrated and to acquire the assets normally required for such a household.

According to the aggregate data available on private transfers, transfers from the Middle East countries accounted for only about half the total remittances in 1981 and 1982. It has been suggested that the country of origin according to which the private transfers have been analysed may not always indicate the true origin of remittances, and that some of the Middle East migrants may be using banking channels in West European countries to remit their money in Sri Lanka. However, given the level of employment of the vast majority of the migrants and the access they may have to banking facilities, it is unlikely that a significant proportion of these migrants use banking channels other than those available in the Middle East. From the data in Table 8, it appears that after 1977 there was a substantial increase in remittances from non-Middle East countries. This might be the consequence of several factors. Professionals who migrated earlier may have finally established a satisfactory financial

TABLE 8. Private Remittances, 1979-1982

Origin	Rs. Million				SDR Million				Percentage Share			
	1979	1980	1981	1982	1979	1980	1981	1982	1979	1980	1981	1982
Middle East	194.4	976.7	2,044.3	3,212.9	9.7	45.4	90.2	140.0	20.8	38.8	46.2	53.4
EEC countries	322.8	739.4	1,116.2	1,477.7	16.0	34.3	49.2	64.4	34.5	29.4	25.2	24.5
North America	189.9	411.8	631.1	641.7	9.4	19.1	27.8	28.0	20.3	16.4	14.2	10.7
Other European countries	51.1	130.7	170.7	168.0	2.5	6.1	7.5	7.3	5.5	5.2	3.9	2.8
Southeast Asia	80.8	78.8	89.3	158.6	4.0	3.7	3.9	6.9	8.6	3.1	2.0	2.6
Far East Asia	26.7	56.7	135.5	113.4	1.3	2.6	6.0	4.9	2.9	2.3	3.1	1.9
South Asia	6.8	25.2	31.0	83.1	0.3	1.2	1.4	3.6	0.7	1.0	0.7	1.4
Central Africa	7.8	28.6	89.8	59.5	0.4	1.3	4.0	2.6	0.8	1.1	2.0	1.0
South Africa	3.3	11.1	23.2	44.8	0.2	0.5	1.0	2.0	0.4	0.4	0.5	0.8
Australasia	38.8	45.9	76.2	21.7	1.9	2.1	3.4	0.9	4.1	1.8	1.7	0.3
North Africa	0.8	2.3	14.4	18.6	.....	0.1	0.6	0.8	0.1	0.1	0.3	0.3
Soviet Bloc	1.6	3.9	2.7	2.8	0.1	0.2	0.1	0.1	0.2	0.2	0.1	.....
Latin America	0.4	1.3	0.8	1.4	.....	0.1	.....	0.1	.....	.....	.....	.....
Other	10.2	5.6	4.6	19.5	0.5	0.3	0.2	0.8	1.1	0.2	0.1	0.3
Total	935.4	2,518.0	4,429.8	6,023.7	46.3	117.0	195.3	262.4	100.0	100.0	100.0	100.0

Source: Central Bank of Ceylon, "Review of the Economy, 1983," p.201.

TABLE 9. Private Remittances from Middle East Countries
(millions of rupees)

Country	1979	1980	1981	1982
Bahrain	12.1	42.0	85.6	130.7
Iran	3.2	4.6	0.9	3.5
Iraq	0.7	10.4	18.9	56.7
Jordan	3.0	19.1	29.6	47.8
Kuwait	31.8	176.8	207.9	377.6
Lebanon		3.8	27.7	54.0
Oman	13.6	63.4	144.7	246.0
Qatar	5.1	25.7	41.0	94.4
Saudi Arabia	76.9	463.9	1208.6	1744.7
UAE	16.6	119.9	150.6	253.0
Others	29.7	47.6	124.1	284.3
Total	194.4	976.7	2044.3	3242.9

Source: Central Bank of Ceylon.

footing in the host countries and thus be able to remit part of their surplus income. But, more important, the government policies to dismantle exchange controls, liberalise the economy, and provide special incentives for Sri Lankan nonresidents to hold foreign exchange accounts in Sri Lanka have all contributed to enhanced flows of private transfers. These policies have virtually eliminated the market for unofficial foreign exchange transactions and closed the gap between the black market and official rates of conversion for hard currencies.

Residents abroad have been allowed to open foreign exchange accounts and operate on these accounts freely. These accounts also earn interest in foreign exchange. Migrants who return to Sri Lanka can continue to operate these foreign exchange accounts for a stipulated period, which is currently ten years. Sri Lankans returning from visits or periods of residence abroad are entitled to import a quota of duty-free goods; quotas vary according to duration of residence abroad. If migrants bring their savings in foreign exchange without fully utilising their quota for imports, they are entitled to higher quotas for the purchase of goods from the duty-free shopping complex, which has been established by the government for Sri Lankans returning from abroad as well as for tourists. These facilities enable migrants to benefit from the scarcity premium for certain types of imported goods and thereby to obtain a higher value for their foreign exchange earnings than the official rate of exchange. Consequently, there is a considerable trade in goods imported by migrants as well as in goods purchased at the duty-free complex with the foreign exchange quotas available to them.

If we discount the possibility of remittances from the Middle East coming through

TABLE 10. Monthly Wages and Salaries for Sri Lankan Migrants by Occupation and Country, 1980/81 (rupees)

	Salary/Wage Range	Countries
High level		
Doctors	26,700–32,700	Oman, Saudi Arabia
Engineers	15,000–28,500	UAE, Saudi Arabia, Nigeria
Accountants	7000–25,900	Saudi Arabia, Bahrain, Zambia
Quantity surveyors	7900–17,000	UAE, Oman
Cargo officers	20,000–22,000	Saudi Arabia
Administrative officers	8200–19,600	Saudi Arabia, Oman
Project managers	36,800–	Bahrain
Mid-level		
Pharmacists	6300– 8600	Saudi Arabia, Oman
Nurses	4600– 7100	Saudi Arabia, Oman
Medical technologists	8700–	Saudi Arabia
Technicians	4200–29,500	UAE, Saudi Arabia, Bahrain, Oman
Foremen	6500–19,000	UAE, Saudi Arabia
Surveyors	8200–28,000	Saudi Arabia, Bahrain, Oman
Draughtsmen	7900– 9100	Saudi Arabia, Bahrain, Oman
Laboratory technicians	6500–13,000	Saudi Arabia, Oman
Clerks	4400– 6300	Saudi Arabia, Oman
Accounts clerks	7200–23,900	Bahrain, Oman
Receptionists	5500– 6700	UAE, Bahrain
Shroffa/cashiers	5000– 6700	UAE, Saudi Arabia, Bahrain
Secretaries	6300–13,500	Saudi Arabia, Oman
Stenographers	7200–12,000	Saudi Arabia, Yemen
Typists	13,100–	Saudi Arabia
Storekeepers	4100–12,700	Saudi Arabia, Kuwait, Oman
Timekeepers	4800– 5000	UAE, Saudi Arabia, Bahrain
Airline-ticketing officers	5200– 8000	UAE, Saudi Arabia, Oman, Qatar
Floor supervisors	7200–	UAE, Bahrain
Garden supervisors	9800-	Saudi Arabia
Sales officers	6600–13,600	Saudi Arabia, Oman
Skilled		
Carpenters	2700– 7300	UAE, Saudi Arabia, Bahrain
Masons	2700– 6800	UAE, Saudi Arabia
Steel fixers	7100–	Saudi Arabia
Plumbers	3700–12,000	UAE, Saudi Arabia, Bahrain Oman
Bar-benders	3800–	Saudi Arabia
Welders	4400– 6400	UAE, Saudi Arabia, Bahrain
Painters	4400– 6400	UAE, Saudi Arabia
Mechanics	4200–13,600	UAE, Saudi Arabia, Bahrain, Oman
Electricians	4300–12,000	UAE, Saudi Arabia, Bahrain
Drivers	2400– 9700	UAE, Saudi Arabia, Bahrain, Oman

(Continued)

TABLE 10 — Continued

	Salary/Wage Range	Countries
Heavy-vehicle operators	2400–8000	UAE, Saudi Arabia, Kuwait, Oman
Telex/telephone operators	4800–8600	UAE, Saudi Arabia, Bahrain,
Cooks	3800–9900	UAE, Saudi Arabia, Bahrain
Roomboys	3300–4600	UAE, Saudi Arabia, Bahrain
Captains (hotel)	5400–5900	UAE, Saudi Arabia, Bahrain
Unskilled		
Housemaids/nannies	2300–4000	UAE, Saudi Arabia, Bahrain, Qatar, Kuwait
Domestic servants	2200–4800	UAE, Saudi Arabia
Labourers	2200–9000	UAE, Saudi Arabia, Bahrain, Kuwait
Cleaners	3500–4800	UAE, Saudi Arabia, Bahrain
Security workers	3300–6000	UAE, Saudi Arabia, Bahrain
Waiters	3900-9700	UAE, Saudi Arabia, Bahrain Qatar
Bar tenders	2800–5900	UAE, Saudi Arabia, Bahrain, Lebanon

Source: Korale et al., "Migration of Sri Lankans for Employment Abroad."

other countries, then the Middle East remittances amounted to 53.4 per cent of total receipts of private transfers in 1982 — approximately the equivalent of 15 per cent of the country's 1982 earnings from merchandise exports. They covered approximately 25 per cent of the import bill for petroleum products and contributed nearly 16 per cent towards bridging the deficit in the goods-and-services account of the 1982 balance of payments. In 1983 remittances from the Middle East increased by 6.5 per cent in special drawing right (SDR) terms and rose to 59.2 per cent of total remittances. These figures, however, do not include transfers in kind and foreign exchange brought by the migrants when they return to Sri Lanka. In Malsiri Dias's study of four Sri Lankan communities, it is reported that "many migrants were known to be saving a part of their earnings to bring consumer articles on their return home." These imports will not be reflected as part of private transfers. It is also likely that foreign exchange brought back by migrants and encashed in Sri Lanka is not always accurately brought to account under private transfers. The foreign exchange benefits accruing to Sri Lanka would therefore be significantly higher than what is represented in the balance-of-payments account under private transfers.

Earnings and Remittances

The information on remittances is not adequate for the purpose of making a reliable evaluation of actual versus potential flows of remittances. Such an assessment would have to compare the earnings abroad with the foreign exchange transferred in money and kind by migrant workers. This comparison would be useful to policy-makers on two counts: one, in ascertaining the effectiveness of incentives to attract the foreign exchange earnings of migrant workers, and, two, in determining whether the full foreign exchange benefits are accruing to the Sri Lankan economy from the migration. The brief analysis that follows attempts to arrive at some indicative estimates regarding the potential earnings of Middle East migrants and the likely proportions of these earnings that are remitted.

The ranges of salaries and wages received by employees in 1980/81 are shown in Table 10. The table was prepared by the Manpower Division, Ministry of Plan Implementation, from several sources: registered employment agencies, advertisements in the national press, and foreign missions that visited Sri Lanka to recruit labour. However, the figures do not represent the total incomes that workers might earn, as they do not include overtime, which is likely to be an important component for skilled and unskilled workers other than domestic helpers. High wages with a wide range of fringe benefits, including free board and lodging, and the consequent possibility of saving and repatriating a large proportion of the incomes earned abroad are the key incentives for migration to the Middle East. A comparison of salaries and wages offered in the Middle East and in Sri Lanka shows the former to be higher by as much as about 300 per cent at the minimum point for professional grades and 3000 per cent at the maximum for some of the lower grades. For many occupations, the salary earned in one month in the Middle East is equivalent to or exceeds one year's salary in Sri Lanka. This would apply to earnings of domestic helpers, cooks, and labourers. Among the high-level manpower, doctors can earn nearly eight times the average Sri Lankan salary for doctors, while engineers can earn three to four times Sri Lankan wages. More recently, the wage differentials for most occupations have contracted as a result of significant increases in Sri Lankan wages. This aspect will be examined further in a later section of this study.

The study conducted by Malsiri Dias provides data on the earnings and remittances of a sample of migrants from four different communities. The sample contains a mix of skills that enables us to derive some broad estimates of the salaries earned abroad. We are, however, cautioned by the author that, first, "questions relating to salary are sensitive," and respondents are reluctant to provide accurate information, and, second, "income from remittances were usually mentioned in approximations."

The range of incomes earned abroad as revealed in this survey (see Table 11) are not significantly different from the salaries given in Table 10 and could be fitted into corresponding occupational categories and salary levels set out in that table. The salary above Rs.10,500 is evidently that of a high-level professional. Most of the managerial and supervisory grades are likely to earn salaries in the range Rs.8500 to Rs. 10,500. The next two lower scales will probably comprise technical workers such as electricians and mechanics as well as clerical workers. Production and construction workers as well as most of the labourers would fall into the scales ranging from Rs.2,500 to Rs.5,500. If we take the approximate average of the salaries earned and that of the remittances sent, the proportion of earnings remitted is likely to be in the region of 70 to 75 per cent. This is quite a high proportion indeed and seems to compare favourably with the proportion of earnings remitted by Middle East migrants from countries such as Bangladesh and Thailand.

TABLE 11. Incomes, Occupations, and Remittances of Sri Lankan Migrants

Monthly Income (rupees)	No. of Migrants	Occupation	No. of Migrants	Monthly Remittances (rupees)	No. of Migrants
Not disclosed	13			Below 1500	5
1500-2500	4	Labourers	29	1500–2500	20
2500-3500	22	Drivers	4	2500–3500	20
3500-4500	15	Production and	27	3500–4500	15
4500-5500	9	construction			
5500-6500	6	workers (masons and carpenters)			
6500-7500	7	Clerical workers	7	4500–5500	11
7500-8500	5	Management and	7	5500–6500	4
8500-9500	5	supervisory		Over 6500	8
9500-10,500	3	Technical and related workers	14	Not disclosed	7
Over 10,500	1	Others	2		

Mean income earned by migrants: Rs.5084; mean remittances: Rs.3662; remittances as percentage of mean income: 72.

Source: Malsiri Dias, "Migration to the Middle East — Sri Lanka Case Study," Tables 17, 23, 24.

These estimates, however, cannot be accepted without a few important qualifications. First, they are derived from two tables in the Dias study that present the data on earnings and remittances separately. The number of respondents in the two tables is not identical; the mix of salary scales in one may therefore be different from the other. If the mix is significantly different, the proportion of earnings remitted could be higher or lower by a considerable margin. Furthermore, it is very probable that the remuneration indicated by respondents did not include additional earnings such as overtime. Respondents are unlikely to have detailed information on the migrants' earnings. As against this, it has to be noted, however, that the estimates given understate the total proportion of income transferred home to the extent that it does not include transfers in kind as well as savings brought home by migrants on their return.

Table 12 presents an independent calculation of potential earnings of migrants in the Middle East based on reasonable assumptions regarding the stock of migrants

TABLE 12. Estimate of Potential Earnings (thousands of rupees)

	Monthly Salary Range	Average Annual Earnings[1]	1980		1981		1982	
			Number[2]	Total Earnings	Number[3]	Total Earnings	Number[3]	Total Earnings
High level	15 –25	240	1046	251,040	1088	261,120	1786	428,640
Mid-level	6 –12	108	3340	360,720	4351	469,908	7144	771,552
Skilled	3 – 7	60	9942	596,520	11,622	597,320	19,082	1,144,920
Unskilled	2.8– 4.2	42	22,058	926,436	30,740	1,291,080	50,478	2,120,076
Unclassified		51[4]	3864	197,064	9389	478,839	15,510	791,010
Total			40,250	2,331,780	57,190	3,198,267	94,000	5,256,198
Adjusted total[5]						3,651,141		5,453,095
Actual remittances as % of potential earnings				42		56		59

1. Weighted average of the mean salaries of selected grades.
2. Based on the proportion of different levels in the migrant outflow for 1979 and the assumption that remittances for 1980 come from a stock of approximately 40,250 migrants.
3. Based on the proportion of the different levels in the migrant outflow for 1980.
4. Based on the assumption that half are unskilled and half skilled.
5. Adjusted for changes in exchange rate — Sri Lanka rupees per US dollar: 1980, Rs. 18.00; 1981, Rs. 20.55; 1982, Rs. 21.32.

and their average earnings. If we use these estimates, we find that the proportion in 1980 was only about 42 per cent, and in 1981 and 1982 had risen to 56 per cent and 59 per cent respectively. It is quite likely that the increase in remittances seen here reflects the real situation; Sri Lankan residents abroad would have responded to the government incentives and transferred their savings with greater confidence as the domestic environment improved and exchange rates moved increasingly in favour of the foreign-exchange earner. The estimates obtained through these calculations are considerably lower than those obtained from the micro-level studies, even if we use the proportions for 1981 and 1982. It should be noted, however, that the aggregate estimates in Table 12 are approximations that are subject to even greater margins of error than those of the micro-level sample. The aggregate estimates come up with an average monthly income of approximately Rs.4500 for 1980, which is lower than that of the sample study. (The salaries for the sample study are for 1982 when the rate of conversion of the rupee was 2.32 per US dollar compared to Rs.18 in 1980.) But the key variable is the stock of migrants, and here we have to be satisfied with estimates based on informed speculation and unverified assumptions regarding outflow and return. If the stock is lower than estimated by 10 per cent, the proportion of earnings remitted rises to 65.4 per cent.

These estimates, therefore, only provide a frame of reference with low and high variants that give some broad indications of remittance flows in relation to the potential. They indicate the importance of obtaining more accurate and reliable information on earnings and remittances. It is interesting to speculate on some of the reasons for the differences in the two sets of estimates that have been presented, apart from the likely errors in regard to the key assumptions. It will be observed that in Malsiri Dias's sample, the proportions for both the high-level manpower and unskilled labour are considerably lower than for the normal migrant flow. It is probable that, for very different reasons, the proportion of earnings remitted at both these ends is lower than for the average. In the case of the top end the migrants have greater opportunities and motivations both for using and retaining their earnings outside Sri Lanka. In the case of those at the bottom end, such as housemaids, it is probable that they do not have ready access to facilities needed for regular remittances, and that much of their earnings are saved, to be brought with them when they return. Furthermore, many of them may invest their earnings on various consumer durables, some of which they can trade on their return at prices that bring them a higher value in local currency than if they had brought their foreign exchange home for conversion. All this confirms the need for further knowledge of the earnings of migrants, their expenditures abroad, and their propensity to save if the foreign exchange benefits of the migration are to be monitored and the full potential realised through appropriate incentives and other measures.

The Use of Remittances

It would not be sufficient to measure the macro-economic effects of the migration merely in terms of the transfers of income and the contribution it makes to the balance of payments and national income and savings. The net benefit of the migration can be evaluated only if we can account for all the transactions arising from the migration, which include outflows of foreign exchange and import leakages that occur as a result of remittances (and the new demand generated thereby). However, no systematic study has been undertaken at the national level to examine the use of remittances in terms of consumption and investment and the impact they are having on different resource flows and different sectors of the economy. The few micro-studies that have been conducted indicate a mixed pattern of consumption and investment.

There is little doubt that the large income increases accruing to the households of migrants would have led to a spurt of consumer spending. A good deal of this spending would have been on imported goods. These incomes came at a time when the economy was being liberalised and the supply of imports was being freed of the exchange and import controls that had been in place since the beginning of the 1960s. Imports rose steeply both in volume and value between 1978 and 1982. The value increased from SDR 774 million in 1978 to SDR 1825 million in 1982, and the volume increased by 80 per cent during this period. Of this, the increases in certain categories of consumer-goods imports was quite substantial. Textiles increased by 87 per cent between 1978 and 1982, and other consumer goods excluding food and drink rose by 120 per cent. In a situation where imports were freely available, the import content of consumer spending by migrant households is likely to have been high.

However, in the absence of detailed surveys of the patterns of consumption and investment of migrants and their families, it is difficult to make reliable and representative generalisations. The micro-studies reveal that the use of the remittances and income from employment abroad depends a great deal on the type of community and the migrants' socio-economic background. One sector in which the income of migrants is making a significant impact is housing. Investment in housing is reported to receive high priority by most migrants and their families. Such invest-ment includes purchase of land, construction of new houses, repairs and extensions of existing houses, redemption of mortgages, and liquidation of debts. In some cases, remittances are used to generate new employment, to invest in an income-earning piece of equipment such as a tractor, truck, or van. In other cases, there are efforts to provide self-employment such as setting up small trading enterprises or grocery stores. Some of the migrants in the construction sector have established themselves as building contractors. Dias refers to a few cases where income from remittances had been used for self-employment. In a sample of 90 migrant households, 3 families had set themselves up in trade, one had opened a lathe workshop providing employ-ment to four others, and another had purchased three acres of agricultural land. Again, these are random observations and no firm conclusions can be drawn regarding the volume of migrant incomes that find their way into investments, and to productive investments in particular.

Many households, particularly those in rural communities, show a prudent use of the new income; expenditure is mainly incurred on the satisfaction of basic needs such as food, housing, clothing, and essential consumer durables for the house as well as to provide better education for their children. At the same time, the proportion of households incurring extravagant expenditure on luxury items and on life-styles inappropriate to Sri Lankan conditions is not inconsiderable. In their survey, Tilakasiri and De Silva find that all migrant households possessed cassette recorders, electric clocks, foreign clothes, and various foreign-made articles. Most households are likely to spend on at least a few expensive consumer durables and household appliances. It must be mentioned here that a large part of the expenditure on consumer durables would have been incurred abroad and the goods transferred to Sri Lanka. This expenditure would not have been a "leakage" from remittances received in Sri Lanka and need not be set off against the remittance flow in estimating the net benefits. In contrast to the findings of Tilakasiri and De Silva, Dias's study of four communities finds less evidence of conspicuous consumption and changes in life-styles. These aspects will be considered further in a later section of this report, which discusses the social and cultural impact of the migration.

The Impact of the Migration on Gross National Product and Gross National Savings

The inflow of remittances as a result of the Middle East migration has had a significant impact on national savings as well as the GNP. The national accounting system in its present form does not take account of the inflow of private remittances. Although remittances are brought into the balance of payments as private transfers, they are not included as a part of the factor income from abroad. If the remittances from nationals employed abroad are treated as an addition to the national income, the rates of growth of GNP during recent years would have been significantly higher than what has been recorded. The differences are set out in Table 13, which provides tenta-tive estimates of the additions to GNP for the period 1980 to 1982. The growth rate for 1981 at constant prices would have risen from 3.9 per cent to 5.8 per cent, and for 1982 from 5 per cent to 6.6 per cent. These increments include remittances from all nationals abroad. The contributions from the labour migrants in the Middle East would have accounted for approximately half of this increment.

Table 14 presents the contribution made by private transfers from abroad to national savings during the period 1979 to 1983. Private transfers were able to sustain savings at a reasonable level when the share of domestic savings was in fact declining. This was a period when there was a significant increase in the outflow of net factor income from foreign investments and other foreign sources. Had there been no substantial inflow of private remittances, national savings would have been lower than domestic savings. As it happened, however, the private remittances were able to raise savings by contributing a significant share that rose from 1 percentage point in 1979 to 3.5 percentage points in 1982. Again, of this contribution, the share of the remittances from the Middle East would have accounted for approximately half.

TABLE 13. Contribution of Migrant Income to GNP (at 1970 factor-cost prices)

	1980	1981	1982
1. GDP	19,575	20,706	21,756
2. Net factor income	−119	−490	−527
3. GNP	19,456	20,216	21,220
4. Private remittances	622.5	1027	1423
5. GNP if remittances of workers earnings are treated as factor income from abroad	20,078	21,243	22,652
6. GNP growth rate on 3 (%)		3.9	5.0
7. GNP growth rate on 5 (%)		5.8	6.6

Source: Central Bank of Ceylon, Annual Report, 1983, p. 8, tables and I and II.

TABLE 14. National Savings, 1979–1983 (at current market prices; millions of rupees)

	1979	1980	1981	1982	1983
1. GDP at market prices	52,387	66,527	85,005	100,140	122,322
2. Domestic savings	7218	7443	9944	11,851	16,598
3. Net factor income from abroad	240	432	1712	2034	3164
4. Net private transfers from abroad	754	2260	3918	5494	6401
5. National savings	7732	9271	12,150	15,311	19,835
6. Domestic savings ratio (2 as a percentage of 1)	13.8	11.2	11.7	11.8	13.6
7. National savings ratio (5 as a percentage of 1)	14.8	14.9	14.3	15.3	16.2

Figures for 1980–1983 are provisional.

Source: Central Bank of Ceylon, Annual Report, 1983.

The Labour Migration and the Domestic Labour Market: High-level, Mid-level, and Skilled Manpower

Several studies on the Middle East migration from Sri Lanka have examined some of the effects of migration on the labour market in selected sectors. It was seen that the outflow to the Middle East has included the whole range of manpower, from high-level professional categories to unskilled labour. The outflow is, of course, heavily weighted towards manual labour — skilled and unskilled — and within this category the predominant share goes to the unskilled category. Even so, the outflow of professional Sri Lankans to the Middle East has not been inconsiderable with regard to its impact on the selected sectors in Sri Lanka.

In the early 1970s the capacity of the Sri Lankan economy to absorb the output of its institutions producing doctors, engineers, accountants, etc., was not adequate to provide full employment to these categories. The large majority of these professionals, especially doctors and engineers, were provided employment in the public sector. Owing to the severe constraints on the government budget, the public sector was not expanding sufficiently fast to absorb the new output, an important factor in stimulating and promoting the brain drain during this period. In the second half of the 1970s, however, the government undertook a massive investment programme that resulted in a rapid expansion of the construction industry with a consequent large increase in the demand for related manpower, from professionals to skilled workers. Correspondingly, the private sector was also growing rapidly and providing new employment opportunities. All this enhanced the demand for manpower in the very categories that were migrating to the Middle East.

According to the estimate of the net outflow in Table 1, the numbers withdrawn from the workforce in 1980 would be as follows:

High-level	1.9 %	2490
Mid-level	7.6 %	9880
Skilled	20.3 %	26,390
Unskilled	53.7 %	69,810
Unclassified	16.5 %	21,450

The outflow of high-level manpower included 37 doctors, 380 engineers, and 356 accountants from 1978 to 1980, when the net outflow was as yet only 57,250. In a net outflow of 130,000, the numbers migrating in the professional grades is likely to be much larger, even if it has not increased proportionately. As can be observed from Table 4, the migration of professionals to the Middle East accounted for only a third of the outflow in this category. Nevertheless, it aggravated a problem that had assumed serious proportions since the late 1960s.

The Middle East migration also resulted in the loss of mid-level manpower — another critical component of the work force. In this category the outflow of white-collar workers in the clerical and service grades did not pose any major problem as these were either easily replaceable or already in surplus. The technical grades, however, constituted a more critical manpower component: Their skills were relatively scarce and were acquired through longer training periods and work experiences. These workers were therefore not easily replaceable. Detailed information on the occupational distribution of the migration is available only for the year 1979. Of 2327 mid-level workers who migrated to the Middle East, 1440, or nearly two-thirds, belonged to nontechnical grades. The balance, 887, belonged to technical categories, which included technicians, foremen, engineering supervisors, surveyors, and draughtsmen. These categories were undoubtedly in high demand for the national economy, both in the construction sector and in land development and irrigation, where investment programmes of unprecedented magnitude were being undertaken.

In terms of numbers, the migration had a larger impact on the categories of skilled labour. For example, the incomplete data available up to the end of 1979 indicate that approximately 2500 carpenters left for the Middle East from 1977 to 1979. The total number of workers in the carpentry trade, as enumerated in the census of 1971, was 27,000. According to data available, the installed training capacity for this category of workers in various institutions accounts for an output of approximately 2500. The migration of skilled labour also included many skill categories that are relatively scarcer and more difficult to replace — mechanics, electricians, welders, heavy-vehicle operators.

The government recognised the impact of the migration on manpower supply and the consequent problems and took remedial measures regarding the mid-level and skilled grades. The government rapidly expanded the available programmes of training, installed new ones, and modified existing courses to provide for accelerated training and speedier replacement of the outflow. A number of public-sector institutions and programmes established in the 1960s and 1970s had increased the output of trained mid-level workers in the technical grades as well as skilled workers who were in high demand.

The National Apprenticeship Board more than trebled its training capacity during the period 1977–1981, from around 2000 apprentices per year in 1977 to about 6500 in 1981. The Ministry of Labour increased its enrolment for training engineering and craft-level trades from 2000 in 1977 to 4400 in 1982. Increased training facilities are also provided by the Ministry of Small Industries, the Polytechnical and Junior Technical Colleges, and the Construction Industry Training Project of the Ministry of Local Government, Housing and Construction. On the recommendations of the Committee on Technical Education (1979), the Ministry of Higher Education increased the number of technical colleges from 15 to 26. Many of the programmes have responded to increased demand by modifying their curricula to provide accelerated training.

However, even with the accelerated training programmes, only a moderate net addition to the existing stock was produced, and this at a time when the demand for skilled labour was rising rapidly in response to Sri Lanka's massive new development programme. The migrants to the Middle East were also from among the more skilled and experienced cadres and could not be replaced even by the accelerated training programmes. There is now a high premium on construction skills at all levels, from architects and engineers down to the semiskilled workers. A severe strain has been imposed on the country's available resources of such skills both by the Middle East drain and by the massive lead projects of the government, such as the accelerated Mahaweli river project, the setting up of industrial processing zones, and the urban development and government housing programmes.

Impact on Unemployment

One of the most beneficial effects of the Middle East migration is the dent it has made in the country's unemployment problem through the withdrawal of surplus labour. The rapid growth of population, the slow growth of the economy, and economic stagnation in the critical growth sectors combined to bring about an unprecedentedly high level of unemployment. In 1977 it reached a peak of almost 25 per cent of the workforce, with approximately 1.25 million unemployed. With the liberalisation of the economy, the accelerated growth that followed, and the massive investment programme that rose to approximately 30 per cent of GDP during the period 1979–1982, the unemployment rate dropped rapidly. It fell to 14.8 per cent in 1978/79 and 11.8 per cent in 1981/82, the latest years for which figures are available from national socioeconomic surveys. The Middle East migration significantly eased the problems of unemployment. We saw that more than 50 per cent of the migrants were unskilled. This outflow would have directly reduced the backlog of unemployment. During the 1970s, female participation in the workforce had increased and the rate of unemployment among females, particularly among the young, had overtaken that of the males. Opportunities for female unskilled workers were, therefore, eagerly seized by the young women. The migration has created job openings in those occupations in which opportunities had become scarce within the country, such as clerks, manual workers, and females with secondary education. On the basis of estimates of the gross outflow of migrants in the Middle East, it had provided job opportunities for approximately 183,000 during the period 1976 to 1982, which amounts to approximately 20 per cent of the net increase in the labour force during this period, or about 15 per cent of the total unemployed in the mid-1970s. It is, however, the net outflow (after making allowance for returning migrants) which is the relevant variable for measuring the impact on employment. If we use the estimate in Table 1 for the net outflow during this period (i.e. 129,000), the employment opportunities abroad amounted to nearly 13 per cent of the incremental workforce. The more recent increase in the annual migrant flow has more significant effects on the employment situation. The gross annual outflow of approximately 55,000 workers for employment abroad accounts for nearly 44 per cent of the annual net increment to the labour force. These figures indicate the importance the migration has assumed in regard to the creation of new employment. Apart from the direct impact of employment in the Middle East, we need to take account of the employment created through investment by migrants, which includes self-employment in various activities such as transport, retail trade, small-scale manufacture, and construction.

It is difficult to come to any firm conclusions about the impact on the labour market and the economy as a whole created by the outflow of scarce skills. As we will see later, the migration contributed to the upward pressure on wages. The shortages of particular skills have undoubtedly created bottlenecks during Sri Lanka's implementation of its major development programmes. But on the whole, many of the programmes have been completed without undue delay. The massive programmes for the accelerated development of the Mahaweli has by and large kept to its time schedule — which by itself is quite an unusual achievement considering the enormous demands on the total national system. These accomplishments were made possible by a combination of policies. On the one hand, the government drew liberally on capacity from abroad and awarded contracts for large components of the work to foreign firms. On the other, it expanded domestic capacity for training and increased supply. The development programmes themselves became a means of providing accelerated training.

At the same time, the impact of the migration on unemployment in Sri Lanka ought not to be exaggerated. It is correct that the additional employment created abroad during the initial stages of the migration brought considerable relief in a situation in which the rate of unemployment was inordinately high. But, as the flow of migration stabilises and migrants return after their contracts of employment, the net outflow and the increase in the Sri Lankan workforce in the Middle East is likely to be significantly lower. This is reflected in the flow of remittances, which after doubling in 1981 and increasing by 50 per cent in 1982, increased only by about 6.5 per cent in 1983. If we assume that the increase in the Sri Lankan migrant workforce will not exceed 15 to 20 per cent per annum, the annual net outflow on a medium-term basis would be in the region of 20,000–25,000 workers. This in itself would be a significant contribution to employment, as it would amount to approximately 15 to 18 per cent of the incremental workforce. But it would certainly not provide the same measure of relief to unemployment as was provided by the migrant outflow of 1979–1982.

Another important consequence of the Middle East migration is the changing pattern of job expectations, especially among the young with secondary and tertiary educations, who until quite recently showed a strong preference for white-collar jobs. The high incomes of skilled workers in the engineering and construction sectors in the Middle East have attracted these youths and helped to transform their job aspirations and attitudes. The social status attached to these occupations has been enhanced, and a demand for training in these and other craft-level skills has been created. While the wages in these occupations have increased two- to fourfold within the country, the wages abroad are as much as 5 to 15 times the prevailing rates.

**Migration and Its Impact
on Domestic Wages and Prices**

By causing shortages in various key sectors, the Middle East migration helped push up wages of the skilled and unskilled grades. In the economic expansion that came after 1977, it would be correct to say that the construction sector led the rapid rise in wages. Several important factors combined to produce these conditions, one of which was the relative scarcity of experienced and skilled workers in the construction trade owing to the labour migration. However, the impact of the Middle East migration on wages and prices (from both the outflow of labour and the consequent remittances)

TABLE 15. Cost Indices for Selected Building Materials and Construction Labour, 1976–1980
(1970 = 100)

	1970	1976	1977	1978	1979	1980 (Jan.–June)	1980 (July–Dec.)
Cement	100.0	164.4	164.4	199.1	291.7	392.0	680.0
Steel (M.S.bars)	100.0	245.6	240.0	257.4	431.0	455.8	492.9
Bricks (hand-moulded)	100.0	164.8	164.8	284.1	301.9	419.7	413.9
Asbestos sheets (corrugated)	100.0	262.3	254.5	290.6	365.6	506.7	573.3
Timber (sawn)	100.0	140.8	140.8	216.7	377.6	634.4	634.4
Metal (3/4")	100.0	148.8	168.5	338.3	533.2	593.3	640.0
PVC pipes (3/4")	100.0	208.4	255.4	318.1	404.1	457.8	457.8
Unskilled labour	100.00	160.3	160.3	226.0	251.4	344.0	411.0
Skilled labour	100.00	179.4	179.4	191.0	228.9	311.2	245.6

Sources: Ministry of Local Government, Housing and Construction; and the IBRD.

has not been subjected to systematic analysis and study. The movement of prices and wages in the construction sector for the period 1977–1980 is set out in Table 15. The price increases for selected building materials ranged from 200 per cent to 428 per cent, while wage increases for skilled and unskilled construction labour rose by 192 per cent and 256 per cent respectively between 1977 and 1980. It is difficult to isolate the specific impact of the migration from the general increases in prices arising from a variety of other factors. The much steeper price increases for materials suggest that the major determinant was the rapid expansion of construction activity and the demand generated thereby. The impact of the withdrawal of labour and the resultant shortfall would have been a less significant factor. In regard to the impact on prices, it is unlikely that the remittances would have had an inflationary impact on the economy as a whole. These remittances provided support to the Sri Lankan balance of payments and became part of the resources in the country's management of its external transactions. In the normal course, the additional domestic income generated by the remittances would have been matched by the supplies made available to the economy as a result of the additional external resources. Any inflationary impact of the external account would have been due to national economic policies as a whole and cannot be specifically attributed to the remittances. On the other hand, the distribution of income domestically as a result of inward remittances would have some effect on the pattern of demand. The augmentation of household incomes was most pronounced in the lower social stata. These households would have come to the market for certain consumer durables and assets that previously had been beyond their reach. Similarly, they would have increased the aggregate demand for certain types of essential consumer goods. How sizeable such increases were and what impact they could have had on the structure of prices has not been investigated.

It is also likely that these households would have added to the demand for land and housing. According to available data, the prices of agricultural land and housing blocks have risen considerably in the regions from which significant numbers of Sri Lankans have migrated. Various micro-studies confirm this conclusion. Tilakasiri and De Silva in their study of a southern village community with a high outflow of migrants, report that land values in the area had risen from Rs.100 per perch (approximately 25 m^2) in 1976 to Rs.500 per perch in 1979. Dias's more recent study of three locations reveals that land values have increased by 250 per cent. Over the past few years urban land values have increased 10- to 15-fold. Foreign remittances appear to have contributed significantly to this trend and to the appreciable rise in the value of agricultural land in certain areas.

The Impact of the Labour Migration on Sri Lanka's Manpower Planning

The Employment and Manpower Planning Division of the Ministry of Plan Implemen-

TABLE 16. Projected Growth Rates for GDP, Productivity, and Workforce 1982-1991

	Annual Growth Rate (%)		
	GDP	Productivity	Workforce
Industrial sector			
Agriculture	4.0	1.5	2.5
Mining and quarrying	7.6	2.0	5.6
Manufacturing	9.1	4.5	9.6
Construction	8.0	3.0	5.0
Electricity, gas, and sanitary services	10.0	2.0	8.0
Transport, storage, communication	6.0	3.5	2.5
Wholesale and retail trade	4.0	1.5	2.5
Banking, insurance, real estate	14.0	2.5	12.5
Other services	5.0	2.0	3.0
All economic activities	6.0	3.5	2.5
Occupational group			
Professional/technical			3.1
Administrative/managerial			2.1
Clerical			5.2
Sales			4.1
Services			4.0
Agriculture			1.1
Productive/transport			3.0

Source: R. B. M. Korale et al., "Manpower: Data Sources, Utilisation Trends and Prospects in Sri Lanka."

tation recently made a detailed study on the trends and prospects relating to manpower and its utilisation. The study includes projections of manpower supply and demand. The projections were made for the period 1983–1991 and are based on annual growth rates of 6 per cent for GDP with varying sectoral rates of growth. The productivity of the economy is expected to grow at 3.5 per cent per annum with varying rates for the sectors. On this basis, the workforce has been projected by the industrial sector, and forecasts for the increase of the workforce by occupational groups have been derived from this projection. Table 16 sets out some of the principal components of these projections.

The study also prepared a set of detailed projections for specific occupations. Table 17 presents the projections for 15 occupations for the period 1983–1991. In constructing these projections, allowance has been made for withdrawals from the labour force through migration. For this purpose, the Manpower Planning Division has used the estimates it prepared for the occupational classification of migration based on emigration data collected from embarkation cards. The largest outflows have taken place among carpenters (2500 from 1977 to 1979), motor-vehicle drivers (2166 from 1979 to 1980) and masons (2640 from 1977 to 1980). In relation to the stocks available, the migration of plumbers (70 per annum from 1977 to 1980),

TABLE 17.   Manpower Projections — Selected Principal Occupations, 1982–1991

	Total Number 1982	Additional Demand									
		1983	1984	1985	1986	1987	1988	1989	1990	1991	Total
Medical doctors	3015	600	600	600	600	600	600	600	625	650	5475
Ayurvedic physicians	8500	250	250	250	275	275	275	300	300	300	2475
Teachers	147,000	5750	6000	6000	6250	6250	6500	6500	7000	7000	57,250
Nurses	8150	1150	1150	1150	1150	1150	1150	1150	1150	1150	10,350
Bookkeepers	10,300	500	550	550	550	600	600	600	650	650	5250
Stenographers	9420	1050	1050	1100	1150	1000	1000	1000	1050	1050	9450
Typists	12,400	1050	1100	1150	1200	1000	1000	1000	1000	1000	9500
Masons	17,500	3000	3000	3250	3250	3000	3000	3250	3250	3250	28,250
Carpenters	15,500	2700	2700	2800	2900	2900	2500	2600	2700	2700	24,000
Plumbers	1000	140	140	150	150	150	150	175	175	175	1405
Welders	6700	450	450	450	450	450	475	475	475	475	4150
Blacksmiths	6600	275	275	275	275	200	200	200	200	200	2100
Electrical wiremen	4400	475	475	500	500	400	400	400	450	450	4050
Auto mechanics/ repairmen	40,800	2100	2100	2100	2100	1900	1900	1900	1600	1600	17,300
Heavy-vehicle drivers	3150	400	400	400	350	350	350	400	400	450	3500

Source: Korale et al., "Manpower: Data Sources, Utilisation Trends and Prospects in Sri Lanka."

welders (190 in 1979/80) and heavy-machine operators (212 in 1979) has also been significant. As for blacksmiths, only 11 have gone abroad for employment during the four-year period (1977–1980). Although auto mechanics have migrated in large numbers, no reliable statistics are available.

It is not indicated precisely how the migrant outflow has been taken into account in the projections, but the growth rates for some of the occupational categories for which detailed projections are provided suggest that both domestic and foreign demands have been included. For example, the growth of the stock of carpenters and masons for the period 1983–1991 has been projected at annual averages of 9.8 per cent and 10.1 per cent respectively. The domestic workforce in the construction sector, which includes these occupational categories, however, will grow only at 5 per cent. Similarly, the demand forecasts for welders, electricians, and other categories are based on significantly higher rates of growth than those for the main occupational group in which they are included.

The growth in demand reflected in these estimates does not appear to present major problems with regard to output and supply of most of these categories to meet both domestic and Middle Eastern needs. The demand for construction is likely to decline, as World Bank forecasts show. Mid-level skills and skills related to production and sophisticated equipment are likely to be in increasing demand. Therefore, manpower planning that takes into account the migrant outflow to the Middle East will require further detailed work on the basis of the framework that has been prepared by the Manpower Division.

As has been stated earlier, certain unskilled and semiskilled components of the outflow (such as unskilled female labour for domestic service) are likely to continue at present levels and even to grow. However, they will not pose problems of manpower planning, as they draw on a large reservoir of surplus labour. What is likely to pose serious problems is the mid-level and skilled manpower required as a result of structural changes and shifts in demand in the Middle East countries. This highlights the importance of more reliable and fuller information on the Sri Lankan labour market as well as the labour markets of host countries. As already pointed out, the key variable is the net outflow, given the turnover the migrant labour in the host countries. Training of cadres for the specific purpose of supplying a foreign market would therefore need to take careful account of the nature of the return flow of migrants and their re-entry into the national workforce as well.

The Regulation and Management of Migration

Channels of Recruitment

Recruitment of migrants for employment in the Middle East takes place through several channels. The two formal channels of recruitment are the Ministry of Labour and private employment agencies. In the matter of foreign employment, the Ministry of Labour functions as both a recruiting agency and the regulating authority. The ministry began operating as a recruiting agency in the early stages of the migration; it initially set up a foreign employment bureau in 1976 and then established it as a ministry division in 1978.

The major share of formal recruitment is handled by private-sector agencies, in keeping with government policy of promoting private-sector participation in this activity. In 1978 and 1979 these agencies were responsible for more than two-thirds of the recruitment. The new business opportunities that the migration provided for employment agencies attracted many entrepreneurs. In 1979 there were 125 such agencies registered with the Ministry of Labour as required by the Fee-Charging Employment Agencies Act No. 31 of 1956. By 1981 there were about 570 such agencies. They played an important intermediary role, establishing contacts with Middle East employers on the one hand and with potential emigrants in Sri Lanka on the other. They were able to obtain orders from employers in the Middle East and to organise the local recruitment. The Ministry of Youth Affairs and Employment has also begun functioning as recruitment agency for Middle East employment. It has made its own contacts with the recruiting firms in the Middle East and has provided services to Sri Lankan job-seekers. Altogether, the formal sources of recruitment accounted for approximately 44 per cent of the estimated migrant outflow during the period 1976–1980 (see Table 18).

TABLE 18. Distribution of Migrants by Recruitment Channel

| | Total[1] | Department of Labour and Licensed Agencies | | | Others (unlicensed agencies, informal channels) |
		D of L	Agencies	Total	
1977	7500	2551	3082	5633	1867
1978	12,500	1941	6141	8082	4418
1979	24,000	809	8614	9423	14,577
1980	27,000			8314	18,686
1981	55,000			12,850	42,150
1982	55,000			14,515	40,485

1. Estimate as given in Table 1.

Sources: Compiled from data in Soysa, op. cit.; Ruhunage, op. cit.; and R. B. M. Korale, "Migration for Employment to the Middle East."

Alongside the registered agencies, there has been a proliferation of unregistered agencies that have been operating since the Middle East migration began and have handled a large volume of migrants. Table 18 presents the available data on the numbers migrating through the different channels. The total flow of migrants has been estimated as indicated earlier. Therefore, the figure for migrants using channels other than the Ministry of Labour and licensed agencies are approximations. This would be applicable particularly to 1977 and 1978. Nevertheless, they are indicative of the importance of the informal networks and unlicensed agencies. It is estimated that even during the early period of their operations between 1976 and 1979, they were able to secure employment for approximately 48 per cent of the workers who migrated during this period. According to available statistics, during the two-year period from 1980 to 1981, approximately 60,000 Sri Lankans found employment in the Middle East through these agencies. Some of these agencies have operated as "mushroom" organisations earning large profits through a few operations, after which they go out of business. This mode of operation makes it difficult for the Ministry of Labour to bring them under the normal regulations. There have been many instances where agencies of this type have defrauded their clientele.

The Employment Division of the Ministry of Labour receives an average of ten complaints a month from Sri Lankans working in the Middle East, of which more than 80 per cent are said to be from housemaids and 65 per cent against unlicensed agencies. Prosecutions have been launched against some of the agencies for irregular practices. However, job-seekers still continue to patronise these agencies as they are able to circumvent some of the time-consuming procedures and regulations and provide ancillary services such as procurement of passports, visas, and travel documents.

Considerable public ire has been aroused regarding the recruitment methods of private agencies. Several instances of exploitation and harassment have been brought to public attention; fees have often amounted to about Rs.15,000; and various clandestine, unregistered agencies have obtained money from prospective migrants on false promises of overseas employment, leaving the victims without any redress. The act that was in force when the Middle East migration began was the Fee-Charging Employment Agencies Act of 1956. This act was amended in 1980 to deal with the new situation arising from the labour migration to the Middle East. A variety of irregularities had occurred during the intervening period. During the parliamentary debate on the amendment, several malpractices and irregularities were pointed out: Exorbitant and unauthorised commissions were charged to applicants, especially women workers; terms and conditions offered in contracts were at variance with actual conditions; agencies often resorted to deceptive descriptions of job conditions, or failed to specify the terms and conditions of work in the contract; and in some instances, the contract of employment had not been properly drawn up, or sufficiently read and explained to the person employed.

Improvement of the Regulatory Framework

The Foreign Employment Agencies Act No. 32 of 1980 was brought into operation on 23 March 1981. The act empowered the government to regulate, supervise, and control the recruitment of Sri Lankans for employment abroad and to provide for measures to protect their interests and promote their welfare. The main improvements brought about by this act are the following:

— The employment agencies are required to obtain new licences upon satisfying new requirements, which include a bank guarantee of Rs.100,000. This guarantee was expected to provide relief to prospective employees and recruits by way of back wages, compensation, and cost of repatriation of recruits in the event of default.
— Employers are prohibited from recruiting employees for overseas employment if the interests of that particular category of workers are not regulated by the labour laws of the host country.
— Regulations made under the act now require agencies to provide contracts of employment that stipulate certain basic terms and conditions and clearly define the nature of the work offered.
— Prospective employees are safeguarded from foreign principals who might recruit personnel illegally and employ them under substandard conditions.
— The fees to be levied by a licensed foreign-employment agency from an applicant recruited for employment abroad shall not exceed Rs.150.

The act and its enforcement has certainly helped to regulate the process of recruitment for overseas employment and to reduce irregularities, but it would not be correct to conclude that the act has eliminated all the malpractices. Accounts given by individual recruits suggest that the recruitment agencies are still charging fees far in excess of the legally permissible fee. Most recruits appear to agree to pay the employment agency, or agent, one month's earnings as the agent's fee. Although the government has sought to prevent the migration of Sri Lankans in occupational categories that are not regulated or protected by laws in the host countries, housemaids and domestic servants who fall into this category and who have no redress under labour regulations in the host countries continue to migrate in large numbers and constitute the largest single category of employment in the Middle East.

It is also important to note that the major flow of migrants to the Middle East occurs outside formal recruitment channels and appears to occur most frequently through informal contacts between migrants and job-seekers in Sri Lanka. This would signify that the networks of friends and relations operate as a very important means of recruitment. This process cannot be brought under governmental regulation. No detailed investigations have been made into these informal processes of recruitment to ascertain the conditions and problems encountered by migrants when they use these channels. The government itself has been reluctant to centralise or formalise the recruitment, as this may lead to all manner of bureaucratic bottlenecks, which in turn could be a source of corruption and exploitation. At present there is a relatively competitive structure in the recruitment of Sri Lankans for employment overseas. This may operate to some extent to the advantage of the applicants if it is underpinned by regular monitoring and control of the recruitment process.

Supervising the Migrants

The government has also made several changes in the administration dealing with the problems of migrants. In 1978 the Ministry of Labour established a separate division headed by a deputy commissioner to deal with foreign employment. Three assistant commissioners, two labour officers, and ten clerks are employed in this division, which is responsible for the regulation and supervision of recruitment activities. Some of the regulatory procedures that have been put into effect are as follows:

- A minimum salary of US$125 with free food and accommodation has been stipulated for female domestic workers and unskilled labourers.
- A standard employment contract has been drawn up for domestic workers.
- Specific recruitment procedures for female domestic workers have been adopted with respect to the UAE, where a Sri Lankan embassy has been set up. According to this procedure, prior clearance of the employer with respect to individual employees is required. Once the recruit is selected, six copies of the contract — approved by the Department of Labour — should be signed by the employer and the employee; these copies are distributed to the employer, the employee, the Ministry of Labour, the relevant Sri Lankan embassy in the host country, the local employment agency, and its counterpart in the host country.
- Special provision has been made in employment contracts for settlement of disputes between migrant workers and the employers, especially in instances where premature termination of employment occurs. These have to be submitted to the government authority in the host country.

The division, therefore, acts in both regulatory and servicing capacities — handling grievances and other problems of migrants. The nature of the complaints received against registered employment agencies is set forth in Table 19.

TABLE 19. Complaints against Registered Agencies, 1982-1984

Requests for repatriation	1200
Adjustment of service conditions	191
Fraud and cheating	152
Underpayment/nonpayment of wages	120
Deaths—compensation	62
Stranded in host country	24
Damages and insurance claims	88

Source: Soysa, op. cit., p. 6.

To facilitate the flow of migration to the Middle East, further administrative measures have been taken by a working group led by the secretary of the Labour Ministry and the Commissioner of Labour. As a result, free services are provided to the migrants for the translation of their birth certificates; special arrangements are made for the issue of visas to recruiting agents from West Asia; representatives of employment agencies are permitted to enter the airport to assist migrants during departure; and migrants employed in countries that have no Sri Lankan embassy are served by embassies in neighbouring countries. The Ministry of Labour has attached four officers to the Sri Lankan missions in Abu Dhabi, Bahrain, Kuwait, and Saudi Arabia who are expected to inquire into and mediate grievances of migrants as well as study the trends in the labour markets in the host countries with a view to promoting the export of manpower.

The passport section of the department has been streamlined to cope with the increase in applications. In 1979 arrangements were made to provide application forms to the general public at the provincial *kachcheries* (secretariats). In 1982 the Immigration and Emigration Department was decentralised. In order to deal with the increasing demand, the activities relating to the issue of passports for Middle East migrants was decentralised and delegated to two districts at the initial stage. Branch offices have been established in Galle and Kandy.

The government has also recently implemented a variety of programmes to prepare and orient migrants for employment abroad, and to assist returning migrants in their efforts to readjust and to find employment and identify income-earning opportunities. The People's Bank, for instance, offers brief orientation programmes for female migrants leaving for domestic service, which includes lessons on the use of modern household appliances, travel formalities, and remittances. The Ministry of Labour organises brief orientation sessions that instruct migrants on the customs and living conditions in host countries, travel procedures, foreign exchange, the use of banking facilities for remittances, and other relevant matters.[3] The programmes for returnees are discussed in the section that follows.

The migration of females for employment as housemaids has been a somewhat sensitive public issue. Several instances of ill-treatment and harassment, even leading to loss of life, have been reported in the press. The Sri Lankan mission in Saudi Arabia, soon after it was established in November 1981, reported that it had received 200 complaints, particularly from Sri Lankan housemaids. These covered a variety of problems, including nonpayment of salaries, violation of terms and conditions contracted for, harassment and torture, assaults, sexual advances, and long hours of work without rest or holidays. Ad hoc missions have surveyed working conditions in the host countries and have made recommendations to the government. The Sri Lankan embassies in this region are expected to deal with problems of migrant employees. Although these embassies can handle problems and issues that affect the migrants as a whole, they do not have the resources to attend to individual needs or to specific grievances on a systematic, large-scale basis.

The major problems relating to working conditions, performances of contracts, and disputes between employers and employees appear to relate mainly to migrant house-maids and domestic helpers. This is probably a special set of problems that is specific to Sri Lankan migrants, as most other countries have now regulated the outflow of migrants to this type of occupation. Individual accounts from migrants in this category reveal severe problems of adjustment both on the part of the migrants and of the employers. The informal nature of the work, the absence of any norms or agreed working conditions such as hours of work and days of rest, communication problems, and culture shock all result in working and living conditions that are on the whole unsatisfactory. At the same time, it has to be mentioned that what receive publicity are the few cases that bring such conditions to light. A representative survey of the working conditions for domestic help has not been undertaken, and the present state of information does not enable us to make any reliable generalisations in this regard. The need for some type of orientation and induction programme for migrants before they leave for employment, in order to prepare them better for the new environment, has been recognised by the government. Some work has been done by voluntary agencies in this field. But there is as yet no regular programme that reaches out to the migrants on a sufficiently large scale.

In addition, a comparative study needs to be done on the terms and conditions of employment in the different countries of the Middle East. First, there appear to be significant differences in the salaries paid for the same occupation in the various labour-importing countries. Salaries in Saudi Arabia and Kuwait are higher than those in Bahrain and the UAE. Second, there are general complaints from migrant employees that the salaries and wages offered to Sri Lankans are lower than those offered to migrants from most other countries. In the case of housemaids, the Sri Lankan mission in Saudi Arabia reported that "the North African countries (Ethiopia, Somalia, Sudan) sending women for household work demand very high salaries ranging from SR 1000 upwards" and recommended that the minimum for Sri Lankan maids be SR 550, which was in fact much higher than what they were paid. It seems that the remuneration policies of the host countries are, to some extent, related to the wage levels of the countries supplying labour and that, as a result, there is a differentiated structure of remuneration.

Returning Migrants: Problems and Issues

Information on the volume of the return flow and the problems of returning migrants is extremely scanty. There is as yet no regular, systematic monitoring of the return flow and the collection of related information. Problems of returning migrants do not appear to be exerting any serious pressures on the Sri Lankan system as yet. There are many possible explanations for this situation. Since the flow of migrants assumed significant proportions in the years 1979 and 1980, the return flow has not yet emerged in its true and fullest dimensions. Also evidence shows that many migrants who return after termination of their first contract are successful in obtaining new contracts of employment. These in all probability are in other Middle Eastern countries. It is likely that migrants establish contacts through their friends and relations or through networks in the Middle East countries themselves. If this is happening on a large scale, and if the flow of migration itself is not being significantly augmented, the system of turnover is not operating as it should — and successive new cohorts of migrants are not receiving the benefits of Middle Eastern employment. At the same time, to the extent that it operates, it reduces the problem of returning migrants. The migrants who do return and remain in the country appear to be being absorbed into the workforce without encountering problems on a scale that demands public attention. The savings they have accumulated and the skills they have acquired appear to have enabled them to re-establish themselves and re-enter the workforce.

Recently, the government has taken some initiatives to identify and deal with the special problems of returning migrants. The Ministry of Labour has established a special unit to examine the problems in this area and to facilitate the rehabilitation of the returning migrants and their re-entry into the workforce. A rehabilitation scheme for migrants has been organised which will be run by the Returnee Migrant Branch of the Labour Ministry. The programme includes self-employment schemes, counselling and career-guidance services, placement in former employment, finding relevant job opportunities, and research into the socioeconomic needs of returnee migrants and their households.

A scheme is also being undertaken with the assistance of the Merchant Bank of Sri Lanka to assist returnee migrants to set up in business or industry by providing consultancy services. The Merchant Bank has, under the auspices of the Ministry of Labour, designed a project to develop the necessary attitudes and skills and to provide the returnees with the required guidance to launch new business enterprises.

A training programme consisting of seminars, workshops, and lectures has also been organised to impart the necessary knowledge and skills. It includes interviews with management consultants, bank officials, and high officials in the public sector as well as a study of the market situation and the structuring and operational aspects of business organisation. These training programmes are conducted at the Ministry of Labour, and more than 100 returnee migrants are reported to have attended them. After eight weeks of training, the trainees are expected to be able to start their businesses. Those who have successfully completed their training are entitled to avail themselves of a special loans scheme run by the Bank of Ceylon, under which they can obtain credit on easy terms. The amount would depend on the nature of the business.

As stated earlier, the dimensions of the return flow are not large enough to make a discernible ecnomic and social impact. Some of the micro-level studies indicate that return migrants have not had major readjustment problems. The studies by Tilakasiri and De Silva as well as Dias tend to support this conclusion. Many migrants do not seem to show any great reluctance to resume the occupation in which they were engaged prior to migration. Some studies have shown, in fact, that either migrants do not bring back any significant new skills or some of the skills they do bring relate to sophisticated equipment that is not available in Sri Lanka. Nevertheless, random observations and interviews with engineers, particularly in the construction industy, suggest that the migration results in an accumulation of skills and competencies of various types that serve to increase the productivity of the domestic workforce. There appears to be a demand for appropriate types of self-employment and small-scale investment opportunities among a significant number of return migrants. This group will combine a degree of entrepreneurial ability with financial resources, and could be potentially important for promoting small-scale business and industry.

The size of the return flow of migrants depends on a number of factors on which further investigation is needed. We need to establish more accurately the prevailing trends relating to both the outward flow of migrants and the extent to which these migrants are being re-employed in the Middle East. It is likely that the return flow will increase to approximately 25,000–35,000 per annum when the termination of contracts begins to affect the labour migrants who found employment in 1980–1983.

The Social Impact of the Migration

The temporary migration to the Middle East is an unusual social phenomenon for Sri Lanka. First, the size of the migration itself is unprecedented. If we accept the estimates of the outflow shown in Table 1, about 180,000 households — or approximately 6 per cent of the country's total — participated in the migration during the period 1976–1982. If we allow for a 20 per cent remigration, the outflow would still amount to nearly 5 per cent of the Sri Lankan population. About 75 per cent of these migrants are drawn from among manual workers and low-income groups. More than 60 per cent of these lower-income migrants are young females who migrate for employment as domestic helpers. Of the 34,472 unskilled and skilled workers who migrated to the Middle East in 1979 and 1980, 21,234 are reported to have belonged to this latter category. Migrants in the skilled and unskilled grades earn incomes between 10 and 20 times what they would earn in Sri Lanka.

These features of the migration indicate the wide-ranging social impact of the outflow: The steep increase in incomes, the relatively long separation of family members, the exposure of low-income social strata to a foreign environment, and the high rate of female participation, taken together, will inevitably generate various social changes, ranging from the lowering of fertility and some alleviation of poverty to an improvement in the status and role of women and changes in life-styles and values. Korale's "Migration for Employment in the Middle East" gives a comprehensive and insightful overview of both the positive and negative social effects of the migration.

Alleviation of Poverty

The income from migration should in the normal course bring about a substantial improvement in the material well-being of the households that participate in the migration. Although it is true that this improvement will primarily occur in those households that have members employed abroad, it could nevertheless result in a relief of poverty on a not-insignificant scale. We can reasonably assume that about 75 per cent of the migrants come from the bottom four income deciles. This means that approximately 11 per cent of low-income households have had an opportunity to move out of poverty during the period 1976–1982. This was easily accomplished as long as a family member was employed abroad, but they could make their temporary well-being more lasting with the prudent use of their newly earned income.

The micro-level studies give somewhat varying accounts of the improvements of households as a result of the migration. Some of the studies confirm that many migrant households have succeeded in improving their living conditions. Tilakasiri and De Silva[4] have made the following observations:
— According to the survey, prior to 1976 only 28 per cent of the households held bank accounts. Now all families having members employed in the Middle East possess bank accounts.
— All households were in possession of cassette recorders, electric clocks, foreign clothes, and various foreign-made articles.
— 55 per cent of the homes had purchased new furniture and 75 per cent obtained electricity.
— There is a greater desire to provide better schooling and tuition for school children.
— Socially, there has been a virtual disappearance of thefts and robberies and village "loafers" or antisocial elements in the area.

Dias's observations were less favourable: "Rural migrants spent their earnings uneconomically, chiefly on short-term improvement of their family's living standards. Only a few embarked on productive economic activities." There was no evidence, however, of "conspicuous consumption"; income from remittances were used for daily household needs. Only a few families were able to save. Commenting on the impact of the migration on the labour-sending communities, she observes: "To an outsider, the impact of remittances is not visible except in a few housing units which have been upgraded. There has been no decrease in the number of food-stamp holders." Only those households where the migrant earned more than Rs.5000 per month (a little more than a third of the sample) showed recognisable signs of newly acquired wealth, such as household goods and a better life-style. In the four communities Dias studied, it appeared that in most cases the well-being was temporary, lasting until the migrant returned. "The majority of the returnees did not have the knowledge to make their money last longer by shrewd investments or entrepreneurship."

Although the micro-studies cited here provide useful insights into the conditions of migrant households, they are limited to specific locations and are not sufficiently representative. For example, the two studies mentioned above did not treat one of the primary aspects of Sri Lanka's labour migration — female labour for domestic service. Therefore, more comprehensive surveys need to be conducted on a more representative scale. Only then will we be able to draw valid conclusions regarding the migration as a whole.

Family Relations and the Role of Women

The human consequences of the migration, in its impact on family relations and the roles of family members, appear to be far-reaching. The micro-level studies draw attention to the effect of the migration on women. Where the male head of the household migrates, women generally have been able to cope with dual responsibilities of mother and chief of the household. Therefore, the migration has served to enhance their role in the household and increase their self-reliance. When a female migrates, her newly acquired status as a major income-earner and the resultant dependence of household members on her transforms her relationships with her family and the society. Dias observes that in "almost every household, a remarkable change was noted in the status of women." Women were attending to responsibilities usually assumed by men — attending to financial transactions, meeting government officers, interviewing bank managers. Women also appeared to be more prudent in their use of the new income. They were not as prone to extravagance and wasteful expenditure. "Whatever luxury articles were displayed in households were the purchases of the husbands who carried the items home when arriving on holiday."

The studies also point to the negative consequences of the long separation of spouses. For example, the incidence of divorce among migrants appears to be above the average. Another harmful impact is the effect of long absences of either parent on children and young adults. The children grow up with only one parent, most of them without fathers, in communities where the male traditionally exercises parental control. On the other hand, studies have pointed out that the migration also tends to strengthen the extended family system, which was gradually becoming weaker as a result of urbanisation, expansion of education, and the greater participation of women in school drop-outs, or serious indiscipline among the young that could be attributed migrates, seeks the assistance of parents or close relations in caring for the family during the migrant's absence. These arrangements have also had the effect of making the migrants share the benefits of their employment with relatives outside the immediate family unit.

Dias concludes that, on the whole, the impact of the migration on rural families has not been adverse. In the four rural communities surveyed, few women complained of difficulties in handling their children in the absence of the fathers. In this sample, researchers did not come across any cases of neglect of children, any unusual increase in school drop-outs, or serious indiscipline among the young that could be attributed to the parent's absence from home. In the more traditional communities, the structures of kinship and extended family relations have, in most instances, been able to cope with the problems. It is in the urban lower-income groups that absence and separation have led to neglect of children and to serious disorganisation of family life.[5] In a sample of 100 female migrants, one researcher found that 64 were able to make arrangements with grandparents or elderly relations for the care of the children left behind. Thirty-four had to leave children with working fathers who could not provide adequate care.[6] The situation as depicted in these studies is, therefore, mixed. For at least a significant minority of the migrant families it is evident that the human cost is heavy.

The migration to the Middle East is likely to have a significant impact on fertility. The large majority of the migrants are young adults. A large proportion of the Sri Lankan migrants in particular are young females who must live under conditions where they cannot marry or live with their spouses if married. This has the direct effect of preventing or at least inhibiting births. The temporary separation of married couples, the increasing age at marriage of both males and females due to their absence from home, the higher incomes, the better living standards achieved through employment abroad are all likely to contribute to a reduction of fertility. The current trends indicate that after a rise in the birth rate from 27.8 in 1975 to 28.7 in 1979, the rate dropped to 26.8 in 1982 and 26.2 in 1983.

The Work Ethic

The labour migration has also had an effect on the work ethic and skills of the Sri Lankan workforce. First, the competition for employment abroad (particularly in the skilled grades) motivates workers to improve their skills and to acquire them through training. The exposure to a foreign setting, the discipline under a work regime different from Sri Lanka's, and the acquisition of skills may all have beneficial effects on Sri Lanka's productivity. Random observations by construction industry professionals indicate that migrants returning to Sri Lanka sometimes organise themselves as small contractors and show great enterprise and efficiency in handling their work. The high wages paid for all types of work abroad have also contributed to changes in attitudes towards specific occupations. Such attitudinal changes can have far-reaching consequences on the status hierarchy of occupations and the pattern of job expectations. This in turn can affect the demands made on the educational system. Although there are indications that many of these factors are already at work, no specific studies have been undertaken to examine these aspects of the migration.

The Migration and Religious Practice

Another aspect that deserves comment is the impact of the Middle East migration on the religious practices of the migrants. The majority of the migrants are Buddhists, who would have little or no opportunity to practise their faith abroad and take part in religious observances. This would apply, to some extent, to the Christian and Hindu migrants as well, although in their case, places of worship are available in some of the Middle East countries. Most of the migrants are from traditional rural and semiurban communities where religion and religious practices occupy a central place in the lives of the people. The absence of facilities for the regular observance of their religious obligations is likely to be felt as a serious deprivation by these migrants.

Sociocultural Consequences of the Migration

These observations regarding the religious problems faced by Sri Lankan migrants lead to another aspect of the migration — the socio-psychlogical impact of migration on the migrant and his family. The migrant is exposed to an entirely new social environment and to new value systems. The new incomes and the opportunities made available by the migration often bring sharp discontinuities with the former life. Many activities that were once central to his life lose their importance and value. Consequently, it is often argued that the migration results in the disorientation of the migrant and his family, uprooting him from his community, and undermining the value system which had organised his life and his relationships with his family and society. Studies have not lent support to this argument.

Of course the migration causes temporary disruptions in the family. In some instances, it leads to the break-up of marriages. Individual migrants may have felt disoriented and uprooted by the experience. But on the whole, migrants and families have been capable of a relatively balanced and stable adjustment to the emigration and its experience. They have not allowed the migration to sever them from their community and their past life. Nor do the studies suggest that the migrant households with their newly acquired wealth become a discordant element in their communities with a demonstration effect that disrupts accepted social values.

Dias records the views of some of the religious leaders in communities that have sent migrants to the Middle East. A Buddhist monk deplores "a general deterioration of the traditional ways among Middle East returnees." But the study goes on to point out that there was no positive evidence of "an increase in the level of modernisation" and expresses surprise at the quick re-adaptation of returnees to village life and their readiness to accept and live with its modest standards. This scene is both positive and negative in that it showsa lack of any major change. If there are no signs of instability and disorientation, there is also no distinct evidence of attitudinal changes, social mobility, and positive innovation resulting from the migration. These observations, however, are limited to a small sample drawn from four locations. It is not possible to draw conclusions that are valid for the migration as a whole. The scale of the migration, its composition, and the income flows generated (according to the aggregate data) suggest that changes — both positive and negative — should be more significant and more visible. These aspects call for further investigation and research.

Conclusion

The export of manpower has become one of the principal sources of foreign exchange income for Sri Lanka in the recent past. The remittance of Sri Lankans employed in the Middle East amounted to approximately Rs.3212 million in 1982 — about 15 per cent of the country's export earnings for that year. The remittances increased to Rs.3751 million, which again was about the same proportion of exports. The positive impact of the migration, both on the balance of payments and on unemployment has been substantial. Recognising these benefits, the government has therefore encouraged and promoted the migrant outflow. Efforts to promote employment abroad have included studies of demand for labour in the host countries. These, however, need to be undertaken on a more detailed and systematic basis, and should attempt to gather much more reliable information on the outflow and return flow of migrants.

In order to adjust to the changing demand for skills, manpower development and training has to look after both the net additional employment abroad and the demand generated in the national economy. In such a strategy it is necessary to ascertain the prospects for migration from Sri Lanka to the Middle East on a more reliable basis. With the drop in oil revenues and the consequent restructuring of ambitious investment programmes in the high-income oil-exporting countries of the Middle East, the demand for expatriate labour has shown a downward trend. This has been particularly evident in the construction sector. However, most projections for manpower demand in the Arab countries, such as those of the World Bank, show that employment opportunities in the service sector are likely to expand as the social and economic infrastructure in these countries steadily improves. Similarly, as the industrial projects now under construction are completed and come into producrion, industrial workers and operatives of various grades will be required. The skill composition of the expatriate workforce needed in the host countries is, therefore, likely to change significantly.

As we saw earlier in this chapter, the labour migration has comprised skills and workers that were easily replaceable. This is not likely to be the case in the future. The skills that are likely to be required abroad will need longer training periods and will be in greater domestic demand in Sri Lanka. Therefore, the manpower planning and development has to address these special problems. The impact of the migration on the labour market and employment require more careful appraisal and monitoring. The changing composition of the expatriate skills that will be in demand in Arab countries is not likely to affect one major component of Sri Lanka's labour migration (on which the country has a near monopoly), female labour for domestic service. Here, if at all, the demand is likely to increase. This trend and government policies regarding this part of the migration need careful evaluation. If Sri Lanka is to allow such migration to continue at present or increasing levels, the government will need to consider how the interests of these migrants can best be protected given their special work conditions, and how the employment contracts for domestic service can be upgraded to give greater self-respect and human dignity to the workers.

All these tasks impose new demands on Sri Lanka's administrative system and call for more efficient manpower planning and policy formulation. An urgent need is a well-designed information system that provides a regular and reliable flow of data required by policy-makers for monitoring the migration and responding adequately to these changes. Such information is also needed for the more immediate tasks of managing and regulating the migration.

If the country is to get the maximum benefit from the migration, the migrants themselves and their welfare and assistance have to be the centre of government policy and attention. The flow of benefits will depend eventually on the migrants, their responses to the steep and sudden increases of their incomes, their propensity to save, the prudence with which they utilise these savings, and, encompassing all this, their ability to adjust to the problems of migration in all its phases. The study discusses the various measures taken by the government to protect the welfare of migrants and to assist them in the various phases. These range from incentives for remittances and regulation of the recruitment process, to schemes of assistance and counselling for investment and re-employment on return. Assisting migrants during the different phases of migration — the preparatory phase, the period of employment abroad, and the return — have all placed new responsibjlities on different parts of the government machinery. These include the Ministry of Labour, the Foreign Ministry, the emigration authorities, the banking system, the Planning and Plan Implementation ministries. As has been described in the study, these agencies have responded in various ways to the new needs that have arisen as a result of the migration. It is, however, necessary to examine the existing arrangements for the coordination of all the activities relating to the migration, and to strengthen and improve the administrative framework for such coordination.

Notes

1. Although 86,000 departures were recorded, only 83,963 cards were available for analysis.
2. Central Bank of Ceylon, *Consumer Finance and Socio-Economic Survey: 1978/79* (Colombo 1983), p. 98.
3. David Soysa, "Country Paper—Sri Lanka—on Overseas Employment Administration," ILO/ARPLA Inter-Country Symposium on Overseas Employment, 21–25 May 1984, Thailand.
4. S. L. Tilakasiri and Asoka S. de Silva, "Socio-Economic Impact of Employment in the Middle East: A Study of Kurunduwatte in Ambalangoda," *Economic Review*, 7 (April 1981): 12–13.
5. Malsiri Dias, "Single-Parent Families" (Colombo: Ministry of Plan Implementation, mimeographed).
6. Dr. Lakshmi Jayasekera, "Children They Leave Behind," *Daily News,* 9 October 1980.

Bibliography

Balasooriya, Tissa. "Migration to the Middle East and the Problems of the Family in Sri Lanka." In *Family Counseling*. Colombo: Sri Lanka School of Social Work, 1982.

Central Bank of Ceylon. *Review of the Economy, 1982*. Colombo, 1984.

Commissioner of Labour Administration Reports, 1977–1983.

Dias, H. D. "Development Policy and Migration in Sri Lanka." *Sri Lanka Journal of Social Sciences*, 1 (June 1978): 37–59.

Dias, Malsiri. "Migration to the Middle East: Sri Lanka Case Study." Colombo: Ministry of Plan Implementation, 1983.

———. "Single-Parent Status Arising from Migration of a Parent to the Middle East." In *Exodus to the Middle East,* pp. 35–38. Dossier 91. Colombo: Centre for Society and Religion, 1983.

Exodus to the Middle East. Dossier 91. Colombo: Centre for Society and Religion, 1983.

Fernando, Denis. "Country Paper: Sri Lanka." In *Emigration for Employment,* pp. 37–62. ARPLA Series, no. 13. Geneva: ILO, 1983.

———. "Conditions Affecting Employment in West Asian Labour Markets Relating to Migrants from Sri Lanka." Paper presented at seminar on Migration of Sri Lankan Labour to the West Asian Region, sponsored by the Ministry of Youth Affairs and Employment, 8–9 March 1983, Colombo.

Gooneratne, John. "Labour-Importing Countries: Their Economic and Social Situation." Paper presented at seminar on Migration of Sri Lankan Labour to the West Asian Region, sponsored by the Ministry of Youth Affairs and Employment, 8–9 March 1983, Colombo.

Korale, R.B.M. "Migration for Employment to the Middle East: Its Demographic and Socio-economic Effects." Colombo: Ministry of Plan Implementation, 1983.

———. "Occupational Distribution of Labour and Sri Lankan Migrants for Employment in the West Asian Region." Paper presented at seminar on Migration of Sri Lankan Labour to the West Asian Region, sponsored by the Ministry of Youth Affairs and Employment, 8–9 March 1983, Colombo.

———. "Prospects for Supplying Manpower to the Gulf States." Colombo: Ministry of Plan Implementation, Division of Employment and Manpower Planning, 1977.

Korale, R.B.M., and I.M. Karunawathie. "Migration of Sri Lankans for Employment Abroad." Colombo: Ministry of Plan Implementation, Division of Employment and Manpower Planning, 1981.

Korale, R.B.M., et al. "Manpower, Data Sources, Utilisation Trends and Prospects in Sri Lanka." Colombo: Ministry of Plan Implementation, Division of Employment and Manpower Planning, 1983.

"Middle East Migration: Special Report." *Economic Review,* 7, no. 1 (Apr. 1981): 3–18.

Ruhunage, L.K. "Migration of Sri Lankans to the Middle East Countries." Colombo: Ministry of Plan Implementation, 1979.

Soysa, G.G.D.P. "External Migration of Labour from Sri Lanka." *Sri Lanka Labour Gazette,* 32, no. 3 (July–Sept. 1981): 43–81.

———. "Labour Administration." In *Overseas Employment Administration in Selected Asian Countries*. Proceedings of the ILO/ARPLA Inter-country Symposium on Overseas Employment Administration, Pattaya, Thailand, 21–25 May 1984. Geneva: ILO, 1985.

Sri Lanka Women. Dossier 92. Colombo: Centre for Society and Religion, 1983.

Tilakasiri, S.L., and Asoka de Silva. "Socio-economic Impact of Employment in the Middle East: A Study of Kurunduwatte Village in Ambalangoda." *Economic Review,* 7, no. 1 (Apr. 1981): 12–13.

"UAE, Sri Lanka Can Help Each Other." *Sri Lanka Labour Gazette,* 32, no. 3 (July–Sept. 1981): 7–8.

REPUBLIC OF KOREA

Hyunho Seok

Chairman, Department of Sociology, Sung Kyun Kwan University, Seoul, Republic of Korea

International labour migration from developing countries in Asia to oil-rich countries in the Middle East is becoming an increasingly important issue not only for the countries involved in the migratory movement but for the global economy as a whole. Its impact on the economic health of labour-supplying countries, their labour markets, unemployment, national savings, balance of payments, and ability to service their external debt have far-reaching implications at both national and international levels. The present study explores the migration of Korean workers to the Middle East and its socioeconomic consequences.

Emigration of Korean workers to the Middle East began in 1974 and has been ac-celerated in the subsequent years. As of August 1983 there were about 170,000 Korean migrant workers in the region, most of whom were engaged in construction work. This figure corresponds to about 1.3 per cent of Republic of Korea's total employed population and about 25.6 per cent of those employed in the construction industry.

During the past two decades Korea has achieved remarkable economic progress and maintained exceptionally high rates of growth. Yet, the country's economy is not as healthy as these indicators suggest. It has to manage its economy with a relatively large current-account deficit in its balance of payments and an increasing burden of external debt. The foreign exchange that Korea has received as a result of the Middle East migration has therefore helped ease the pressures on its external account. At the same time, the export of manpower has helped to reduce unemployment and upgrade technology in the industrial sector.

However, the benefits of the migration are often overstated and its negative impact on the labour-supplying country is not properly evaluated. Emigration of Koreans to the Middle East is highly selective in favour of young, skilled construction workers. This means that the country has exported workers from the most pro-ductive part of the labour force in the construction industry, a sector that has played a key role in the country's economic development. Remittances sent by migrant workers have improved their families' well-being, but they often drift into patterns of conspicuous consumption, contributing thereby to domestic inflation. In addition, the human cost of the migration is indisputable. Korean migrant workers have a harder time than other international migrants to Arab countries in adjusting to a new environment, totally different from their home country. Their readjustment after returning can be difficult as well. Above all, nearly all the migrants have to reside in enclaves where board, lodging, and other amenities are provided by the firms employing them, and where ordinary civilian life as they had known it at home is severely restricted. At home, most of the families left behind have to adjust to the separation from spouse and parent, and manage without the household head.

The present study examines these and related problems within the framework prepared for it collectively by the team of consultants from seven Asian countries who participated in the comparative study on Asian migrant workers in the Gulf region. The framework covers 12 aspects of the labour migration, including psychological, cultural, sociological, political, and economic issues. The study has been organised in four parts: The first analyses the special characteristics of the Korean migration to the Gulf region in its historical context; the second part deals with determinants of the migratory movement and some characteristics of the migrants; the third explores problems of adjustment in host country and at home after migration; and the final part examines the socioeconomic effects of migration on the labour-supplying country. First, however, I will discuss some theoretical guidelines for the study and describe the sources of data and their limitations.

Key Characteristics of the Migration Process: A Definitional Framework

By definition, every act of migration involves an actor, an origin, a destination, and a movement from origin to destination. The act of migration and its effects are, therefore, determined by a complex of factors including the individual actor's attributes, factors associated with the areas of origin and destination, and those lying in between the two areas.[1] However, what is not self-evident is the nature of each factor and the complex interrelationships among them, since different disciplines conceive of the factors affecting migration in different ways and every conceptualisation has its implications and risks for interpretation and analysis.

This study follows some of the theoretical guidelines suggested by Mangalam and Schwarzweller.[2] They place migration within the context of human interaction and define the migration system as consisting of donor and recipient subsystems, linked by the subsystem of the migrating collectivity. The donor and recipient subsystems are the social systems at origin and at destination respectively, and the subsystem of migrant collectivity refers to the specific social subsystem of the migrants themselves.

According to this conception of the migration, the donor system that operates in the emigration of Koreans to the Gulf region can be described as relatively open, represented by a free labour market, while the recipient system is closed in the sense that the migrants are housed within work camps. The migrants constitute a collectivity of both contract labour and inmates in a work camp.

The Spatio-temporal Frame of Reference

In defining different types of migration, it is important to bear in mind the spatio-temporal framework. Migration is usually defined as a permanent or semipermanent change of residence. However, this definition is riddled with ambiguity, since there is no ultimate criterion to delimit duration of stay and boundaries of residence.[3] It excludes what we call temporary migration. This temporary migration often exerts significant influences on migrants as well as on the socioeconomic systems of both the sending and receiving areas. Therefore, two types of migration must be differentiated with reference to the duration of stay: namely, temporary and permanent migration. Cross-cutting the duration of stay, the other basic criterion in the typology of migration is the boundary of residence. In this regard, various types of migration can be identified, but for this study it is sufficient to distinguish between internal and international migration.

In the history of Korean international migrations before the outflow to the Middle East, the predominant pattern was one of permanent settlement. Although many of these emigrants have returned, their return in most cases was induced primarily by political factors in the country of destination. But the labour migration to the Middle East is temporary: it presumes return to the country of origin within a specified contract period.

Main Migratory Forces

The categorisation of possible factors affecting migration will enable us to develop a typology of migration. Petersen[4] constructs such a typology that combines major migratory forces with the characteristics of the migrants. He identifies the main categories of migratory forces as ecological push, migration policy, higher aspirations, and social momentum. He divides migrant characteristics into two categories — conservative and innovative. With reference to the four main categories of migratory *force,* he classifies the four types of migration: (1) primitive migration resulting from the ecological push, (2) impelled and forced migration induced by a migration policy, (3) free migration activated by higher aspirations, and (4) mass migration generated by social momentum. In the first two types the volition of the migrants is relatively unimportant, while in the third, the migrant's will is decisive; in the last type, mass migrations, it is relatively important, but not so important as in the third. Earlier migratory flows are usually made up of innovative people with high aspirations, called pioneers; later migrations tend to be mass movements stimulated by social momentum.

According to this typology, the Koreans' emigration to the Middle East is not a conservative settlement type of outflow but an innovative, temporary phenomenon.

Linked with forces behind migration is the selection process whereby migrants gain access to employment abroad. Therefore, the characteristics of migrants, their motivation to migrate, and their capacity to work and reside in the labour-importing country should be assessed in two socioeconomic contexts: first, the home country and, second, the country of destination.

The Social Unit of Migration

We can distinguish three social units of migration: individuals, families, and organized nonfamilial groups. These groups can migrate according to economic orientation — that is, movements of people can be production-oriented or consumption-oriented.[5] We have thus constructed a typology of migration by combining the social unit of migration with an economic orientation, thereby providing a useful basis for studying migrations in their socioeconomic context. According to the typology, the emigration of Koreans to the Gulf region is a production-oriented, organized-group migration — in other words, an "organized labour migration."

The Korean migrant workers are sent, as an organised group, to a working place where not only the physical environment but also the sociocultural conditions are vastly different from those in their home country. They have to adjust to the extreme heat that prevails for the greater part of the year. Furthermore, they are integrated into residential-cum-working units that regulate their lives both during and after work and control their relations with the world outside.

This environment can be depicted as a "total institution," in the sense used by Goffman.[6] A total institution is defined as a place of residence and work where a large number of individuals, cut off from the wider society for an appreciable period of time, together lead an enclosed, formally organised life, e.g. prisons, hospitals, work camps. Its encompassing or "total" character finds expression in various clearly defined barriers to social intercourse with the outside world.

Goffman lists five groups of such institutions, one of which consists of those that are purportedly established to pursue a given set of tasks and that justify themselves only on these instrumental grounds. The work camps in the Middle East where Korean migrant workers are situated fall into this category. In a total institution, all aspects of life are organised and occur in the same place and come under the same authority; each phase of a member's daily activity is carried on in the immediate company of numerous other workers and is governed by uniformly applicable rules; the day's activities are tightly scheduled and are part of a single, rational plan aimed at fulfilling the objectives of the institution.[7]

In total institutions there is a clear differentiation between the large managed groups, conveniently called "inmates," and the small supervisory staff. Upon entrance to the institution, the inmate is immediately stripped of the support provided by certain social arrangements in his homeland. He is systematically, if often unintentionally, mortified.

Many facets of the life in the total institution can be found in the work camps established by Korean firms for Korean migrant workers in the Middle East, although their actual situation may deviate in some key characteristics from Goffman's ideal construct, which was formulated primarily from his observations of mental hospitals and prisons. Nevertheless, the concept of the total institution helps us to depict the distinctive adjustment problems faced by Korean migrant workers in the Gulf region.

Repeated and Return Migration

Every migrant worker is expected to return upon the termination of his contract, although the contract can be extended or renewed. This can be regarded as a forced migration in that the labour-importing countries of the Middle East do not permit the naturalisation of migrants. Voluntary return migration takes place for various reasons, such as dissatisfaction with the working conditions, improvement in economic conditions at home, or personal and family problems. Migrants may decide to return having attained the objectives they originally pursued. However, in the case of international labour migration, which takes place on a contract basis, the most important factors determining return movement would be termination of contract and adverse immigration laws in the host country. Therefore, a more important question regarding the return migration is not why they return, but how they readjust once they do return.

Most of the returnees may have great difficulties in their economic readjustment, especially in their efforts to re-enter the workforce. They are likely to be temporarily unemployed after their return. Although they may have obtained more skills overseas, suitable job opportunities for them may be limited and, if available, the wages may be significantly lower than they were in the Middle East. Therefore, some of the returnees will have to seek employment in new fields, while those who fail to find suitable jobs or are dissatisfied with those that are available might re-emigrate. In fact, repeated migrations to the Gulf region are common.

Sources of Data

The data for this report are obtained from primary and secondary sources. The former include a sample of 144 personnel records obtained from a large Korean construction company which has sent about 45,000 workers to the Middle East, scheduled interviews with 22 returnees, and informal interviews with a number of government and business officials who deal with the Middle East emigration. Secondary sources consist of published government statistical reports and academic research papers on emigration to the region.

Data on migrants' characteristics and migration experiences are obtained from a random sample of individual records mentioned above. The data cover a wide range of information on the migrant workers, including age, educational attainment, marital status, family size, occupation, reasons for migrating, identity of the host country, experience with repeated migrations. However, it should be noted that the sample from which the data are compiled is not national but merely drawn from one of many construction companies that have sent migrant workers to the Middle East. Therefore, the data cannot claim to represent the entire body of migrants. In addition, the data are incomplete, since the individual records are marked by various gaps and erratic information. Therefore, our data must be seen as approximations rather than as accurate measures.

The second set of data on the migration and its effects on migrants and their migration and its effects on migrants and their families were obtained from scheduled interviews with 22 return migrants. The interviews were divided into four parts: (1) socioeconomic characteristics of the workers before migration such as age, marital status, education, job-training, occupation, place of birth, family background, motives for migrating, and difficulties encountered in the process; (2) the situation of the migrant workers while abroad — adjustment to the host country, pre-migration knowledge about it, difficulties during the first months and the ways to resolve them, contacts with the host society and attitudes towards natives, communication with families and their own problems, satisfaction with daily life, leisure, and recreation, health, friendships, social activities, relationships with supervisor and staff, wages, remittances and their uses, remittance channels, other family income and expenditures, plans after return; (3) the effect of the migration on the migrants' economic situation, changes in skills and work attitudes and world views, changes in the role of their wives and the behaviour of their children; and (4) post-migration status — readjustment problems such as unemployment and employment, reasons for unemployment, current occupation and income, reasons for job transfer, other problems of readjustment, plans and reasons for re-migration.

The third set of data — interviews with government officials and business executives — concern general information on emigration procedures and regulations, the recruitment system, service institutions for emigrants, work organisations at destination, and emigration policy in Korea.

As for the secondary sources, it should be noted that neither government agencies nor private companies with business concerns in the Gulf region have published official reports on the labour migration. They are reluctant to disclose such information to the public primarily because the government does not want competing countries to obtain recent information on the Korean emigration. This is also true for companies, which do not want to disclose sensitive information. The data they did provide are, therefore, not current.

Published research reports on the labour migration also are limited. The first extensive research on Korean emigration to the Middle East was conducted by Korean social scientiests under the sponsorship of the Korean National Commission for Unesco.[8] It addressed various matters relating to the migration, including the emigration pioneers, adjustment to the host country, and the economic and cultural effects on the home country. Although the research was extensive, it did not analyse the problems in depth. In addition to the Unesco report, two reports published by the Korea Institute for Industrial Economics and Technology will be used in this study.[9]

Migration to the Middle East

Historical Overview

The first massive emigration of Koreans began with the Japanese colonial rule of the Korean peninsula. During the colonial period (1910-1945), the main emigration flows were to Manchuria and Japan. Three million or more Koreans participated in these migrations during Japan's colonial rule (about 1.3 million to Manchuria and about 1.9 million to Japan).[10] More than half of those who migrated to Japan returned to the country before 1945, but most of the migrants to Manchuria remained at least until the liberation of the country from colonial rule. About half of those who migrated to Japan in the later stage of colonial rule (1939-1944) were mobilised labour conscripted by the Japanese colonial government's Labour Draft Plan of 1939, which sent about 700,000 Korean workers to Japan from 1939 to 1944. This was "impelled migration" in Petersen's term — the type of migration in which the people involved retain some power over the decision to leave but their will is relatively unimportant.

As of 1940 there were about 2.7 million Korean migrants in Japan and Manchuria, including children born there. The number corresponds to about 10 per cent of the total Korean population at that time. As might be expected, this large migratory movement had significant effects on both the sending and receiving countries. Although the effects have not been explored fully, we can draw some inferences. First of all, the movement contributed to the economies of the receiving countries but detracted from that of Korea. In fact, the movement was caused by a migration policy devised to facilitate the colonial exploitation of the country. Such a massive emigration might have produced the salutary effect of reducing Korea's population, but it did not improve its domestic employment opportunities, because the new jobs emerging as a result of Korea's development as Japan's hinterland were mostly taken by Japanese immigrants. The number of Japanese immigrant workers in the country amounted to about 283,000 as of 1940. They were "privileged migrants," and were mostly engaged in higher status occupations.

One of the migration's more significant impacts on Korea appeared not during the colonial period but afterwards. The collapse of Japan's colonial rule in 1945 called forth a massive international return-migration. All Japanese immigrants in Korea returned to Japan, and more than half the Korean emigrants and their children were repatriated. The number of repatriates into the Republic of Korea, including political refugees from the Democratic People's Republic of Korea, is estimated at about 2.5 million. Before these repatriates settled down, the Korean War broke out (1950-1953), creating massive exchanges of populations between the two territories. The number of refugees from the north was estimated at about 646,000, while those who were drafted or forcibly taken to the north are estimated at about 286,000.[11]

The influx of repatriates and refugees during this chaotic period exerted prolonged effects. One of the most visible effects was a population redistribution in favour of large cities, as most of the dislocated population preferred to settle down in urban areas. As a result, the urban service sector and squatter settlements expanded enormously.

During the postwar period, when Korea had still not recovered from the damages of war, there was no significant outflow. As conditions improved and as political and economic relations between South Korea and the United States became closer, increasing numbers of Koreans began to emigrate to the States. This migratory flow was accelerated after 1967, when the U.S. government began to permit immigration for those with needed skills or with a close relative with U.S. citizenship or permanent residence. In the 1970s, the annual number of Korean immigrants in the United States who obtained permanent-residence status was estimated at 20,000 to 30,000.[12]

However, this type of emigration for permanent settlement typically exerts little positive effect on the sending country. It is to be viewed as a type of "brain drain," whose effect on the country can hardly be positive. Along with this settlement type of emigration to the United States, there was also a significant, temporary labour emigration to other countries, starting with the emigration of miners to the Federal Republic of Germany in 1963. It increased considerably during the Viet Nam War as the South Vietnamese government sought Korean workers, mostly stevedores. In addition to these, there also developed a special type of contract-labour migration in which Korean seamen were employed on foreign ships. Table 1 presents the numbers of these contract-labour migrants by destination. The labour emigration to Viet Nam, which began in 1966, was virtually terminated with the end of the war in 1974, and the emigration to the Federal Republic of Germany declined gradually, while the emigration of sailors to various countries tended to increase.

The same table also shows that emigration of Korean workers to the Middle East

TABLE 1. Annual Number and Percentage of Korean Migrant Workers by Destination, 1966–1975

	1966	1967	1968	1969	1970	1971	1972	1973	1974	1975
Middle East	—	—	—	—	—	—	—	—	395	6466
									(2.7)	(30.8)
East Asia	9	185	250	323	464	393	469	821	2096	1521
	(.1)	(2.2)	(2.9)	(5.9)	(5.3)	(4.2)	(4.5)	(6.9)	(14.4)	(7.2)
South Asia	312	221	176	150	266	807	991	616	595	1345
	(2.4)	(2.7)	(2.1)	(2.7)	(3.0)	(8.7)	(9.6)	(5.2)	(4.1)	(6.4)
North America	24	234	582	413	914	844	736	973	608	358
	(.2)	(2.8)	(6.8)	(7.5)	(10.5)	(9.1)	(7.1)	(8.2)	(4.2)	(1.7)
Fed. Rep. of Germany	1520	428	94	847	3022	2731	1728	2120	2416	910
	(11.7)	(5.1)	(1.1)	(15.4)	(34.6)	(29.4)	(16.7)	(17.9)	(16.6)	(4.3)
Foreign ships	978	1861	1307	1577	2874	4089	6199	7278	8403	10,323
	(7.6)	(22.4)	(15.3)	(28.7)	(32.9)	(44.0)	(60.1)	(61.4)	(57.8)	(49.2)
Viet Nam	10,097	5328	6046	2131	1134	355	88	8	6	1
	(78.0)	(64.1)	(70.9)	(38.8)	(13.0)	(3.8)	(.8)	(.1)	(.0)	(.0)
Others	7	57	73	51	108	61	109	47	19	62
	(.1)	(.7)	(.9)	(.9)	(1.2)	(.7)	(1.1)	(.4)	(.1)	(.3)
Total	12,947	8314	8528	5492	8728	9280	10,320	11,863	14,538	20,986

Figures in parentheses are percentages.

Source: Institute for Middle East Studies, *Current Status of Labour Migration to the Middle East* (Seoul: Institute for Middle East Studies, 1976), 8–9.

began in 1974 and that within two years it became one of the two main flows of emigration. In 1975 Korean migrants to the region — mostly construction workers — numbered about 6500, corresponding to about 31 per cent of the total temporary migrant workers in the year. Thereafter, the labour emigration to the Gulf region has greatly accelerated. The total number of Korean migrant workers in the Middle East as of August 1983 is estimated to have reached about 170,000, constituting about 85 per cent of the total stock of Korean migrant workers who have labour contracts.

Volume of Migration to the Middle East

The only available data presenting a total picture of overseas migration for Koreans are the reports compiled by the Immigration Office. Table 2 presents the numbers of annual departures and arrivals for 1974–1982. It should be noted that these figures include not only permanent and temporary migration but other kinds of travel, such as business travel, tourism, and studies.

From the table, however, we can discern some distinctive features of the migration. First, a very large increase has occurred in the number of annual departures and arrivals. Between 1974 and 1982, annual departures quadrupled from 122,000 to 500,000. Second, the ratio of arrivals to departures increases with the number of departures, indicating that the most of the recent departures are made by persons travelling abroad and returning home. Finally, the net balance between departures and arrivals has also increased considerably. This can be attributed largely to the labour migrants, since permanent emigration of Koreans has not increased significantly. In fact, the yearly number of permanent emigrants for the same period has remained around 30,000, most of whom have moved to the United States.

Table 3 presents the distribution of the Korean outflows by destination. We should note that the figures for each region cover only departures for the major host countries in the region, as indicated in the footnotes to the table; minor destinations are subsumed under "others." In 1974, when the labour migration to the Middle East began, the main destinations of the migrants were East Asia and North America. In the same year, about 47 per cent of the total departures were for East Asia, about 37 per cent for North America. But since 1976 the percentage shares of the departures for the two regions have decreased considerably, with a sharp increase in the share of those migrating to the Middle East and the others. As a matter of fact, between 1978 and 1980 departures for the Middle East constituted the largest outflow of Koreans, about 37 per cent of total departures. In 1982 the total number of migrants to the Middle East (including those departing for Libya, Iraq, and the United Arab Emirates, which have absorbed increasing numbers of Korean migrants but which are included under "others" in the table) had climbed to about 160,000 or about 32 per cent of the total departures. It should also be noted that since 1976 Saudi Arabia, Japan, and the United States have been the main destinations for departing Koreans.

Table 2. Annual Departures from and Arrivals in Korea, 1974–1982 (thousands)

	1974	1976	1978	1980	1982
Departures	122	165	260	339	500
Arrivals	76	96	183	264	431
Balance	46	68	76	75	69
Ratio of arrivals to departures	.62	.58	.70	.78	.86

Source: Economic Planning Board, *Monthly Statistical Report of Korea* (Seoul: EPB), vol. 20, no. 6 (June 1978), 6–7, and vol. 25, no. 5 (June 1983), 6–7.

TABLE 3. Percentage Distribution of Departures from Korea by Destination, 1974–1982

	1974	1976	1978	1980	1982
Middle East[1]	.9	14.8	36.3	38.6	26.0
East Asia[2]	47.0	38.9	28.4	26.7	36.5
South Asia[3]	1.2	1.1	1.4	1.4	1.5
North America[4]	37.3	35.4	23.2	19.0	18.2
Europe[5]	6.3	3.3	4.6	4.2	3.4
Others[6]	7.4	5.9	6.1	10.2	14.4
Total	100.0	100.0	100.0	100.0	100.0

1. Saudi Arabia, Kuwait, Jordan, Qatar, Iran, Bahrain
2. Japan, Taiwan, Hongkong
3. Indonesia, the Philippines
4. United States, Canada
5. United Kingdom, Federal Republic of Germany, France, Spain
6. Iraq, Libya, United Arab Emirates, others

Source: Economic Planning Board, *Monthly Statistical Report of Korea* (Seoul: EPB), vol. 20, no. 6 (June 1978), 6–7, and vol. 25, no. 5 (June 1983), 6–7.

With regard to Korea's temporary labour migration, it appears that since 1977 the Middle East migration has been the predominant flow (see Table 4). When this migratory movement began, in 1974, Korean seamen employed on foreign ships constituted Korea's main category of migrants. Thereafter, the relative number of the seamen has decreased steadily with the steep increase in the migration to the Middle East. In the period 1978–1981, the Middle East migrants comprised more than 80 per cent of Korea's stock of migrant workers. A slight decrease in the share after 1980 is largely due to the advent of labour migrations to such Asian countries as Indonesia and Malaysia, not to an absolute decrease of migrants to the region.

Table 5 shows the annual number of Korean migrant workers in the Middle East by

TABLE 4. Percentage Distribution of Korean Migrant Workers by Destination, 1974-1982

	1974	1975	1976	1977	1978	1979	1980	1981	1982
Middle East	2.7	30.8	57.2	75.0	80.4	81.9	82.3	80.0	76.9
Asia	18.6	13.7	4.7	2.3	.9	.6	2.7	5.2	6.3
North America	4.2	1.7	1.4	.7	.7	.2	.1	–	.4
Foreign ships	57.8	49.2	35.2	20.2	17.8	17.0	14.8	15.7	16.1
Europe	16.6	4.3	1.0	1.1	.1	–	–	–	.1
Others	.1	.3	.4	.6	.1	.2	.1	–	.1
Total	100.0	100.0	100.0	100.0	100.0	100.0	100.0	100.0	100.0

Source: Rae Young Park, "Effects of Labour Migration to Middle East on the Domestic Labour Market," *Overseas Migration of Koreans: A Case of Migration to the Middle East* (Seoul: Korean National Commission for Unesco, 1983), 63.

country. It can first be noted that the migration to the Middle East began with 395 migrant workers in 1974 and increased steadily to nearly 160,000 in 1982. Second, Saudi Arabia has been the main recipient of Korean labour from the beginning. In 1979, when migration to Saudi Arabia was at its peak, the migrants to that country comprised over 81 per cent of the total migrants to the Middle East. Third, in the earlier years Iran was the second major destination, but due to the revolution in 1979, the migration dropped sharply. The distribution of the migrants in 1982 shows that Saudi Arabia continued to absorb the most Koreans, recording 71 per cent of Korean migrants in the Middle East. Iraq was second with 12 per cent, Libya, with 10 per cent, and Kuwait with 3 per cent. Besides these countries, no other country in the same year absorbed more than 1 per cent, although some countries had previously absorbed a relatively greater number of migrants, as in the case of Iran.

Return and Repeated Migrations

The migration of Korean workers to the Middle East is, as discussed earlier, an organised, temporary migration taking place on the basis of labour contracts between the migrant workers and the companies employing them. When the contract period is over, the migrants must return to their home country. Most contracts are for one year, but some migrants return home before the termination of their contract, while others extend their contracts beyond one year. Some of them are first-time migrants, while others have migrated on more than one occasion, after returning home on completion of their contract.

In one of the largest construction companies, which sends more than a thousand workers to the Gulf region every month, it is observed that 65.3 per cent of their employees have stayed for less than one year, 29.3 per cent stayed one to three years, and 5.4 per cent more than three years. From these figures it is estimated that on the average the current migrants have stayed about one year. This means that the average expected total duration of stay in the region will be considerably more than one year.

On the other hand, our sample estimates of returnees from the Middle East show that on the average they moved to the region twice and stayed there about two years. Most migrants stayed exactly one year for every move, and, hence, the number of years stayed nearly equals the number of moves (see Table 6). Among the total sample of 144 returnees, about 54 per cent moved to the Gulf region twice, and about 27 per cent moved there more than three times. Those who stayed for less than one year comprise only 15 per cent of the total returnees, while those who stayed for three years or more, made up about 28 per cent.

Table 7 shows the duration of migrant stays in Korea between moves. Among a total of 136 cases of remigration, about 63 per cent of the migrants appear to have stayed in Korea for one to two months between moves; only 4 per cent of them stayed

TABLE 5. Number and Percentage of Korean Migrant Workers to the Middle East by Country, 1974–1982

	1974	1975	1976	1977	1978	1979	1980	1981	1982
Saudi Arabia	218	3593	15,855	32,478	56,161	80,787	99,441	112,963	113,186
	(55.2)	(55.6)	(74.5)	(62.2)	(68.5)	(81.5)	(78.1)	(73.5)	(70.8)
Iraq	—	9	84	—	428	1063	161	6265	19,701
		(.1)	(.4)		(.6)	(1.1)	(.1)	(4.1)	(12.3)
Libya	—	—	—	677	1018	2046	3757	15,264	16,114
				(1.3)	(1.2)	(2.6)	(3.0)	(9.9)	(10.1)
Kuwait	—	48	462	4657	8646	7155	10,927	9060	5290
		(.7)	(2.2)	(8.9)	(10.5)	(7.2)	(8.6)	(5.9)	(3.3)
Jordan	—	90	486	1651	1418	902	2404	1840	1261
		(1.4)	(2.3)	(3.2)	(1.7)	(.9)	(1.9)	(1.2)	(.8)
Qatar	—	—	636	1491	1915	1854	1356	1980	1242
			(3.0)	(2.8)	(2.3)	(1.9)	(1.0)	(1.3)	(.8)
UAE	—	39	155	804	2689	3503	6758	2957	1111
		(.6)	(.7)	(1.5)	(3.3)	(3.5)	(5.3)	(1.9)	(.7)
Iran	177	2402	1630	6264	7418	64	30	198	441
	(44.8)	(37.2)	(17.1)	(12.0)	(9.1)	(.1)	(.0)	(.1)	(.3)
Others[1]	—	285	1961	3717	2116	1540	2489	3174	1556
		(4.4)	(9.2)	(7.1)	(3.0)	(1.6)	(2.0)	(2.1)	(1.0)
Total	395	6466	21,269	52,247	81,987	99,141	127,323	153,699	159,950
	(100.0)	(100.0)	(100.0)	(100.0)	(100.0)	(100.0)	(100.0)	(100.0)	(100.0)

1. Egypt, Yemen, Bahrain, Oman, Sudan

Source: Unofficial data

more than five months. For most of the re-migrating workers, stays in Korea may simply mean a vacation from difficult working conditions for continuous periods of a year or more. Therefore, it can be argued that repeated migrations are closely related to interruptions in employment owing to the terms of a labour contract rather than to changes in socioeconomic conditions in the home or host countries, or in the migrants' socioeconomic situation.

TABLE 6. Duration of Stay in the Middle East for Korean Migrant Workers by Number of Moves

Duration (months)	Number of Moves					Total	
	1	2	3	4	5	Number	%
1–11	15					15	10.4
12 (1 year)	39					39	27.1
13–23	12	1				13	9.0
24 (2 years)		30				30	20.8
25–35		7				7	4.9
36 (3 years)		1	12	3		13	9.0
37–47			11	4		14	9.7
48 (4 years)				4		4	2.8
49–59				1	1	4	2.8
60 (5 years)				1	2	2	1.4
61 and over						3	2.0
Total	66	39	23	13	3	144	100.0

Source: Migrants' personnel records.

TABLE 7. Repeat Migrants to the Middle East: Duration of Stay in Korea between Moves

Duration (months)	1st-2d Move	2d-3d Move	3d-4th Move	4th-5th Move	Total	
					Number	%
1–2	48	23	11	3	85	62.5
3–4	22	13	5	—	43	31.6
5–6	3	—	—	—	3	2.2
7–12	1	3	—	—	4	2.9
13 and over	1	—	—	—	1	.7
Total	78	39	16	3	136	100.0

Source: Migrants' personnel records.

The Motives for Labour Migration and Characteristics of Migrants

The Employment Situation in Korea

Despite increasing population pressure on the labour market, the employment situation in Korea during the past two decades has improved steadily. People of working age (15–64) increased from 54 per cent of the population in 1960 to 62 per cent in 1982. Yet the country's economy has expanded considerably so as to maintain a high labour-participation rate, which increased from 55 per cent in 1963 to 57 per cent in 1982. During the same period, unemployment declined from 8 to 4 per cent (see Table 8). These notable achievements were attained mostly before 1974, when emigration to the Middle East began.

However, it should be noted that Korea's actual employment situation has not been as stable as the statistics suggest, because the rates of labour participation and employment fail to account for "disguised under-employment," especially for the agricultural sector and females. Disguised under-employment for males in the non-agricultural sector is less serious. Nevertheless, the unemployment rate for males in this sector has been fairly high, ranging from 5.3 to 8.5 per cent. This suggests that the overseas migration of Korean workers, composed almost entirely of males, takes place partly in response to the unfavourable employment situation in their home country. The instability of employment in the domestic construction industry can also be considered an important factor in the migration of this category of labour to the Middle

TABLE 8. Labour Participation and Unemployment: All Households and Non-farm Households, Korea, 1973–1982

	All Households			Non-farm Households		
	Population 14 and older (in 1000s)	Labour Participation Rate	Unemployment Rate	Population 14 and older (in 1000s)	Labour Participation Rate	Unemployment Rate
1973	20,438	56.8	4.0	11,694	50.6	6.8
1974	21,148	57.1	4.1	12,164	51.8	6.8
1975	21,833	56.5	4.1	12,779	52.2	6.6
1976	22,549	57.9	3.9	13,421	53.3	6.3
1977	23,336	57.6	3.8	14,313	54.0	5.8
1978	24,024	58.0	3.2	15,290	54.6	4.7
1979	24,678	57.6	3.8	16,186	54.4	5.6
1980	25,335	57.1	5.2	17,066	54.4	7.5
1981	25,959	56.6	4.5	17,656	53.8	6.5
1982	26,531	56.8	4.4	18,683	54.7	6.0

Source: Economic Planning Board (EPB), *Monthly Statistical Report of Korea* (Seoul: EPB), vol. 20, no. 6 (June 1978), 69, and vol. 25, no. 6 (June 1983), 70.

East. Most of the males employed in the domestic construction industry (about 72 per cent) are temporary or daily workers, while the corresponding figure for all employed males is only 17 per cent (see Table 9).

The Korean government has tried to promote the export of entire construction services with migrant workers to the Middle East. This would not only ease the pressure on the domestic labour market but also earn foreign exchange. The government began to implement various policies directed towards this objective immediately after a few Korean construction companies started to develop businesses in the region. Since then the government has continuously reinforced these measures by strengthening the administrative machinery required for its promotional efforts as well as by strengthening diplomatic and economic ties with the Middle East countries.[13]

The Korean government has established many organisations for such services: the Committee for Middle East Economic Cooperation (a coordinating agency); the Office for Management of Middle East Economic Cooperation, in the Ministry of Construction; and the Overseas Labour Guidance Division of the Ministry of Labour. In addition, the government has established or enlarged such government-supported institutions as the Institute for Middle East Studies (currently developed as the Korea Institute for Industrial Economics and Technology), the Korea Overseas Development Corporation, the International Craftmanship Development Association, and the Training Institute for Construction Technology.

The second important measure was the enactment of the Overseas Construction Development Law. By this law, the government not only approves and regulates overseas construction companies but also supports their businesses. Related measures include the implementation of several schemes such as the payment guarantee, insurance, and tax incentives.

The various government measures in addition to the favourable domestic labour market situation have enabled Korean construction companies to expand their businesses in the Middle East. The total value of contracts undertaken during the four-year period 1973–1976 was $3,293 million,* but it increased to $27,884 million for the period 1977–1980. Saudi Arabia, which is the greatest importer of Korean labour, has been the main contractor with Korean companies, absorbing about 74 per cent of Korean contracts (see Table 10). When the annual value of contracts undertaken in each country is examined in conjunction with the annual flow of migrant workers (see Table 5), each Middle East country has absorbed Korean migrant workers in proportion to the value of contracts made in the country.

---

* References to dollars ($) are to US dollars throughout this paper.

TABLE 9. Percentage of Employed Males by Industry and Class of Worker, Korea, 1975

	Total Employed (in 1000s)	Self-employed	Employer	Family Worker	Regular Employee	Temporary Employee	Daily Employee
Construction	459	5.6	3.2	0.8	18.7	13.2	58.6
Agriculture	3281	58.8	1.6	27.7	2.8	2.7	6.4
Mining	89	1.2	2.7	0.5	67.0	18.7	10.0
Manufacturing	1377	7.9	6.3	2.1	63.2	13.9	6.7
Electricity	32	2.8	2.8	0.1	82.8	6.4	5.1
Sales	979	58.2	8.4	5.1	17.1	7.4	3.9
Transport	386	6.0	5.0	0.5	68.2	12.7	7.6
Finance	118	24.5	0.9	4.9	61.5	5.3	2.7
Services	980	7.5	2.0	3.1	70.0	6.8	11.0
Total	7702	35.9	13.2	3.8	30.1	7.2	9.9

Source: Economic Planning Board, *Population and Housing Census Report of Korea*, vol. 2, no. 3-1 (Seoul: EPB, 1978), 281.

TABLE 10. Work Contracts between Korean Companies and Middle East Countries, 1973–1981 (in millions of US dollars)

	1973–1976	1977	1978	1979	1980	1981 Jan.-Oct.	Gross Amount	Gross %
Saudi Arabia	2752.8	2410.6	6404.1	4741.2	5283.7	5888.4	27,435.9	73.8
Libya	–	46.4	169.7	175.0	1366.1	1689.2	3446.3	9.3
Kuwait	205.8	257.5	528.1	461.6	378.8	85.3	1917.1	5.2
Iraq	–	30.4	43.7	8.7	431.1	764.0	1277.3	3.4
UAE	15.9	141.6	112.9	230.1	227.0	126.1	853.5	2.3
Iran	53.8	326.5	281.9	12.5	63.1	–	601.9	1.6
Bahrain	173.3	99.0	68.5	10.8	7.1	23.1	381.8	1.0
Qatar	8.4	48.5	88.9	161.6	33.2	6.8	333.8	0.9
Jordan	58.0	2.1	79.2	83.7	18.3	82.2	323.5	0.9
Yemen	–	–	85.7	78.9	23.1	37.4	225.1	0.6
Sudan	–	20.0	88.3	2.3	–	9.7	120.4	0.3
Egypt	10.0	4.5	31.1	17.5	107.1	15.7	185.8	0.5
Oman	–	–	0.2	–	52.0	–	52.2	0.1
Total	3293.2	3387.0	7982.4	5958.4	7819.4	5977.2	37,154.7	100.0

Source: Hee Woo Kim, Industrial Export to Middle East and Government Policy Measures (Seoul: Korea Institute for Industrial Economics and Technology, 1982), 22.

Costs and Benefits of Migration

The previous section described employment situations and migration policies in Korea. This section will examine the motivating factors in the migration to the Arab countries.

Table 11 presents the average monthly earnings for migrant workers and domestic workers employed in production and production-related work. The average earnings of the migrants from 1978 to 1981 were more than twice those of nonmigrants. Concerning the trends in earnings, it is worthwhile to note that substantial increases in the average earnings for migrants and nonmigrants in 1979 were largely due to the construction boom in both the Gulf region and Korea, combined with a relative shortage of experienced construction workers in the latter.

Table 12 shows the income differences between migrants and nonmigrants by occupation. Somewhat greater differences are seen between the two in Table 12 than in Table 11, since the latter compares average earnings for migrants with those for nonmigrants with similar levels of work experience. Table 12, on the other hand, compares earnings of all workers, whose average work experience is less than that of migrant workers. Nevertheless, it demonstrates that none of the occupations in the Middle East earns less than the same category in Korea.

Almost all living expenses of the migrants during their stay in the Middle East are borne by the companies employing them. A former director of the general affairs department in a large Korean overseas construction company indicated that the company's outlay for wages comprises only about half of the total costs for their employees in the Middle East. The other half includes food, housing, recreation, insurance, and round-trip airfare. According to the informant, the costs for food and housing per worker amounted to about $250 per month, and insurance fees for each worker amounted to $600 year. When we include these benefits in the migrant's earnings, the average monthly earnings of a migrant worker in recent years have been about $1,050, or more than three times the average monthly earnings for domestic workers with similar work experience.

Of course, migrants' main motive in migrating to the Middle East is increased earnings. According to our sample data, about 70 per cent of the prospective migrants who answered the question regarding motives said their main motive was "to earn a round sum of money." Most of the others had similar economic reasons such as "to prepare own house" and "for better economic life." Only 10 per cent pointed to noneconomic reasons such as "to learn new skills" and "for new experience."

We should note, however, that to obtain the economic benefits of migration, migrant workers are required to work in more demanding conditions than at home. The migrants' living conditions in the Middle East are less comfortable than in their home

TABLE 11. Average Monthly Earnings for Korean Migrant Production Workers and Domestic Male Production Workers with 5–9 Years' Work Experience, 1978–1981

| | Migrant | | Domestic | | Ratio of Migrant to Domestic |
	US$	Won (1000s)	US$	Won (1000s)	
1978	686	333	258	125	2.7
1979	734	356	361	175	2.0
1980	752	436	316	183	2.4
1981	756	509	316	213	2.4

Earnings for domestic workers in US dollars and for overseas workers in Korean won are obtained by applying the following exchange rates: $1 = W485 in 1978–1979, W580 in 1980, W674 in 1981.

Source: Rae Young Park, op. cit., 84–86.

TABLE 12. Average Monthly Earnings: Korean Migrant Workers and Domestic Workers by Occupation, 1976 and 1980 (in 1000 Korean won)

| | 1976 | | | 1980 | | |
	Migrant	Domestic	Ratio	Migrant	Domestic	Ratio
Carpenter	340	63	5.4	425	163	2.6
Electrician	314	90	3.5	458	176	2.6
Welder	328	64	5.1	499	147	3.4
Pipe fitter	295	92	3.2	455	157	2.9
Engine operator	279	85	3.3	523	202	2.6
Other skilled	398	87	4.3	436	230	1.9
Unskilled	—[1]	54	—	365	166	2.2

1. Unknown.

Source: Rae Young Park, op. cit., 84, 88; Ministry of Labour, *Statistical Yearbook of Labour* (Seoul: Republic of Korea, 1981), 215–217.

country. Every migrant works longer hours than he would in Korea: The migrants are known to work about 60 hours per week— about seven hours more than the normal work week for nonmigrants working in the construction sector. The Middle East allowance for overtime is much greater than that for regular work, and, hence, all the migrants are eager to work overtime. The migrants work not only longer than nonmigrants but also harder. In recent years, most Korean construction companies in the Middle East have introduced a special kind of subcontracting system in order to reduce non-wage expenses. This system disburses wages not on the basis of hours worked but on the amount of work that should be completed by contract. Naturally, this payment system results in harder work and more sustained effort.

The costs of migration comprise monetary costs for moving and non-money costs, including income forgone and psychological health. The money costs of migration to the Middle East are negligible since migrants' entire round-trip fare is paid by their companies. Yet the amount of income forgone in preparing for migration and during the job-seeking period after returning appears to be substantial. Our interview data indicate that preparation for migration to the Middle East takes at least one full month, and that most returnees are not able to get a new job right after return. Among 22 returnees interviewed, only 9 found jobs within a month. The rest of them sought jobs for a few months or even more than one year. On the average, they were unemployed for about three months. If these situations are taken as typical, the average income forgone for this period (four months) is about $1300 on the basis of the average wage in 1981 for production workers with five to nine years of experience. In this connection, it should be noted that although the amount of income forgone due to the migration is considerable, the money return is far greater.

The data inform us that the psychological costs of migration are also considerable, although not quantifiable. Nearly all the migrants had strong feelings of anxiety, stress, and even regret prior to their departure for the Middle East. Among the 22 returnees, only one said he had had no such feelings. These premigration anxieties, however, are not as serious as the problems encountered during their stays in the Middle East, problems that need to be considered as part of the significant non-economic costs borne by migrants.

Characteristics of the Migrants

Korean migrant workers in the Middle East can be classified into two groups: those employed by overseas Korean companies and those employed by foreign companies. In 1980 the latter comprised only 1.3 per cent of Korean migrants in the Middle East. No detailed information regarding their working conditions or other experiences is available. These migrants moved out upon their employer's direct request. What is known about them is that their average wage is almost twice that of migrant workers employed by Korean companies and that their educational and skill levels are much higher than those employed by Korean companies.

The migrant workers employed by the overseas Korean companies can themselves be classified into two groups: regular and temporary employees. Regular employees make up less than 10 per cent of the migrants. The majority of them are professional and managerial workers, while nearly all the temporary employees are engaged in production and related work. In this section, as in the others, we are concerned only with the temporary, production-related workers.

Some of the socioeconomic characteristics of the migrant workers obtained from our sample are shown in Tables 13 to 18. These migrants had been sent to the Middle East by a Korean construction company between 1976 and 1983 and their characteristics were recorded before departing for the region. All the Korean migrants to the region are male workers temporarily employed by the construction company.

According to the sample, the average age of the migrants at the time of departure for the Middle East was about 32, which was also the average age for domestic male construction workers. However, when we compare the ages of the migrant workers with those of domestic workers, it is clear that the labour migration to the Middle East is selective in favour of the young adult. About 80 per cent of the sample of 143 migrant workers were between 25 and 39 years of age, but the corresponding figure for the domestic construction workers in 1980 was about 51 per cent (see Table 13).

TABLE 13. Age Comparison of Korean Migrant and Nonmigrant Workers, 1980 (percentages)

	Migrant Workers	Nonmigrant Workers		
		Total Employed	Production	Construction
19 and under	2.8	5.9	8.5	2.8
20–24	4.9	11.1	14.9	8.8
25–29	34.3	15.9	21.1	17.0
30–34	25.9	14.7	17.2	17.7
35–39	19.6	12.9	13.4	16.5
40–44	11.9	12.4	10.8	14.7
45 and over	.7	27.1	14.1	22.5
Total	100.0	100.0	100.0	100.0

Sources: Migrant personnel records; and Economic Planning Board (EPB), *1980 Population and Housing Census Report of Korea,* vol. 2, no. 3-1 (EPB, 1982), tables 1, 4, and 5.

The average educational attainments of the migrants to the Middle East appear to be higher than those of the domestic employees in construction (see Table 14). Among the migrants, more than 75 per cent had received middle-school education or more. The figure for nonmigrant workers is about 58 per cent. It should be noted that data on the migrants includes only skilled and unskilled production workers in construction, while the data on nonmigrant workers comprise the entire workforce, including professional and managerial workers whose educational levels are certainly much higher than those of manual workers. Thus, if we compared the migrants' educational levels with those of nonmigrants with the same occupation, the disparities would be even greater.

We can therefore conclude that the labour migration to the Middle East favours young adults with better education. However, this does not mean that the economic status of migrants in general is higher than that of the nonmigrants in the same occupation.

TABLE 14. Educational Levels of Korean Migrant and Nonmigrant Workers, 1980
(in percentages)

	Migrant Workers	Nonmigrant Workers		
		Total	Production	Construction
No school	1.4	9.9	5.2	5.7
Primary school (1–6 years)	23.2	30.7	31.5	36.5
Middle and high school (7–12 years)	73.9	48.8	62.2	49.0
College and over (13 years and over)	1.4	10.6	3.0	8.9
Total	100.0	100.0	100.0	100.0

Sources: Migrants' personnel records; and Economic Planning Board (EPB), *1980 Population and Housing Census Report of Korea,* vol. 2, no. 3-1 (EPB , 1982), table 10.

TABLE 15. Familial and Economic Statuses of Korean Migrant Workers

	Number	%
Marital status		
married	77	59.7
not married	52	40.3
Total[1]	129	100.0
Relationship to household head		
household head	79	59.4
eldest son	35	26.3
other	19	14.3
Total[1]	133	100.0
House ownership		
own	22	45.8
rent	26	54.2
Total[1]	48	100.0
Economic assets		
less than $8500	21	67.8
$8500–$17,000	5	16.1
$17,000 and over	5	16.1
Total[1]	31	100.0

1. Excluded are unknown.

Source: Migrants' personnel records.

TABLE 16. Fathers' Educational Levels and Residential Origins of Korean Migrant Workers

	Number	%
Fathers' educational level		
none	5	11.6
primary school	28	65.1
middle school	7	16.3
high school	2	4.7
college	1	2.3
Total[1]	43	100.0
Place of birth registration		
large cities[2]	39	27.1
medium and small cities[3]	10	6.9
towns[4]	26	18.1
villages	69	47.9
Total	144	100.0
Residence before migration		
large cities[2]	76	52.8
medium and small cities[3]	30	20.8
towns[4]	16	11.1
villages	22	15.3
Total	144	100.0

1. Excluded are unknown.
2. Population over 500,000.
3. Population 50,000–500,000.
4. Population 20,000–50,000.

Source: Migrants' personnel records.

Although we do not have comparable data for the nonmigrants, data in some of the tables that follow suggest that their economic status might be lower than that of the nonmigrants. About 60 per cent of the migrants are married, and about 86 per cent are either household heads or eldest sons, who are usually responsible for the management of household affairs. Yet their economic assets are minimal, as indicated by the fact that about 54 per cent of the migrants did not have their own houses and about 68 per cent had economic assets valued at less than $8,500 (see Table 15). In connection with the migrants' ownership of houses, it is worth noting that at the national level about 87 per cent of all households own their own houses. The educational level of the fathers of the migrants indicates that most migrants originated from lower social strata; and most of them were rural-to-urban migrants (see Table 16). Another indicator of the migrants' economic status is that a considerable number of them were jobless before departing for the Middle East (see Table 17).

The majority of the migrants were engaged abroad in the same occupation that they had before migration, perhaps because the most important criterion of the Middle East recruitment is the kind of skills in demand. Unskilled migrant workers in the region comprise only about one-fourth of the total migrants throughout the period 1977–1982 (see Table 18).

TABLE 17. Occupations of Korean Migrant Workers at Origin and Destination

	Number		Percentage	
	Origin	Destination	Origin	Destination
Carpenter	9	16	6.2	11.1
Painter	5	7	3.5	4.9
Scaffold setter	4	10	2.8	6.9
Welder	13	27	9.0	18.8
Pipefitter	4	13	2.8	9.0
Machine fitter	4	5	2.8	3.5
Electrofitter	3	8	2.1	5.6
Mechanic	—	4	—	2.8
Engine operator	1	5	.7	3.5
Cook and camp service	3	8	2.1	5.6
Clerk	3	3	2.1	2.1
Other	14	38	9.7	26.4
Not classifiable	50	—	34.7	—
Unemployed	31	—	21.5	—
Total	144	144	100.0	100.0

Source: Migrants' personnel records.

TABLE 18. Percentage Distribution of Korean Migrant Workers by Occupation, 1977–1982

	1977	1978	1979	1980	1981	1982
Construction	57.0	56.7	50.2	51.1	50.5	48.2
Driver, mechanic	16.1	11.6	12.8	12.6	13.1	14.3
Nurse	.6	.5	.5	.1	.3	.4
Sailor	1.7	.9	.3	.3	—	.3
Unskilled	14.4	13.4	21.7	23.4	23.4	18.1
Other	10.2	17.0	14.4	12.4	12.6	18.7
Total	100.0	100.0	100.0	100.0	100.0	100.0

Source: Rae Young Park, op. cit., 74.

Adjustment and Readjustment: The Migrant Worker in the Middle East and at Home

The Physical Environment and Social Setting

The physical and social environment abroad under which Korean migrant workers must live for one or more years is entirely different from that of their homeland. The Middle East is much drier and hotter than Korea, and the temperature disparities between day and night are also much greater. Korean migrants often suffer from fatigue, loss of appetite, sunstroke, and cold. Islamic culture differs greatly from Korean culture. It prohibits the drinking of alcoholic beverages and eating pork, which most Koreans enjoy, and it also imposes strict codes for religious and sexual behaviour. Any violations of these regulations are subject to punishment, even within the work camp.

The work camp seems to have developed partly as a response to the demand by Middle East government officials, who felt that the growing number of non-Arab migrants in their country might erode their national and cultural identity. Birks and Sinclair[14] see the use of Oriental labour in "work camps" as a means of resolving two apparently conflicting objectives: economic and industrial development concurrent with the preservation of a distinctive culture and identity. However, the institution of the work camp also seems to be preferred by Korean employers in the region, since it is regarded as a suitable mechanism for utilising their workforce efficiently.

Most Korean work camps are near the work site and far away from the residential areas of the Arab population. The camps are usually enclosed by some sort of physical structure, a fence or natural barrier. The accommodation in such work camps is similar to that provided by the military. A typical camp has living quarters for the staff (regular employees) and for the temporary employees, a mess-hall, a first-aid station, and other service facilities. The living quarters for the staff are separated from those for the temporary workers, and, of course, are of higher quality. A barrack for temporary workers is usually divided into two or four large rooms, and each room is shared by 10 to 40 workers.

The staff not only supervises the workers in the workplace but also controls their everyday life. Like other "total institutions," there are house rules controlling the workers' conduct and a system of rewards and punishments supporting the rules. The most important rules are prepared by the Ministry of Labour of the Korean government and appear in the employment contract between employer and employee. The contract states that the employee may be subject to reprimand, reduction of salary, or dismissal when he commits the following offences:

1. misconduct against national dignity or policy;
2. divulging an employer's confidential information;
3. gambling or other harmful behaviour in violation of public morals leading to

deterioration of discipline and the work ethic;
4. misconduct such as violence, destruction of property, and instigation of sabotage;
5. violation of the laws of the host country resulting in diplomatic problems;
6. any conviction during employment;
7. harmful behaviour against the employer or violation of the employer's rules and contracts;
8. disobedience against rightful orders from superiors;
9. job transfer without the employer's agreement;
10. forgery of documents; and
11. work absenteeism of more than 12 days without legitimate permission.

Besides these regulations, the employers impose a number of additional rules, most of which concern the regulation of life and conduct within the work camp. These rules include, among others, prohibitions of long hair, violence against co-workers, drinking alcoholic beverages, visiting disreputable localities, and leaving camp without permission.

By imposing these rules, the employers maintain discipline in work camps and control their employees. Those who violate the rules are subject to commensurate punishment, while those who observe them fully are rewarded. The employers evaluate their employees' performance in terms of their conformity to these rules and their work achievements, and use the resulting score as an important criterion for the renewal of contracts.

The organisation based on the above rules is quite authoritarian. In the organisation there is a basic differentiation between the regular employees (the staff) and the temporary employees (the inmates). The staff comprises a director and a number of managerial and technical officers. In the work place, a technical officer (engineer) directs a number of working units, each of which is supervised by a foreman. In the camp an executive manager regulates all aspects of the inmates' lives, and a number of chief inmates from each of the barracks help the manager. The chief inmates play dual roles as the communicators of the management decisions and orders and as representatives of the workers in the labour-management council, called Sae-Ma-Uel Ja-Chi-Hoe. No other formal association is allowed, although there are a few informal groupings for social and religious activities.

The workers' everyday life is tightly scheduled. They must get up early in the morning and go to bed late at night. They start to work at around 6 a.m., take a siesta for two to three hours after lunch, and finish their regular working day at 6–7 p.m. Regular working hours are eight hours per day, 48 hours per week. But nearly all of the migrants work overtime for two or more hours after dinner, since the overtime allowance is 50 per cent higher than the regular hourly payment. The workers enjoy one day's leave for a month and eight days of vacation leave in a year. Yet most of them work even on days off and vacation because they have no other activities to occupy them.

On Sundays the migrants do not work but spend most of the day within their work camp. The employers allow them to go out of the camp on Sunday and occasionally provide them with transport. They also provide them with various recreation facilities and occasionally entertain them with movies and outdoor games. Yet during the week working hours are so long that the workers have no leisure time.

Adjustment to the Work Camp

Before departing for the Middle East, the migrant workers follow a series of complicated procedures: application for overseas employment, physical examination, education from their employers as well as from the Overseas Development Corporation, and application for passport. Upon departure they are required to carry a set of standardised personal belongings. However, they are not allowed to take Bibles, pornographic literature, alcoholic beverages, or playing cards. Upon arrival at the work camp, they receive an introduction to the house rules and are assigned to prearranged work units and living quarters. As in the "total institution" described by Goffman, the worker is shaped and coded into an object that can be fed into the administrative machinery of the institution and treated as an input into a routine operation.

This trimming procedure may not mortify the workers in the same manner as the inmates of a prison, mental hospital, or army barracks. Most of the workers are familiar with such procedures through their experience with military service. Yet the barriers the work camp erects between the inmates and the wider world or their homeland are strong enough to lead to feelings of alienation and a diminution of self-esteem. For this and other reasons, migrants become anxious about leaving their homeland or even regret their decision to move as the time for departure arrives.

In the early stage of the camp life, the most difficult problem that the migrant workers face seems to be the physical adjustment to the new climate. Due to the temperature difference between origin and destination, most of them find it difficult to sleep and eat well. Some feel anxious or miss their families. In the early stage, the psychological problems, however, seem to be outweighed by the physical ones.

With time, both psychological and physical problems seem to affect them with similar force. Most of the returnees interviewed complained they often suffered not only from such physical problems as fatigue, loss of appetite, and sleeplessness but also from stress, loneliness, and depression.

The staff of the work camp are a totally different group from the workers. They form a better educated, highly paid managerial and professional cadre of regular employees. They run the work organisation according to its rules, and in doing so they develop what may be described as a "theory of human nature."[15] This theory rationalises activity, provides a subtle means of maintaining social distance from workers and of stereotyping them, and justifies the treatment accorded to them. Typically, the theory covers the "good" and "bad" possibilities of the conduct of workers, the disciplinary value of privileges and punishments, and the essential difference between staff and workers.

The workers, on the other hand, are less educated and low-paid skilled and unskilled workers who are temporarily employed. They are a relatively homogeneous group in terms of socioeconomic status. They rationalise their migrant-worker status only in terms of economic benefit. Their "true self" resides in their homeland and especially in their families left behind. In such situations, the superior staff appear essentially as enforcers of rules and discipline in the manner of officers of a military establishment.

A number of returnees who were interviewed stated that while the staff held the view that they had taken care of the inmate workers well, the workers themselves held contrary opinions. Most of the workers (15 out of 22) replied that the labour-management relationship was not friendly but rather antagonistic. According to them, the main reason for such antagonism was incorrect accounting for overtime work and repressive management. The most frequent dispute between the managers and the workers arises from the calculation of working hours, which is often unfavourable to the workers. Overt conflicts between management and workers do not occur frequently, since the workers usually are in a weak bargaining situation. Most of the interviewees (17 out of 22), however, felt that their superiors were authoritarian or even despotic in their management of the workforce.

The labour-management council mentioned earlier is not held in high esteem by the workers, who view it as a mechanism for controlling the inmates and hence as protective of the employer's interests rather than those of the employees. The employer does not permit any formal organisation other than the official one. Although the workers form various kinds of informal organisations, mostly friendship associations, their participation in such organisations appears to be very low. Instead, they form strong friendships with their co-workers, most of whom meet each other at the work camp. When they need help, they ask their friends rather than their superiors. They enjoy conversing with their friends about their work, family, and plans. These personal relationships seem to be one of the important means of protecting their personality as individuals. However, the relationships with co-workers are not always positive. They occasionally quarrel and fight, or are victims of violence and robbery at the hands of their co-workers.

The migrant workers scarcely make friends with the nationals of the host country and other foreign co-workers. They go out of their work camp only two or three times a month for shopping and sightseeing. Therefore, relations with foreigners and contact with the native society are a negligible part of their life. Their "soul," above all, resides not in the Middle East but in their homeland.

Their main preoccupation is the well-being of their families. They live in their expectations. Most interviewees reported that they wrote letters to their family or friends more than once a week. In this connection, it is noteworthy that a major cause of anxiety is their fear of the infidelity of their wives. The most satisfying time for the migrant workers was the time they spent writing letters to their families. One of the returnees reported that whenever news or a rumour of the misconduct of a fellow-worker's wife spread in the camp, a panic-stricken atmosphere developed.

The migrant workers expressed strong dissatisfaction about the inequitable privilege system adopted by their employers. A considerable proportion of the returnees (10 out of 22) aspired to start their own businesses rather than be simply employed, although most of them eventually became employed again. This aspiration can be explained partly as a response to the repressive management techniques in the Middle East and their desire to be free of an authoritarian employer. Most of those interviewed suggest that the staff should be more democratic and concerned with rights of workers.

However, the "house rules" of the work organisation do not allow democratic relationships and they permit little freedom. The staff control the inmates through the mechanism of reward and punishment. They evaluate individual workers' performance and occasionally reward those who conform to the rules. On the other hand, those who violate the rules are often punished by temporary layoffs without payment or compulsory deportation from the Middle East. Further, they utilise the individual performance score as an important criterion of contract renewal or re-employment. As shown in Table 19, 91 per cent of the migrant workers who got a high score during their first contract period could make the renewal one or more times, but none of the migrants with low scores obtained renewals.

Under the privilege system, the inmates engage in what Goffman calls "removal activities."[16] Some activities are collective such as field games and card playing; some are individual but rely on public materials such as newspapers, magazines, and TV sets. Still others may constitute secondary adjustments by forbidden means such as gambling and "highs" and "jags" achieved with industrial alcohol. Modes of adaptation to the work camp among the inmates are diverse and vary from worker to worker. Furthermore, the individual worker may change his mode from time to time. He may also occasionally challenge the institution directly by a flagrant refusal to cooperate with the staff or may retreat from everything except events immediately around himself. The latter two cases may result in either compulsory expatriation or voluntary return migration before the termination of the contract.

Our sample data from an overseas construction company includes information on premature returns — that is, returns before the termination of the contract. According to the data, the rate of premature return is about 15 per cent (see Table 20). This high rate does not seem to be uncommon. An informant who had served

TABLE 19. A Comparison of Korean Migrants' Contract Renewals with Performance Scores during the First Contract Period

Number of Contracts	High (over 79 points)		Middle (60–79 points)		Low (under 60 points)		Total	
		Score						
1	4	(8.9)	16	(47.1)	21	(100.0)	41	(41.0)
2	12	(26.7)	17	(50.0)	–		29	(29.0)
3	16	(35.6)	1	(2.9)	–		17	(17.0)
4	11	(24.4)	–		–		11	(11.0)
5	2	(4.4)	–		–		2	(2.0)
Total	45	(100.0)	34	(100.0)	21	(100.0)	100	(100.0)

Figures in parentheses are percentages.

Source: Migrants' personnel records.

TABLE 20. Premature Returns and Completed Terms among Korean Migrant Workers

	Number	%
Premature	22	15.3
Completed	122	84.7
Total	144	100.0

Source: Migrants' personnel records.

TABLE 21. Reasons for Premature-Return Migration

	Number	%
Familial	4	18.2
Personal	6	27.3
Loss of work incentive	3	13.6
Illness	4	18.2
Injury	3	12.6
Contract violation	2	9.1
Total	22	100.0

Source: Migrants' personnel records.

as a personnel manager in one of the largest companies told us that the rate in his company varies from one work camp to another but ranges from 10 to 20 per cent. These rates suggest that the migrants' adjustment to the working and living conditions is unusually difficult.

The data also include reasons for the premature returns (see Table 21). Some of the reasons, as recorded in the personnel files, are not mutually exclusive, especially in cases of personal and family reasons. The most prevalent personal reasons for premature returns appear to be the infidelity of a wife or lover, or the misuse of remittance money by family members. Nearly half of the premature returnees appear to have terminated their contracts for such reasons. Loss of work incentive and violation of the contract also figure prominently in premature returns. Also, about a third of the premature contract-terminations were caused by illness and injury, indicating again the difficulty involved in adapting to the physical and working conditions in the host country.

The socioeconomic characteristics of premature returnees and of the migrants who completed their contract term are not much different in terms of marital status and education, but differences in community origin and economic status seem to be significant. The data indicate that migrants from large cities and those whose economic status is lower are less likely to return prematurely. This suggests that migrants from more adverse socioeconomic conditions are likely to have stronger economic incentives to remain for full term. Second, although there is no difference in the premature-return rate between married and ummarried migrants, the *reasons* for the premature returns in the two categories are quite different. Married workers returned primarily for personal and familial reasons, while the unmarried leave primarily because of loss of work incentive, a loss most often explained by the fact that an unmarried worker has less of an incentive to make money and is therefore more willing to withdraw from an unpleasant situation.

Readjustment to Korea after Overseas Employment

The return from the Middle East to Korea means switching from the total institution to an open labour market. Therefore, the first serious problem faced by the returnees is the economic readjustment. For most of the migrants, the social and psychological problems are not so serious since the return means a homecoming, a return to the known and familiar environment. Our interview data with 22 returnees show that about half of them were jobless for over three months after returning and that more than one-third had to change jobs. Furthermore, their earnings decreased substantially. About half of them reported that their earnings after returning fell more than 40 per cent. For these and other reasons, a third of the returnees want to remigrate.

Before leaving for the Middle East, about half of the migrants expressed a desire to have their own business. Yet most of them failed to accomplish this goal, perhaps because their savings were not adequate for the purpose. Besides, half of them stated that their physical health had worsened because of the hard work in the Middle East.

However, this does not mean that their family economy did not improve or that their attitudes had become more pessimistic. More than half of them said their family economy has improved, while only two said they were economically worse off than before. For most of the migrants, the overseas experience gave them a more optimistic world view and more positive attitudes towards work, although there were a few exceptions.

Finally, the readjustments of the migrants' families need to be considered briefly. As we have mentioned earlier, most migrant workers are either household heads or played otherwise dominant roles in the household. Their absences therefore changed the roles of their wives and affected their children's behaviour. Their wives may have assumed dual roles, that is, the usual role of wife in addition to the new role as household head. Obviously, working mothers have a more difficult time than nonworking mothers, especially in managing the household economy and in disciplining their children.

Our interview data suggest that about half of the migrants' wives acted as the sole decision maker for the family during their husbands' absence. Important decisions were usually discussed by letter with their husbands. Their responsibilities became greater. The same data also show that some of the migrants' children had poorer academic records, and in some cases there was a lowering of discipline. According to one report, the migrants' children experienced greater difficulties with their peers, suggesting a less than ideal socialisation process.

However, these familial problems (except for the incidences of divorce brought on by migration) seem to be well resolved with the return of the migrants. Our data suggest that the migrant's attachment to his family tends to be stronger and his children's academic records better when he returns from the Middle East. Above all, the economic improvement wrought by the migration appears to contribute considerably to the family's sense of well-being.

Effects of Migration

Earnings, Remittances, and Their Uses

The average monthly earnings for temporary employees (base wage plus overtime) have increased from about $520 in 1973 to about $756 in 1982 (see Table 22). The overtime allowance constitutes 46–55 per cent of the total earnings. This average earning is about 2.5 times greater than that of construction workers in Korea with similar experience (see Table 12).

According to government regulations, all the migrant workers employed by Korean overseas companies are required to remit more than 80 per cent of their total earnings to Korea via the Korean banking system. Those who do not meet this requirement get a warning from the Korean overseas councillor, and often lose chances to renew their contracts, visit Korea, or change host country. On the other hand, those who remit more than the average are honoured and guaranteed a contract renewal.

TABLE 22. Average Monthly Earnings for Overseas Korean Production Workers, 1976–1982

	1976	1977	1978	1979	1980	1981	1982
US dollars							
Base wage	280	331	341	358	354	339	339
Overtime	239	292	345	376	398	418	418
Total	519	623	686	734	752	756	756
Won (1000s)[1]							
Base wage	136	161	165	174	205	228	244
Overtime	116	142	167	182	231	281	300
Total	252	302	333	356	436	510	544

1. The amounts in Korean won are obtained by applying the following exchange rates: US$1 = W485 in 1976–1979, W580 in March 1980, W674 in March 1981, W720 in March 1982.

Source: Rae Young Park, op. cit., 84–86.

In fact, nearly all the migrants remit about 90 per cent of their earnings to Korea. The estimated average remittance per migrant worker in 1976 was about $5600 and about $8200 in 1982. Since the average migrant tour in the Middle East is about two years, the average total remittance per person was about $11,000 in 1976 and about $16,400 in 1982. They remitted such a large portion of the earnings not only because the government implemented the regulations to discourage consumption in the host country, but also because their travelling costs and living expenses in the Middle East are paid by their employers.

Only 10 per cent of the migrants' earnings is spent in the host country. Most expenditures appear to be for the purchase of consumer durables for personal use, such as TV sets, cassette tape recorders, and cameras and gifts for family and friends such as cosmetics and wristwatches.

On the average, about 60 per cent of the migrants' earnings while they were in the Middle East were saved or invested. This means that only about 30 per cent of their earnings went toward their families' living expenses. The families saved or invested such a large portion of the remittances partly because the remittances were large enough and partly because most families had other sources of income. The interview

248

TABLE 23. Annual Value of Contracts Made Abroad by Korean Construction Companies by Region, 1977–1982

	Up to 1977	1978	1979	1980	1981	1982	Total
US dollars (millions)							
Middle East	6680	7982	5958	7831	12,674	11,392	52,518
Southeast Asia	642	91	378	409	838	1921	4279
Pacific region	151	10	14	4	2	–	185
Latin America	21	36	–	–	–	–	67
Africa	22	25	1	15	166	–	229
Total	7516	8145	6351	8259	13,681	13,383	57,336
Percentage							
Middle East	88.9	98.0	93.8	94.8	92.6	85.1	91.6
Southeast Asia	8.5	1.1	6.0	5.0	6.1	14.4	7.5
Pacific region	2.0	0.1	0.2	*	*	*	0.3
Latin America	0.3	0.4	*	*	*	*	0.1
Africa	0.3	0.3	*	0.2	1.2	*	0.4
Total	100.0	100.0	100.0	100.0	100.0	100.0	100.0

* Less than 0.05 per cent

Source: Unofficial data

data also shows that about three-fourths of the returnees spent their remittance money as planned.

According to the same data, the migrants' post-migration earnings were far lower than their earnings in the Middle East. On the average, the returnees make about half of what they made in the Middle East, but their post-migration earnings are greater than their earnings prior to migrating, perhaps because some of them improved their skills while others invested their remittance in profitable businesses.

As a result, the economic situations of most migrants improved considerably. Among the 22 returnees we interviewed, only two workers reported that their economic situation had deteriorated; only one returnee reported that his family's consumption had somewhat decreased. These exceptional cases seem to have been primarily due to misuse of remittance money or improper investment.

Effects on Economic Growth

The export of Korean construction industry to the Middle East started with a contract of $24 million in December 1973. The annual value of contracts made in the region has grown rapidly, reaching $11.4 billion in 1982 (see Table 23). The total amount of contracts made during the ten years 1973–1982 is estimated to be about $53 billion. This figure corresponds to 92 per cent of the total contracts made abroad.

Table 24 presents the annual contribution to the national economy made by the exportation of construction industry, labour, and cargo services to the Middle East. The first category indicates the business profits from contracts, the second, remittances sent by the migrant workers. (However, a part of the gain in the second category is mistakenly included in the first category, resulting in an over-estimate of the total gain. This misreported portion is known to be negligible.)

According to the data, the total gain from the Middle East in 1974 was only about $2 million. Thereafter, the gain increased substantially, reaching $3.5 billion in 1980. During the entire period covered in the table (1974–1980), the total gain amounts to about $11.5 billion. Of this gain, about 70 per cent came from the business profits of the overseas construction companies and about 27 per cent from remittances. Unfortunately, the same data is not available for 1981 to 1983. The annual gain, however, can be estimated at nearly $4 billion, based on the number of contracts made in the recent years.

Table 25 presents the contribution of the monetary gain from the Middle East to the nation's economic growth for the period 1976-1980. According to the estimates given in the table, the gain in 1976 contributed to the economic growth by only about 1.2 per cent, but the percentage contribution increased sharply in the subsequent years, ranging from 6 to 12 per cent. In terms of GNP growth rate, in 1976

TABLE 24. Annual Monetary Gains from Construction and Labour Exports to the Middle East, Republic of Korea, 1974-1980

	1974	1975	1976	1977	1978	1979	1980	Total
US dollars (millions)								
Construction	–	14	478	1199	2123	1990	2346	8150
Labour	2	35	115	278	585	995	1102	3111
Cargo service	–	4	5	29	35	41	88	202
Total	2	53	598	1505	2743	3026	3536	11,462
Percentage								
Construction	–	26.4	29.9	79.7	77.4	65.8	66.3	71.1
Labour	100.0	66.0	19.2	18.5	21.3	32.9	31.2	27.1
Cargo service	–	7.5	0.8	1.9	1.3	1.4	2.4	1.8
Total	100.0	100.0	100.0	100.0	100.0	100.0	100.0	100.0

Source: Byeong Ho Park, "Economic Effects of Industrial Export to the Middle East," in Korean National Commission for Unesco, op. cit., 29.

the gain from the Middle East contributed only 0.2 per cent, but in the subsequent two years it accounted for more than 1 per cent.

Accompanying the export of the construction industry and labour migration to the Middle East, the trade between Korea and the region has grown considerably (see Table 26). In 1973, when the first construction contract was made, the Republic of Korea exported only $59 million worth of commodities and imported about $247 million of crude oil, resulting in a total deficit of $215 million. Yet in 1980 exports had gone up to about $2077 million, while imports had risen to $5789 million, resulting in a deficit of $3712 million. In addition, in 1973 the exports to the Middle East made up only 1.8 per cent of the country's total exports, but since 1976 the proportion has risen to more than 10 per cent.

We can observe from the above data that the trade deficit with the Middle East increased considerably. However, the current account with the region shifted from a negative to a positive balance in 1977. As shown in Table 27, from 1973 to 1976 the total current account between Korea and the Middle East recorded a deficit of about $2 billion, but in the subsequent four years, it was converted to a surplus of $4.5 billion. Obviously, the shift of the current balance was entirely due to the invisible trade with the region, that is, the net gain from the export of construction industry and migrant workers.

TABLE 25. Percentage Contribution of Construction and Labour Exports to the Middle East to the Republic of Korea's Economic Growth, 1976–1980

	1976	1977	1978	1979	1980
GNP (in US$ millions)	25,090	31,488	47,396	50,408	42,278
Growth rate	15.5	10.3	12.5	6.4	−6.2
Growth rate by labour migration	.18	1.02	1.51	.38	.61
Contribution of labour migration to economic growth	1.17	9.79	12.10	5.91	9.82

Source: Byeong Ho Park, op. cit., 31.

Table 28 shows the contribution from the exports of the construction industry, commodities, and labour to Korea's economic growth. As shown in the table, in the first part of the period (1973–1975) the contribution to the annual economic growth was 0.6 to 3.6 per cent. In the subsequent three years (1976–1978), however, the percentage contribution increased remarkably, reaching more than 14 per cent in both 1977 and 1978. After 1979 the country's economy became depressed, recording negative growth in 1980 in spite of a continuous gain from the Middle East. This means

TABLE 26. The Republic of Korea's Trade Balance (total and Middle East only), 1973-1980 (in millions of US dollars)

	1973	1974	1975	1976	1977	1978	1979	1980
Export								
Total	3225	4460	5081	7715	10,047	12,711	15,056	17,505
Middle East	59	195	446	903	1328	1501	1627	2077
Middle East %	1.8	4.3	8.7	11.7	13.2	11.9	10.8	11.9
Import								
Total	4240	6852	7274	8774	10,811	14,972	20,339	22,292
Middle East	274	991	1318	1631	1987	2247	3185	5789
Middle East %	6.4	14.4	18.1	18.5	18.3	15.0	15.5	26.0
Total trade balance	−985	−2391	−2193	−1058	−764	−2261	−5283	−4787
Trade balance with Middle East	−215	−796	−872	−728	−659	−746	−1558	−3711

Source: Beyong Ho Park, op. cit., 34.

253

TABLE 27. Trade, Invisible Trade, and Current Balance of the Republic of Korea, 1973-1980 (in millions of US dollars)

	1973	1974	1975	1976	1977	1978	1979	1980
Trade								
Total	-566	-11,934	-1671	-591	-477	-1781	-4396	-4384
Middle East	-215	-756	-872	-728	-659	-746	-1558	-3711
Invisible Trade								
Total	67	-308	442	-72	266	224	-195	-1386
Middle East	—	2	53	598	1505	2743	3026	3536
Current								
Total	-309	-2023	-1887	-314	12	-1085	-4151	-5321
Middle East	-215	-794	-819	-131	846	-1997	1467	175

Source: Byeong Ho Park, op. cit., p. 37.

TABLE 28. Percentage Contribution of Total Economic Gains from the Middle East to the Republic of Korea's Economic Growth, 1973-1980

	1973	1974	1975	1976	1977	1978	1979	1980
Growth rate of GNP	16.7	8.7	8.3	15.5	10.3	12.5	6.4	-6.2
Growth rate by Middle East gains (%)	.16	.05	.29	.86	1.51	1.82	.60	.84
Contribution to economic growth by Middle East gains (%)	.99	.64	3.64	5.32	14.79	14.64	9.32	13.49

Source: Byeong Ho Park, op. cit., 48.

that if there had been no gains from the region, the country's economy would have further deteriorated, as indicated by the fact that in 1979–1980 its contribution to the national economy ranged between 9 and 13 per cent.

Effects of Migration on the Labour Market

In this final section, the effects of migration to the Middle East on the domestic labour market will be explored by breaking down the entire period of migration into three distinctive phases of economic growth. The first phase (1974–1975) was an extension of the period of stable economic growth that began in the first half of the 1960s. The second phase (1976–1978) is known for the unprecedented prosperity of Korea's economy, and the final one (1979–1982) is recognised as a period of economic depression.

The first two years of migration to the Middle East may be termed a pioneering stage. At this stage the number of migrants was rather small. In 1974–1975 the total number of migrants to the region amounted to about 7000 (see Table 5), which corresponds to only 0.06 per cent of the total employed population, and to 1.4 per cent of the male workforce in the construction sector in 1974 (see Table 29). This small number could hardly exert a significant effect on the domestic labour market.

In the second period (1976–1978) the national economy grew at an exceptionally high rate. The previous two years had seen an 8 per cent growth rate, but in the second period it ranged from 10 to 15 per cent. At the same time, the labour demand from the Middle East also increased sharply. The number of migrants in the region during the three years nearly quadrupled, from 21,000 to 81,000. In 1976 they constituted 0.2 per cent of the total employed population and 4 per cent of the male employed population in the construction sector; by 1978 the corresponding figures had increased to 0.6 per cent and 9.5 per cent, respectively.

This increase in migration to the Middle East seems to have improved the domestic employment situation considerably. Although it is impossible to measure its extent, all the indicators of the employment situation in the period 1976–1978 show a substantial improvement. During the three-year period the labour-participation rate reached its highest level, about 58 per cent, while unemployment dropped from 4 to 3.2 per cent. The average monthly wage for all workers increased from $129 to $229, and the wage for construction workers from $237 to $459. Such a sharp rise in wages was primarily due to the rapid growth of the national economy. But a substantial part of it can be attributed to a relative shortage of labour due to the migration to the Middle East.

After 1979 the national economy declined sharply. In 1980 its growth rate recorded −6 per cent, and the recovery from such a deep depression has been rather slow. In spite of such a serious economic recession, the labour-participation rate dropped only

TABLE 29. Percentage of Migrant Workers to Various Domestic Workers, Republic of Korea, 1974–1982

	1974	1975	1976	1977	1978	1979	1980	1981	1982
Total employed (1000s)	11,601	11,851	12,593	12,999	13,592	13,765	13,861	14,240	14,632
Total migrants (%)	.1	.2	.3	.5	.8	.9	1.1	1.3	1.4
Mideast migrants (%)	—	.1	.2	.4	.6	.7	.9	1.1	1.1
Employed males (1000s)	7290	7508	7773	8196	8449	8530	8617	8889	8990
Total migrants (%)	.2	.3	.5	.9	1.2	1.4	1.8	2.2	2.3
Mideast migrants (%)	—	.1	.3	.6	1.0	1.2	1.5	1.7	1.8
Employed in construction(1000s)	465	532	556	715	923	957	996	1067	1039
Total migrants (%)	3.2	3.9	6.5	9.8	11.1	12.6	15.6	18.0	20.1
Mideast migrants (%)	.1	1.2	3.8	7.3	8.9	10.4	12.8	14.4	15.4
Males in construction (1000s)	442	507	540	646	860	893	924	998	981
Total migrants (%)	3.4	4.1	6.9	10.8	11.9	13.5	16.8	19.2	21.2
Mideast migrants (%)	.1	1.3	3.9	8.1	9.5	11.1	13.8	15.4	16.3

1. Base populations include both domestic employed and temporary migrant workers.

Sources: Compiled from Economic Planning Board (EPB), *Monthly Statistical Report of Korea* (Seoul: EPB), vol. 20, no. 7 (July 1978) 59, and vol. 25, no. 7 (July 1983), 70, and table 5.

1.2 percentage points and the unemployment rate increased by the same amount. This can be attributed largely to a continuous increase in labour migration to the Middle East. Between 1979 and 1982 the number of migrants to the region increased from 99,000 to 160,000. In 1979 they constituted 0.7 per cent of the total employed population and 11 per cent of males employed in the construction sector; by 1980 the corresponding figures had increased to about 1 per cent and 16 per cent, respectively. Nonetheless, the employment situation has not improved at all, largely because of the economic recession and partly because of a continuous return migration from the Middle East. This has resulted in a surplus of skilled construction workers. As our interview data and other sources reveal, many returnees failed to get jobs in the construction sector. This problem will become more serious as the construction boom in the Middle East declines.

Conclusion

This study has inquired into the process of Korean labour migration to the Middle East and its effects, utilising the available reports as well as new data from various sources. The inquiry covers the analysis of migration at both individual and social levels. At the social level the socioeconomic conditions of migration and its effects on the national economy are examined. At the individual level, the motives for migration, the migrants' characteristics, their adjustment, and the changes in their socioeconomic situations are analysed.

The migration of Korean labour to the Middle East has taken place almost entirely as the labour component of the contracts for construction projects undertaken by Korean firms in the Middle East. Consequently, Korea's labour migration to the Middle East is distinguished in several aspects from migration flows to the Middle East from other Asian countries. The study examines in some detail various institutional features that have accompanied this migration from the Republic of Korea to the Middle East and the way in which the migrant community is managed in the host country. These aspects of the Korean migration had important implications both for the adjustment of the migrants in their countries of destination have and for their readjustment when they re-enter the Korean workforce upon their return.

The study proceeds to examine in some detail the benefits that have accrued to households as a result of the migration and the gains made by the national economy in relation to the balance of payments, international trade, and employment. The analysis of data shows that these gains have been considerable, and that if the opportunities in the Middle East countries had not been available in the second half of the 1970s, the Korean economy would have performed more poorly than it actually did. Current trends, however, indicate that the construction boom in the Middle East countries is coming to an end and that the demand for expatriate labour in these countries will, therefore, change in regard to the composition of skills required,

and in all probability will also decline. These developments will have important repercussions on Korea's economy and its labour market. They may result in a net return
flow of migrants from the Middle East, which will call for readjustments at both the
sectoral and the national level.

Although the Korean labour migration has been a significant factor in the growth
of the economy, not much research has been done on all its important aspects.
Therefore, the data and the analytical material available are not adequate for a full and
reliable evaluation of its effects. The study draws attention to the paucity of
information and points to the urgent need for more systematic research and
analysis of the migration of Korean labour to the Middle East.

Notes

1. Everett Lee, "A Theory of Migration," *Demography* 3 (1966): 47–57.
2. J. J. Mangalam and Harry K. Schwarzweller, "Some Theoretical Guidelines toward a
   Sociology of Migration," *The International Migration Review* 4 (1970): 5–21.
3. William Petersen, *Population* (New York: Macmillan, 1975), 41–44.
4. Ibid., 317–328.
5. Simon S. Kuznets, "Introduction," in Hope T. Eldridge and Dorothy S. Thomas, eds.,
   Population Redistribution and Economic Growth: United States 1870-1950, vol. 3
   (Philadelphia: The American Philosophical Society, 1964), xxiii–xxxv.
6. Erving Goffman, *Asylums* (New York: Doubleday, 1961), 3–124.
7. Ibid., 6.
8. Korean National Commission for UNESCO, *Overseas Migration of Koreans: A Case of
   Migration to the Middle East* (Seoul: Korean National Commission for UNESCO and
   the Population and Development Studies Centre, 1983).
9. Institute for Middle East Studies, *Current Status of Labour Migration to the Middle
   East* (Seoul: Institute for Middle East Studies, 1976); and Hee Woo Kim, *Industrial Export
   to the Middle East and Government Support* (Seoul: Korea Institute for Industrial Economics
   and Technology, 1982).
10. Tai Hwan Kwon et al., *The Population of Korea* (Seoul: Population and Development Studies
    Centre, Seoul National University, 1975), 29.
11. For the estimate of repatriates and refugees, see Kwon, op. cit., 35.
12. Hagen Koo and Eui-Young Yu, "Korean Immigration to the United States." Papers of the
    East-West Population Institute, no. 74 (Honolulu: East-West Population Institute, 1981),
    2–4.
13. For detailed information on these policies, see Institute for Middle East Studies, op. cit.,
    39; and Hee Woo Kim, op. cit., 32–99.
14. J. S. Birks and C. A. Sinclair, "The International Migration Project: An Inquiry into the
    Middle East Labour Market," *International Migration Review* 13 (1979): 122–135.
15. Goffman, op. cit., 87.
16. Ibid., 68–69.

THE PHILIPPINES

F. R. Arcinas
Chairman, Department of Sociology, College of Social Sciences and Philosophy,
University of the Philippines

In the past, permanent Filipino emigrants to Canada and the United States accounted for the major share of Philippine emigration. In recent years, however, the temporary migration of Filipinos for employment in the Gulf region has become far more significant. Since 1975 the Middle East has become the largest recruiter of Filipino labour. In 1981 workers bound for this region accounted for 87 per cent of land-based work placements, a proportional increase of 47 per cent from 1976. The increasing importance of temporary employment in the Gulf region is reflected in the proliferation of recruitment agencies in the Philippines and in the long queue of rural and urban residents in search of the opportunity to participate in the Middle East labour market.

In light of the growing significance of this migration to the Gulf region, this chapter attempts to assess several aspects of Filipino employment in the Middle East; in particular, the eventual repatriation of these migrants. In general, little scholarly work has been done in the Philippines on the labour migration to the Gulf region. Publications of institutions under the Ministry of Labor (e.g. the Institute of Labor and Manpower Studies — ILMS), a few survey reports and papers, and news and feature articles are about the only sources of information regarding overseas employment in the Middle East. Moreover, some of the published information lumps contract Gulf-area workers with workers employed elsewhere.

This paper is divided into two parts. The first part evaluates the availability and quality of information on selected topics and summarizes the published data. The second part identifies urgent research problems on which very little or no information exists at present.

Number of Migrants and Returnees

The Total Stock of Filipino Emigrants in the Middle East and Other Countries

Although attempts have recently been made to monitor closely the movements of Filipino migrants, it has been difficult to ascertain their exact numbers. One estimate places the total number of overseas Filipinos at 1.3 million.[1] Another places it at 1.6 million, or exactly 1,674,722 in 1979, distributed by destination as follows: Africa 4,438, Asia 77,679, Europe 50,741, the Middle East 145,183, Oceania 21,069, the Americas 1,220,753, the Trust Territories 6,686, and other countries 3,004.[2]

As of 1983 the Middle East was still the principal market of newly hired and rehired Filipino workers.[3] Close to 82 per cent of the former group and 91 per cent of the latter can be found in the area. On the whole, the Gulf region's aggregate market share of land-based workers is about 85 per cent. Asia has the second-biggest share, a low 10.73 per cent, followed by the Americas (1.48 per cent), the Trust Territories (.81 per cent), Europe (.76 per cent), and Oceania (.55 per cent).

Estimates of the total stock of Filipino migrants in the Middle East vary widely. Assuming a three-year maximum period of employment and granting a failure to place 20 per cent of the workers processed in 1981, my estimate places the 1981 stock figure at 205,000 in Saudi Arabia alone. The Bureau of Employment Services (BES) and Overseas Employment Development Board (OEDB) — which are now under the Philippine Overseas Employment Administration Office (POEA) — on the other hand, estimated a total of about 206,000 Filipino workers for the entire region from 1975 to mid-1980. Table 1 presents the estimates of these offices.

For the 1980s, the estimated proportion of workers in the Gulf region also varies. Gamboa and Cuayo claim that 90 per cent of all workers were concentrated in Kuwait, Saudi Arabia, and the United Arab Emirates (UAE) in 1981.[5] Gibson gives a slightly lower estimate (83 per cent).[6] In general, the available information on the total stock of emigrants has two important limitations. First, existing estimates are calculated on the basis of outflow figures only, because there is absolutely no information on migrants who have returned, died, or become permanent residents of the host countries. The formula used to estimate the stock of Filipino workers in the Gulf region, for instance, merely assumes that migrants return after three or five years, and do so at an even rate. The second limitation is that data on annual outflows, which form the basis of all calculations, may actually underestimate the number of departing migrants. In the case of contract workers bound for the Middle East, the POEA asserts the possibility of illegal transmission of documents between its office and the Ministry of Foreign Affairs. This means that workers who obtained travel papers on the basis of false documents are not represented in the Labor Ministry's outflow figure. Aside from illegal departures, Filipinos who go abroad initially as tourists or students but who, through extralegal means, end up joining the workforce of the host country, are not taken into account in the government estimate outflow.

TABLE 1. Distribution of Filipino Labour Migration by Region, 1975 to Mid-1980

	BES	OEDB	Total	%
Africa	2311	2231	4542	1.6
Asia	39,343	4484	43,831	15.4
Europe	7639	3199	10,838	3.8
Middle East	158,613	46,909	205,522	72.0
Oceania	226	1091	1317	.5
The Americas	10,837	1758	12,595	4.4
Trust Territories	6054	633	6687	2.3
Total	225,023	60,309	285,332	100.0

Source: Virginia Sinay-Aguilar et al., "Effects of Temporary Employment of Professionals and Skilled Manual Workers in the Middle East on the Labor Market," p. 33.

Annual Rates of Outflow and Inflow

The figures from the POEA's 1983 annual report (Table 2) show that the total number of workers exported annually rose from 36,035 to 434,207, an increase of more than 1000 per cent, in just eight years.

Annual Rate of Inflow

As noted earlier, there are no empirical data on permanently returning migrants. Thus, the annual rate of inflow is estimated on the basis of assumptions about the even rate of return throughout a specific time period. Assuming a five-year stay abroad, Abella estimates a 20 per cent return flow per year.[7]

The Demographic and Social Characteristics of Filipino Labour Migrants

Extensive information (except for family income) on the labour migrants is available from various surveys. More detailed data on specific characteristics of workers in the Gulf region are also available in unprocessed form from the POEA. These data, which consist of completed job requisitions from Middle East companies, reflect the occupational and educational characteristics of migrant workers in the region.

Two points are worth noting in relation to the demographic and social information on the migrants. First, some of the more important studies (like the Institute of

TABLE 2. Overseas Contract Workers Processed through the POEA, 1975–1983

	Land-based	Sea-based	Total
1975	12,501	23,534	36,035
1976	19,221	28,614	47,835
1977	36,676	33,699	70,375
1978	50,961	37,280	88,241
1979	92,519	44,818	137,337
1980	157,394	57,196	214,590
1981	210,936	55,307	266,243
1982	250,115	64,169	314,284
1983	380,263	53,944	434,207

Labor and Manpower Studies' *Profile of Overseas Workers*) do not refer specifically to contract workers in the Middle East. However, since this region has continued to absorb close to 80 per cent of all contract workers, it can be safely assumed that these workers are generally representative of all temporary Filipino workers in the Gulf region. The findings of such general studies have therefore been incorporated in the summary below. The second point is that discrepancies in the figures from the different surveys are a result of sampling differences.

The following summary is based on the records of the Ministry of Labor and Employment (MOLE), the surveys of Go, Postrado, and Ramos-Jimenez (1983), of Abella (1979), of Lazo, Teodosio, and Sto. Tomas (1982), and of Gibson (1982), and news and feature articles in various Filipino newspapers.

Age and Sex

Most Filipino migrants are in the prime age of the workforce and have long been so. In contrast to the country as a whole, where workers in the 25-to-34 age bracket constitute only 25 per cent of the labour force,[8] close to 50 per cent of migrant workers fall into this age category.[9] Although estimates of the distribution of workers by age vary considerably from one study to another, the fact that about half of the workers abroad are between their early 20s and mid-30s is a point of consensus among different researchers.[10]

There are also variations in average age. In Gibson's sample, the mean age of respondents is 33. The Stahl and Smart surveys in 1980[11] yield the same results, while the 1978 ILMS survey of Filipino migrant workers in Iran presents a slightly higher mean age (−35).[12]

About three out of four workers in the Middle East are male, owing to the demand for men in the construction sector. Female migrant workers, on the other hand, tend to be concentrated in some European countries, the United States, Hong Kong, and

Iran, where the demand for nurses, household help, and other service workers is high.[13]

Education

The educational attainments of contract workers are far above the Filipino norm. The national census statistics show that one out of every five employed workers in the Philippines in 1975 had completed high school. In contrast, four out of five in a sample of workers who were placed overseas between 1975 and 1977 by the Bureau of Employment Services were high-school graduates.[14] The ILMS's 1981 survey gives a more conservative figure of 40 per cent, but this is still much higher than the national figure.

While one out of eight employed workers (12.5 per cent) in the Philippines has some college education, about 20 per cent of overseas workers had been to college.[15] The ILMS survey gives a higher figure. Close to 45 per cent of land-based workers had obtained a college degree, and slightly less than half had reached the college level but did not complete the requirements. It should be noted that about 12 per cent of the migrant workers have even reached the graduate-school level.[16]

Both the OEDB's 1980 survey and the Gibson study reached similar conclusions. As comparisons in Table 3 show, half of the sample migrants took at least some college units.

The figures on college education would certainly be too high for the Filipino migrant workers in the Gulf region when one considers that the bulk of them are construction workers.[17] They would, however, accurately reflect the educational characteristics of, say, Filipino domestic and hotel workers in Hong Kong, Singapore, and Europe. A more detailed description of educational attainments by occupation should be incorporated in future research to give a more accurate picture of the educational attainments of Filipino migrant workers.

Occupation

Contract workers are drawn from the professional/technical category and the group of

TABLE 3. Educational Level of Migrants (percentages)

	ODEB	Gibson
College graduate or some college courses	50	52
High-school graduate and some units	39	29
Vocational courses	5	15
Others	6	4

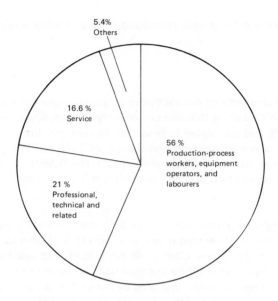

FIG. 1. Percentage Distribution of Overseas Filipino Migration by Major Occupational Groups, 1975–mid-1980 (After V. Sinary-Aguilar et al., "Effects of Temporary Employment of Professional and Skilled Manual Workers in the Middle East on the Labour Market.")

production and related workers.[18] While the national average for professional and technical workers in the labour force is one out of thirteen, Figure 1 shows that about one out of five migrant workers is either a professional or a technician; the proportion was even higher for previous years. Slightly more than half of the total manpower in 1975 belonged to this category as opposed to only 19 per cent in 1979 and 16 per cent in the first semester of 1980. The decline in the proportion of professionals overseas through the years is contrary to government expectation that the proportion of professionals and highly skilled workers would rise. The percentage of relatively highly paid professionals is going down, while there is a sustained rise in the number of ordinary production workers and labourers (see Table 4). The data presented in Table 5 basically supports this conclusion, although it shows a very slight increase in the proportion of professional and technical workers and a negligible decline in the proportion of production-process workers from 1980 to 1983.

Among the professionals bound for the Middle East, the most commonly contracted occupational group consists of those in the medical field. Table 6 shows that, except for 1977, medical professionals made up about half of the group of overseas professional and technical workers. Engineers and surveyors, on the other hand, constituted the second-largest occupational group. The "other" category in section

TABLE 4. Overseas Migration by Major Occupational Group, 1976–mid-1980 (percentages)

	1975	1976	1977	1978	1979	1980
Professional, technical, and related	53.3	35.3	18.3	22.2	19.4	16.1
Managerial, executive, and administrative	.6	.4	.6	.6	.6	1.2
Clerical	1.8	1.9	2.6	2.9	3.7	3.2
Sales	.1	.1	.1	.2	.2	.3
Agricultural, animal husbandry, foresters, and fishermen	12.1	9.8	.3	.1	.2	.2
Production, transport-equipment operators, and labourers	9.7	32.1	65.5	58.4	61.1	59.1
Total	100.0	100.0	100.0	100.0	100.0	100.0

Source: Sinay-Aguilar et al., op. cit., p. 29.

A of Table 6 (comprising 13 per cent of all professionals and technical workers deployed from 1975 to 1979), includes teachers, performing artists, lawyers, photographers, and athletes.

Throughout the late 1970s and early 1980s close to 36 per cent of the labour migrants were highly skilled workers.[19] A great variety of skills, ranging from electrical linemen to bartenders, are involved in the outflow of migrant workers.

Because of the construction boom in Saudi Arabia, Iran, Kuwait, Bahrain, and the United Arab Emirates, the most important group of skills in terms of the number of workers is construction.[20] Around 8000 migrants are classified as craftsmen, construction, and production-process workers (i.e. mechanics, machinists, electricians, welders, plumbers, pipefitters, carpenters, sheet-metal workers, weavers, spinners, and related skills).[21] The 1981 Labor Statistics Service (LSS) official statistics indicated that 66 per cent of all contract workers were in production and construction, while the Gibson survey showed 54 per cent in this group (see Table 7).

Nearly three out of four construction workers are employed in the Middle East, and about the same proportion of truck drivers, aircraft mechanics, and telecommunications technicians are also in the region.[22]

Table 6 shows that of the total 59,591 Filipino migrant workers in the production, transport, and equipment group, about one-third had carpentry skills. One out of ten workers were either electricians or machine operators, while two or three out of ten workers were either foremen and supervisors or machinists, welders, and steelworkers. Painters constituted the smallest sector of this group.

TABLE 5. Land-based Contract Workers by Major Occupational Grouping, 1975–1983 (percentages)

	1975	1976	1977	1978	1979	1980	1981	1982	1983
Professional, technical and related	38.1	15.2	7.2	10.3	10.4	7.5	5.6	6.0	10.4
Entertainers and managerial	15.4	20.1	5.6	12.0	9.0	7.9	6.8	5.4	3.5
Administrative	.6	.4	.6	.7	1.6	.5	.9	.6	.5
Clerical	1.8	1.9	2.6	3.0	3.1	3.4	1.2	3.4	3.7
Sales	.4	0.0	0.0	.1	.3	.3	2.2	5.6	.6
Service	22.0	20.3	12.5	15.5	15.2	14.8	15.7	17.3	15.3
Agricultural, animal husbandry, foresters and fishermen	.9	.4	.3	.1	.2	1.0	.6	.3	.4
Production, transport-equipment operators, and labourers	21.0	41.6	71.1	58.4	60.2	64.2	68.7	66.4	65.6
Total	100.0	100.0	100.0	100.0	100.0	100.0	100.0	100.0	100.0
Total number	12,501	19,221	36,676	50,961	92,519	57,934	210,936	250,115	380,263

Source: Philippine Overseas Employment Administration Annual Report, 1983, p. 31. The original table presented frequencies.

TABLE 6. Distribution of Professionals and Skilled Workers in the Middle East by Occupation, 1975–1979 (percentages)

	1975	1976	1977	1978	1979	1975–1979
A. *Professional, Technical, and Related*						
Medical field	63.54	73.63	19.46	44.98	51.65	51.41
Engineers/surveyors	26.17	12.97	43.11	25.02	22.10	23.25
Accountants	1.82	1.55	3.74	8.43	5.44	5.29
Architects	1.06	0.69	0.90	1.71	1.59	1.44
Technicians	0.61	2.23	0.30	2.49	4.94	3.61
Draftsmen/commercial artists	4.08	5.49	2.25	2.44	—	1.47
Others	2.72	3.44	30.24	14.93	14.29	13.53
Total	100.00	100.00	100.00	100.00	100.00	100.00
Total number	661	1164	668	2170	6123	10,786
B. *Production Process Workers, Transport and Equipment Operators and Labourers*						
Foremen/supervisors	2.71	2.29	2.46	1.82	2.95	2.48
Mechanics	8.25	8.28	8.28	4.39	11.06	8.39
Electricians	11.82	8.82	8.52	11.28	12.06	10.81
Machine operators (all types of equipment)	7.02	10.13	3.71	9.42	14.50	10.36
Machinists/welders	8.13	4.98	5.01	1.72	1.69	2.78
Plumbers/ribbers	16.50	14.40	8.62	6.55	5.98	7.59
Steelworkers	0.49	2.91	1.99	3.23	2.65	2.66
Carpenters/masons	9.61	29.14	31.44	29.96	32.53	30.99
Painters	—	1.40	1.25	2.30	0.37	1.16
Others	35.47	17.65	28.72	29.33	16.21	22.78
Total	100.00	100.00	100.00	100.00	100.00	100.00
Total number	812	5561	12,557	16,077	24,784	59,591

Source: Sinay-Aguilar et al., op. cit., p. 42.

Marital Status

A wide disparity exists in the available figures on marital status of migrant workers. One sourse claims that between 1975 and 1979, 86,164 (52.4 per cent) of the Filipino migrants were single, 76,241 (44.63 per cent) were married, 9,170 (3.36 per cent) were widowed, and 5 (.002 per cent) were separated.[23] Another report states that 70.7 per cent were married, 28.1 per cent were never married, the rest were widowed or separated.[24] A 1982 migrant survey with a sample of 100 respondents, on the other hand, yielded the following results: never married, 29 per cent; married/de facto, 69 per cent; once married/not stated, 2 per cent.[25]

TABLE 7. Distribution of Contract Workers by Occupation (percentages)

	1981 LSS Official Statistics	1982 Gibson Survey
Professional, technical, managerial and administration	13	22
Clerical, sales	4	5
Service	16	17
Agriculture	1	—
Production and construction	66	54

Premigration Employment Status

The employment status of migrant workers is difficult to ascertain. However, it is reasonable to assume that a large proportion of migrant workers were previously employed, because foreign-recruitment teams carefully monitor the applicant's work history and prefer to tap those with experience.[26] This assumption is supported by empirical evidence. The ILMS study of Filipino migrant workers in Iran[27] showed that only 4.5 per cent were not employed in the Philippines at any time before they departed for Iran. The same study reveals that of those who were previously employed in the Philippines, about 44 per cent had at least four years of experience. The average length of employment at their most recent job in the Philippines was 5.4 years.

A study conducted by the OEDB in 1977[28] shows that all overseas-job applicants recorded in the labour-service exchanges had previous employment in the Philippines or overseas. Finally, Gibson's survey (1982) shows that the majority of the sample migrant workers were employed in the Philippines before migration; more than two-thirds of them had worked for 2 to 22 years in their last jobs. Of the 80 interviewed, two-thirds were employed in the enterprises that involved more than 50 workers, and very few worked for firms with 5 employees or less.

These findings have significant implications. Contrary to popular belief, overseas contract employment has not absorbed the unemployed members of the labour force. It has recruited from a skilled, employed component of the workforce. The impact that the withdrawal of these employees has had on the labour market and employment creation has to be closely examined before conclusions are drawn.

Social Status by Province, Community, and Ethnic Group

The majority of the contract workers come from Luzon, particularly Manila and the provinces close to it. Taken together, Metro Manila, Rizal, Cavite, and Pampanga account for more than half of all placed workers. Tabel 8 presents the provincial distribution of Filipino contract workers. It should be noted that many people now living in Manila and adjacent cities are themselves migrants from other regions.[29] The preponderance of workers originating from Pampanga in central Luzon is interesting, for this province produces the finest carpenters and construction workers in the country.

The Gibson survey seems to support the claim that workers are, in the main, drawn from an established working and petit-bourgeois class. Her sample size, however, is too small. The author herself suggests that the survey results should be regarded merely as illustrative. More than two-thirds of her respondents owned no land, one-fifth owned residential lots, and only a small number had access to agricultural plots.

Ownership of agricultural land among the parents of Gibson's respondents was a little higher. Almost half of them owned or had owned land. Compared to migrants themselves, a higher proportion of their fathers were self-employed agricultural workers, suggesting that about a third of the sample may have originated from the rural peasantry. On the whole, however, the majority of the fathers of migrants were either wage workers in skilled occupations or wage workers and self-employed in the commerce and small-business sectors.[30]

Domestic Demand for and Supply of Labour

There are few systematic accounts of the domestic demand for labour, the existing supply of workers, and wage trends. Data in the form of yearly projections and reports of government institutions like the National Manpower and Youth Council (NMYC) are available. The projections of the Wage Council can also be used to a limited extent to infer changes in the wage structure.

Demand for and Supply of Labour by Occupation

In 1978 the NMYC projected that of the 8.4 million members of the Filipino labour force in 1982, 47.6 per cent were to be absorbed in agriculture, 14.6 per cent in industry (10.5 per cent of whom were to be in manufacturing), and 37.8 per cent in the service sector. The total unemployed population was projected to increase from 667,000 in 1978 to 755,000 in 1982, of whom 71 per cent were to be found in the rural areas. In industry, 439,000 workers were projected to be unemployed in 1982. Although the bulk of this unemployment will be in manufacturing, which is based mainly in urban areas, the estimate includes the unemployed in rural industries such as mining, quarrying, and logging.[31] A more detailed analysis of the demand component of the labour market can best be done, however, by looking at the employment opportunities, quit rates, number of vacancies, and cost of training.[32]

The defunct Bureau of Employment Services (BES) of the Ministry of Labor and

TABLE 8. Distribution of Filipino Contract Workers by Region and Province of Origin

Region/Province	Number	Region/Province	Number
Ilocos	*1480*	*Western Visayas*	*390*
Abra	19	Aklan	13
Benguet	60	Antique	9
Ilocos Norte	74	Capiz	20
Ilocos Sur	123	Iloilo	147
La Union	200	Negros Occidental	201
Mountain Province	89		
Pangasinan	915	*Central Visayas*	*223*
		Bonol	25
Cagayan Valley	*140*	Cebu	164
Batanes	6	Negros Oriental	34
Cagayan	46		
Ifugao	3	*Eastern Visayas*	*58*
Isabela	37	Leyte	42
Kalinga-Apayao	22	Southern Leyte	6
Nueva Vizcaya	26	Eastern Samar	8
		Western Samar	2
Central Luzon	*4229*		
Bataan	439		
Bulacan	411	*Western Mindanao*	*28*
Nueva Ecija	138	Sulu	2
Pampanga	2243	Zamboanga del Norte	12
Tarlac	262	Zamboanga del Sur	14
Zambales	736		
		Northeastern Mindanao	*231*
Southern Luzon	*11,019*	Agusan del Norte	34
Batangas	659	Agusan del Sur	18
Cavite	1655	Bukidnon	18
Laguna	502	Lanao del Norte	19
Marinduque	10	Lanao del Sur	8
Metro Manila	6267	Misamis Occidental	13
Occidental Mindoro	16	Misamis Oriental	70
Oriental Mindoro	28	Surigao del Norte	11
Palawan	10	Surigao del Sur	40
Quezon	186		
Rizal	1683	*Southeastern Mindanao*	*218*
Romblon	3	Cotabato	14
		South Cotabato	79
Bicol	*124*	Davao del Norte	4
Albay	46	Davao del Sur	104
Camarines Norte	26	Davao Oriental	17
Camarines Sur	34		
Catanduanes	5		
Masbate	1	*Not Reported*	*965*
Sorsogon	12		

Source: Rebecca B. Jayme, "A Study on the Effects of Temporary Worker Outflows from the Philippines" (M.A. thesis, University of the Philippines, 1979), pp. 56-57.

Employment conducted a series of studies on occupational outlooks, including the number of vacancies and quit rates. Since these are the most systematic studies undertaken so far, the following discussion summarizes some of the relevant findings. The BES studies contain detailed occupational projections based on industry employment trends and an occupational staffing pattern by industry presented in an occupation-industry matrix. The demand for particular members of this group increased with the government's infrastructure program, expanded health services, and the further development of the industrial sector. In the medical profession, the growth rate of employment opportunities ranges from moderate to rapid. The overall increase in opportunities is attributed to the extension of health services in the rural areas and the high turnover rate of nurses who leave the country for better-paying jobs abroad.

The demand for technicians, engineers, and architects is also projected to increase. A growing concern over the environment, an increasing demand for chemical products, and the acquisition of advanced equipment are some factors cited to account for the demand for technicians. The massive urban-development projects of the Philippine government prior to the present political and economic crisis account for the demand for engineers and architects. Aside from the three occupational groups, the BES also projects an increasing need for accountants, cashiers, and personnel managers as accounting processes become more complex. In general, the BES findings show that practically all professionals have bright employment prospects for 1983.

There is very little discrepancy in the employment prospects of professionals and skilled workers. The increase in government projects and the demand for specific products such as electrical devices and machine goods has resulted in the growth of employment opportunities for selected, skilled occupations. There is a moderate to rapid growth in employment opportunities for plumbers, carpenters, masons, and painters because of massive construction activities in both public and private sectors. Job openings for electrician, machinists, and steelworkers are also projected to increase with the demand for equipment and household appliances.

Two points are worth noting in relation to the BES projections of local employment opportunities. First, their projections are based on 1975 and 1978 data, but those bright prospects for Filipinos in the 1980s must be reassessed in light of the current economic and political crisis. The restrictions on importation of raw materials in October of 1983, for instance, have had tremendous impact on the capacity of industrial firms to retain their employees. The professional sector has been the most severely hit by the current economic crisis that began to be more pronounced towards the second half of 1983. With the tight credit situation and the virtual freeze in the imports of raw materials, many establishments, including financial companies, have ceased operations. Consequently, an increasing number of clerks, bookkeepers, and junior managers are finding themselves without jobs.

The second point is that the local demand for workers in some of the occupations mentioned above may be affected by the demand from overseas labour markets. In 1977, 668 professional, technical, and related workers out of a total of 67,799 workers in this category in the Philippines were absorbed in the Middle East market. By 1978, 21,170 migrated out of a total of 112,465 professionals and technicians who obtained employment. The proportion of professionals and technicians abroad increased from 0.985 to 1.929 per cent in the two-year period. Although the overall proportion is low, the increase of almost 100 per cent from 1977 to 1978 and the possible outflow of more migrant workers as government institutions intensify the search for jobs abroad warrant a closer examination of the impact of temporary overseas migration on the local structure of employment opportunities.[33] Statistics on quit rates can indicate, albeit in an indirect way, the labour demand for specific jobs. Quit rates not only help explain the labour turnover in particular occupations; they also help identify the types of work that have job openings for the increasing workforce.

The construction industry apparently has the highest quit rates (see Table 9). The figure reached 9.22 per cent during the first quarter of 1980. Quit rates for the construction industry are generally higher than the overall industry average. Construction workers tend to seek employment abroad, where pay is high and working conditions are perceived to be more stable.

With regard to job vacancies, Table 10 shows that, of all professional occupations, accounting jobs have the highest number of vacancies. Among skilled occupations,

TABLE 9. Quit Rates in Twelve Industries in the Metro Manila Labour Market, First Quarter 1979 to Second Quarter 1980 (percentages)

	1st Quarter 1979	3rd Quarter 1979	4th Quarter 1979	1st Quarter 1980	2nd Quarter 1980
Metal manufacturing	3.68	2.60	3.61	2.03	3.71
Chemicals manufacturing	1.56	2.81	3.20	4.24	0.71
Wood/furniture manufacturing	4.72	4.00	4.95	4.17	4.21
Wood manufacturing	2.62	2.22	2.02	2.54	3.36
Textile	3.33	3.49	3.15	3.39	3.52
Wearing-apparel manufacturing	2.82	3.06	3.68	5.35	4.27
Cosmetics manufacturing	2.40	2.44	3.00	4.12	7.68
Construction	4.12	5.68	7.81	9.22	2.09
Transportation services	2.28	1.14	2.92	2.28	3.71
Bankng institutions	2.33	2.10	3.46	3.50	2.51
Restaurants	2.71	3.66	4.55	3.30	3.87
Hotels	3.58	5.55	3.19	4.56	5.33
All industries	3.01	3.23	3.80	4.06	3.28

Source: Sinay-Aguilar et al., op. cit., p. 63.

TABLE 10. Reported Vacancies in Selected Occupations
(Professionals and Skilled Workers), 1975

	Number	%
Professional		
Civil engineer	318	10.4
Accountant	2064	67.3
Architect	119	3.9
Draftsman	564	18.4
Total	3065	100.0
Skilled		
Electrician	1064	12.6
Machinist	1100	13.0
Plumber	1014	12.0
Steelworker	406	4.8
Carpenter	4480	52.9
Painter	400	4.7
Total	8464	100.0

Source: Sinay-Aguilar et al., op. cit., p. 64.

on the other hand, carpentry has the most vacancies, owing to the high turnover in this sector.[34]

Identification of Occupations with Excess Demand or Excess Supply of Labour

Identifying the specific occupations with an excess demand or supply of labour is a difficult task given the lack of systematic data for all occupations. A rough picture may be derived, however, from a summary of the supply of and demand for workers in specific occupations for which data have been gathered, and from a general description of labour demand abroad, particularly in the Middle East.

About 10,000 engineers have already migrated permanently, and the construction boom in the Middle East will attract many more. Estimates place the number of engineers in the Philippines at 68,000 after adjusting for deaths and retirement. The combined number of graduates for some lines of engineering for which data are available (civil, mechanical, electrical, mining, and sanitary) average 5632 a year for the period 1964–1972, or a growth rate in supply of about 8 per cent a year. Very rough estimates indicate that the stock of mining engineers will grow at a faster rate than they can be employed.

According to the Professional Regulation Commission (PRC), there are only 612 registered agricultural engineers, as the yearly output of such a line of engineering is small. This is cause for concern because of government plans to irrigate 1.3 million hectares of land between 1974 and 1984.[35]

As for doctors, given the population growth rate of 2.8 per cent a year, it will take some 16.5 years to produce the physicians needed to attain what is thought to be the desirable level of health service of at least one physician for every 2000 people. However, if the present emigration rate of Filipino physicians continues, it will take 26 years for the local supply to reach this "ideal" ratio.[36]

The Bureau of Forestry has 766 foresters in its employ to take care of 16.7 million hectares of forestland. Because of the urgent need to rebuild and protect the Philippines' forests, the government is now very concerned that the PRC has registered only 791 foresters.

In the area of commerce, some 200 establishments had openings for 1752 salespeople but could not fill them with appropriately qualified employees. It is difficult to establish surpluses or shortages for blue-collar workers since no government agency administers tests for such skill categories. It is reported, however, that 1251 positions for textile workers are open in 138 establishments for which there are no qualified people. The government's labour-export policy has been blamed for the loss of experienced blue-collar workers such as heavy-equipment operators, machinists, welders, and electricians. Between 1975 and early 1977, 28,000 contract workers in this category were placed overseas, in addition to 44,000 seamen, the majority of whom were manual workers.[37]

Except for some lines of engineering, the foregoing discussion suggests a lack of skilled workers rather than an excess labour supply. The shortages of labourers in some areas of work may be exacerbated by the attractiveness of Middle East employment opportunities.

Table 11 shows the number of Filipinos employed in the Middle East as a proportion of Filipinos employed domestically in 1977 and 1978 for selected occupations. The percentages for all occupational categories in the table increased in the two-year period except for machinists, which declined by 0.03 per cent. Painters had the highest proportional increase, followed by plumbers, electronic workers, and bricklayers. If the projected annual increment in the ratio of professional and skilled workers demanded in the Middle East to the total employed in the Philippines exceeds the estimated increase in the annual supply of these occupations relative to the total workforce, policymakers will have a serious problem on their hands.[38]

Researchers have already noted the short supply of professional/skilled workers in the Philippines to fill the jobs vacated by migrant workers and that the country is losing badly needed manpower. The government has usually argued that since the country's labour force is not fully employed and is growing at a relatively fast pace, the

TABLE 11. Number of Workers in Selected Skilled Occupations Employed in the Middle East in Relation to the Number Employed in the Philippines, 1977 and 1978

	1977			1978		
	Philippines	Middle East	Mid-East as % of Philippine Employment	Philippines	Middle East	Mid-East as % of Philippine Employment
Electronic fitters/electronic workers (electricians)[1]	156,545	1069	0.68	89,123	1813	2.03
Machine fitters, assemblers, precision instrument makers (machinists)	233,240	629	0.27	115,884	276	0.24
Plumbers, welders, sheet-metal/ structural erectors (plumbers, sheet-metal workers-welders)	87,242	1333	1.53	52,587	1573	2.99
Bricklayers, carpenters, and other construction workers (carpenters/masons)	477,524	3948	0.83	303,966	4817	1.59
Painters (painters)	71,706	157	0.22	32,673	370	1.13

1. Terms in parentheses are the Middle East job classification.

Source: Sinay-Aguilar et al., op. cit., p. 81.

advantages of employing workers overseas far outweigh the disadvantages of losing skilled labour at home.[39]

As pointed out earlier, however, the unemployed are mostly unskilled and are therefore in no position to fill the jobs left by skilled migrant workers. Thus, it is not surprising that local industries have begun to complain of slackening productivity owing to the loss of their skilled technical workers to higher-paid jobs abroad.[40] In a dialogue sponsored by the Overseas Employment Development Board in 1976,[41] representatives of the construction industry illustrated the loss of skilled manpower by noting that although 50 painters readily formed a queue for vacant positions, hardly anyone was of the same calibre as the master painter who emigrated. In their study of the effects of international contract labour, Go, Postrado, and Ramos-Jimenez observed similar trends.[42] The outflow of skilled workers from one community adversely affected the labour supply of a medium-scale business firm located there. It should be noted, however, that the lack of trained personnel in some areas of Philippine society is not solely due to the migration of skilled manpower. In another dialogue sponsored by the OEDB towards the end of 1976, it was concluded that despite migration the absolute number of health personnel was sufficient to meet national health targets. The critical problem is the maldistribution of doctors and nurses across regions because of the low remuneration for health personnel outside Metro Manila.[43]

Training Costs for Migrant Workers

The National Manpower and Youth Council (NMYC) conducts regular training sessions for skilled, semiskilled, and unskilled workers. A number of private entrepreneurs have also opted to train their personnel in NMYC training centers or in other institutions. The Atlantic, Gulf and Pacific Co. and Engineering Equipment, Inc. (EEI), for instance, employ trade schools to train their workers, and, in return, they promise to upgrade the schools' facilities.

The cost of training varies. EEI spends ₱2000 per worker for training alone. The NMYC's total training costs increased by 82 per cent from 1975 to 1978 (see Table 12). With the rising cost of training, any depletion in the labour supply, skilled or otherwise, can have a tremendous impact on retraining costs. It is important to note that the training costs for migrant workers are not borne solely by the recruiting companies or the NMYC. The corporations employing the contract workers prior to their stint abroad also unwittingly subsidize their training. To illustrate this, an eight-year study (1976–1983) conducted by the Philippine Long Distance Co. reveals that out of the ₱30 million it spent on training costs, nearly ₱18 million was spent on workers who eventually migrated. On the average, each employee who left the company for a job abroad received between ₱4300 and ₱5060 in training.[44]

The Impact of the Labour Migration on Wage Trends in the Philippines

Again, there has been no scientific study of the effects of emigration on wage trends in the Philippines. Although a 9.1 per cent improvement in real wages was reported for 1970–1974, without supporting data this cannot be attributed to the increase in overseas employment. The projections of the Wage Council reveal interesting trends that can be correlated with the labour outflow, but these are still inadequate for the purpose of establishing causal relations. Despite the paucity of information, however, some tentative hypotheses can be drawn from an examination of the wage structures of the Philippines and the Middle East. Table 13 presents the monthly salary ranges for identical occupations in the Philippines and the Middle East. Salaries are stable in the Middle East, while those in the Philippines are erratic; a wide divergence also exists in the level of wages in the two places. In the Middle East, doctors receive about $923* per month, or $356 more than the highest salary level of doctors practising in the Philippines. Craftsmen in the Philippines make about $283 less per month than their counterparts in the Middle East.

TABLE 12. The NMYC's Costs for Training Skilled Workers, with the Number of Workers Trained in Selected Skills, 1975–1978

	1975	1976	1977	1978
Training costs (thousands of pesos)				
Including staff development, seminars, symposia, publication, etc.	11,495	15,418	20,162	25,379
Personnel services only	8377	8469	10,166	10,760
Number of workers trained in selected skills				
Lineman, barangay electrician, electronics, automotive, refrigeration, welding	—	1405	1409	1500
Mining and quarrying	2375	3050	4150	4700

Source: NMYC Annual Report (Manila: NMYC, 1979), cited in Sinay-Aguilar et al., op. cit., table 17, p. 67.

The difference in the wage levels of skilled workers in the Philippines and of workers in the labour-importing countries (e.g. the Middle Eastern nations) has potential effects on the domestic wage structure. In his study of wages behaviour in the construction industry in Metro Manila, Abella concludes that wages for skilled workers in demand overseas have grown faster than wages of common labourers and workers whose skills are not in demand abroad (Table 13 shows the comparative real-wage rate indices used by Abella). The experiences of some other firms and industries further support Abella's conclusion. In one of the Philippines' oil companies (Caltex), emigra-

---

* References to dollars ($) are to US dollars throughout this paper.

TABLE 13. Comparison of Monthly Salaries of Professionals and Skilled Manual Workers in the Philippines and Middle East (in US dollars)

	Philippines[1]	Middle East
Professional, Technical, and Related Workers		
Senior officer		
Engineer	95—878	986—1733
Architect	88—586	
Junior officer		
Bookkeeper	76—293	631—730
Accountant	146—659	986—1243
Medical staff		
Laboratory technician	59—169	654—749
Nurse	54—205	
Midwife	47—118	687—795
Medical technician	49—178	
Doctor	49—567	623—1155
Production-process workers, transport and equipment operators and labourers		
Heavy-equipment operator	48—177	561—640
Craftsmen		
Carpenter	48—131	
Mason	48—131	430—522
Electrician	48—147	
Pipefitter	51—163	

1. Philippine data were adjusted from 92 hours to 208 hours to make them comparable to the total working hours per month in the Middle East.

Source: Sinay-Aguilar et al., op. cit., p. 77.

tion has provided strong leverage for the workers seeking improved local contracts. In 1976 the company acceded to the workers' demands for promotion, improved pension schemes, and mid-year wage adjustments in exchange for a clause that bound the workers to inform the company of foreign-work plans six months before departure.[45]

Although one can talk about the effects of emigration on wages in specific firms or industries, it is still difficult to assess the impact of emigration on the domestic wage structure as a whole. Such conclusions must be based on aggregate data. On this level of analysis, however, the impact is hard to assess because the labour outflows are still relatively small.

Institutional Arrangements for Vocational Training

The NMYC has been assigned the task of providing a training program in the re-

TABLE 14. NMYC Training Graduates,
1974–1978[1]

	Number
1974	1044
1975	689
1976	1828
1977	2085
1978	2205

1. In electronics, mechanics, refrigeration, and welding.

Source: National Manpower and Youth Council.

quired skills for land-based workers (see Table 14). The National Maritime Polytechnic Institute, on the other hand, is in charge of establishing a training plan for seamen. In general, however, badly needed skills are taught by the companies in which workers are employed prior to their overseas jobs. Some of these companies have begun to demand government subsidies since they claim that they are, in effect, subsidizing the training of workers whose services are used by overseas corporations and firms.

These demands for government subsidies may have been partly responsible for the creation of an NMYC–World Bank vocational training project that aims to provide subsidies in the form of training contracts. Under the training-contract scheme, the government, through NMYC, is supposed to reimburse 70 per cent of the training costs incurred by the eligible firms. These firms fall under the eleven priority sectors identified by the government: construction; metals and engineering; footwear and leather goods; wood products; automotive; garments; hotel and restaurant; land transportation; power, electricity, water, and gas; printing; and coal mining.

As of September 1983, 125 training contracts had been awarded to private firms and training institutions. About 2000 trainees have graduated from the approved programs, and another 600 are still undergoing training.[46]

The Process of Migration

The Channels of Recruitment

The labour recruiters in the Philippines can be classified into two groups: government agencies and private agencies. Unlike other Asian countries, the Philippines has more than enough private recruiting agencies. Although the Ministry of Labor and Employment is attempting to reduce the number of licensed recruiters to around 200, approximately 800 agencies are still in existence. The government, which deploys 2000 to 3000 workers a year, can easily be compared to one big private recruitment agency. The preponderance of private enterpreneurs in the labour-recruiting business, each with his own estimate of hidden and overt costs, makes it difficult to offer conclusive statements about the actual premigration expenses of overseas workers.

The amount of authorized fees paid by a prospective migrant worker depends on whether he was recruited through a manning office, a private agency, or a government-authorized agency. Manning offices are not allowed to charge any fees. Private agencies, on the other hand, can charge a maximum of $179 (₱2500), while authority-holders can legally charge a maximum of $50 (₱700) to cover medical examinations, psychological testing, trade/skill testing, passport/visa, clearances, inoculation, airport terminal, and other fees. In addition, the worker is required to pay a performance-bond premium — not to exceed a $21.45 (₱300) to guarantee his faithful compliance with the employment contract. The maximum price of the performance bond is about $714 (₱10,000). These fees are to be collected (for which receipts must be issued) only after approval of the hired worker's "notice of employment" by the POEA. The agencies are required to advance the repatriation costs, collectible from the bonding or surety company should there be a need for immediate repatriation of any worker.[47]

Nearly half of all workers paid more than the cost of the legal contract ($45). Around 24 per cent of all workers and a third of the workers processed by the now defunct Bureau of Employment Services (BES) paid more than $180. Given the many job applicants and the limited employment opportunities abroad, private recruiting agencies exploit prospective migrants by overcharging.[48] Overseas workers have been known to pay as much as $140.[49] In general, workers who are not sponsored by well-established foreign or Saudi firms are the worst victims of corruption in the recruiting business. Whereas the costs of importing manpower used to be borne by the labour recruiter, the worker now shoulders all the expenses of obtaining entry papers into Saudi Arabia. A worker therefore pays an exorbitant amount to his recruiter in order to buy a job.[50]

Regulating the Migration: Public and Private Institutions

The recruitment and placement of overseas workers have been the responsibility of both public and private sectors in the Philippines. Until 1982 the Overseas Employment and Development Board (OEDB) and the National Seamen's Board (NSB) were the government agencies charged with securing employment opportunities for land-based workers and seamen respectively, ensuring the best working terms, protecting Filipino workers, and maximizing remittances. The OEDB recruited workers on a government-to-government basis, while the Bureau of Employment Services supervised the recruiting and placement activities of private, fee-charging agencies that mainly recruit workers for private employers abroad.

The reorganization of the Ministry of Labor and Employment (MOLE) on 1 May 1982 resulted in the creation of the Philippine Overseas Employment Administration (POEA) and the Welfare Fund Administration (WFA). The POEA took over the functions of the OEDB and the National Seamen's Board (NSB), and those of the BES that were relevant to overseas employment. The WFA, on the other hand, became an independent financial agency in charge of managing the welfare fund for overseas workers.[51]

The three major offices of the POEA are (1) the Market Development and Placement Office, in charge of conducting systematic manpower marketing, (2) the Workers Assistance and Adjudication Office, which is involved in the promotion and protection of overseas workers and their families, and (3) the Licensing and Regulation Office, which is mainly responsible for inspection and standard development.[52]

In addition to these three offices, the POEA maintains a regional labour center in Jeddah for the Middle East and Africa to maximize employment and contracting opportunities for Filipino workers and companies, and to coordinate those activities of labour attachés that revolve around employment promotion and workers' protection.[53] Furthermore, attached to the POEA is the One-Step Documentation Center, an interagency body run by MOLE, the Ministry of Foreign Affairs, and the Ministry of Tourism. The center hopes to cut down time taken by Filipino contract workers in migration procedure by consolidating all processing and documentation services under one roof.

To ensure that all departing contract workers have proper and complete documentation, the Labor Assistance Center was set up at Manila International Airport. Operating on a 16-hours-a-day schedule, 7 days a week, the center is charged with keeping track of returning workers and providing them with relevant information on new rules on labour, immigration, and related matters.

The POEA has also set up regional extension units in selected areas where the volume of overseas employment and related concerns warrants. There are now units in Baguio, Bacolod, Cebu, Zamboanga, and Davao to assist in the POEA's information compaign on its overseas employment program. They hold seminars on illegal recruitment and form regional manpower pools.[54] POEA reports that as of 1983, the number of authorized participants in the overseas employment program totalled 1023 – 679 recruitment agencies, 164 manning agencies, 49 service contractors, and 231 construction contractors.[55]

All Filipino overseas workers are entitled to the services of the Welfare Fund Administration (WFA), to which they contribute funds as fixed rates depending on their assignments, i.e. whether they are sea- or land-based. The WFA's board of trustees formulates policies and programs; its secretariat administers fund-collection and other functions. The secretariat has three departments: (a) the resource management department, which is responsible for the proper accounting and use of funds, (b) the worker's benefit department, which develops and implements programs to promote workers' welfare, and (c) the administrative department, which takes care of personnel management and other general services. Aside from the POEA and the WFA, other agencies like the International Labor Affairs Services (ILAS); the National Council on Illegal Recruitment, Ministry of Foreign Affairs; the ministries of Tourism, Education and Culture, and Industry; the National Manpower and Youth Council; and the National Study Commission on Overseas Employment and Contracting are also involved in overseas labour.

The ILAS maintains and supervises a corps of labour attachés deployed in major countries of employment. The attachés monitor and record developments affecting Filipino overseas workers and the social and economic developments in their foreign posts that may be of interest to the Philippine government.[57]

The Ministry of Foreign Affairs not only takes charge of processing travel papers but also of taking care of emergency situations at work sites, while the Ministry of Tourism, in coordination with MOLE, polices travel agencies and prosecutes those engaged in illegal recruitment and allied activities. The Ministry of Education and Culture and the NMYC, on the other hand, review educational opportunities. The NMYC is also involved in certifying the skills of workers going abroad. Finally, the National Study Commission on Overseas Employment and Contracting is charged with preparing a master plan for the labour-export industry. Their research is aimed at helping the government formulate labour policies that will strengthen the country's competitive advantage in negotiations.[58]

Government Rules and Procedures

Since 1972 the government has taken a more active part in controlling and regulating employment as well as emigration. It sets and maintains standards for employers and recruiting agencies. The minimum for the terms and conditions of employment abroad were set in the Labor Code of 1974.[59] The terms include the following:

1. Wages should not be less than the prevailing rates in the country of employment for the same skills and occupations, and in no case shall they be less than the prevailing legal minimum in the Philippines. The minimum wage set by the government for overseas employment is $200.
2. Employers must shoulder the passport and travel expenses of their workers and must provide free passage to and from the country of employment, free medical insurance, and free repatriation of remains in case of death.
3. Generally, the employer is required to observe the eighthour workday and to give the employee one whole day of rest per week.
3. Generally, the employer is required to observe the eight-hour workday and to give the employee one whole day of rest per week.
4. All contracts of employment must be approved by the Ministry of Labor. Without

the proper approval, passports witll not be issued by the Ministry of Foreign Affairs.

Model employment contracts for different labour-importing countries and service agreements are being developed by the Standards Division of the POEA, which takes into account basic Philippine requirements for the workers' welfare as well as the laws, customs, traditions, and working and living conditions in the host country. Model employment contracts for all Filipino contract workers and all domestic helpers bound for Saudi Arabia and Papua New Guinea have been recommended to the governments of these countries.[60]

Aside from setting standards, the government exerts control over the labour exportation by requiring recruitment agencies to obtain licenses. Licensing puts constraints on illegal transactions since firms refrain from actions that may jeopardize their government-bestowed right to recruit workers. It should be noted, however, that government control over licensing is restricted only to registered agencies. It has virtually no hold over illegal recruitment agencies. These agencies do not bother to legitimize their operations — even if they have foreign clients — because they want to avoid bureaucratic red tape and what they perceive to be unreasonable requirements in the licensing or registration of their companies. Besides the many documents that should be completed, the prospective recruiter is also required to have a competent staff for interviewing applicants and an office that the licensing agency can inspect at any time. Moreover, the processing of licenses can take as long as a year.[61]

In the Philippines, illegal labour recruiters include travel agencies that either work independently or in connivance with other illegal recruiters. These agencies legalize the overseas travel of job-seekers on tourist visas by assuring the would-be worker that the agency can easily convert a tourist visa to a working visa once the labourer arrives at a job site. It is safe to assume that of the 2000–2500 tourists issued passports daily by MOFA, a majority are actually workers in disguise. Article 26, chapter 2, book 1 of the Philippine Labor Code prohibits travel agencies and airline sales agencies from engaging in the recruitment and placement of workers for overseas employment, whether for profit or not. But working with sister placement firms, some travel agencies pass off the "tourist" worker as "individual name hires" — workers who got employed overseas through their own efforts — to get around this prohibition. As such, their papers could be processed for approval by the OEDB. Although the employer is legally required to provide free airfare to the worker, the "tourist" worker is actually made to pay for his own transportation by the travel agency.

Some training centers have also participated in illegal recruitment. They offer courses that teach skills in demand overseas like hotel administration. Prospective migrants are entitled to enrol because of the oral assurance that they will be given priority for placement abroad. Trainees are charged exorbitant fees upon enrolment but are left to their own devices after graduation. Centers that actually undertake placement activities usually do so without authority and only after collecting another round of exorbitant fees.

In general, the Labor Code prohibits direct hiring by foreign employers except for certain internationally recognized organizations that may be exempt by MOLE. The MOLE office has been receiving reports, however, that foreign agents, holding offices in plush hotels, conduct interviews and offer jobs to applicants. Their activities include the collection of guaranteed fees averaging from ₱2000 to ₱3000 per recruit.

Illegal recruitment is sometimes done through correspondence and misleading advertisements in the newspapers. Applicants are asked to apply directly and are required to remit payment by money order for brochures, application forms, and shipping and handling.

The process of "legalizing" what could otherwise be an illegal recruitment process is documented by Abrera as follows.
— Applicant companies register with the Securities and Exchange Commission or Bureau of Domestic Trade to establish a legal personality.
— The companies apply for accreditation as licensed agencies, submitting some of the necessary documents including "job contracts" or "memoranda of understanding" to show that they have established offices overseas.
— On the basis of submitted papers, these companies start recruiting workers and collecting fees from applicants without the proper authorization. They assure the applicants that they are just awaiting approval from the MOLE office.
— Sometimes, the agencies ask applicants to buy shares in the corporation to ensure the consideration of their application. When the applicant tires of waiting, the agency asks him to apply for a passport so he will be given priority by "affiliates" overseas. The credibility of the agency is not completely undermined by its failure to place a large number of applicants because they know how to use one or two success stories to bolster the confidence of their "clientele."

Illegal recruitment is reinforced by the pool of workers who are willing to pay any price to obtain the much-sought-after first job abroad.

Because of the high incidence of violations of basic recruitment and employment rules, several proposals have been suggested by different people and institutions:
— Illegal recruitment should be categorized as a crime against the state, i.e. as a form of economic sabotage.
— Rules on recruitment must be updated to meet the needs of the times and to lessen, if not do away with, the confusion of worker applicants. Legislation should make it easier for legitimate recruiters to get official sanctions.
— The processing time for documents should be shortened and fair queueing for workers should be enforced to lessen the use of money to get priority listing.[63]

— The recruitment trade must be nationalized to eliminate the "profit motive" and thereby remove the cause of many of the exploitative practices in this trade. Abella does not agree with this suggestion. He asserts that, rather than nationalization, recruitment transactions should be brought into the open and within the reach of the law given the present realities. This implies a more liberal attitude towards licensing new, private recruiting agencies as long as heavy penalties are enforced for rule violations. Legitimate establishments should be encouraged to enter the trade, but they should be supervised very closely. Abella further proposes that these establishments be required to post a sizeable performance bond which would be confiscated if the agency is found to have defrauded a worker. The present policy not to renew the license of any agency found to be guilty of fraud should be complemented by serious threat of criminal prosecution whenever appropriate.[64]

— The recruitment operations of private agencies and MOLE must be consolidated under a semi-governmental corporation to ensure proper control and direction and, at the same time, to maximize foreign-exchange earnings for the country. This corporation should establish a manpower pool from which Filipino workers sought by foreign governments and private institutions can be drawn. A microcomputer system should be set up to facilitate rapid and immediate determination of available manpower for each position classification. Besides maximizing foreign-exchange remittances, illegal recruiters would be eliminated and illegal practices of legitimate recruiters would be stopped by a computerized and integrated recruitment system. Finally, adoption of a microcomputer system in the Philippines compatible with Middle East computer centers would facilitate a much faster transfer of computer data through diskettes.[65]

An organization of labour-exporting countries on an international scale has also been proposed. Such an organization would have three primary functions: (1) It would serve as a forum for concerns relative to overseas-employment programs. (2) It would facilitate mutual-assistance arrangements whenever necessary, e.g. in cases of worker imprisonment, death, or some such similar circumstance. If this mutual-assistance scheme were institutionalized among labour-exporting countries, costs could be minimized and workers assured of protection and representation at all times. It could set up common strategies for meeting issues like terms and conditions of work. It could also set minimum standards that would keep labour-exporting countries from competing with each other. And (3) it would serve as a medium for exchanging knowledge relative to overseas employment.[66]

Actual and Contractual Terms and Conditions for the Migrant Worker

The information on the actual and contractual terms of work for Filipino labourers in the Middle East, while extensive, is not based on detailed research into the day-to-day structure of relations and informal agreements between workers and their employers.

Thus, while the terms of the legal contract are observed, other arrangements emerge, unknown to the Philippine government, which are in most cases detrimental to the worker.

Variations in the Contract

Political factors influence the legal agreements between contract workers and employers and between the Philippine government and the labour-importing Arab nations.[67] The usual one- or two-year contracts for Filipino workers in the Middle East clearly keep them from staying on in the host country after the completion of the project for which they were recruited.[68] However, in recent years there have been newspaper reports of workers who were forced to leave their original, contractual employers. As a result, numerous free-floating workers are reported to be doing odd jobs here and there in the Gulf region. Such workers are most vulnerable to victimization by unscrupulous employers. Although some government employers in the region extend three-year contracts with a provision of a midterm home leave in the eighteenth month, staying on in the host country is still prevented by specific provisions. The worker must fly home at the end of the contract to renew it or to reapply for overseas employment.[69] It should be noted that in recent years some Middle East employers have begun granting career-employment contracts, which leave the duration of the overseas stint open to the Filipino workers.[70]

On the whole, the worker has no recourse but to abide by the laws of the host country when it comes to the termination of the contract, the granting of compensation benefits, and other general behaviour at the worksite. The Philippine government has jurisdiction only over the resolution of labour disputes.[71] These points are well-emphasized by the companies dealing with migrant workers. In its briefing sessions with prospective migrants, for example, Engineering Equipment, Inc. warns workers against activities such as taking pictures without permission, staring at women, and possessing Israeli materials or pornographic articles, since these are considered crimes in Saudi Arabia.

Wage Structure for Filipino Migrant Workers

The average earnings from foreign employment for Philippine professionals and technical workers are eight times what they would earn in the Philippines (see Table 15). Even the highest-paid professional in the Philippines receives only a third of what he could earn abroad as a contract worker.

Compared to professionals, the disparity in the earnings of manual workers in the Philippines and their counterparts abroad is much greater. Service workers such as chambermaids, waiters, and domestic helpers abroad earn close to 20 times what they can expect to earn at home. Production and transport workers earn more than ten times what they receive locally. If one considers the fact that for many of the overseas workers, board and lodging are free, then the effective earning differential is even greater.[72]

In general, comparisons of nominal earnings are unsatisfactory, because the purchasing power of a currency differs in various countries. Real income differences should provide a more realistic measure of the economic advantage of working abroad. In the Philippines, real wages have declined steadily since the 1950s, reaching their lowest level in 1973. Thus, while the trend in money wages has been upward, increases in consumer prices have been much more rapid.[73] In contrast, real wages in most of the economically advances countries where Filipino workers work have grown positively.[74]

TABLE 15. Comparative Mean Monthly Earnings of Workers in the Philippines and Abroad, by Major Occupational Groups (in pesos)

	Philippines		
	NCSO[1]	Tan[2]	Overseas
Professional, technical, and related	400	1184	4125
Managerial, executive, and administrative	1000	1294	2700
Clerical	400	436	3000
Sales	240		4050
Service, sports, and related	150		3000
Agricultural	160		2550
Transport and communication/craftsmen, production and construction	300		3225

1. Based on the NCSO Statistical Survey of Households, February 1975.
2. Based on salaries of University of the Philippines graduates in 1975 (see E. Tan. "Careers of the College of Educated," IEDR Discussion Paper, 76 – 14, School of Economics, University of the Philippines, 1976).
3. Based on reported salaries of Filipino contract workers sent overseas during the period July 1975-June 1977 (OEDB); conversion rate is US$1 = P 7.50.

Source: Jayme, op. cit., p. 97.

Work and Living Conditions for the Migrant Worker

Work schedules of Filipino migrant workers depend on the employers' practices and the type of industry — although employers often adhere to the standards set by the ILO of eight hours of regular work per day or a maximum of 48 hours a week (six workdays). Some countries require five workdays a week. In the Middle East, work hours are usually from 7 a.m. to 3 p.m. This schedule does not hold for hospital, airport, and hotel workers, who generally follow strict shift schedules.[75]

Overtime pay based on the current wage rates at the work site — which is normally time and a half of the basic pay — is made for every hour worked beyond eight hours.

Pay is often double for rest days and holidays. Filipino workers in the Middle East render an average of two hours of overtime work per workday, although in some cases they work four extra hours per day.[76]

Vacation and sick leave are the two types of paid leave enjoyed by Filipino contract workers. Labour laws of the host country are usually the basis of vacation-leave provisions. In the Middle East, vacation is normally 30 days for every year of continuous service. This leave may be extended at the end of each contract period. Therefore, a worker who has been in continuous work for 11 months may enjoy vacation leave in the twelfth month.[77]

Workers may spend their paid, 30-day vacation in their home country or secure the money equivalent of the airfare home. Some spend this money for vacation elsewhere, subject to company policy. For two-year contracts, this is commonly referred to as the worker's "midterm leave."[78]

Specific sick-leave provisions vary depending on the employer, but usually it is given for 15 days per year. Accumulated sick-leave benefits paid in its money equivalent are generally allowed in some Persian Gulf countries, but in Saudi Arabia such benefits can be enjoyed only under specific conditions.[79]

Depending on the type of company, living conditions for workers overseas vary. Larger companies provide air-conditioned housing with two workers sharing one room and bath. Smaller companies billet more workers in a room with electric fans, bunk beds, and common washrooms.[80]

In the United Arab Emirates, workers sleep in four-person, fully carpeted rooms with air conditioners, heaters, furnishings, and shower and bath facilities with hot and cold water. Linen and soap are also supplied by the employers, together with free laundry service.[81]

Large companies provide recreational facilities for tennis, basketball, squash, billiards, and in some cases even swimming. They also have video machines for their workers. These are nonexistent in small companies, in which case workers resort to chatting, exchanging news from home, and writing and reading letters for their leisure.[82]

Filipinos working in big, organized camps are said to eat in common, clean, and well-equipped self-service mess halls together with other expatriate workers. American and European dishes are served. A typical meal consists of two main courses of beef, turkey, chicken, or fish and cooked or raw vegetables. Those whose job sites are far from the mess halls arrange for a specially packed lunch with a canteen or thermos bottle of water. Dacanay claims that it is not unusual for foreign employers to hire Filipino cooks to serve Filipino working communities. Some of the more organized work camps are also said to import fresh foodstuffs from the Philippines.

Data on living conditions must be taken with caution. Researchers tend to draw a rosy picture. It may be the case that some workers enjoy comfortable surroundings, but there is evidence that other workers are, indeed, exploited. Teachers and other educated workers employed in households overseas are known to have complained about sexual abuses and maltreatment at the hands of their employers.[83] The problem is that very few studies have documented the various forms of exploitation in the Gulf region. The lack of systematic data on the real working conditions of Filipino workers overseas, particularly in the Middle East, underscores the need for further research using a more representative sample of workers from different work sites.

Wages and Work Conditions According to Nationality

Although overseas workers are recruited on the basis of their skills, they are paid on the basis of their country of origin; wages therefore vary.[84] Three general payrolls are maintained in the Middle East. the American/European payroll, the local payroll for the countries' own nationals, and a payroll for Third World nationals, which includes Filipinos and other Asian nationalities. Such disparities in wage scales are explained in terms of the different levels of incentives needed to attract a particular nationality to work in a certain country.[85]

The large number of unemployed in the Asian and African countries who are competing for jobs in Saudi Arabia exert sustained downward pressure on wage levels, affecting mainly unskilled labour. Filipino manpower is experiencing fierce competition from at least six Asian countries at a time when the labour market in the Gulf region has peaked and demand is no longer as keen as it was in the late 1970s because the major programmes of infrastructure development started in the 1970s are nearing completion.[84]

Information on how the wages for different nationality groups in the Middle East compare is inconsistent. Abella says that Filipino construction workers in the region are known to receive better wages than their Asian counterparts. Gibson claims, on the other hand, that the pay scale of Filipinos falls between the South Koreans, who are the most highly paid Asian workers, and the Bangladeshi and Pakistani workers, who are the least paid.

Renewing Contracts: Possibilities and Problems

The prospects of renewing contracts for Filipino workers in the Gulf region are not at all promising. At present, Saudi Arabia requires all travel documents of Filipino workers on the job sites to be authenticated by no less than Malacañang Palace and the Ministry of Foreign Affairs. This policy is said to have been triggered by the number of Filipinos involved in criminal cases in Saudi Arabia.[87] The government has noted numerous arrests of Filipinos involved in attempts to smuggle drugs and firearms, gambling paraphernalia, liquor, and other prohibited articles.[88] The Saudi policy is definitely posing problems for the renewal of contracts.

Even more serious is the recent drop in oil revenues and the new domestic goals in the Middle East, which are affecting the demand for labour.[89] Wide-ranging austerity measures are being implemented in Gulf Cooperation Council countries with the exception of Kuwait. These are taking the form of cutbacks on construction projects, deferment of projects even in identified expansion areas, deferment or stretching of contract payments for government projects, review of government subsidies, requirements that foreign contractors subcontract 30 per cent of their jobs to local companies, and so on.[90]

Smaller firms are especially hard hit by the tougher labour regulations of 1983. The UAE, for instance, stipulates that workers finishing a contract must stay out of the country for at least a year before seeking a new job. There was a time when contractors could hire labour for a new job straight from a just-completed one and be assured of a skilled workforce already familiar with local conditions. With the new regulations, labour has to be recruited from outside the UAE, causing further delays as most new workers require a training period — ultimately reducing efficiency.[91]

All these measures have adversely affected the Philippine position, causing substantial loss of job opportunities for Filipino workers. Two Saudi contractors employing nearly 500 Filipinos have started to demobilize. Filipinos, South Koreans, and other "medium-cost" workers are expected to be displaced in the nonskilled or low-skilled job categories. On the other hand, there is also the possibility that medium-cost workers may displace Americans, Europeans, and Japanese for the administration, technical, supervisory, submanagerial, and managerial levels.[92]

Trends in Skill Composition

The near completion of the infrastructure and other public works projects in the Middle East signals a shift in the labour demand away from construction and manual work and toward the services sector: higher-level employees such as managers, executives, and computer and other experts.[93] Another notable trend is the employment of many Filipino clerical workers in the Gulf region. More than 67 per cent of all those who left the Philippines to work in clerical positions ended up working in the Middle East.[94]

Earnings and Remittances

Several studies have paid close attention to the remittances from contract workers. Gamboa and Cuayo focused solely on the topic when they analysed OEDB's 1981 survey data. Go, Postrado, and Ramos-Jimenez also discussed this report on the effects of international contract labour. The ILMS study of the socioeconomic consequences of labour migration from the Philippines and the Lazo et al. *Contract Migration Policies in the Philippines* both provide extensive data, except on annual earnings of migrants and the proportion of remittances spent on domestic goods versus imported goods. None of the existing studies, on the other hand, address the macro-economic issues relating to remittances. The conclusions of these studies are not confined only to the workers in the Gulf region. However, as previously argued, since most of the overseas contract workers are concentrated in the Middle East anyway, the trends in remittances mainly reflect the responses of this group.

Annual Earnings of Migrants

On the average, overseas workers earn an annual income of between $4000 and $8000. The figures vary widely. The ILMS report puts the mean annual income at around $4900, while Gamboa and Cuayo make it much higher ($8500). However, the income distribution of the latter's sample is skewed since half of the workers in the sample earn less than $5000.

There is no breakdown of the annual earnings of migrants by specific occupation. The generalized data are only for broad occupational categories. It is possible, however, that the original data sets include detailed occupational groups. Among the land-based employees, service workers earn the least: more than half have an income of less than $3240 a year. The yearly earnings of transport and clerical workers are between $2100 and $6000. Craftsmen generally have slightly higher incomes — approximately $2500 to $6500 per annum according to the ILMS report. As expected, however, professional and technical workers tend to fall into higher income brackets: close to 70 per cent earn at least $5400 annually.

Level of Annual Remittances

The average overseas worker remits about half of his earnings, mostly in cash, with a smaller proportion in the form of merchandise for personal use, such as clothing, electronic goods, and household items.[95] The average cash remittance is about $3500, while the mean value of merchandise remittance for the reference period is $1050.[96]

Remittances are also recorded by the Central Bank under the "services including personal income" category of invisible receipts. From 1976 to 1979 dollar inflows from services ranged from $319.53 million to $711.63 million (or an average of $520.94 million). Remittances in this category accounted for about 17.6 per cent of total invisible receipts. In 1982 Central Bank figures indicated a total of $800 million remitted by overseas contract workers. In 1983 there was an increase of 19.3 per cent, bringing the total amount of remittances to $955 million and making the overseas employment sector one of the biggest contributors to the country's foreign exchange reserves.[97]

The remittances of land-based workers manifested a substantial annual increase from $34.4 million in 1976 to $452.6 million in 1979. Although these figures include remittances of permanent migrants, it can be assumed that, on the average, the contribution of this latter group would be less than of temporary migrants. This observation is based on the fact that during the observed years, 68 per cent of Filipinos abroad were contract workers as oppsed to only 32 per cent permanent emigrants. It has also been argued that permanent migrants are more concerned with establishing themselves in the host country, while migrant workers accumulate savings to send home to the Philippines.[98]

As previously noted, none of the existing studies has data on the approximate amount of cash remittances and value of merchandise transferred specifically from Filipino workers employed in the Middle East. The POEA 1982 annual report, however, cites the fact that about 84 per cent (or $1017.24 million) of the $1211 million total *pledged* foreign exchange remittances of Filipinos in the referred period was from workers employed in the Middle East. The remaining 16 per cent came from workers based in Africa, Asia, Europe, Oceania, the Trust Territories, and the Americas.

Potential Remittances

Information on unremitted savings is extremely limited since data on the allocation of income that remains with the worker are not available. However, it is safe to assume that some workers retain part of their earnings as savings. This can be inferred from the fact that about 70 per cent of Go, Postrado, and Ramos-Jimenez's sample have been visited by overseas labourers who brought home cash averaging about $230 per household.[99]

The Channels of Remittances

Overseas contract workers are mandated to remit a portion of their basic salary (70 per cent for seamen and construction workers with free board and lodging, and 50 per cent for domestic and other workers whose contracts do not stipulate free board and lodging) through the Philippine banking system, since the law prohibits direct payment to beneficiaries. The portion of basic salary to be remitted was increased to 80 per cent starting January 1984. There is agreement in the literature that most workers make use of bank-to-bank transactions. However, complaints about delays and the unfavourable exchange rate have made overseas workers (who are mostly the main income-earners of their families) look for alternative remittance channels. About 15 per cent of the OEDB sample migrants rely on friends or relatives to bring home their remittances, while 20 per cent had their remittances automatically deducted from the payroll.[100] A few use the postal system.

It is worth noting that owing to the perceived drawbacks of the Filipino banking system, some of the remitted dollars do not enter the official channels. Gamboa and

Cuayo cited the report of a Central Bank team sent to Saudi Arabia to monitor the remittances of construction workers. The team claimed that a portion of total workers' remittances end up in the black market.[101]

A MOLE study showed that, despite inherent risks, overseas workers still prefer to send their remittances through informal channels. Computations made by the Central Bank in 1980 revealed that only 50 per cent of the dollar remittances of overseas workers passed through banking channels,[102] although private-sector leaders believe the official estimate of total labour remittances sent through the banks represents only a fourth of the total foreign exchange earnings sent home.[103] The Philippine National Bank booked 12,000 remittances, an insignificant number considering the 250,000 Filipinos working in Saudi Arabia today.[104]

The primary considerations of overseas Filipino workers in sending their remittances are speed, cost, and safety. Any undue delay in the receipt of remittances can mean unnecessary suffering for their families. Remitting money through the banks is constrained by several factors. There are no banking facilities in a number of work sites in the Middle East. Because of this, there is a delay of three to six weeks before money is received by beneficiaries. In Saudi Arabia there are only three Philippine banks — the Philippine National Bank (PNB), the Allied Banking Corp., and the Philippine Commercial and International Bank (PCI) — which could not even operate on their own without tie-ups with Saudi banks or, in case of PNB, without performing other functions (PNB officials also double as attachés of the Philippine embassy in Jeddah).

Delays in the receipt of remittances by families of migrant workers can also be caused by inefficiencies in the remitting bank, such as faulty transmissions of messages, incomplete details, or lack of knowledge on the part of the remitting bank as to the correct procedure to follow.[105]

For their part, local banks are not too willing to act as conduits for migrants' remittances. The costs involved in remitting relatively small amounts are high. A worker's $500 remittance requires as much time and attention as a ₱3 million transaction. One bank has complained that telex costs alone are prohibitively high.[106]

Because of the inefficiency and high cost of basic banking, the only groups actively involved in remitting the earnings of migrant workers are foreign exchange black-market dealers and dollar-salting Filipino outfits. Not only are they more effective than the official channels; they are also cheaper and their exchange rates are higher. They pledge delivery of money to the families in seven days, charging a minimum remittance fee of ₱95.40, and a maximum of ₱159, which is even lower than the minimum fee of ₱190 charged by Saudi banks. They also promise door-to-door delivery and signed receipts from the workers' families.[107]

Both the ILMS (1983) report and the Go, Postrado, and Ramos-Jimenez survey draw the same conclusion. Most of the overseas workers are married; more than half remit their earnings to their spouses. Close to a third remit to their parents, while the rest are distributed to other family members; disputes over who should receive the workers' remittances have been reported.

Uses of Remittance

Remittances are used primarily to purchase consumer goods. According to the Gamboa and Cuayo report, part of the money remitted is used for education and debt payment. A 1978 ILMS study of Filipino migrant workers in Iran indicated that 78 per cent of the remittances was used for food, education, and housing, and only 22 per cent for savings and investments in economic ventures.[108] High-level investments of about $4000 or more were found only among administrative and managerial migrant workers.

The way remittances are utilized reflects the absence of more productive investments on the part of workers and their families. It has been pointed out that the sheer volume of foreign exchange earnings has caused many governments to close their eyes to the nonproductive use of foreign income.[109] There are no reports of buying shares in joint stock companies or of establishing businesses. Gamboa and Cuayo assert that very few workers use remittances to improve business. However, 70 per cent of the workers did save part of their cash remittances in the banks either as savings or time deposits.

Social, Psychological, and Cultural Issues

Compliance with the terms and conditions of work abroad itself is one of the major problems confronting the overseas employment program. Overseas workers are subject to the relevant labour legislation at the job site.[110] Between 1975 and 1979 there were 283 reported cases of labour violations by employers of Filipino contract workers in the Middle East.[111] During the same period, nine disputes arising out of wage rates and payments were reported. Other sources of disputes ranged from housing problems to alleged maltreatment. There were also 262 reported disputes under the category of "others," which included illegal termination and dismissal, unfair labour practices, sexual abuse, separation pay, etc.[112]

In June 1978 the Permanent Unit on Illegal Recruitment (PUIR) was formed to take care of the complaints raised by employees. From July 1978 to December 1979 this office registered the complaints and sworn statements shown in Table 16.

The PUIR estimates that only 10 per cent of the victims actually report abuses, and only half of those are willing to submit sworn statements. Among those who do not report are workers who obtained overseas employment through illegal means, who are embarrassed to report their own gullibility, who managed to slip out of the country as tourists, whose losses are quite small, or who got stranded in foreign countries and can no longer rely on official channels for redress of their conditions.[113]

The impact of temporary overseas emigration on migrants and their families is the subject of a growing number of surveys, theses, and papers. The following discussion summarizes some of the key findings of this research. The fun-loving Filipino finds adjusting to the alien culture of the Middle East, particularly that of Saudi Arabia, most difficult. Forbidden to indulge in coping devices such as gambling, drinking, and night life, he finds the Middle East a harsh, hostile place where the problems associated with separation from his family (e.g. loneliness, worry, jealousy) become especially acute. Because of poor communication, feelings of neglect, and suspicions of infidelity, separation from loved ones has led to feelings of depression on the part of the migrant worker and in some cases a total break-up of his family.[114]

Culturally disoriented, the predominantly Christian Filipino worker finds the inability to worship freely disconcerting. The situation in the more fundamentalist Moslem countries of the Middle East is said to be comparable to that of the early Christians in pagan Rome. Religious services are disrupted, religious objects are confiscated or desecrated, and people are forced to convert.[115]

Many Filipinos have gone to jail for incidents such as bumping another car, a commonplace in the Philippines but punishable by automatic imprisonment in Qatar.[116]

The difficulty of work and grouchy supervisors are other complaints among Filipino workers. And in cases where the medical facilities are inadequate, the Filipino worker would rather go home to his family when he becomes ill, thereby breaking his work contract.[117]

Filipino workers in Qatar bewail the absence of a Philippine diplomatic office to assist them. Women who suffer abuse and rape have nowhere to go for help — sometimes such incidents are just not reported.[118]

TABLE 16. Number of Complaints by Migrants

Complaints	July–Dec. 1978	Jan.–Dec. 1979	Total
By sworn statements	220	422	642
By concerned citizens	135	819	954
Total	355	1241	1596

The worker's family, which lays out a large amount of money for the worker's departure (often selling property or borrowing from moneylenders), experiences severe financial crisis in the first three months, during which time no earnings have been remitted. There are cases where the distribution of the remitted money among the worker's wife, his mother, or his mistress causes rifts in the family and in the community while causing anxiety on the part of the worker abroad.

Wives of overseas workers worry about the responsibility of being the sole parent to their children. A special source of anxiety is the disciplining of older children. Cases of infidelity have also been reported and of women spending their husbands' hard-won earnings on their lovers or on extravagant shopping sprees.[119]

The Impact of the Labour Migration on the Family

The overseas contract worker phenomenon has affected the norms of behaviour of the country.[120] Some young boys have dropped out of school in order to be overseas contract workers. The idea that a good education is not all that is important in acquiring a well-paid job abroad is gaining ground. Among schoolchildren, the attraction of overseas work is so strong that even grade-school boys aspire to be contract workers.[121]

In the communities studied by Go, Postrado, and Ramos-Jimenez, wives of overseas workers were generally able to cope well with the added responsibilities of the households. Their financial-management abilities were also enhanced during their husbands' stay abroad. It was pointed out, however, that some wives tended to be "extravagant." The same conclusions were reached by the Javier study.

Social Mobility and Attitudes toward Life

Children of overseas contract workers in one of the barrios observed by Go, Postrado, and Ramos-Jimenez felt that their status was improved by their father's migration. Objectively, employment abroad has improved the social status of families in that they eat better, enjoy amenities such as household appliances, and also have some money on the side for needs beyond basic subsistence.

An ILMS study of Filipino migrant workers in Iran in 1978 showed that of the total number of workers studied, 37 per cent said they were well-satisfied with their present job conditions, while 30 per cent were less satisfied. The study also concluded that job satisfaction among the workers was significantly and positively associated with the amount of skill involved in a job, the enhancement of existing skills, the acquisition of new skills, and good health conditions.[122]

In letters sent to wives and children, some workers write that the loneliness, the heat, and the generally difficult life they have abroad become more bearable with the

296

knowledge that they are earning about three times what they would be earning at home, enabling them to repair their houses, buy more things, save for their children, and have a better future.[123]

Orientation and Support Programmes

The main types of programmes for overseas workers may be classified into orientation programmes and support programmes. The former, which are conducted by recruiters, contracting companies, and the MOLE office, include familiarization with the following aspects:
— *Physical and environment*: geographical location of the country involved, time of travel, distance from Manila, climate, weather, season of the year, average temperature, living conditions, workers' quarters, kind of food, water available, mailing procedures, recreation, and forms of entertainment allowed.
— *Economic and political*: standard of living, rate of currency exchange order, persons in power, political overview, and a primer on the country's criminal, civil, and labour laws.
— *Social and cultural*: way of life, customs, and traditions, standard of good manners, social taboos, social institutions and practices relevant to the workers' role in society, cultural overview including a short historical background, religious practices, events, and other matter of religious importance.

Support programmes take many forms. Labour-attaché services extended by the MOLE provide assistance for the workers in negotiating better terms, conciliating disputes, and counseling those with problems in adjusting to the new environment. Labour attachés generally serve as the link between the workers and the Philippine government. There are fifteen attachés stationed in thirteen cities so far: Hong Kong, Jakarta, Tokyo, Tehran, Cairo, Jedda, Bonn, London, Madrid, Rome, Ottawa, New York, Washington, Guam, and Geneva.[124]

The Seamen's Assistance Division of the NSB takes care of seamen's problems — facilitating adjustments, giving personal and professional advice.[125]

There are also support programmes consisting of recreational projects such as basketball, bingo nights, chess tournaments, films, and videotape movies. Some companies provide communication support via telex and the pouch system,[126] and open bank accounts for the workers' families.

There are no programmes for families, but some companies say that families of workers are free to approach them and assistance is given when needed.[127] In cases of emergency, workers and their dependents are granted aid and access to the companies' telephone and telex facilities.[128] The Engineering Equipment, Inc., one of the construction firms doing business in the Middle East, periodically organizes a dependents' forum.[129] Dumez, a French multinational in the Philippines, has planned a novel project of providing job opportunities for wives of Filipino workers stationed in the Middle East: ₱1 million monthly will be appropriated by the company to establish cottage industries to generate jobs in areas where there are at least 200 migrant spouses.

A more aggressive and creative support programme for the total well-being of the worker is a church project involving monthly taping of worship services, inspirational talks, songs, and messages by fellow parishioners for the benefit of relatives and friends in the Middle East.[130]

Auxiliary bodies bringing additional services to workers and to their dependents such as the Worker Welfare and Training Fund, which was started in 1977 by the BES, OEDB, and NSB, aim to meet welfare problems of overseas workers as well as cultural and other social problems.[131]

The Returning Migrants: Prospects and Scenarios

The return of contract workers from overseas can be either voluntary or involuntary. Voluntary returnees usually return on the termination of their contract. Involuntary returnees include sizeable numbers of workers who are forced to come home owing to various circumstances outside their control, such as premature termination of work for contract violations, business failures, national disasters, etc.[132]

Information on overseas placement for the last two and a half years shows that one-fourth of the workers' contracts are for less than six months, while about half are for one year. Because employment contracts are often renewed right after expiration, the length of a worker's stay abroad cannot be determined by the original contract.[133]

In general, no systematic data on returning migrants are available. Interviews with households whose migrant workers have returned are about the only reliable source of information.

A Demographic Profile

One important argument in favour of labour export is that it provides an opportunity for workers to acquire new and higher skills. A substantial number of Filipino workers, however, assert that this is not necessarily the case. Some have even indicated that they had to teach workers from other countries. Considering the relatively high level of education and skill among the Filipino workers, this situation is not altogether unexpected. It should be noted, however, that there are no serious studies on skills acquired by Filipino workers overseas and what they do with such skills when they return home.[134]

One effect of temporary migration may be an increasing turnover in the local labour market, affecting labour costs, wage rates, and production techniques. The returnees' job expectations may also have risen. A major problem is having to readjust to the peso salary, and a low one at that. The returnee may waste a significant amount of time looking for a job that pays more than his salary overseas. Discouraged by the usually lower pay for his skills, many workers often reapply for overseas work and the cycle continues.[135]

The returnee stands out in his community with all the manifestations of success — his cassette tape-recorder, stereo and appliances, the toys for his children, and nice clothes. Although many workers do spend money on the education of their children and on a house and lot, some go back to drinking and other vices, losing their hard-earned cash, ending up no better-off than before.[136]

The migrant worker finds life, although difficult, better than it used to be — the future brighter. With a better income, he can get his house fixed, buy more clothes, and save for his children.[137] Most migrant workers look forward to returning to work in the Philippines. They look forward to being with their families and generally express a sense of hope and well-being. Those who had misgivings about their eventual return home cited their apprehensions about the low pay.

The land-based workers' substantial work experience prior to their first overseas employment probably accounts for their confidence about finding employment when they return to the Philippines. Because there are fewer employment opportunities for women in the Philippines, men appear more confident than women about getting jobs upon their return despite the latter's relatively higher educational qualifications. Those who anticipate some difficulty in finding work cite the general unemployment situation and competition among workers with similar occupations and background.[138]

Migrant workers who hope to invest their savings generally prefer investing in a small store or some form of trade.[139] The survey data on the actual use of remittances show, however, that their earnings have not yet been utilised for productive purposes.

Notes

1. Manolo I. Abella, *Export of Filipino Manpower* (Institute of Labor and Manpower Studies, Ministry of Labor, Manila, 1979), p. 1.
2. OEA, *A Special Report on Profile of Filipinos Overseas* (Office of Emigrant Affairs, Ministry of Labor and Employment, 1980), p. 2. It should be noted that the Philippine Overseas Employment Administration (POEA) data for 1983 indicate a slight shift in the skills demanded from lower skills to higher-level ones. While the most demanded categories of workers were production-process workers, transport-equipment operators, and labourers, there was a bigger share of workers in the professional, technical, and clerical categories in 1983 than in 1982. See Table 5.

3. *Annual Report 1983,* POEA, p. 6.
4. Virginia Sinay-Aguilar et al., "Effects of Temporary Employment of Professionals and Studies, Manual Workers in the Middle East on the Labor Market" (paper submitted to the Program in Development Economics, School of Economics, University of the Philippines, in partial fulfillment of the requirements for the Certificate in Development Economics, April 1980), pp. 32–33.
5. Eduardo D. Gamboa and Edelana M. Cuayo, *Analysis of the OEDB Survey Data on Overseas Workers' Remittances* (Research for Development Department, Development Academy of the Philippines, 1982), p. 9.
6. Katherine D. Gibson, "Contract Labor Migration from the Philippines: Preliminary Field Work Report," 1983, Table 1.
7. Abella, *Export of Filipino Manpower,* pp. 55–56.
8. *Philippine Census 1975,* Table 2.
9. Gibson, "Contract Labor Migration," Table 2.
10. OEA, *Special Report,* p. 5; Gibson, "Contract Labor Migration," p.6.
11. Gibson, "Contract Labor Migration," Table 1, citing Stahl and Smart survey, 1980.
12. M. Robosa and A. King, "Filipino Temporary Migrant Workers in Iran (Insight into Temporary Migration," *Philippine Labor Review* 4 (Second Quarter 1979): 48.
13. Rebecca B. Jayme, "A Study on the Effects of Temporary Worker Outflows from the Philippines" (M.A. thesis, University of the Philippines, 1979), p. 58.
14. Ibid., pp. 55, 58.
15. Ibid., p. 58.
16. Ibid.
17. Ibid., p. 42.
18. Abella, *Export of Filipino Manpower,* p. 14.
19. OEA, *Special Report,* pp. 5–6.
20. Abella, *Export of Filipino Manpower,* p. 13.
21. Ibid., p. 14.
22. Ibid.
23. OEA, *Special Report,* p. 6.
24. Robosa and King, "Filipino Temporary Migrant Workers in Iran," p. 48.
25. Gibson, "Contract Labor Migration," Table 3.
26. Jayme, "Temporary Worker Outflows" p. 58.
27. Robosa and King, "Filipino Temporary Migrant Workers in Iran," p. 48.
28. Jayme, "Temporary Worker Outflows" p. 82, citing C. Eco and R. Tiamzon, *Manpower Availability Study: 1975–1976* (Overseas Employment Development Board, February 1977).
29. Abella, *Export of Filipino Manpower,* p. 88.
30. Gibson, "Contract Labor Migration," p. 18.
31. L. S. Lazo, V. A. Teodosio, and P. A. Sto. Tomas, "Contract Migration Policies in the Philippines" (working paper issued by the International Migration for Employment Branch, International Labour Organisation, 1982), pp. 6–7.
32. Sinay-Aguilar et al., "Temporary Employment," p. 49.
33. Ibid., p. 59.
34. Ibid., pp. 62, 65.
35. Abella, *Export of Filipino Manpower,* p. 33.
36. Ibid., p. 30.
37. Ibid., p. 38.
38. Sinay-Aguilar et al., "Temporary Employment," p. 60.
39. Abella, *Export of Filipino Manpower,* p. 21.
40. *Bulletin Today,* 24 August 1982.
41. Jayme, "Temporary Worker Outflows," p. 94, citing *Dialogue with the Construction Industry* (Overseas Employment Development Board, 1976, mimeographed).
42. Stella P. Go, Leticia T. Postrado, and Pilar Ramos-Jimenez, *The Effects of International Contract Labor,* vol. 1 (Integrated Research Center, De La Salle University, Manila, 1983), p. 134.
43. Jayme, "Temporary Worker Outflows," p. 91, citing *Industry Dialogue on the Availability of Health Manpower* (Overseas Employment Development Board, 1976, mimeographed).

44. Carlo R. H. Magno, "Implications of the Export of Manpower to the Telephone Industry" (paper presented at the University of the Philippines–Institute of Industrial Relations panel "Manpower Export: Unexplored Issues," March 1984).
45. Jayme, "Temporary Worker Outflows," p. 106.
46. *Business Day,* 13 October 1983.
47. "Placement Fees for Overseas Workers," *Manpower Exchange* 2, p. 4.
48. ILMS, *Socio-Economic Consequences of Contract Labor Migration in the Philippines* (Manila: Ministry of Labor and Employment, 1983), pp. 83–84; *Bulletin Today,* 6 September 1983.
49. Go et al., *International Contract Labor,* pp. 209–210.
50. *Bulletin Today,* 6 September 1983.
51. ILMS, *Socio-Economic Consequences,* pp. 26–27.
52. Lazo et al., "Contract Migration Policies, p. 23.
53. Ibid., p. 14.
54. *Annual Report 1983,* POEA, p. 22.
55. Ibid., p. 4.
56. ILMS, *Working Abroad: The Socio-Economic Consequences of Contract Labor Migration in the Philippines* (1984), p. 16.
57. Lazo et al., "Contract Migration Policies," p. 14.
58. *Bulletin Today,* 24 May 1983.
59. "The Philippine Overseas Employment Program" (paper presented at the ILO/ARPLA Symposium on Overseas Recruitment for Senior Officials in East Asian Countries, Manila, 14–19 April 1980); published earlier in *Philippine Labor Review* 4 (Second Quarter 1979): 11–16.
60. *Annual Report 1983,* POEA, p. 13.
61. Alcestis Abrera, "Illegal Recruitment: The Philippine Experience," *Philippine Labor Review* 4 (Second Quarter 1979): 35–37.
62. Ibid., pp. 37–38.
63. Ibid., pp. 39–41.
64. Abella, *Export of Filipino Manpower,* p. 79.
65. *Bulletin Today,* 6 August 1983.
66. Blas F. Ople, "Toward a Just and Equitable Manpower Movement" (speech delivered during the opening ceremony of the ILO/ARPLA Symposium on Overseas Recruitment Procedure for Senior Officials in East Asian Countries, Manila, 14 April 1980); published earlier in *Philippine Labor Review* 4 (Second Quarter 1980): 4.
67. Gibson, "Contract Labor Migration," p. 13.
68. Ibid., p. 14.
69. Ibid.
70. Regina B. Dacanay, "Work Conditions of Contract Workers Abroad," *Philippine Labor Review* 6 (Second Quarter 1982): 43.
71. Ibid. Because of increasing incidences of misbehaviour and criminal involvement of Filipino contract workers overseas, the POEA issued a "Code of Discipline for Overseas Workers," contained in memo circular No. 4, series of 1983, which took effect on 16 March 1983. The code spells out the responsibilities of the overseas worker to his family, his coworkers, his country, his agency, employer, and host country. It also lists behaviour that the POEA penalizes. Penalties range from stern warnings, payment or refund of the cost of repatriation, confiscation of performance bond, suspension, or permanent disqualification from overseas employment.
72. Jayme, pp. 98–99.
73. Ibid., p. 99, citing M. Mangahas, *Measuring Quality of Life: Philippine Social Indicators* (Development Academy of the Philippines, 1975).
74. Jayme, "Temporary Worker Outflows," p. 99.
75. Dacanay, "Work Conditions," p. 45.
76. Ibid.
77. Ibid., p. 50.
78. Ibid., p. 51.
79. Ibid.

80. Patricia B. Licuanan, "Beyond the Economics of Overseas Employment: The Human Costs," *Philippine Studies* 30 (1982): 266.

81. Dacanay, "Work Conditions," p. 52.

82. Licuanan, "Beyond the Economics," p. 267.

83. R. Benavides, "Skilled Filipino Laborers: Those Dream Merchants Are Still Hauling 'Em In," *WHO,* 4 April 1981, p. 13. Interviews with Filipino workers on various job sites by a POEA fact-finding team indicate that among the problems common to many are: lack of Arabian lawyers with competent arbiters to settle labour disputes at the plant site or even at diplomatic level; the need for more aid from the embassy and the regional labour center on work-related problems; inadequate predeparture orientation being given to departing workers, particularly on what to expect upon arrival in Saudi Arabia; delayed salary payments; delayed salary remittances through banks or employers; lack of adequate banking facilities and poor service of existing ones; unsatisfactory meals; maltreatment such as molestation and rape; poor postal service in the Philippines; homesickness; discrimination; professional jealousy; crimes committed by fellow workers; lack of recreational facilities; lack of reading materials in Pilipino; lack of videotaped recordings of Filipino films and T.V. programs; illegal exaction of fees by recruitment agencies before deployment; and fear of being unemployed after expiration of work contracts (source: *Manpower Export* 1 (9), p. 3.).

84. Gibson, "Contract Labor Migration," p. 17.

85. Dacanay, "Work Conditions," p. 47.

86. *Bulletin Today,* 6 September 1983.

87. "Bleak Prospects Seen for Jobs in the Middle East," *Bulletin Today,* 17 December 1982.

88. "Tighter Screening of Workers Proposed," *Bulletin Today,* 17 December 1982.

89. *Bulletin Today,* 8 August 1983; *Business Day,* 22 August 1983.

90. *Business Day,* 22 August 1983.

91. *Manpower Exchange* 3 (1), p. 2.

92. *Business Day,* 22 August 1983.

93. *Bulletin Today,* 15 August 1983.

94. Abella, *Export of Filipino Manpower,* p. 16.

95. Gamboa and Cuayo, *OEDB Survey Data,* p.5.

96. Ibid., p. 6.

97. *Annual Report 1983,* POEA, p. 4.

98. Sinay-Aguilar et al., "Temporary Employment," p. 80.

99. Go et al., *International Contract Labor,* pp. 99–100.

100. Gamboa and Cuayo, *OEDB Survey Data,* pp. 6–7; ILMS, *Working Abroad,* p. 117.

101. Central Bank of the Philippines records show the official peso-dollar rate during the period 1975 to 6 June 1984 to be as follows:

1975	— ₱7.24	1982	— ₱ 8.54
1976	— ₱7.44	Year-end 1982	— ₱ 9.17
1977	— ₱7.40	10 May 1983	— ₱10.00
1978	— ₱7.36	23 June 1983	— ₱11.00
1979	— ₱7.37	5 October 1983	— ₱14.00
1980	— ₱7.51	6 June 1984	— ₱18.00
1981	— ₱7.89		

For obvious reasons, the source of data on the black-market rate cannot be pinpointed. Despite speculations and conflicting estimates, it has been reported that the prevailing rate from 1975 to 1979 was about ₱0.20 to ₱0.30 over the official rate. From 1980 to the present, it has been as follows:

1980	— ₱ 7.80
1981	— ₱ 8.20
1982	— ₱ 9.00 to ₱9.20
January 1983	— ₱10.05
July 1983	— ₱11.50
October 1983	— ₱16.00 to ₱18.00
January 1984	— ₱22.00 to ₱23.00
February 1984	— ₱20.00 to ₱21.00
March 1984	— ₱19.50

April 1984	— ₱ 22.00
May 1984	— ₱ 23.00
June 1984	— ₱ 23.50
End of June 1984	— ₱ 24.00 to ₱ 25.00
July & August 1984	— ₱ 20.00
September 1984	— ₱ 21.00

102. "Why Workers Don't Remit Thru Banks," *Business Day,* 21 June 1982.
103. "Dollar Earnings of Overseas Workers Grow in Importance," *Business Day,* 11 January 1982.
104. *EO 857 Filipino Overseas Workers' Remittances: The Multi-Billion Dollar Question,* Kaibigan Research Series, no. 1 (Friends of Filipino Migrant Workers, Inc., p. 14.
105. Ibid., p. 15.
106. "Despite EO No. 857, Workers Won't Remit Thru Banks," *Business Day,* 23 December 1982.
107. Ibid.
108. Robosa and King, "Filipino Temporary Migrant Workers in Iran," p. 50.
109. R.M. Inokhonda, "New Dimensions in the Brain Drain Problem," *RIHED Bulletin* 10 (4), p. 18.
110. "The Philippine Overseas Employment Program," p. 15.
111. Ibid., p. 20.
112. Ibid.
113. Abrera, "Illegal Recruitment," p. 33.
114. Licuanan, "Beyond the Economics," p. 267: *Bulletin Today,* 29 August 1982.
115. Patricia B. Licuanan, "Enhancing the Socio-Psychological Well-Being of Overseas Workers and Their Families" (paper presented at the National Congress on Overseas Employment, Manila, 20 July 1982); also published in *Manpower Forum MFI* 2 (2), p. 5.
116. *Bulletin Today,* 29 August 1982.
117. Licuanan, "Beyond the Economics," p. 267.
118. *Bulletin Today,* 29 August 1982.
119. Licuanan, "Beyond the Economics," p. 268; Go et al., *International Contract Labor,* pp. 54–55; Lourdes M. Javier, "The Changing Life Style of the Families of Overseas Filipinos: A Case Study" (D.Ed. diss., Centro Escolar University, 1983), pp. 126–127.
120. Josefa S. Francisco and Pilar Ramos-Jimenez, eds., *The Effects of International Contract Labour,* vol. 2, *Community Studies* (Integrated Research Center, De La Salle University, Manila, 1983), pp. 52–53; Javier, "The Changing Life Style," pp. 128–129.
121. Francisco and Ramos-Jimenez, *International Contract Labour,* pp. 52–53, 281; Javier, "The Changing Life Style," pp. 128–129.
122. Robosa and King, "Filipino Temporary Migrant Workers in Iran," p. 52.
123. Licuanan, "Beyond the Economics," p. 265.
124. Abella, *Export of Filipino Manpower,* p. 82.
125. Lazo et al., "Contract Migration Policies," p. 36.
126. Licuanan, "Socio-Psychological Well-Being," p. 9.
127. Ibid., p. 10.
128. Cynthia Santiago, "The Lure: Irresistible Incentives," *HR Magazine,* July 1982, p. 27.
129. Ibid.
130. Licuanan, "Socio-Psychological Well-Being," p. 10.
131. Lazo et al., "Contract Migration Policies," p. 36.

References

Abella, Manolo I. *Export of Filipino Manpower.* Institute of Labor and Manpower Studies, Ministry of Labor, Manila, 1979.

Abrera, Alcestis. "Illegal Recruitment: The Philippine Experience." *Philippine Labor Review,* vol. 4, no. 2 (2nd quarter 1979).

Benavides, Richie. "Skilled Filipino Laborers: Those Dream Merchants Are Still Hauling 'Em In." *WHO* (Liwayway Publishing, Manila), 4 Apr. 1981.

Campania, V. *The Incidence of External Migration on the Philippine Labor Supply.* 1977.

Central Bank of the Philippines. "Convenient Ways to Send Something to Somebody in the Philippines: Deposit in Philippine Bank." Manila.

Dacanay, Regina B. "Work Conditions of Contract Workers Abroad." *Philippine Labor Review,* vol. 6, no. 2 (2nd quarter 1981).

De la Cruz, Jonathan. "The Philippine Overseas Employment and Contracting Program: Policies and Programs Influencing Overseas Labor Migration." Ministry of Labor and Employment, Manila, 1982.

Fernandez, Perfecto V. "Regimentation of Labor in an Open Economy." *Philippine Journal of Industrial Relations,* vol. 5, nos. 1–2 (1983).

Francisco, Josefa S., and Pilar Ramos-Jimenez, eds. *The Effects of International Contract Labor.* Vol. 2, *Community Studies.* Integrated Research Center, De La Salle University, Manila, 1983.

Gamboa, Eduardo D., and Edelana M. Cuayo. *Analysis of the OEDB Survey Data on Overseas Workers' Remittances.* Commissioned by the Overseas Employment Development Board, Ministry of Labor and Employment. Research for Development Department, Development Academy of the Philippines, 1982.

Gibson, Catherine D. "Contract Labour Migration from the Philippines: Preliminary Fieldwork Report." Department of Human Geography, Research School of Pacific Studies, Australian National University, Canberra, 1983.

Go, Stella P., Leticia T. Postrado, and Pilar Ramos-Jimenez. *The Effects of International Contract Labor,* vol. 1. Integrated Research Center, De La Salle University, Manila, 1983.

Gupta, M. L. "Outflows of High Level Manpower from the Philippines, with Special Reference to the Period 1965–1971." *International Labor Review,* vol. 7, no. 2 (Feb. 1973).

Inciong, Amado G. "The Filipino Workers: Development with Justice in the New Society." *Fookien Times,* 1977.

Inokhonda, R. M. "New Dimensions in the Brain Drain Problem." *RIHED Bulletin,* vol. 10, no. 4 (Oct.–Dec. 1983).

Institute of Labor and Manpower Studies (ILMS). "Overseas Placement Volume/Industry Distribution of Contract Workers."

——. *Socio-Economic Consequences of Contract Labor Migration in the Philippines,* vol. 1. Ministry of Labor and Employment, Manila, 1983.

——. *Working Abroad: The Socio-Economic Consequences of Contract Labor Migration in the Philippines.* Ministry of Labor and Employment, Manila, 1984.

Javier, Lourdes M. "The Changing Life Style of the Families of Overseas Filipinos: A Case Study." Ed.D. dissertation, Centro Escolar University, Manila, 1983.

Jayme, Rebecca B. "A Study on the Effects of Temporary Workers' Outflows from the Philippines." M.A. thesis, University of the Philippines, 1979.

Kaibigan (Friends of Filipino Migrant Workers, Inc.). *EO 857 Filipino Overseas Workers' Remittances: The Multi-Billion Dollar Question.* Research Series, no. 1. Kaibigan, Manila, 1983.

Kalaw-Tirol, Lorna. "Petro-Dollars Go a Long Way, but Not Long Enough to Ease the Pain of Loneliness." *Panorama,* 26 Sept. 1982.

Lazo, L. S., V.A. Teodosio, and P. A. Sto. Tomas. *Contract Migration Policies in the Philippines.* International Labour Organisation, Manila, 1982.

Licuanan, Patricia B. "Beyond the Economics of Overseas Employment: The Human Costs." *Philippine Studies,* vol. 30 (1982).

——. "Enhancing the Socio-Psychological Well-Being of Overseas Workers and Their Families." *Manpower Forum MFI,* vol. 2, no. 2 (Sept. 1982).

Magno, Carlo R. H. "The Effects of Labor Export on the Employment Situation in the Philippines." Sept. 1983.

——. "Implication of the Export of Manpower to the Telephone Industry." Paper presented at seminar-conference on Export of Manpower: Some Unexplored Issues, 24 Mar. 1984, sponsored by the Institute of Industrial Relations, University of the Philippines.

Manpower Exchange. "Improvement Procedures in Recruitment, Placement, and Enforcement of Labor Contract Overseas." *Philippine Labor Review,* vol. 4, no. 2 (2nd quarter 1979).

Office of Emigrant Affairs (OEA). *Special Report on Profile of Filipinos Overseas.* Ministry of Labor and Employment, Manila, 1980.

Ople, Blas F. "Toward a Just and Equitable Manpower Movement." *Philippine Labor Review,* vol. 4, no. 2 (2nd quarter 1979).

Philippine Overseas Employment Administration (POEA). *Annual Report 1982.*

————. "Basic Information on Overseas Employment and Illegal Recruitment." Workers' Assistance and Adjudication Office, POEA, Ministry of Labor and Employment, Manila.

Reyes, Melissa. "Overseas Employment: Rich Economic Vein or Development Brain?" *HR Magazine,* July 1982.

Robosa, M., and A. King. "Filipino Migrant Workers in Iran (Insights into Temporary Migration)." *Philippine Labor Review,* vol. 4, no. 2 (2nd quarter 1979).

Santiago, Cynthia. "The Lure: Irresistible Incentives." *HR Magazine,* July 1982.

Sto. Tomas, P. A. "Project Proposal: Studies into the Effects of Temporary Labor Migration in the Philippines." Prepared for the International Development Research Center, Aug. 1981—Dec. 1982.

Sarmiento, Loida. "Preliminary Study on Families of Migrant Workers."

Sinay-Aguilar, Ma. Virginia, Julie Q. Casel, Joan Amor F. Palafox, and Sofronio V. Amante. "Outflow of Scarce Skills in the Philippines, 1975–1982." Research and Publication Program, Institute of Industrial Relations, University of the Philippines, Quezon City, 1983.

Sinay-Aguilar, Virginia, Gloria B. Caromen, Carmelita Baquiran, A. Laqui, H. Luwalhati, Nenta Retiro, and Edna Macarrubo. "Effects of Temporary Employment of Professional and Skilled Manual Workers in the Middle East on the Labor Market." Submitted to the Program in Development Economics, School of Economics, University of the Philippines, in partial fulfilment of the requirements for the Certificate in Development Economics, 1981.

Smart, John E. "Saudi Demand for Filipino Workers: Labour Migration Issues in the Middle East." *Asian and Pacific Census Forum* (East-West Center, Honolulu, Hawaii, USA), vol. 9, no. 1 (Aug. 1982).

Stahl, Charles W. "International Labor Migration and the ASEAN Economics." Working paper. ASEAN-Australian Economic Relations Project.

"The Philippine Overseas Employment Program." *Philippine Labor Review,* vol. 4, no. 2 (2nd quarter 1979).

THAILAND

Witayakorn Chiengkul

Lecturer, Department of Sociology and Anthropology, Faculty of Social Sciences,
Chiang Mai University, Chiang Mai, Thailand

Historical Background of the Thai Labour Migration

The emigration of Thai workers to the Middle East began in the early 1970s. The
first Thai migrants to go to the Middle East were the skilled workers who had been
employed by the U.S. construction firms based in Thailand during the Viet Nam War.
Following the withdrawal of the U.S. armed forces from Viet Nam, these construction
firms had to wind up their activities and retrench their Thai employees. These firms,
however, soon found new opportunities in the Middle East, where massive investment
programmes were being undertaken. The U.S. firms that succeeded in obtaining large
contracts under these programmes had to go outside the Gulf region in order to
recruit the necessary workforce because these countries did not have the required
manpower. The previous links with Thailand provided a ready source of labour — both
among former Thai employees as well as other Thai workers who possessed the needed
skills. The wages offered were very attractive, being many times the domestic wage,
and the Thai workers were naturally eager to seize these opportunities for employment
in the Middle East.

The flow of migrant Thai workers to the Middle East from 1971 to 1974 was relatively
small. Since the demand for foreign labour in the region far exceeded supply, at the
outset of the migration recruiting agencies had to offer strong incentives to attract the
first groups of migrant workers. Although living and working conditions in the Middle
East were exacting, the remuneration averaged four to five times the wage for
equivalent grades in Thailand. By the latter half of the 1970s the high wage incentives
had become so attractive that rapidly increasing numbers of workers were drawn into
the emigration process.

The migration to the Middle East was gathering momentum during a period when the
Thai economy was suffering from the combined effects of the withdrawal of American
troops and the closure of military bases in Thailand as well as the growing world

306

economic crisis following the steep increases in the price of oil in 1973. Nearly 100,000 Thai workers were left unemployed as a result of the withdrawal of U.S. troops. With a rapidly growing labour force and an unstable internal political situation — resulting in a lowering of investment between 1973 and 1974 — Thailand faced record levels of unemployment and underemployment. It was during this period that the demand for expatriate labour in the Gulf region was rising rapidly. The first return flow of migrants from the region was bringing information about the highly remunerative jobs there. More and more workers began to compete for employment in the Middle East.

In this situation of keen competition, brokers and other intermediaries who secured employment for the job-seekers often charged exorbitant commissions and fees, which usually ranged from 2000 to 3000 baht (approximately $100 to $150*). Soon thereafter, recruitment agencies also established themselves as profit-making ventures and charged fees for their services. At first, the commissions charged by the recruiting agencies were paid by the companies who employed the migrant workers. Since then, however, the process of securing employment in the Middle East has become more complex. Unscrupulous elements began exploiting the situation and making unconscionable profits at the expense of the workers. Commission charges increased to $200 or $300; in certain instances, they went as high as $750.[1]

As the flow of expatriate migration expanded rapidly and brought a variety of problems in its wake, the Thai government began to recognise, on the one hand, the substantial benefits of exporting labour to the Middle East and, on the other, the need to introduce better systems and more effective controls to realise the full potential of the migration. In August 1977 the Department of Labour issued its first decree on the exporting of Thai labour to employers in foreign countries. The department cautioned workers to contact only licensed job agencies and to submit a job description and a copy of the job contract for inspection by the Department of Labour.

In practice, however, the unlicensed private job agencies who controlled approximately half the market, were able to continue in business. The Department of Labour did not have the necessary resources to monitor the activities of even the licensed job agencies. Furthermore, the penalties imposed on the agencies in breach of regulations were surprisingly low and did not act as effective deterrents. For example, the maximum fine was 1000 baht ($50) or imprisonment for not more than one month. Greater attempts are now being made to control illegal practices and harmful competition among the private agencies. It is expected that penalties for illegal practices will become more severe and will be enforced more strictly.

---

* References to dollars ($) are to US dollars throughout this article.

Current Knowledge about the Labour Migration

As the emigration of Thai workers to the Middle East began to receive serious national attention only a few years ago, no extensive research has been carried out on the various aspects of the phenomenon. It was not until 1978 that research of any significance was undertaken on the issue.[2] Currently, there are three main sources of information and research data on the emigration issue:
- The Wages and Employment Planning Sector of the Population and Manpower Planning Division, National Social and Economic Development Board (NESDB)
- The faculties of Economics, Thammasat and Culalongkorn universities, and their papers on this subject at a workshop series on the New International Economic Order, 27 April 1982
- Other sources, including the Bangkok Bank and journal and magazine articles.

The majority of the studies and research work have been conducted by economists or writers focusing on the economic issues. These researchers have been mainly concerned with the various economic aspects of the export of labour to the Middle East, both positive and negative, at the macro as well as the micro level. Some researchers have been concerned with the technical and efficiency problems of exporting Thai labour to foreign countries. There are, however, few studies on the impact of returned workers, and none as yet on the socio-psychological and cultural effects of this process.

The Migration and the Return Flow — Volume and Composition

Number of Migrants and Returnees

Tables 1 and 2 give an indication of the flow of emigrants from Thailand to the Middle East and other countries during the period 1975-1981.

Thailand has a dual system of labour export whereby labour is exported both by private recruitment agencies and by a government organisation, the Department of Labour. However, owing to the openness of the national system in which competitive private enterprise plays a key role, more than 95 per cent of the total Thai labour exports are carried out by private firms. These include both licensed and unlicensed organisations. As of 1981 there were 223 licensed and 232 unlicensed agencies in operation.

The free and nearly uncontrolled export of Thai labour means that the actual total export (both yearly and cumulative) is nowhere recorded or registered. Only the portion channelled through the Department of Labour by government and private firms appears on record, constituting only a small part of the total flow. Some sources tentatively estimate that the number of Thai workers exported through the Labour

Department between 1975 and 1982 could not constitute more than 20 per cent of the total exported to the Middle East.[3]

Another study by the chief of the Wage and Employment Planning Sector of the National Social and Economic Development Board has arrived at a different estimate, using the concept of surveyed average and recorded remittances. This estimate reveals

TABLE 1. Number of Thai Workers Sent to the Middle East through the Department of Labour, 1975–1981

	1975	1976	1977	1978	1979	1980	1981
Bahrain	968	960	776	1050	75	306	388
Saudi Arabia	16	327	2855	8502	7657	9990	9806
Dubai	—	—	239	—	—	—	—
Iran	—	—	—	3199	—	—	—
Kuwait	—	—	—	2176	188	958	608
UAE	—	—	—	262	146	757	59
Qatar	—	—	—	76	165	1070	2538
Yemen	—	—	—	—	6	215	—
Jordan	—	—	—	—	110	33	—
Israel	—	—	—	—	100	—	—
Iraq	—	—	—	—	174	988	1979
Libya	—	—	—	—	—	6492	10,189
Oman	—	—	—	—	—	—	5
Total	984	1287	3870	15,265	8522	20,809	24,472

Source: Department of Labour.

TABLE 2. Estimate of Thai Workers in the Middle East, 1980–1981

	1980	1981
Bahrain	5000	5000
Saudi Arabia	60,000	100,000
Kuwait	5000	5000
UAE	2000	3000
Yemen	—	1000
Qatar	2000	3000
Jordan	2000	2000
Iraq	10,000	20,000
Libya	10,000	20,000
Total	98,000	159,000

Source: Department of Labour

that, on average, a labourer working a full year abroad (12 months) had remitted 102,928 baht (approximately $5000) annually between 1973 and 1981.[4] Since then, annual earnings during the study period have shown little variation, and it may be assumed that average annual remittances in 1981 are the same as for the previous period. The total annual remittance estimated for 1981 amounted to 7000 million baht; thus, the amount of labour abroad should have been approximately 70,000 to 100,000 workers.

This figure is much smaller than the Labour Department's estimate of 159,000 workers for the same year. The difference is attributable to the methodology applied. For example, the Department of Labour seems to derive its figure from the number of visas issued by all countries concerned; the estimated total of Thai migrants to the Middle East is, therefore, inevitably overstated.

TABLE 3. Thai Workers Sent Overseas by the Department of Labour, 1982

Country	Number[1]	%
Saudi Arabia	88,271	81.3
Libya	9034	8.3
Iraq	3140	2.9
Qatar	2825	2.6
Singapore	1975	1.8
Brunei	960	0.9
Kuwait	611	0.6
Jordan	580	0.5
Israel	362	0.3
UAE	310	0.3
Malaysia	199	0.2
Algeria	150	0.14
Japan	41	0.04
Macao	31	0.03
South Yemen	20	0.02
Bahrain	10	0.01
Total	108,519	100.0

1. Includes workers sent directly by the Department of Labour and the employers, who account for 1 per cent in any case.

Since 1982 the process of registering Thai overseas workers has been improved by one external factor: the new requirement by most labour-importing countries that Thai migrants should have obtained a Police Clearance Certificate (PCC). As a result, there is a new record of the number of Thai labourers exported to the Middle East by private agencies channelled through the Department of Labour. In 1982, this was as high as 108,127 (Table 3), a big jump from the 24,750 estimated in 1981.[5] However, even in 1982 not all Thai workers who went to the Middle East were channelled through the Department of Labour. Nevertheless, even after the procedure was introduced, the correct actual total of current outward migration of workers cannot be obtained, since some countries do not require the PCC for visa application.

In the first stage of labour export, the destination was limited to two Middle Eastern countries — Saudi Arabia and Bahrain. Later, the labour migrants have been more widely distributed throughout the Middle East and have also gone to Singapore and Brunei. Saudi Arabia remains the largest importer of Thai labour. Other important labour-importing countries include Libya, Iraq, and Kuwait. Other less important countries include the UAE, Qatar, Jordan, Israel, and Algeria. For the majority of the entire exporting period, more than half the total number of Thai workers abroad have worked in Saudi Arabia (81.3 per cent in 1982), while the remainder were divided among Libya, Iraq, Kuwait, and Bahrain, respectively.

The total number of Thai emigrant workers in countries other than the Middle East is difficult to determine. Before the emergence of the Middle Eastern labour market boom in the mid-1970s, a moderate number of Thai workers migrated to the United States and the United Kingdom for employment. Between 1966 and 1977 approximately 23,219 immigrant visas were reported to have been issued by the U.S. embassy in Thailand for Thais intending to work in the United States. If those illegally employed are included in the total number of Thais working in the United States during this ten-year period the total would reach 43,000 to 44,000 workers.[6] In 1981 the U.S. embassy in Thailand reported that an average of 200 persons per month applied for immigrant visas. The remittances in 1981 and 1982 from the United States totalled 2358 and 2206 million baht respectively (approximately $1000 million). These figures account for only 15-20 per cent of the total remittances from all countries.

The Bank of Thailand study also reveals that between 1972 and 1977, 1743 Thais applied for work in the United Kingdom. This number exceeded the 293 workers applying for United Kingdom jobs between 1973 and 1977 as recorded by the Thai Department of Labour. Fewer and fewer Thais have been emigrating to work in the United Kingdom since 1976 owing to restrictions there on foreign labour. The number of those illegally employed is not known.

Another market for Thai emigrant workers is other Asian countries — namely, Singapore, Brunei, Malaysia, Hong Kong, and Japan. In 1978, 250 Thais were sent to Singapore for contract employment. This number rose substantially to reach 1851 workers in 1979.[7]

The National Economic and Social Development Board (NESDB) estimated that at the end of 1982 there were 6070 Thai workers in Singapore. The annual rate of inflow (permanently returning workers) is not known, as there exist no records and little research on the subject to date. There is no reliable information regarding the return flow of migrants.

Individual research studies of migrants who have returned indicate that the vast majority of these workers wish to return to the Middle East for re-employment. Only about 20 per cent of those interviewed were planning to stay and were not seeking re-employment abroad. These figures, however, do not help us to ascertain the number of migrants who return annually after they complete their contracts. It is possible to estimate the return flow on the basis of the average stay in the Middle East and the annual migration, but these estimates are bound to be very tentative as they are derived, as we saw, from widely varying estimates from different sources. However, we could assume that if the annual flow is in the region of 150,000 workers and the period of stay is approximately 18 months (see Table 4) the annual inflow could be as high as 125,000 per annum in any given period.

TABLE 4. Period of Employment of Thai Workers in the Middle East

Time (years)	%
1	49.3
2	28.5
3	14.8
4	5.0
5	1.4
More than 5	1.1
Total	100.0
Average time (years)	1.85

Source: NESDB Survey, 1981.

Composition of the Migrant Population

Sex. Almost all Thai workers in the Middle East are male. The conditions in the labour-importing countries have discouraged the migration of female workers. Most of the job opportunities for females are confined to domestic service. Labour laws in the Middle East countries do not cover this category of employees and reports of ill-treatment of domestic female workers by their employers have not been un-common.

Age. In 1977 and 1981 the average age for Thai workers overseas was approximately 32 years. In other words, workers between 25 and 35 years of age constituted roughly half of the total outward migration to the Middle East. This means that the selection of eligible workers was from the age group which was neither too young nor too old but were physically energetic and able to withstand hard work and the rigours of a harsh climate. (See Table 5.)

TABLE 5. Thai Workers in the Middle East by Age Group (percentages)

	1977	1981
Below 20	1.7	0.4
21–25	13.0	17.3
26–30	22.8	27.8
31–35	26.4	23.6
36–40	21.1	16.9
41–45	10.2	8.0
46–50	4.3	2.6
Over 50	0.8	0.4
Not reported	0.7	3.0
Total	100.0	100.0
Average	—	31.90

Source: Department of Labour

TABLE 6. Thai Workers Classified by Education (percentages)

Grade 1–4	83.2
Grade 4–high school	14.4
Vocational and certificate	2.0
Bachelor degree and above	0.4
Total	100.0

Source: Survey by Population and Manpower Planning Division, NESDB, 1981.

Education. According to a 1981 survey by the NESDB, the majority of sampled workers had received an education only through grade 4 — that is, the minimum required to read and write simple Thai (Table 6). They were supposedly able at least to sign their names on relevant documents, including contracts translated from English into Thai.

Region. Based on registration by the Department of Labour in 1981, out of the total number of Thai workers in the Middle East, 39.5 per cent were from the northeast; 38.0 per cent were from the central plains, mainly the Bangkok area; 22 per cent were from the north; and only 0.5 per cent were from the south. However, Bangkok has acted as the main centre for job-seekers from all parts of the country; therefore, at any given time Bangkok workers may not be Bangkok residents but migrants or temporary visitors for the specific purpose of securing employment abroad. Further, many of the workers temporarily in Bangkok have moved from the north and northeast. This would indicate that the predominant majority of workers come from the rural areas of the northeast, north, and central plains. (See Table 7.)

TABLE 7. Thai Workers in the Middle East by Domicile (percentages)

	1977	1981
Bangkok	22.6	14.84
Udonthani (N.E.)	14.5	20.08
Chonburi (central)	13.1	3.50
Lampang (north)	12.4	6.60
Ubonratchathani (N.E.)	5.9	—
Rayong (central)	5.4	1.52
Nakhonratchasima (N.E.)	3.3	5.46
Samutprakan (central)	2.3	2.31
Nongkhai (N.E.)	1.6	2.56
Nakhonphanom (N.E.)	1.6	2.56
Sakonnakhon (N.E.)	1.2	2.08
Nakhonsawan (north)	1.5	2.27
Other provinces	14.6	38.78
Total	100.0	100.0

Source: Department of Labour

According to the same Department of Labour 1918 registration, the breakdown of the data by province reveals that Udon Thani (where the U.S. army base had been located) is the major source of Thai overseas workers, followed by Bangkok, Lampang, Nakhon Ratchasima, Chonburi, Tak, Khon-Kaen, Nongkai, Samuth Prakarn, Nakhon Sawan, and so forth. Interestingly, almost no workers came from the south. The fact that the workers in this area enjoy a relatively higher per capita income, better wages, and year-round employment opportunities may have contributed to the low level of migration from this area.

Marital status. According to the 1981 NESDB survey, the majority of emigrating workers (88.2 per cent) were married. Only 10.2 per cent were bachelors. This was probably due to the pressure on married males, when faced with economic difficulties, to find income to support their families. The high percentage of married workers abroad may also be due to the fact that rural, less-educated male and female workers tend to marry earlier than the more educated urban residents. However, when comparing married and single returnees, it was found that the latter showed more tendency to work in the Middle East a second time than the married returnee. This may be explained by that fact that without marriage-related dependents, single workers could take more risks, including living and working abroad. (See Table 8.)

TABLE 8. Thai Emigrant Workers by Marital Status, 1981 (percentages)

Bachelor	10.2
Married	88.2
Widower or divorced	1.6
Total	100.0

Source: Survey by the Population and Manpower Division, NESDB, 1981.

TABLE 9. Thai Workers in the Middle East by Previous Occupation, 1981 (percentages)

Farmer	46.82
Trader	5.83
Wage worker	4.77
Carpenter	6.18
Construction	7.78
Welder	1.77
Electrician	1.77
Mechanic	3.53
Metalworker	0.88
Pointer	1.06
Driver	7.42
Cook	0.71
Other	11.48
Total	100.00

Source: Population and Manpower Planning Division, NESDB Survey, 1981.

Occupation. According to the 1981 NESDB field survey, farming remained the most common previous occupation for all the emigrants surveyed. Nevertheless, such other occupations as general employment construction work, driving, and carpentry also accounted for significant percentages (Table 9).

Employment status. According to Department of Labour figures, skilled and semi-skilled workers together accounted for 77.0 per cent, 53.2 per cent, and 69.6 per cent of total migrant workers in 1978, 1980, and 1981 respectively (Table 10). Unskilled workers, however, accounted for only 23.0 per cent, 36.8 per cent, and 30.4 per cent during those years. This categorisation and grading may not be entirely accurate or reliable. When a breakdown by position held abroad for 1981 is taken into consideration, it is found that the labourer category was largest, followed by mason, carpenter, ironworker, electrician, and foreman, respectively. In conclusion, regardless of the skilled or unskilled nature of the labour, most Thai workers abroad were engaged in construction activities. (See also Table 11.)

Family income. Field research in two northeastern villages in 1982[8] revealed that the majority of emigrant workers came from middle- and low-income families. The average annual income for emigrants' families (prior to migration) was 20,012 baht, while that for nonmigrants' families in the same areas was 57,399 baht.[9]

Other characteristics. The 1981 NESDB field survey reported that the majority of migrant workers came from large, dependent families. On average, each migrant family surveyed had six members, three of whom were employed in the labour force, and

TABLE 10. Percentage of Thai Workers in the Middle East by Category and Occupation, 1978–1981 (percentages)

	1978	1980	1981
Unskilled	23.00	36.37	30.44
Semiskilled and skilled	77.00	63.23	69.56
Total	100.00	100.00	100.00
Labourer	10.80	20.74	18.67
Janitor	—	2.76	0.85
Cook's helper	—	1.80	2.01
Porter	—	2.83	0.78
Join worker	—	5.85	4.80
Electrician	3.5	2.46	2.80
Welder	8.3	3.59	2.06
Mason	6.2	9.53	9.64
Carpenter	8.8	9.21	7.21
Tile-layer	—	2.94	1.64
Welder	5.6	2.09	1.33
Foreman	—	4.08	2.73
Driver	—	3.33	6.22
Cook	—	0.62	1.30
Other	—	28.17	37.96
Total	100.00	100.00	100.00

No data for 1979.

Source: Department of Labour.

316

TABLE 11. Thai Workers in the Middle East by
Occupation (percentages)

Labourer	13.2
Service	4.4
Carpenter	18.5
Construction	19.2
Mechanic	2.0
Electrician and welder	7.7
Other skilled	7.1
Driver	11.4
Foreman	4.1
Cook	3.9
Other	8.5
Total	100.0
Number interviewed	562

Source: NESDB Survey, 1981.

the others were dependent (i.e. children or aged people). The majority (98.8 per cent)
of the interviewed migrant workers were Buddhists; there was no report whatsoever
of religious discrimination.

The Domestic Labour Market: Supply and Demand by Occupation

Of the total Thai labour force of 23,810,000 in 1981, the number of unemployed was
286,000; the number underemployed (working less than 20 hours per week) was 6.3
million; and the number of seasonally unemployed was approximately 3.5 to 4.0
million. It is estimated that there are 500,000 to 600,000 new job-seekers each year.
Thus, even if detailed domestic labour supply-and-demand statistics are not available
by occupation, it may be said that in general the labour supply far exceeds the
demand. This is particularly true of agriculture and other industries using unskilled and
semiskilled labour.

Some statistics currently available may show part of the overall supply-and-demand
picture. As yet, no detailed research has been undertaken on whether or not the
emigration of unskilled and semiskilled Thai workers to the Middle East has caused
labour shortages or has led to wage increases. The impact may be difficult to identify,
since the percentage of workers migrating to the Middle East accounts for less than
1 per cent of the total labour force (Table 12). It is believed by most Thai economists
that the export of Thai workers to the Middle East relieves domestic unemployment.
Although the majority of migrant workers have held some form of job before moving
to the Middle East, most of those working abroad did not have sufficient year-round
employment.

Even migrant full-time workers would be largely, if not wholly, replaced by the unemployed. There is then the question of skill requirements and the unavailability of certain skills in this process of replacement. In answer to this question, it has to be pointed out that with the exception of very highly skilled labour, there should be no problem with such replacement and, in fact, the second or third best can usually take up the post. In response to this problem, a process of on-the-job training and promotion is available. In brief, as yet there have not been any discernible problems in the labour market as a result of the migration.

One NESDB study[10] argued that the problem of a shortage of skilled labour has not actually occurred yet. It was reasoned that the income incentive is not the only factor influencing migrants' decisions but that a number of other factors exist. These include the size of current income (a future opportunity cost in the case of positive decision making), work security and benefits, working conditions, living environment, and various types of hardships and psychological costs suffered in working abroad. As a result, only those skilled or semiskilled workers who are seasonally employed, self-employed, or underemployed in all categories and with a rather low income level are actual and potential emigrants. Moreover, from the demand side, it also appears that the requirement for skilled workers (many of whom are available both from Thailand and other competing countries) is not unlimited. Thus, the eventual outcome is that Thailand has not yet reached the point of a serious shortage of skilled labour, let alone of unskilled labour, although temporary bottlenecks in special categories of labour can occur. A small mailing survey of construction companies conducted by the Wages and Employment Planning Sector in 1981 revealed some shortages in certain types of semiskilled labour, particularly in the construction industry. But this survey and other random inquiries with the more active recruitment agencies showed that, in the case of recruits drawn from construction-company employees, labour-shortage problems were temporary during the transition period and were eventually solved satisfactorily. The negligible impact of the labour migration is also attributable to the current sluggishness of the economy, causing lay-offs and a slackening of demand for workers.

TABLE 12. Comparison of Number of Thai Workers Overseas with the Total Thai Labour Force and Unemployment, 1981

Total labour force	23,810,000
Open unemployed	286,000
Overseas workers	
Estimated number	100,000
As % of total labour force	0.42
As % of number of open unemployed	34.96

Source: NESDB Population and Manpower Planning Division figures and NESDB estimates.

The commonly held view that there is an excess supply of workers in nearly every occupation except medical doctors is supported by the statistics in Table 13. Research, however, has not been done yet on the estimated cost of producing skills in excess of demand. The influence of labour migration on wage trends in the Thai economy is not clearly seen, or at least has not yet been systematically investigated. In addition, there is as yet no solid research on shortages of skilled and semiskilled labour as a direct result of the emigration to the Middle East. Training in ordinary skills is provided by the Department of Labour at several centres. This training is divided into four branches: pre-employment training, upgrading, on-the-job training, and nontechnical training. The number of trainees in 1980 was 11,541 and in 1981 reached 13,540.[11] There is an even greater number of vocational students training under the Ministry of Education programmes. At present, the output of these programmes appears to be more than adequate to meet the current demand.

The Process of Migration

In Thailand, the export of labour to the Middle East is initiated and managed by private firms. While one might say that there has been a dual system of export,

TABLE 13. Projection of Additional Manpower Requirements and Supply in Key Occupations during the Fifth Plan, 1982–1986

Field of Study	Demand	Supply	Difference
Medicine	3600	3166	− 434
Pharmacy	1320	1643	+ 323
Dentistry	725	1045	+ 320
Agriculture (B.A.)	6260	9382	+3122
Education (B.A. and higher)	45,135	76,824	+31,689
Teacher training (below B.A.)	74,307	78,598	+4291
Engineering	9454	10,635	+1189
Science	6207	8523	+2316
Vocational education	334,870	584,310	+249,440
Certificate level	*258,720*	*431,510*	*+192,790*
Agriculture	5050	21,300	+16,250
Industry	122,900	141,040	+18,140
Commerce	100,700	253,700	+153,000
Home economics	30,070	35,470	+5400
Diploma level	*76,150*	*132,800*	*+65,650*
Agriculture	9830	12,160	+2330
Industry	37,820	58,280	+20,460
Commerce	20,690	43,570	+20,460
Home economics	7810	10,790	+10,980

Source: Subcommittee on Manpower Assessment, NESDB.

whereby actual labour exports are carried out by private recruitment agencies and the Department of Labour, more than 95 per cent of total labour exports are carried out by both licensed and unlicensed private firms.

The Overseas Employment Service Division (OESD) has been established within the Department of Labour to facilitate the processing of overseas employment. Apart from controlling the private employment agencies engaged in overseas recruitment, the OESD also functions as a recruiter for foreign employment. However, this organisation has a very limited function due to the lack of financial resources and manpower.

Cost of Job-Finding

Since more than 95 per cent of Thai migrants to the Middle East are recruited by private agencies, the cost of securing a job in the Middle East is quite high in proportion to the average income of Thai nationals. Most emigrants must borrow money from private sources and pay high interest rates. According to an NESDB study in 1981,[12] the total cost of getting a job, excluding interest costs, was 20,498 baht ($1000) per person, or 25,954 baht ($1200) including interest charges. The other major expenditures were for travel and accommodation during the entire period of job application, which sometimes took months or even a year of waiting. Passport-issuance fees might be considered the third important expenditure. This averaged 1628 baht, of which 1000 baht was the official passport fee.

It will be observed that interest costs were approximately 5456 baht each. The average monthly interest rate was as high as 9.3 per cent and varied from place to place in accordance with the degree of risk involved. This average interest charge is obviously unacceptably high compared to that charged by banks or other financial institutions. There was a close correlation between high interest-rate fees and quick repayments. In other words, due to high interest rates imposed by lenders, migrant workers who borrowed tended to send as much of their monthly earnings back home as possible for debt repayment. This means that, among all payments, debt repayment received the highest priority. Despite this high priority for low-income workers, it took quite a long period for them to settle their debts — as much as one year of work. For this reason, and for the net monetary gain to benefit their families, they would attempt to have their contract renewed or extended as many times as possible.

A comparison of costs incurred by the low-income and high-income brackets shows that much higher costs were incurred by labourers than, for example, by mechanics — 32,607 baht and 17,632 baht respectively. As already mentioned, the major reason for this was the keen domestic and international competition for jobs among unskilled workers. Furthermore, low-income workers tended to finance costs by borrowing, resulting in higher interest costs.

The last element of the total economic cost of emigration is the opportunity cost. The average monthly income of emigrants within Thailand was 2251 baht (roughly 27,000 baht per yeat) during the surveyed period. If this sum is added to the total financial cost of migration, the overall economic cost of migration, the overall economic cost per person comes to 52,954 baht. If the net income gain accruing to a migrant is estimated by subtracting the total cost of migration from the total annual remittance, there is a net gain of 49,974 baht, or approximately 94.4 per cent of the total economic costs—or 185.1 per cent of the forgone income (opportunity cost) Where the worker is employed for more than a year, the gain is much higher.

Forms of Exploitation and Government Controls

One of the major problems in the recruitment process is the widespread exploitation of workers. Despite considerable efforts by the government to curb exploitative practices, it is unlikely that they can be eliminated altogether owing to the willingness of so many job-seekers to go along with unscrupulous recruiters in order to compete for jobs abroad.

Exploitative practices relating to overseas recruitment may be classified into four major types. The first includes false employment offers, whereby workers are charged sizeable fees for nonexistent jobs by spurious employment agents during application. The Middle Eastern boom has given rise to a very lucrative recruiting business, attracting many licensed and unlicensed job agencies into the trade.

Despite laws specifying allowable fees, all private agents normally demand much higher fees, most of the time with the cooperation of the workers, who are convinced that it is the price which must be paid if they are to succeed in obtaining such jobs. Although there are some complaints regarding fraud and irregularities, there is little the government is able to do by way of redress or punishment due to difficulties in tracing these unlicensed agents, who quickly close down their offices after the money has been taken.

There are various corrupt practices during the preselection, interview, and selection process for employment, which result in additional costs to the job-seekers. Often exaggerated and unrealistic information on terms and conditions of employment is given by licensed recruiters, officials, or middlemen. This type of illegal practice creeps in during the selection and hiring stages. Some middlemen demand further payments from workers to reduce the waiting period and obtain job allocations. Those who refuse to make such payments may have their waiting period prolonged.

Other forms of corruption crop up after selection. Gratifications might be paid to government by recruiting agents to obtain approval for work contracts that are below official standards. All such costs are generally transmitted to the workers. In addition, there are cases where workers pay more than the fees due in order to obtain passports and visas for travel overseas. There have been instances where workmen have been overcharged even for their airfare.

In the host country, migrant workers face other forms of exploitation. New contracts may be substituted for the original contracts with terms and conditions altered to the disadvantage of the employee; procedures for presentation and settlement of grievances in the workplace could be unsatisfactory; reliable facilities for remittances might not be easily available, and workers consequently may become victims of fraud. These problems generally occur in the case of workers who have obtained jobs through unlicensed agencies without going through the regular channels. Work contracts are most often signed without proper understanding or full knowledge of the actual terms and conditions of work.

There is, however, little substantiated evidence and data on the incidence of corruption and illegal activities relating to the Middle East migration. This may be primarily because workers who are keen on securing employment abroad normally accept the terms imposed by dishonest recruiters, middlemen, or government officials even though they know the terms are unlawful. Such unlawful activities may thus operate without detection or punishment as long as workers are allocated jobs abroad. Some complaints are made when workers are defrauded, but it appears that even such victims are often afraid or too embarrassed to admit that they have been exploited. As a result, most of the irregularities and malpractices are neither detected nor controlled. Therefore, in the prevailing situation, it is difficult to estimate, control, or eliminate such recruitment malpractices.

Government Controls and Procedures

There are three government agencies connected with the export of Thai labour. The Department of Labour assumes the key role in the process and is in charge of inspecting contracts for their terms and conditions of work, granting permission for the export of labour, skill testing, worker training and orientation, and protection of workers. The second agency, the Ministry of Foreign Affairs, takes responsibility for issuing passports to workers and protecting them while abroad. The third agency, the Police Department, handles the screening process for applicants for the Police Clearance Certificate (PCC) and issues a clearance certificate to those workers having a clean police record.

The Department of Labour also directly exports labour to the Middle East. However, its share of the total is less than 5 per cent. In 1981 the Department of Labour recruited and sent 1824 workers to the Middle East, while in 1982 only 167 were sent. In reality, prior to 1982 the Department of Labour played only a limited role. In 1981 the number of migrant workers recruited by various agencies and channelled officially through the Labour Department was only 24,730, compared to the estimated 76,000 sent by private firms without the inspection or approval of the

Department of Labour. Unlicensed private firms recruiting labour numbered at least 232 in 1981 as compared to 223 licensed firms, 134 of which were engaged in exporting labour. However, since March 1982, when all countries in the Middle East, except Iraq, made it mandatory for all emigrant workers to hold a PCC, the situation has improved somewhat. The number of emigrant workers channelled through the Department of Labour has risen steeply. In 1982 the department channelled 108,172 workers, compared to 24,730 in 1981.

There are many reasons why licensed and unlicensed private recruitment firms attempt to avoid sending emigrant workers through the Department of Labour. The main reason is the high level of competition among private firms, which induces them to try cutting costs to the minimum and maximising profits. These firms do not wish to waste time with government procedures. They are ready to accept substandard wages and working conditions in order to avoid going through departmental channels. In addition, those avoiding government procedures are more easily able to evade taxes. On the other hand, one reason the Thai workers accept substandard contractual terms, including low wages, is that they expect to earn more by overtime work. One study reported that approximately 80 per cent of migrant Thai workers worked overtime, and that the income they received from overtime work was nearly 50 per cent of their regular salaries.[13]

In summary, the widespread nature of recruitment malpractices is largely due to the following three factors: (1) the lack of adequate information regarding job prospects and competition for overseas employment, which enables unscrupulous agents to take advantage of job-seekers; (2) the slow-moving and lenient legal processes, which are ineffective for prevention and control of irregularities and malpractices; and (3) cumbersome and time-consuming procedures for processing job applications which make the majority prefer the speedier illegal processes despite the other disadvantages and costs.

Working and Living Conditions in the Host Country

Establishment of Standards

One measure to prevent worker exploitation, particularly at the job site, is the establishment of standards for employment contracts and the review and approval of such contracts before passport or visas are issued. The setting and enforcement of standards are intended to prevent possible future disputes between workers and employers as well as to prevent exploitative employers from paying their workers below acceptable minimum standards. Established standards for work contracts include a minimum employment term of 12 months; an eight-hour workday; overtime payment; paid holidays and sick leave; roundtrip airfare; free board, lodging, and medical facilities; workman's compensation and life insurance; disposition of employees' remains and effects in case of death; and so forth. Minimum standards for employment contracts are determined by the Department of Labour, including the establishment of a minimum wage rate per hour for each occupational category. These minimum wage rates are to be applied to those employed in Saudi Arabia and Bahrain and can be used as guidelines for other Middle Eastern countries as well.

Thus far, no detailed information on enforcement measures has been given. However, it is accepted that problems arising from employment contracts with migrant workers are largely due to the loosely worded contracts together with weak controls and enforcement in some countries. It is often suggested that a better-designed system of work standards and their enforcement is necessary. These may include the following:

1. the limitation of the initial contract period, allowing the chance for renewal in order to provide flexibility for the improvement of employment terms and conditions based on actual experience in the place of work;
2. the restriction of the transfer of workers to avoid the problem of "pirating" among employers;
3. the verification of the employment offers, including inspection of the living and working conditions at the job site before the contracts are approved;
4. establishing the accountability of recruiting agents in the event of contract violations committed by employers, to be laid down and enforced through cash bonds;
5. minimum disparity in wages, salaries, and other terms of employment among workers with the same skills, undertaking the same jobs, and moving to the same country;
6. the enlargement and strengthening of the role of labour attachés and other government representatives in order to alleviate the problems of migrant workers in their countries of employment.

All of the suggestions above, if implemented, will greatly reduce the number of disputes normally arising over job contracts. However, it must be noted that the enforcement of such standards will not be effective unless the host countries are willing to cooperate. Agreements between sending and host governments on methods for dealing with various types of contract violation, and on the use of host-country facilities for contract enforcement, will be indispensable.

Work and Living Conditions of the Migrants

Systematic research on this subject has not been conducted, except for investigations and studies based on interviews with returned workers. According to one study by the Industrial Unit of the Bank of Thailand's Research Department,[14] some migrant workers were unable to adapt to living conditions in the Middle East, where the climate is hotter than Thailand's and the food, shelter, work procedures, and working conditions are different. Thai workers, in general, had difficulty in communicating with their employers. Workers were also depressed by the strict lifestyle that prohibited alcohol, gambling, or other entertainment, quite different from the relaxed atmosphere of Thailand.

However, interviews with 556 sampled returnees revealed that 73.38 per cent wanted to work again in the Middle East, while 18.88 per cent were uncertain and 7.74 per cent did not want to return.[15] These statistics imply that living and working conditions in the Middle East were tolerable for a majority of Thai workers and that the prospect of higher income offset the adversities they had to endure.

It has been reported that Thai migrant workers are usually lower-paid than migrant workers from Sudan, Lebanon, Iraq, and other Middle Eastern countries (although, according to a Saudi Arabian newspaper report,[16] Thais are the second most efficient workers, after Koreans; there have also been other reports indicating that Thai workers in general are disciplined and reliable). However, there are no reports about the difference in pay scales among East Asian migrant workers.

Social and Psychological Problems

According to the survey (as illustrated in Table 14) the major psychological problem for most migrants is homesickness. The second most important problem is contract violation by the employer, i.e. payment of lower wages than had been specified in the contract. Other important problems include language and cultural barriers, sometimes leading to Thai violations of legal or religious prohibitions, such as gambling, drinking of alcohol, stealing, and fighting.

Contract renewals are always a possibility for Thai emigrants who do not violate contracts. NESDB's 1981 survey of 562 returned workers showed that more than 50 per cent of those interviewed had been to the Middle East more than once.

Earnings Abroad and Remittances

According to the data available from the Bank of Thailand (see Table 15) the remittances from the Middle East increased from 511 million baht in 1978 to 10,326 million baht in 1982. Statistics from the Bank of Thailand (the central bank) differ somewhat from those given by the commercial Bangkok Bank. Although remittances sent through the Bangkok Bank are probably approximately 80 per cent of the total remittances from the Middle East, the actual total in 1981 was slightly larger than the total remittances recorded by the Bank of Thailand (7125 million baht as compared to 6977 baht). This is probably because the method of data collection differs between the two organisations. The Bank of Thailand has probably recorded remittances according to the country of origin, thus excluding remittances sent by Thai migrants in Libya and Iraq through employer companies in Italy, France, and other countries. However, the Bangkok Bank recorded all remittances sent by Thai migrants, including

TABLE 14. Problems Encountered by Thai Emigrant Workers

	No. of Cases	%
Violation of contract by employer	157	11.9
Abuse by employer	109	8.3
Abuse and exposure to ridicule by people in host country	127	9.6
Language problems	146	11.0
Problems arising out of laws and customs of host country	121	9.2
Problems and hardships concerned with shelter and food	132	10.0
Homesickness	458	34.6
Information alleging infidelity of wives	36	2.7
Job security	12	0.9
Poor welfare services	8	0.6
Abuse by fellow Thai workers	8	0.6
Financial problems, e.g. difficulties in remitting income	8	0.6
Total	1322	100.0

Source: Purathep Roongshivin et al., July 1982.

TABLE 15. Remittances from Thai Workers Abroad, 1976–1982 (in million baht)

	1976	1977	1978	1979	1980	1981	1982
Bahrain	—	—	—	0.4	0.1	—	17.5
Cyprus	—	—	—	0.3	0.7	0.2	1.2
Jordan	—	—	0.1	—	1.6	4.3	8.7
Kuwait	—	0.2	2.7	10.8	29.6	57.2	177.3
Libya	—	—	0.1	—	21.2	232.3	286.3
Qatar	—	—	5.8	7.1	22.2	39.9	39.5
UAE	0.1	2.2	16.5	5.4	14.6	10.6	20.2
Oman	—	—	0.9	7.6	16.2	27.7	23.4
Egypt	—	—	0.2	2.3	3.8	9.9	7.8
Iran	3.0	9.3	16.5	36.6	8.8	0.6	0.3
Israel	0.3	—	0.1	1.3	181.1	358.0	40.2
Lebanon	—	—	0.2	0.1	0.7	1.8	14.1
Saudi Arabia	11.6	76.0	468.4	1212.2	3874.5	5814.4	9143.0
Syria	—	—	—	0.3	0.1	—	—
Iraq	—	—	0.2	11.6	47.2	190.5	443.6
Yemen	—	—	—	—	21.3	231.1	3.8
Subtotal (Middle East)	15.0	87.7	511.7	1296.0	4243.7	6977.5	10,326.8
USA	367.5	591.5	1189.0	1842.4	2161.3	2358.5	2206.7
Singapore	8.1	12.1	25.0	37.5	107.3	110.1	221.6
Others	94.6	220.3	385.9	642.4	1190.7	982.1	1466.6
Total	485.1	911.6	2111.6	3818.3	7703.0	10,428.2	14,221.7

Source: Bank of Thailand.

foreign currency brought back with them and exchanged at the Bangkok Bank's offices.[17] Total remittances from the Middle East in 1982 are recorded by the Bank of Thailand as 10,326 million baht.

Annual Earnings of Migrants

An NESDB-conducted survey revealed that, on average, a labourer with a full year (12 months) of work abroad remitted 102,928 baht annually during the survey period from 1973 to 1981. This represents about 70 per cent of total earnings abroad. Remittances were usually made on a monthly basis except for the last few months, when workers preferred to retain their income for shopping prior to return as well as to spend on their return either for a month-long vacation or permanent stay. About 79.9 per cent of monthly earnings were remitted home, and the portion brought during the return trip was about 20.1 per cent.

The monthly earnings of ordinary Thai labourers in the Middle East averaged approximately 5135 baht per person, and those of semiskilled and skilled workers were 10,213 baht per person. However, the overall average monthly earnings of all Thai workers were estimated to be 8522 baht per person. This figure is considerably higher than the average earnings of about 2251.36 baht per month per person available in Thailand. Needless to say, this large wage difference acts as a strong incentive for Thai workers to leave home and family for overseas assignments.

According to a survey by the Population and Manpower Planning Division, around 81.4 per cent of the migrants worked overtime and received an average overtime income of 3742 baht per month. As classified by occupation, labourers received an average of 3070 baht per month in overtime pay, carpenters 4182, masons 4741, mechanics 4130, welders 5976, electricians 4647, and so on (Table 17). The income from overtime work is roughly equivalent to 43.28 per cent of these workers' monthly salaries. Generally, Thai emigrants who have been working for one year will receive a one-month's salary bonus. On average, 69.3 per cent of Thai emigrant workers receive their bonus, each getting approximately 7475 baht.

According to the previously mentioned study in two villages in northeastern Thailand, a Thai worker in the Middle East remitted approximately 8676.19 baht per month to his family.

Low Remittance Levels

Those Thai migrants working in Libya and Iraq found it more difficult to send remittances home due to strict rules on foreign-currency transfers in these two countries. For example, migrant workers were not allowed to remit more than 30 per cent of their incomes, and the process took three to six months. Another reason for relatively low level of remittances is that many Thai migrants tend to be poorly

327

educated and not familiar with the banking system; therefore, they prefer to keep the money with them and take it home upon their return.

Remittance Channels

Nearly 80 per cent of all remittances were sent by bank draft, and 20 per cent reached

TABLE 16. Distribution of Contracts by Income Class

Baht per contract	%
Less than 50,000	10.6
50,000–100,000	20.4
100,001–150,000	24.3
150,001–200,000	17.1
200,001–250,000	9.2
250,001–300,000	6.5
300,001–350,000	3.8
350,001–400,000	3.1
More than 400,000	6.0
Total	100.0
Average income	169,575.50

Source: NESDB Survey, 1981

TABLE 17. Monthly Salary, Overtime Earnings, and Total Income of Thai Workers in the Middle East (in baht)

Occupation	Salary	Overtime	Total income[1]
Labourer	5135	3070	7729
Janitor	5336	2682	6963
Carpenter	8273	4186	13,555
Mason	8119	4741	12,636
Plumber	9961	3686	12,307
Mechanic	12,004	4130	17,445
Welder	9131	5976	15,536
Electrician	9691	4647	13,532
Painter	9015	3981	14,020
Driver	11,295	4595	13,749
Cook	7192	5555	14,634
Foreman	11,416	5793	16,737
Other	9133	4127	13,070
Average per worker	8522	3742	12,553

Source: NESDB Survey, 1981.

1. Not identical to salary plus overtime because of other unclassified receipts included here.

TABLE 18. Monthly Remittances to Migrant Households in Two Northeastern Villages

Baht	Total		Udorn Province		Korat Province	
	No.	%	No.	%	No.	%
Less than 5000	107	26.9	76	41.5	31	14.5
5000–10,000	157	39.8	76	41.5	82	38.3
10,001–15,000	38	14.6	4	2.2	54	25.2
15,001–20,000	15	3.8	4	2.2	11	5.1
20,001–25,000	5	1.3	0	0	5	2.3
More than 25,000	1	0.3	0	0	1	0.5
No remittance	53	13.4	23	12.6	30	14.0
Total	397	100.0	183	100.0	214	100.0

Source: Sumalee Pitayanond et al., 1982.

Thailand in the possession of the worker. Most (70–80 per cent) of remittances sent by bank draft were sent through the Bangkok Bank. The rest were sent through foreign banks such as the Bank of Hong Kong and Shanghai or the Bank of America, sometimes with the help of employer companies.

Use of Remittances

A major proportion of income earned by Thai workers in foreign countries is sent back to pay debts and support their families. While it certainly helps ease hardships, it is doubtful that the money is always wisely utilised. According to surveys conducted, much of the money is not being spent economically. A large amount goes towards the purchase of such luxury goods as home appliances. Also, since most of the products purchased are imported, the money represents an outflow offsetting much of the foreign income sent into the country by Thai workers. The families of successful migrant workers have purchased a number of luxury goods, particularly stereos, radios, television sets, refrigerators, cameras, and various electric appliances. A significant number of these items are purchased abroad and brought back on home leave. Some migrants have even bought colour T.V. sets, still a novelty for well-to-do urban dwellers, let alone the rural poor.

The figures in Table 20 show that of the total number of migrants' families surveyed, approximately 24 per cent purchased refrigerators, 41 per cent stereos, 29 per cent television sets, 18 per cent sewing machines, and so on, out of the total earnings abroad. A part of the purchases result from the migrants' desire to demonstrate their improved circumstances. Many families of successful migrant workers used the major portion of savings from earnings abroad for housing improvements and purchase of consumer durables. Families with sufficiently large savings often constructed new houses. Those already possessing a house of reasonable standard or with smaller savings undertook renovations, including repainting, furnishing, alteration, extensions, and even gardens. From Peerathep Roongshivin's field experiences, the priority given to housing improvement in the use of remittances is clearly evident. Part of the remittances went toward expenditures on land — both for farming and housing — on agricultural equipment and other capital inputs for agricultural improvements,

TABLE 19. The Effect of Remittances on Consumption Patterns of Migrant Families

	Udon Thani		Nakhon Ratchasima		Total	
	No.	%	No.	%	No.	%
Meat						
High increase	31	17.7	16	9.2	48	13.6
Moderate increase	98	51.1	48	27.7	146	41.2
No change	41	22.7	86	49.7	127	35.9
Decrease	2	1.1	10	5.8	12	3.4
Other	—	—	—	—	—	—
Not known	8	4.4	13	7.5	21	5.9
Total	181	100.0	173	100.0	354	100.0
Dairy						
High increase	13	7.2	10	5.8	23	6.5
Moderate increase	67	37.0	16	9.2	83	23.4
No change	35	19.3	75	43.4	110	31.1
Decrease	1	0.6	8	4.6	9	2.5
Other	—	—	3	1.7	3	0.9
Not known	65	35.9	61	35.3	126	35.6
Total	181	100.0	173	100.0	354	100.0
Beverages						
High increase	9	5.0	7	4.0	16	4.5
Moderate increase	66	36.5	14	8.1	80	22.6
No change	43	23.8	79	45.7	122	34.5
Decrease	3	1.7	9	5.2	12	3.4
Other	—	—	1	0.6	1	0.3
Not known	60	33.1	63	36.4	123	34.7
Total	181	100.0	173	100.0	354	100.0
Clothes						
High increase	63	34.8	13	7.5	76	21.5
Moderate increase	80	44.2	55	31.8	135	38.2
No change	31	17.1	87	50.3	118	33.3
Decrease	1	0.6	3	1.7	4	1.1
Other	—	—	—	—	—	—
Not known	6	3.3	15	8.7	21	5.9
Total	181	100.0	173	100.0	354	100.0

TABLE 19 (continued)

	Udon Thani		Nakhon Ratchasima		Total	
	No.	%	No.	%	No.	%
Recreation						
High increase	20	11.0	3	1.7	23	6.5
Moderate increase	63	34.8	6	3.5	69	19.5
No change	40	22.1	80	46.2	120	33.9
Decrease	35	19.3	6	3.5	41	1.6
Other	—	—	5	2.9	5	1.4
Not known	23	12.7	73	42.2	96	27.1
Total	181	100.0	173	100.0	354	100.0
Education						
High increase	65	35.9	42	24.3	107	30.2
Moderate increase	68	37.6	40	23.1	108	30.5
No change	29	16.0	57	32.9	86	24.3
Decrease	3	1.7	1	0.6	4	1.1
Other	—	—	—	—	—	—
Not known	16	8.8	33	19.1	49	13.9
Total	181	100.0	173	100.0	354	100.0

Source: Wages and Employment Planning Sector, NESDB Survey, 1981.

and on investments in some type of business. Part of the remittances is used for improvement of living standards, education, and other investments that are beneficial both to migrant workers and their families and to the community as a whole.

The Effect of Remittances on Savings

The same survey also revealed that approximately 62.7 per cent of the migrants' families surveyed saved money by depositing it in banks. Monthly bank deposits in villages surveyed were 5901.31 baht in Udon Thani, and 7571.34 baht in Nakhon Ratchasima. In addition, some savings are kept in the household and not deposited. However, the survey does not provide information on this. (See Table 21.)

Community Development and Improvement of Living Conditions

Income earned by Thai migrant workers in the Middle East has contributed to significant improvements in their housing, food, and other forms of consumption; to their investment in education; and to economic investments by their familes. At the same time, these remittances have a great impact on community development. As already calculated, on average, a single, successful migrant worker has sent back roughly 100,000 baht annually, with the total of 100,000 workers abroad remitting home the

TABLE 20. Purchase of Consumer Goods from Earnings Abroad

	% of migrant families purchasing goods from earnings abroad to total families owning the goods	% of migrant families purchasing goods from earnings abroad to total migrant families	
		%	Rank
Bicycle	39.4	17.8	6
Motorcycle	45.4	11.3	9
Small passenger car	25.0	0.3	
Pickup	29.4	1.4	
Multipurpose car	27.3	0.9	
Ploughing machine	13.6	2.3	
Refrigerator	65.9	24.0	4
T.V.	51.7	29.4	3
Stereo	85.3	40.9	1
Turntable	50.0	1.4	
Electric fan	53.6	37.8	2
Radio	36.8	20.1	5
Clock	36.8	5.9	10
Sewing machine	41.7	17.8	6
Electric fan	33.0	19.8	5
Electric/gas stove	65.3	18.1	8
Camera	76.8	14.9	7
Electric cooker	67.6	12.9	8

Source: NESDB Survey, 1981.

sum of 10,000 million baht in 1981. After deducting 25,954 baht per worker as costs incurred in obtaining employment, a net balance of 7046 million baht represents the additional income accruing to these communities in 1981. This additional income together with its multiplier effects represents the total impact that the employment of migrant workers has had on villages and communities for the year 1981 alone.

A part of the remitted money, apart from private use, was donated for the improvement of school buildings, other educational facilities, and religious institutions in the migrants' villages.

Government Revenue

Apart from Thailand's foreign exchange earnings, the migration has increased the Thai government's revenue from three sources: fees for issue of passports, revenue from airfare (via the state-owned Thai International Airlines), and taxes. The fee for issuance of a passport valid for five years is 1000 baht. It is estimated that the total annual revenue from the issue of passports to the 400,000 Thais seeking employment abroad (many of these did not actually find employment) is 400 million baht, with about 360 million baht accruing from the issuance of passports to workers bound for the Middle East.

Revenue from Thai International Airlines accruing from the labour migration between Bangkok and the Middle East is estimated at about 650 million baht in 1982. Two types of tax are connected with the migration of labour to the Middle East. The first is the business-turnover tax that job-training and recruitment agencies are supposed to pay to the government based on the volume and value of business during a given period. The second type of tax is income tax, which must be paid annually by both income-earning persons and corporate bodies. According to the tax estimates, collection from income tax should have reached to 500 million baht, and business-turnover taxes 150 million baht for 1982 (based on an estimated 140,000 migrants in that year). However, both the business-turnover tax and the income tax actually collected fell below these estimates. This is due both to widespread tax evasion and failure on the part of revenue-collecting authorities to mount a determined effort to bring these taxable individuals and firms into the tax net. The potential for revenue collection from the migration is, however, significant and can be realised depending on more effective government action.

Sociopsychological and Cultural Issues of Migration

Very little research has been done to date on this topic. The psychological costs to the worker are one type of adverse impact of overseas employment. This may be two-sided, affecting both the migrants and their families. However, it is natural for the former to suffer greater psychological costs than the latter. The host countries where most Thai overseas workers must live and work for at least a year — especially in the Middle East — differ from Thailand in almost all respects. Thai workers have found difficulty in adapting to the extreme of heat and cold in these climates. Differences in culture, tradition, religion, laws, and lifestyles present even more formidable problems. Insufficient or total lack of recreation facilities is a common complaint. Further, workers are compelled to live celibate lives while living away from their families. Gambling and drinking of alcohol, in which they indulge at least occasionally in Thailand, are prohibited by religion in the Middle East. Boarding and accommodation also tend to be problematic, particularly if the workers are unfortunate enough to work with small, unorganised companies; no Thai food is available, and the accommodations provided by such companies might lack air-conditioning.

In itself, living far from home may constitute part of the psychological costs of working abroad. Workers are constantly subject to homesickness and anxiety about the family, especially concerning the health and well-being of wives and children. Another set of problems deal with cases of misbehaviour and infidelity on the part of the spouse left behind. Facilities for regular communication with the families are not always readily available, and letters take considerable time to reach their destination,

TABLE 21. Investments Made from Savings Abroad

	Whether undertaken	Udon Thani		Nakhon Ratchsima		Total	
		No.	%	No.	%	No.	%
Bank deposits	Yes	105	59.0	117	67.6	222	62.7
	No	13	40.3	48	27.7	121	34.2
	No response	3	1.7	8	4.7	11	3.1
Average/month (baht)		2,352.50		7,571.34		5,901.31	
No. of replies		40		89		129	
Land purchase	Yes	32	17.7	24	13.9	56	15.8
	No	146	80.7	138	79.8	284	80.2
	No response	9	1.6	11	6.3	14	4.0
Average (baht)		23,233.33		82,846.15		50,910.71	
No. of replies		30		26		56	
New house construction	Yes	30	16.6	28	16.2	58	16.4
	No	147	81.2	132	76.3	279	78.8
	No response	4	2.2	13	7.5	17	4.8
Average (baht)		54,055.54		124,186.24		92,426.93	
No. of replies		24		29		53	
House renovation	Yes	40	22.1	44	25.4	84	23.7
	No	137	75.7	117	67.6	254	71.8
	No response	4	2.3	12	7.0	16	4.5
Average (baht)		7,535.56		64,936.67		44,544.17	
No. of replies		27		56		83	
Debt repayment	Yes	128	69.6	92	53.2	218	61.6
	No	51	28.2	67	38.7	118	33.3
	No response	4	2.2	14	8.1	18	5.1
Average (baht)		21,541.49		54,977.88		38,079.92	
No. of replies		80		92		178	
Agricultural land development	Yes	17	9.4	31	17.9	48	13.6
	No	161	89.0	128	74.0	289	81.6
	No response	3	1.6	14	8.1	17	4.8
Average (baht)		1,970		10,443.12		8,089.46	
No. of replies		10		27		37	
Livestock	Yes	14	7.7	15	8.7	29	8.2
	No	163	90.1	144	83.2	307	86.7
	No response	4	2.2	14	8.1	18	5.1
Average (baht)		8,836.36		23,052		17,467.71	
No. of replies		11		17		28	

TABLE 21 (continued)

	Whether undertaken	Udon Thani		Nakhon Ratchsima		Total	
		No.	%	No.	%	No.	%
Commerce	Yes	7	3.9	9	5.2	16	4.5
	No	171	94.5	150	86.7	321	90.7
	No response	3	1.6	14	8.1	17	4.8
Average (baht)		4,000		28,499.67		21,293.87	
No. of replies		6		13		19	
Jewellery purchase	Yes	21	11.6	23	13.3	44	12.4
	No	157	86.7	141	81.5	198	84.2
	No response	3	1.7	9	5.2	12	3.4
Share bidding	Yes	2	1.1	3	1.7	5	1.4
	No	176	97.2	162	93.6	338	95.5
	No response	3	1.7	8	4.6	11	3.1

Source: NESDB Survey, 1981.

whether from or to the Middle East. To most Thai workers, communication through letter-writing is a difficult and unfamiliar task, given their level of education and the fact that at home, situations requiring communication by letter very rarely arise.

One of the privileges enjoyed by workers with contracts extending beyond one year is a month's home leave after eleven or twelve months of work, with return airfare paid by the employer. In some firms, although short home visits during the year may be possible, they are at the worker's own expense, which the majority cannot afford. In some cases, workers can afford to have their families come and visit them abroad, but in a majority of countries in the Middle East (such as Saudi Arabia) this is not possible since their entry is restricted.

Workers' families also face social problems due to the absence of the head of the family. There are cases where remitted funds are misspent on wasteful consumption such as nightclubs, gambling, and alcohol. Instances of infidelity have also been reported, leading to the break-up of families. Delinquency among the children of such families also appears to take place.

While Thailand has faced the same problem of insufficient data in attempting to estimate the total number of workers overseas as have other labour-exporting countries, the following tentative estimates may prove useful. It was found that, during the study period, there was little variation in Thai workers' annual earnings. Therefore, the first assumption to be made here is that the average annual remittances by workers after 1980 were the same as those in preceding years.

Conclusion

This brief survey indicates that the migration of Thai workers to the Middle East has had far-reaching effects on Thailand's economy and rural society. The positive effects of the migration are evident in several areas. The total foreign exchange earned through the migration increased from approximately 511 million baht in 1978 to 10,326 million baht in 1982. The earnings of migrant workers made a signficant contribution to the balance of payments during the second half of the 1970s, when Thailand's current-account balance was running into deficits of increasing magnitude. We also saw that the net additional income that flowed into the rural areas was considerable, reaching approximately 7000 million baht in 1982. This had a significant impact both on the improvement of living conditions of households and on the development of communities.

Since most Thai workers involved in the migration to the Middle East could be replaced fairly easily by unemployed workers in Thailand, the impact of the migration on the domestic labour market and on the supply of skills in demand was negligible. The total stock of migrant labour in the Middle East has not amounted to more than 1 per cent of the total Thai workforce. With regard to the positive impact of the migration on unemployment, the figures relating to open unemployment may exaggerate the effect of the migration.

According to the survey conducted by the National Statistics Office, only about 250,000 workers were openly unemployed in 1981. The impact of migration on these figures has however been disputed by various researchers, scholars, and international organisations who have placed the figure at a much higher level, around 1 million or approximately 7 per cent of the workforce. An NESDB study has argued that the majority of migrant workers come from rural areas, where seasonal unemployment in most years can be as high as 4 million. Apart from this category, underemployed workers are estimated to be in the region of as many as 4 million. With this reservoir of unemployed and underemployed, the migration is not likely to have any negative impact on the labour market, particularly as the types of labour that migrate are easily replaceable with accelerated training for the already available workers.

The migration has also had an impact on upgrading the skills of the Thai workforce. Most Middle East countries have undertaken development projects calling for a high level of technology. These include oil and chemical industries, road and highway construction, high-rise buildings, hospitals, airfields, housing, and so on. Thai workers have been engaged in these diverse activities in the Middle East and have been able to acquire some of the skills required at operative and manual levels. This is likely to be of considerable benefit for the development of the Thai economy. Thailand is likely to undertake investments in the oil and petrochemical industries in the not too distant future, and the migrant workforce that has returned to Thailand will become a valuable asset for development projects in this field. Thailand is currently developing the oil, gas, and petrochemical industries as an important part of the Eastern Seaboard Development Programme.

However, despite the substantial benefits accruing to the national economy and to Thai households as a result of the migration, there is no doubt that Thai overseas employment has had some negative effects at the community and national levels. However, as yet no empirical study has been conducted to evaluate these aspects. They may include, for instance, possible shortages of skilled labour; loss of national prestige in the case of deviant behaviour by Thai workers abroad; the disruption of families; the "demonstration effect" in the consumption of luxury goods; increases in land prices; and increased opportunity for and incidence of corruption. Corruption and its effects on poor rural families who are victims of it are among the more pressing problems of the migration, calling for urgent and prompt remedial action.

Notes

1. Banbue Santhumaitree, "Way of Life and Work in Arab Countries: Problems and Solutions" (in Thai), *Rang Ngan Sampon,* July–August 1980.
2. Bank of Thailand, Industrial Unit, Research Department, "Thai Labour in Foreign Countries" (in Thai; 1978).
3. Interview with unidentified government official at the Department of Labour, *Siam Mai* magazine, 10 July 1982.
4. Peerathep Roongshivin, *Some Aspects of Socio-Economic Impacts of Thailand's Emigration to the Middle East* (paper for the ASEAN/Australian Population Project: Institutional Development and Exchange of Personnel, October 1982).
5. Peerathep Roongshivin and Suchai Piyaphan, *Schemes for Expansion of the Foreign Market for Thai Labour* (in Thai; NESDB, 21 April 1983).
6. Bank of Thailand, "Thai Labour in Foreign Countries."
7. Sumalee Pitayanon, *Overseas Employment Procedures in East Asian Countries* (ILO/ARPLA, March 1981).
8. Sumalee Pitayanon and Watana S. Janjaroen, *Thai Overseas Employment Short-Term Contracts' Economic Impact on Families and Communities: A Case Study in Northeastern Villages* (in Thai; Chulalongkorn University Faculty of Economics, July 1982).
9. Peerathep Roongshivin, *Some Aspects of Socio-Economic Impacts.*
10. Ibid.
11. Department of Labour, Ministry of the Interior, *A Handbook of Labour Statistics* (August 1982).
12. Peerathep Roongshivin, *Some Aspects of Socio-Economic Impacts.*
13. Wages and Employment Planning Sector, NESDB, *Thai Labour in Foreign Countries: Problems and Solutions* (in Thai; June 1982).
14. Bank of Thailand, "Thai Labour in Foreign Countries."
15. Yothin Sawangdee, 1978.
16. *Saudi Gazette,* 10 March 1979.
17. Sukitti Krajangyao, *Go to the Middle East,* Bangkok Bank occasional paper, no. 1 (in Thai; 1982).

CONCLUSION

Godfrey Gunatilleke

The country studies on the Asian labour migration to the Arab countries have identified some of the critical gaps in the data base as well as in the policy framework and administrative systems available for managing migration. The authors prepared a list of recommendations appropriate to each national situation and these were discussed at two workshops convened for the purpose. This concluding chapter will examine some of the more important recommendations.

The recommendations can be broadly grouped under two categories. The first deals with the management of the migration at the national, macro-economic level and examines how the migration's social and economic benefits can be maximised. The second set of recommendations deals with the invidial migrants and considers how their welfare and that of their families can best be protected and served. These two categories cannot be considered independently of each other; they are closely related. The management of the migration at the national level so as to ensure that the maximum benefit accrues to the economy also depends crucially on the capacity of the migrants to protect their interests and make proper use of their earnings.

The recommendations in the first category include measures and policies that relate to the management of the labour market and the supply of manpower in the context of the migrant inflow, flow of remittances, channelling of remittances to savings and investments, and promoting the export of manpower. The second category addresses the welfare of the migrants, such as the regulation of the recruitment process, the simplification of procedures for migration, arrangements in the host country to deal with migrant grievances and problems, and rehabilitation of returnees and their reabsorption into the workforce. The recommendations therefore deal with the migration process as a whole and include the stage of preparation for the migration, the period of employment abroad, and the stage immediately after the return of the migrant.

The recommendations could also be examined more specifically in terms of the management system that is envisaged. One set of recommendations concerns the government policies on various aspects of the migration, such as its implications for the country's balance of payments and the labour market; the need to regulate migration and recruitment procedures so as to protect the migrants' welfare; and the need to cope with the sociocultural aspects. Another set of recommendations deals with the institutional framework and the systems and procedures governing the migration. These would include machinery required to monitor and regulate the migration and the institutions that manage the migrants at different stages, both within the country of origin as well as in the host country. A third set deals with the need to improve the information-gathering system and the monitoring of the migration process in regard to the stock of migrants, the outflow, and the return flow. Again, these recommendations cannot be considered separately. They have to be seen as interrelated parts of a total system for managing the migration in all its important aspects. The recommendations offered in the studies, however, do not provide such a system. To develop such a system, countries need to be better equipped to evaluate the macro-economic and social impacts of the migration as well as the needs of the migrants. This in turn requires more knowledge and information on various aspects of the migration. What the studies have been able to do at this stage of the inquiry is to indicate what sorts of policies, institutions, and actions might be required in the different countries to develop the necessary capacities.

The studies highlight the important role migration has come to play in the economies of all the countries studied in this volume. Of course, the contribution made by the migration varies from country to country. If we use remittances as a criterion, we find, for example, that Pakistan is much more critically dependent on the income from remittances for the management of its balance of payments than India or Bangladesh. Although the Middle East contracts have become an important source of foreign exchange earnings for South Korea, the country is not vitally dependent on them. Countries like Sri Lanka and the Philippines, however, have begun to regard the migration as a major source of foreign exchange and have thus come to give it the attention accorded an important export commodity. The effort and resources that have to be deployed for the improvement of systems and the institutional framework will, therefore, differ from country to country according to the role of migration in the management of the economy as well in the country's future development. Many studies underscore the uncertainty and vulnerability that the labour migration has built into the economies of the labour-supplying countries. Any significant contraction of demand for migrant labour in the host countries would create serious repercussions because of their high degree of dependence on the migration, in terms both of the balance of payments and of employment. Therefore, the efficient management of the migration is crucial to the development strategies of these countries. They need to be constantly mindful of the inevitable trade-offs involved in the migration and to manage these trade-offs so as to enhance the long-term health of the domestic economy. This would require, among other things, policies and incentives that channel a large part of the additional resources into savings and sound, productive investments that will rapidly increase employment and income-earning opportunities. Most of the studies, therefore, emphasise the importance of market studies and forecasts in order to design a long-term strategy in relation to the migration.

Here, two sets of factors need to be taken into account. One relates to the structural changes in store for the host countries and the effect these would have on the demand for migrant labour in terms of volume and skill composition. On the one hand, the big spurt of economic growth and investment resulting from the massive increase in oil revenues is likely to taper off in response to the international oil market as well as the conclusion of the development phase that required large infrastructural investments. On the other hand, the host countries will naturally want to contain and reduce their dependence on a migrant workforce, most likely resulting in technological improvements that will reduce labour inputs and raise the level of automation. At the same time, the changes in the structure of the economy will change the skill composition of the workforce.

The second set of factors relates to the changes that will take place in the economies of the labour-supplying countries. If these countries can maintain reasonable rates of growth, the structural changes that follow will be reflected in the demand for skilled manpower and the increase in real wages — processes that will combine to reduce the pressure for employment abroad; this can already be seen in the case of the migration from the Republic of Korea. It is necessary to examine this changing scenario of the migration in order to design policies that benefit both the host countries and the labour-supplying countries. These call for policies and actions at the national, regional, and interregional levels. The recommendations in the studies, therefore, include actions required at the regional and interregional levels as well.

The following recommendations include many items that have already been implemented in one or several of the countries discussed in this book. They have been listed because they could be suitably adapted for the specific conditions of countries that have not implemented them.

Recommendations Relating to National Benefits and Costs of the Migration

Manpower Policies

The overall policy on migration ranges from a relatively open and unregulated system, as in Sri Lanka and the Philippines, to a more closely managed system as in the Republic of Korea. These differences can be seen in the various chapters in this book. Many of the authors agree that policy should be differentiated in regard to the outflow: it should discriminate between unskilled labour, which is in surplus, and skilled and professional manpower, the outflow of which could create serious bottlenecks and shortages in the labour-supplying country.

A specific recommendation suggests that the migrant flow should be managed in terms of three categories. The first category, comprising labour that is in surplus in the domestic economy, should be assisted in finding employment abroad. The second category includes manpower not in surplus but whose supply could be increased at short notice without great cost. This will include, for example, certain categories of skilled labour such as masons and carpenters for which accelerated training programmes could be implemented, and white-collar workers, such as salesmen and teachers. The third category consists of skilled labour that is in high demand and short supply in the domestic economy: high-level professional manpower as well as certain grades of mid-level technicians and skilled labour.

Among the first requirements for the formulation of a sound manpower policy are a reliable data base and a regular flow of information on the different aspects of the migration. This includes information, first, on the outflow, on the stock in host countries, and on the return flow in terms of both volume and skill composition. Second, the effects of the migration on different segments of the labour market must be ascertained. (This recommendation is discussed in greater detail in the section on information-gathering below.)

Manpower in Short Supply

It is evident from the data that have been presented in the studies, that the migrant outflow in many countries includes several levels of skill and professional capability. One example is the outflow from Sri Lanka. Although unskilled female labour there comprises a major share of the migration, considerable numbers of skilled workers, mid-level manpower, and high-level professionals continue to form part of the outflow. National governments would need to design policies appropriate to each. In some countries, such discriminatory policies regulating the outflow of high-level manpower and scarce skills are already in operation. India, for example, follows a procedure with considerable advantages. It makes skill distinctions at the time a passport is issued and categorises the passport-holders who may need emigration clearance. Several countries, however, have no such controls. They have a more open system and permit the market forces to regulate the outflow for all categories.

The effectiveness of administrative controls that regulate the outflow have to be carefully assessed. Most countries have had considerable experience with the outflow of high-level manpower; such migrations began long before the trek to the Middle East. Although the demand in the Middle East market may have augmented this outflow, it must be viewed as part of the larger problem of the brain drain to destinations other than the Gulf countries. Most countries have attempted to implement policies and measures to cope with this problem. In some of these measures, the main thrust has been to improve the career prospects and incentives for employment at home to mitigate the attraction of employment abroad. Some of these policies must be re-examined in the light of the Middle East migration. One particular aspect of the Middle East migration is that it is strictly time-bound and most often excludes the family, thereby providing strong incentives for a return migration. The professional migrants working in the Middle East, therefore, differ markedly from the earlier highly skilled outflow. Consequently, their labour abroad has been more beneficial in terms of transfers of income and return flow. These benefits need to be taken into account in formulating policies that deal with the migration of high-level manpower to the Middle East.

Exportable Manpower

The larger component of the migration, however, is either surplus labour or is needed domestically but can be supplied within a relatively short period. This component of the migration calls for a systematic promotional effort that will require manpower-development programmes geared to employment abroad.

First, such a promotional effort requires a regular flow of information about the labour markets in the labour-importing countries. These markets must be studied in order to identify the manpower needs and the changes in demand so that labour-exporting countries can adjust the supply accordingly. Second, a systematic effort in manpower development must be made to supply these markets. This would include, on the one hand, accelerated programmes for training and skill-formation in order to supply the markets of host countries while maintaining an adequate supply of labour at home. Most countries have launched accelerated training programmes and have gained considerable experience in the field. Accelerated training minimises losses in productivity and imparts the essential skills on which a trainee can speedily build; such programmes need to be further developed. This is an area in which technical cooperation among developing countries is appropriate. The institutional framework for accelerated training will have to include private-sector firms and nongovernmental organisations — all of whom can collaborate in a national programme.

On the other hand, these programmes should also equip the migrants to adjust to the environment in host countries and acquire the basic competence to provide services of acceptable quality to their employers. This would include occupations of various types which are categorised as unskilled such as domestic aides but which nevertheless require basic knowledge and operative skills involved in a variety of tasks. Finally, a code on behaviour and discipline of the migrants should be established to promote high-quality service and satisfactory fulfilment of contracts. The Philippines appears to be taking action in this area, with awards for migrants with exceptional performance records and disincentives for errant workers.

Remittances: Flow and Utilisation

Augmenting the Flow of Remittances

All the country studies emphasise the importance of providing incentives to augment the flow of resources. These incentives will vary according to the system operating in each country for the management of its foreign exchange resources. The incentives range from premium rates, as in the case of Bangladesh, to special bank accounts in convertible currencies bearing attractive interest rates, as in Sri Lanka. The need for incentives will, however, depend on the particular circumstances of each country and the way in which it manages its exchange-rate system. The problems in this area are twofold — relating to motivation for transferring income to the home country, and to doing so through legal channels that will benefit the country's balance of payments. The preponderant majority of migrants need to transfer part of their income while employed abroad and to return with their savings on completion of contract. Therefore, the motivation to transfer savings is strong except in special circumstances where migrants want to retain their earnings abroad for such purposes as the education of children abroad.

When a large black market exists for foreign exchange transactions and where black-market rates of conversion are much higher than the official rates, there is the possibility of large leakages of migrant income into the black market. The chapter on the Philippines draws attention to this danger. The payment of a premium rate or a separate foreign exchange market for migrant remittances (as in the case of Bangladesh) could help to divert remittances to the official market. In the case of the premium, if the operation is to be self-financing, the foreign exchange bought at a premium rate has to be sold at a matching rate. The Bangladesh mechanism achieves this by tying the foreign exchange earned through remittances to a class of imports.

The Sri Lankan incentive works not through a higher rate but through a facility that enables the migrant to retain his remittance in the form of foreign exchange, up to a specified period, in addition to paying interest on it. This discourages the retention of earnings abroad. Combined with an exchange-rate policy that has drastically cut back the black-market operations, it has been effective in attracting a large flow of remittances. The retention of savings in the form of foreign exchange for a relatively long period enables savers to make prudent use of their savings and avoid hasty financial decisions. Each country should examine the problem of remittances and work out effective incentives after evaluating the incentive policies used by other labour-exporting countries.

Another aspect that has a bearing on remittances concerns the facilities that are available to the migrant in both the host country and at home for the transfer of funds, the opening of bank accounts, and the deposit of savings. This entire process has to be streamlined and facilitated if the remittance flow is to be maintained at satisfactory levels or augmented. This calls for special attention.

Utilisation of Remittances

Remittance income amounts to a substantial share of national savings; in Pakistan it was as much as 8 per cent of GDP in 1981; in Bangladesh and Sri Lanka it is approximately 3.5 per cent and 6 per cent, respectively. This represents a very large increase of household incomes in a small proportion of households, and therefore offers a high potential for savings and investment. A comprehensive national programme for the mobilisation of these savings and channelling them into productive investments is essential. For such a programme to be effective, several activities need to be coordinated:

— Institutions and agencies must be established do educate migrants and to offer them investment councelling and guidance.
— Migrants should be offered special investment opportunities in the form of small-scale projects, including self-employment projects.
— Migrants should have ready access to a portfolio of investments designated for the purpose.

These activities could be assumed by existing development banks — which could create special units for the purpose — or special institutions could be created and charged with mobilising remittance incomes for investment. Such institutions could take the form of a development bank for overseas workers or a company in which the state, the private sector, and migrants could participate, undertaking and promoting investment. The Overseas Pakistan Foundation provides a model for such activities. In some countries, the regional concentration of migrants offers opportunities for developing regional programmes in which groups of migrants could participate to promote development in their own areas.

Some of the studies have recommended greater control of the entire process of migration through a central authority — either a board or a corporation in which both the state and the private sector could collaborate. It is argued that such an authority could better monitor the outflow and return flow, regulate the process of recruitment, and implement a well-designed manpower policy for the migration. At the same time, it could secure for the national economy the maximum benefits from the migration by taking measures to augment the flow of remittances. For example, the migrants would be placed in employment through the central authority, which would also arrange through the employers for a regular remittance of a portion of the migrants' earnings. This approach which offers means of monitoring the migration process as well as making necessary interventions may have several advantages. But centralisation to this degree is certain to bring in its train other consequences that might run counter to the open policies favoured by certain countries. Some of these issues are discussed later. Many of the problems connected with the use of remittances must also be

344

considered as part of the management of migrants and are also further discussed in the next section.

The Sociocultural Impact

The sociocultural impact of the migration is not easily amenable to policy intervention. It is also not easy to isolate this impact from the other agents of sociocultural change. Therefore, few specific policies and actions have been recommended. What is first required is a clearer understanding of the processes at work as a result of the migration and the positive and negative effects it has on income distribution, social status, community life, leadership patterns, prevailing value systems, and lifestyles. The responses to the problems that have arisen would have to be made on a wide national front, and would require the participation of a large number of agents, including state organisations such as ministries of culture and education, the educational systems as a whole, the media, religious institutions, and nongovernmental organisations. The orientation programmes for both migrants and returnees would have to pay attention to these aspects of the migration.

At present there is no evidence of any attempt at an organised or systematic programme in this area. Such a programme, however, is urgently needed. It could be initiated by bringing together a few key agencies concerned with this problem under the aegis of a Ministry of Culture or the national body that addresses social and cultural affairs related to migration. Such a group could be constituted into a task force that could map out a strategy involving the various agencies that have been enumerated.

Recommendations Relating to the Migrants' Welfare

The recommendations dealing with the welfare of migrants cover all three stages of migration — the preparatory process, the period abroad, and the return. The recommendations in the different chapters reflect the differences in the national situations. For example, in the South Korean labour migration, migrants are organised under a firm that obtains a contract in the Middle East. The working conditions and indeed the entire life of the migrant are therefore regulated by the firm. The firm provides all the required amenities. The regional origins of the migrants vary significantly among countries. In some countries the migration includes large flows from the rural areas and is widespread; in others the migration appears as yet to be concentrated in the more urbanised parts of the country. Similar differences could be seen in the skill composition and educational levels. In the case of the Philippines, for example, the migration is increasingly confined to the more skilled categories and appears to comprise large proportions of workers who were already employed. The educational levels of the workers migrating from India, Sri Lanka, and the Philippines are higher than those of Bangladesh, Pakistan, and Thailand. In the case of Sri Lanka the migration includes numerous females, who work as domestic employees in households in the host countries. Each of these situations calls for appropriate policies and programmes for meeting the particular needs of the different categories of migrants. Rural migrants require an orientation including basic information and rudimentary skills to help them adjust to changes in environment. Migrants in domestic service encounter an entirely different set of problems. The working conditions and the responsibilities and tasks assigned to them will vary from household to household. Their work area is outside the purview of industrial legislation, and their experience in their own country does not adequately equip them for the discipline and contractual obligations implicit in employment contracts abroad. Therefore, this particular category of employee will face a complex range of problems in regard both to cultural adjustment and to the working conditions.

The Preparatory Phase of Migration

The authors indicate that in most countries a great deal has yet to be done to streamline and systematise the procedures that apply to the preparatory phase of the migration. This would include the following:

1. A re-examination of existing emigration laws and procedures, and their better adaptation to the current needs if this task has not already been done. This is one area in which countries could benefit from each other by a fuller exchange of information about the legal instruments that have been developed to deal with a variety of problems. Many countries are examining existing laws on emigration and are adapting them to meet the new needs that have arisen with the Middle East migration. India has already prepared legislation for the revision of its existing emigration law. The Thai government also has revised its Employment Services Act. This important task should be undertaken by all the labour-exporting countries.

2. The regulation of private recruitment agencies in order to eliminate irregularities as far as possible and to minimise the costs of migration to the migrant; establishing ceilings on fees or commissions charged to migrants; monitoring the activities of recruitment agencies by departments of labour (this includes registration of all contracts of employment with the labour department, as is done in Sri Lanka).

3. Systematic dissemination of information to the migrants about all relevant aspects of the migration: employment contracts, migrants' rights, comparable levels of remuneration, and conditions in the host country. These services should be performed by a migrants' centre. Such a centre would have to be readily accessible to the migrants and should hand out information of various kinds, including model contracts, handbooks, and other relevant material.

4. Simplification of procedures for the clearance of migrants, the issuance of passports and visas, and various other formalities governing the migration. Most of the authors

recommended that the management of this aspect of the migration could be greatly facilitated with the creation of a one-step service centre. The rendering of assistance at airports for completion of travel formalities was also recommended.

5. A system of loans through banking institutions to help the migrant finance the cost of his migration.

6. Programmes of orientation, induction, and training designed to serve the needs of different categories of migrants. Such programmes would include information on the completion of travel formalities, the opening of bank accounts, the use of travellers' cheques, the transfer of remittances, and so on. Part of these needs could be served by informative, well-designed handbooks. These programmes would also have to be adapted to different literacy levels.

Employment Abroad

The period of employment abroad raises a variety of problems for both the migrant and his family.

1. The main recommendation for the migrant is the strengthening of each country's embassy and its capacity to service the migrants. Most chapters refer to the labour attachés now assigned to many of the Gulf countries in order to look after the migrants' interests. This office needs to be strengthened and its role in relation to the host countries more clearly defined through negotiation with the host countries. Procedures must be adopted for registration of migrants at the embassy so that it has complete information on them. This procedure is followed by some of the labour-supplying countries. Arrangements should be made for the labour attachés and their units to respond to inquiries and representations made by the migrants. Documentation of work conditions in the host country, facilities for medical care, banking, travel, and so on should be readily available to the migrants. If these services are rendered efficiently and the migrants fully benefit from them, it would be possible to levy a charge on the migrants for the proper discharge of these functions.

2. At home, appropriate institutional arrangements need to be made to help the migrants' families with their own adjustment problems, which will include the smooth and regular flow of remittances, banking facilities, and other welfare measures relating to such special problems as working mothers, care of young children, and so on. In many of these areas, nongovernmental organisations could be motivated and mobilised. Examples cited in the studies offer models for programmes of this kind. The Welfare Administration Service in the Philippines could be developed to perform a variety of functions relating to the welfare of migrants and their families.

3. Some of the chapters point out that in order to ensure that the welfare of migrants is adequately taken into account, it would be necessary to create institutions in which

the migrants and the migrant families themselves participate. Associations of migrant families could act collectively on a number of issues. They can also be represented in the national welfare administration.

The Return Migrants

Many of the chapters stress the importance of a strong institution that can deal with the problems of returning migrants. This could take the form of a foundation for rehabilitating migrants. It could be financed with contributions from migrants and the government. In this connection, it has been suggested that the labour-supplying countries should explore the feasibility of a fund to which everyone — employers, governments of host countries and labour-supplying countries, and the migrants — contribute. The various aspects of the return flow that need attention include the placement of returnees in the workforce, counselling and guidance for returnees in regard to their savings and investments, and the availability of investment opportunities and small-scale projects.

The institutional framework for such activities can take various forms. One could be the Pakistan model, which is an umbrella-type organisation that promotes the welfare of migrants and identifies investment opportunities, and provides assistance for re-entry and rehabilitation. Another option would be to use the existing institutions, such as the banks and nongovernmental agencies, and develop capacities within them to perform some of these functions. The choice of agencies would depend on the conditions in each country, such as the availability of a good banking network, active nongovernmental organisations, and so on. Where such infrastructure is weak, the state may have to play the main role in providing these services.

Recommendations on Information-Gathering and Institutional Frameworks

Information Support

Streamlining the Information Flow and Designing an Information System

Each recommendation has repeatedly stressed that the formulation of policies must be supported by an adequate and reliable information system. All the studies stress the importance of improving the existing data base and point to large deficiencies and gaps. The information system for policy-making should be able to monitor and provide a regular flow of information on the following aspects of the labour migration:
— the outflow of migrants, the stock in host countries, and the return flow — broken down according to skill composition and geographical distribution in relation to both origin and destination;
— the impact of the migration on various segments of the domestic labour market;

— the demand for migrant labour in host countries, particularly the trends in regard to skill composition and volume;
— remittance flows — sources, volume, savings, bank deposits, investments.

These flows of what can be regarded as "hard" data could be organised so that a more or less automatic supply comes from various points at which the migrants come in contact with the administration or other formal organisations: the immigration and emigration authorities, authorities concerned with authorisation and clearance, labour departments, the foreign office and embassies, customs, the banks, and employment agencies. The problem needs to be researched in each country situation, as the regulations on travel abroad and foreign employment differ widely. In the relatively unregulated or open systems, the collection of data is likely to present greater difficulties. Certain countries have centralised procedures for clearance and authorisation. For example, in Thailand a police-clearance certificate is required for employment in Middle East countries. In Pakistan, migrants obtaining employment abroad have to register with the Bureau of Emigration. Even countries that do not wish to impose any form of restriction or regulation on the outflow could adopt a simple registration procedure that requires migrants to file relevant information on both their departure and return. This could then be a central point for the collection of required data.

Several countries are already developing and improving their information-gathering on the migration, including computerisation. Designing a regular and, where possible, automatic flow of information to a national centre from the numerous points of contact migrants have with agencies and servicing centres deserves high priority. The designing of such a system could form a technical-assistance programme in selected countries, and systems designed under such a programme could be replicated and adapted in others.

Research and Surveys

Besides information of the kind described above, countries need to develop well-coordinated programmes of research and periodic surveys on the utilisation of remittances, effects of the migration on important segments of the labour market, the sociocultural impact of the migration, etc. Given the fact that the migration has become a major socioeconomic variable for many of these countries, information on the migration and the migrants could be included as a regular component in the periodic consumer and socioeconomic surveys undertaken for more general purposes. Other types of periodic surveys specific to the migration would have to be built in as part of an information system on the migration.

For effective policy analysis, however, the data that flow more or less automatically from certain information-generating sources will not be adequate but will need to be supplemented by information of a different kind — "soft data" from more specific knowledge-gathering activities. These will include research on particular aspects of the migration phenomenon and will cover a wide range of issues — the utilisation of remittances, the impact of the migration on the local community in terms of income distribution, changes in social structure, alteration of lifestyles, entry of new values. It might be argued that the socioculture area, while it is of great importance, is not readily amenable to policy interventions, and that in a policy-oriented programme it would not command high priority. Such an argument, however, ignores the crucial importance of ascertaining as clearly as possible the full social outcome of the migration. Policies in regard to the management of the migration, its promotion or regulation, will depend on what we observe as the outcome of the migration in social and human terms. Such information and knowledge is essential if national policies are to minimise the social costs of the migration. Although policy intervention for this purpose is not easy to design, the problem has to be first discerned and understood in its most important human dimensions and characteristics in order to formulate an overall national policy for migration.

The methodology for the surveys and research, particularly if they are to be adequately representative of various aspects of the migration, will present numerous problems. Drawing a representative sample will not be an easy task, particularly with respect to returnees. The task will be easier if there are services that migrants will use at various points in their migration, from the time they prepare for migration to the period after they return and seek re-entry into the workforce. Such servicing activities will provide opportunities for collecting the required information.

The Institutional Framework

Each of the major recommendations has also emphasised the need for an institutional framework that covers all important aspects of the migration and serves the migrants in the different phases of the migration.

Centralised Regulation of the Migration

In India, for example, emigration is regulated from the time of the issuance of passports. In other countries, such as Sri Lanka, the situation is more open and no special procedures are in force for clearance of migrants for emigration. Several chapters recommended greater centralisation and state control of the migration. It is argued that such control would ensure that the problems associated with the migration are dealt with in a systematic and coordinated manner. First, this arrangement would make it possible to implement migration policy and to distinguish between the different categories of migrants and to apply different degrees of control according to the levels of skill and the needs of the domestic economy. Next, it will help to regulate the recruitment and ensure that norms are observed by all recruiting agencies, thereby reducing exploitation. The acceptability of such a centralised approach to the labour migration would, however, depend on the national policies. A great deal of migration is taking place through informal channels. Some governments that are eager to promote the export of manpower would hesitate to interfere in this process. This would probably apply to Sri Lanka. A centralised arrangement may tend to bureaucratise the entire process and create various bottlenecks as often happens with state machinery. This would defeat the purpose of both promoting the export of manpower and safeguarding the welfare and interests of the migrants. An alternative approach would be to deal with the different sets of problems independently through legislative measures, where necessary, and through appropriate institutions set up for the purpose.

Institutions for Serving Migrants

In regard to providing services for the migrants, a wide variety of institutions were recommended for dealing with specific needs. These include one-stop centres for clearance and travel formalities; centres for orientation and induction; strengthening the labour attachés' offices in the embassies of labour-supplying countries; an institution to deal with the welfare of migrants and their families; a rehabilitation fund for returnees; facilitation and promotion of associations among migrants and families of migrants; and mobilisation of nongovernmental organisations to help manage migrants and their families. Many of these ideas are drawn from systems that already exist in some countries but are not yet available in others. Taken together, they provide the basis for developing an effective institutional network that covers the important aspects of the migration, as well as the needs of the migrants.

Coordinating Machinery within Government

Within the government itself there has to be a clearly defined focal point and a co-ordinating agency for the migration. Its functions would include, among other things, the formulation of national policies on migration, the coordination of the migration policies of different sectors and institutions, manpower-planning development for export. These functions are distinct from the administration of the migration. Some countries have recognised the distinction and established separate units for handling the different responsibilities. An example is the division of functions between the Research and Planning Division and the Foreign Employment Bureau in Sri Lanka's Labour Ministry.

Most countries have responded to the problems by creating an agency specifically concerned with employment abroad; this has normally been located under the labour ministry.

In an attempt at rationalisation, many countries have suggested a national body to oversee the migration process. The thinking in Sri Lanka and Bangladesh is that such an organisation should be participatory in character and should include the state, the migrants, and private-sector recruitment agencies. Its scope and objectives should be developmental and promotional, including the promotion of employment abroad, welfare of migrants, and productive use and investment of remittance incomes. It should provide for the representation of the main interest groups involved in the migration and by this means should act as a tripartite forum in which the interests of government, entrepreneurs, and migrants could be reconciled for their mutual benefit. Developing an apex institution of this type and defining its functions and scope is a challenging task. Whatever the institutional choice, a government has to give high priority to developing a comprehensive institutional framework that can effectively attend, on the one hand, to the policy and planning needs of the migration and, on the other, to the needs of the migrants and their welfare.

Recommendations on Regional and Interregional Cooperation

Most of the authors in this book argue that the efficient management of the migration requires the labour-supplying countries to cooperate among themselves and to negotiate with the host countries. The specific recommendations regarding cooperation vary from institutionalised collective action to more informal arrangements such as the exchange of information and experience. The proposal for a formally constituted association of labour-supplying countries exclusively concerned with protecting and promoting their interests needs to be approached with some caution. Organised, unilateral action of this type by labour-supplying countries is likely to engender conflict and distrust between labour-exporting countries and labour-importing countries. It could become counterproductive and serve to inhibit cooperation between the two groups in working towards the management of the migration in their mutual interest. The effort should therefore be directed at more positive forms of cooperation between the two groups of countries.

Planning for Interdependence

As stated earlier, considerable interdependence exists between the two groups of countries, and it is possible to develop modalities for cooperation based on this reality. First, the future scenario for migration suggests a number of changes and shifts. These need to be taken into account by both the labour-importing and supplying countries. It is therefore essential that both groups of countries begin to collaborate on a study of the migration and its future. Such a study could highlight their interdependencies, and the ways in which these could be managed in the best interests of both groups of countries. Second, because of the special conditions in host countries, it is in their interest to employ a well-disciplined, transient migrant workforce that does not become an entrenched component of the population. In order to create conditions for an orderly turnover as well as for the transition to the future migration patterns, both labour-supplying countries and host countries could work together to facilitate the return flow by establishing facilities for the security and reabsorption of returnees — such as the rehabilitation or welfare fund suggested earlier. Such a fund could also enable the host countries both to participate more positively in the whole process of migration and to manage it so that their interests complement those of the labour-supplying countries. Finally, cooperation of this kind will also provide for a better and more systematic flow of information about changes in the labour markets of host countries and shifts in demand, thereby enabling labour-supplying countries to make the necessary adjustments.

The migration should be seen, then, as an important element in the growth, diversification, and development of the economies of the host countries as well as in the development and self-reliance of the labour-supplying countries. Forms of cooperation between these two groups of countries should extend to the negotiation of conventions on working conditions, settlement of grievances and disputes, recruitment procedures, and principles governing remuneration.

Sharing Experience and Information among Labour-Supplying Countries

At the level of cooperation among labour-supplying countries, the countries could organise a more systematic flow of information on the migration process in all its aspects. This can lead to a sharing of experiences from which all labour-supplying countries can benefit. The policies, the legal instruments, information systems, and the various institutional frameworks developed by the countries could provide a wealth of knowledge capable of strengthening and improving the management of the migration. A number of policies and institutions developed in one country could be transferred to another. It is therefore a fruitful field for technical cooperation among developing countries, and could be initiated through study programmes for policy-makers and administrators to enable them to study each other's systems. Such exchanges of information may point to the need for a more institutionalised intergovernmental programme on migration that could either form part of an existing regional body or be established independently. Such a regional programme, for example, could undertake a market study on the export of manpower from the region, which could inform and strengthen the national programmes.

Complementarities and Changes in Supply among Labour-Supplying Countries

The internal changes taking place within the economics of the labour-supplying countries will also change the character of the migration. As stated earlier, structural changes will lead to an increasing domestic demand for the skills that are now being exported. At the same time, wage levels will rise and the differentials between income from employment abroad and employment at home will narrow. These changes will take place at different rates in the different countries and will provide new opportunities, if due account is taken of their changing supply capacities. It is likely, for example, that East and Southeast Asian migration will change rapidly, providing a different set of opportunities for the South Asian countries. Cooperation among the labour-supplying nations of Asia should focus on these aspects, as they will emphasise areas of complementarity and help to contain the competitive character of the migration so that all labour-supplying countries can benefit.

The annexed tables contain a selective summary of the recommendations discussed. The full significance of the recommendations, however, will not be apparent when tabulated as items in abbreviated form, and, therefore, they should be read with the relevant sections of this chapter. The listed recommendations have to be seen as options from which countries would need to select their package depending on their overall national policies — whether these are oriented towards control and regulation of the economy or are more liberal and open. For example, recommendations (i)(d) and (ii)(d) in the "Policies and Programmes" column and (i)(b) in the "Institutions" column would receive greater emphasis in a regulated system than in a flexible system.

Selective Summary of Recommendations

Major Issues	Policies and Programmes	Information System	Institutions
1. *Managing the migration to maximise national benefits and minimise national costs* (i) Manpower policy and planning	For skills in short supply (a) Reappraisal of existing policies of brain drain, in relation to Middle East migration. (b) Taking account of special characteristics in Middle East migration such as turnover. (c) Incentives for both retention and return. (d) Some degree of regulation of outflow. For manpower that is in surplus or easily replaceable (a) Market studies, assessing market demands, shifts in demand, changes in skill composition, new opportunities (b) Accelerated training programmes and programmes for promoting employment abroad. (c) Basic training to improve quality of service. (d) Code for good behaviour of migrants; incentives for migrants with meritorious record; disincentives for errant workers.	(a) System for gathering information on outflow, stock and return flow, composition of skills, geographical distribution, etc. (b) Information on effects of migration on important segments of labour market where skills are in short supply	(a) A focal point in government for coordinating migration policy — e.g., unit in Labour Ministry. (b) A semigovernment overseas employment board or authority with representation from government, private sector, and migrants. (c) A centre within the coordinating unit to receive a regular flow of information on all important aspects of migration. (d) Labour attachés in embassies to be strengthened to obtain information on labour market in host countries. (e) A unit or special institutional arrangements for coordinating and implementing accelerated training programmes in both government and private sectors.

Major Issues	Policies and Programmes	Information System	Institutions
(ii) Remittances			
(a) Augmenting inflow	Incentives to augment flow of remittances — options:	(a) System for monitoring remittances into banking system	(a) Special arrangements in banking system to deal with incentives (a), (b), and (c) at left
	(a) Premium rate on separate foreign exchange market resulting in higher exchange rate for conversion of remittances	(b) Information on non-bank transfers and transfers in kind	(b) Institutional arrangements as in (b) in section (i) above, strengthened by (d), to deal with incentive
	(b) Foreign exchange accounts bearing interest		(d) at left
	(c) Streamlining banking system for facilitation of remittances		
	(d) Regulating earnings and remittances through central recruiting agency.		
(b) Productive use of remittances	(a) Investment counselling and investment advisory services	(a) Ready access to relevant documentation	(a) Special servicing centre for returnees
	(b) Investment portfolios for migrants	(b) Research to obtain more data on use of remittances	(b) Units in existing banking institutions to cater to needs of migrants
	(c) Small-scale turnkey projects for investment or for entrepreneurial self-employment		(c) An umbrella body such as the Pakistan Overseas Employment Foundation, or as part of the authority recommended in (b) in section (i) above.
	(d) Regional programmes for migrant groups from the same locality.		
2. *Welfare of migrants*			
(i) Preparation phase	(a) Strengthening and revision of legal framework for regulation of recruitment and protection of migrants with norms and provisions regarding fees, contract of employment, settlement of grievances, etc.		(a) Strengthening of law-enforcing agency.
	(b) Preparation of migrants through orientation programmes, induction programmes		(b) Service centre for migrants

(c) Dissemination of information regarding rights of migrants, host country conditions, etc., through handbooks, model contracts, other documentation	Ready availability of handbooks, model contracts, documentation to migrants	(c) Special arrangements in existing banking system
(d) Bank loans for financing cost of migration		(d) Strengthening of rural banking system
(e) Simplification of procedures and formalities governing emigration and travel abroad.		(e) One-stop centre for clearances and emigration and travel formalities
(ii) Employment abroad		
(a) Action to safeguard migrant interests in host country – performance of contract by employer, settlement of grievances	(a) Ready availability of handbooks and documentation to migrants	(a) Strengthening of embassies in host countries, in particular through liaison officers such as labour attachés
(b) Provision of services through embassy by processes of registration, establishment of formal links between embassy and migrants. Services to include facilitation of remittances, promotion of cultural activities, recreation and social life outside workplace.	(b) Regular flow of information on entry and departure of migrants to embassies in host countries	(b) Welfare administration agency
(c) Arrangements for welfare of migrants' families		(c) Nongovernmental agencies
		(d) Associations of migrants and migrant families
(iii) Return migrants		
(a) Facilitating re-entry of returnees to workforce	(a) Surveys to obtain more data on return migrants and their readjustment process (in addition to recommendation (a) in section 1 (i) above)	Special programmes/service centres for returnee migrants. Nongovernmental agencies to be mobilised for work in this area.
(b) Re-orientation and readjustment programmes		

Major Issues	Policies and Programmes	Information System	Institutions
	(c) Action already recommended regarding use of remittances (ii)(b).		
3. *Socio-cultural impact*	(a) Systematic attention to sociocultural impact in orientation programmes for outgoing migrants, returnees, families of migrants	Research needed to gain further knowledge of sociocultural impact	Task force including Ministries of Culture, Education and selected nongovernmental agencies to spearhead programmes
	(b) Mobilising agencies working in fields of culture, education to deal with the relevant sociocultural problems		
4. (i) Inter-regional cooperation between host countries and labour-supplying countries	(a) Identifying areas of interdependence and mutual interests for cooperation in managing migration, providing for orderly turnover and agreed norms and conventions on key problems	A system for exchange of information	(a) Initially a collaborative programme between research institutions leading to intergovernmental contacts.
	(b) Joint market studies on structural changes and shifts in demand and joint work on future scenarios of migration		(b) Study tours for administrators and policy-makers
(ii) Regional cooperation among labour-supplying countries	(a) A programme of technical cooperation for sharing information and knowledge on migration		(c) An institutionalised network at the regional level or regional centre on migration, for exchange of knowledge, information and studies of labour markets, etc.
	(b) Cooperation in relation to internal changes affecting supply and skill composition of migration		